SOUND ALIGNMENTS

Duke University Press *Durham and London* 2021

SOUND ALIGNMENTS

Popular Music in Asia's Cold Wars

EDITED BY MICHAEL K. BOURDAGHS,
PAOLA IOVENE & KALEY MASON

© 2021 DUKE UNIVERSITY PRESS. All rights reserved
Text design by Courtney Leigh Richardson
Cover design by Matthew Tauch
Typeset in Garamond Premier Pro and Din by Westchester Publishing Services

Library of Congress Cataloging-in-Publication Data
Names: Bourdaghs, Michael K., editor. | Iovene, Paola, [date] editor. |
Mason, Kaley, [date] editor.
Title: Sound alignments : popular music in Asia's cold wars /
edited by Michael K. Bourdaghs, Paola Iovene, and Kaley Mason. Description:
Durham : Duke University Press, 2021. | Includes index. Identifiers: LCCN
2020038419 (print) | LCCN 2020038420 (ebook)
ISBN 9781478010678 (hardcover)
ISBN 9781478011798 (paperback)
ISBN 9781478013143 (ebook)
Subjects: LCSH: Popular music—Asia—History and criticism. |
Popular music—Political aspects—Asia. | Cold War. |
Music—Asia—History and criticism.| Music—20th century—
History and criticism. | Music—Social aspects—Asia.
Classification: LCC ML3500.S68 2021 (print) | LCC ML3500
(ebook) | DDC 781.63095/0904—dc23
LC record available at https:// lccn.loc.gov/2020038419
LC ebook record available at https:// lccn.loc.gov/2020038420

Cover art: Performer-wait staff sings for customers at the East Is Red
restaurant, Beijing, June 7, 2014. Photo by Kaley Mason.

Duke University Press gratefully acknowledges the University of Chicago
Humanities Council and Center for East Asian Studies, which provided funds
toward the publication of this book.

Contents

Acknowledgments · vii

INTRODUCTION · 1
MICHAEL K. BOURDAGHS, PAOLA IOVENE, AND KALEY MASON

Part I. **ROUTES**

1. MUSICAL TRAVELS OF THE COCONUT ISLES AND THE SOCIALIST POPULAR · 43
JENNIFER LINDSAY

2. VEHICLES OF PROGRESS: The Kerala Rikshawala at the Intersection of Communism and Cosmopolitanism · 69
NISHA KOMMATTAM

3. EAST ASIAN POP MUSIC AND AN INCOMPLETE REGIONAL CONTEMPORARY · 93
C. J. W.-L. WEE

Part II. **COVERS**

4. SEARCHING FOR YOUTH, THE PEOPLE (*MINJUNG*), AND "ANOTHER" WEST WHILE LIVING THROUGH ANTI-COMMUNIST COLD WAR POLITICS: South Korean "Folk Song" in the 1970s · 131
HYUNJOON SHIN

5. COSMOPOLITANISM, VERNACULAR COSMOPOLITANISM, AND SOUND ALIGNMENTS: Covers and Cantonese Cover Songs in 1960s Hong Kong · 153

HON-LUN YANG

Part III. **FRONTS**

6. SONIC IMAGINARIES OF OKINAWA: Daiku Tetsuhiro's Cosmopolitan "Paradise" · 173

MARIÉ ABE

7. COSMAHARAJA: Popular Songs of Socialist Cosmpolitanism in Cold War India · 201

ANNA SCHULTZ

8. YELLOW MUSIC CRITICISM DURING CHINA'S ANTI-RIGHTIST CAMPAIGN · 231

QIAN ZHANG

AFTERWORD: Asia's Soundings of the Cold War · 249

CHRISTINE R. YANO

Bibliography · 263
Contributors · 285
Index · 289

Acknowledgments

The editors would like to thank the University of Chicago Humanities Council and the China Committee and Japan Committee at the Center for East Asian Studies at the University of Chicago for their financial support of this publication. We are also grateful to Taylor and Francis for granting permission to include a revised version of Anna Schultz's chapter, originally published as "Translated Fronts: Songs of Socialist Cosmopolitanism in Cold War India," *History and Anthropology* 28, no. 1 (2017): 1–22. Max Nikol and Danlin Zhang provided editorial assistance in preparing the manuscript for publication. Ken Wissoker, Nina Foster, and their colleagues at Duke University Press were remarkably supportive throughout the submission and publication process, and we are especially grateful to two anonymous referees for the press, whose careful reading and numerous suggestions made this a better book.

The conference from which this volume derived was funded primarily by the University of Chicago Beijing Center, whose staff members provided tremendous support in making the arrangements for the event. We also thank the following University of Chicago entities for providing additional financial support for the conference: the Japan Committee and the China Committee at the Center for East Asian Studies, the Committee on Southern Asian Studies, the Humanities Division Visiting Committee, and the Departments of East Asian Languages and Civilizations and Music. Finally, we would like to acknowledge the valuable contributions of a number of conference participants whose work is not included in this volume, including Sascha Ebeling, Jeroen Groenewegen, Andrew Jones, Ward Keeler, Liu Fei, Liu Sola, Shuang Shen, and Zhang Boyu.

INTRODUCTION

MICHAEL K. BOURDAGHS, PAOLA IOVENE,
AND KALEY MASON

The series of events that led up to the book you are now reading turned out unexpectedly to provide the editors with a new appreciation of the need to rethink the relationship of popular music to the Cold War(s) in Asia. This volume began in an international conference held at the University of Chicago Beijing Center in June 2014. The event was designed to bring together scholars from across the Asia-Pacific region, North America, and Europe to explore different aspects of popular music across Asia during the Cold War era. Originally, the conference also had an official cosponsor in China, but just days before our scheduled meeting, we were informed that that cosponsoring institution had abruptly withdrawn. No official reason was given, but it became apparent that the problem of the Cold War was politically too hot to handle in 2014 China—especially in the month that marked the twenty-fifth anniversary of the suppression of the Tiananmen Square protests. It was as if a wall had gone up around the Cold War, rendering it forbidden territory—at least for scholars in some parts of Asia.

This reinforced an impression we already had: that the Cold War continues today to take on a variety of different meanings in different locations. To paraphrase William Faulkner (a sometime cultural ambassador to Asia during the height of the Cold War), in Asia the Cold War past is not dead; it is not even past yet. As Odd Arne Westad has argued, our present global order is in many ways the living progeny of Cold War geopolitics.[1] Accordingly, following Heonik Kwon, it makes more sense to think of the end of the Cold War as "a slowly decomposing process that involves a multitude of human actions arising from concrete, structured conditions within and across defined locales" rather than as a finished event that exists in a past discontinuous with our present moment.² We are, we learned, still living in the long fade-out of the Cold War.

We received another jolt a few days later. The withdrawn cosponsorship took down with it a scheduled performance by local musicians that our former cosponsors had arranged. The local staff at the Chicago Beijing Center scrambled to find an alternative event to fill the gap in our schedule and came up with something even more interesting. In place of the canceled choral concert, we found ourselves sitting around two large tables in the East Is Red, a vast restaurant located on the Fifth Ring Road East in the Haidian District.

The restaurant was decorated with posters and banners from the Cultural Revolution, and the staff wore replicas of the uniforms of Red Guard youths. The waitstaff also doubled as singers and actors for the floor show, which consisted of re-creations of "red songs" from the Cultural Revolution, complete with slogans, choreographed routines, and condemnations of foreign imperialists. The climax was a staged resurrection of the people rising up into heroic action after the martyrdom of a young Chinese woman at the hands of Japanese imperialist invaders. But in this simulacrum performance, the most overly political of Cold War popular musics was seemingly drained of all politicality. We wondered if we were witnessing a remarkable demonstration of ironic kitsch—until we saw the responses to the performance by other audience members, mostly large family groups. They stood and danced and sang along; grandmothers and grandfathers enthusiastically taught the proper steps to toddler grandchildren. They were, of course, reveling in the soundtrack of their youths. Somehow, popular music made it possible to feel a warm nostalgic glow for what was officially the worst era in China's Cold War. From the other side of the Iron Curtain, a soft and fuzzy version of the Cold War echoed toward us. The wall that blocked academic resurrections of the Cold War proved unable to stand up to the emotional attractions of popular songs.³

At the conference and the performance, we were learning that a different Cold War emerges when we lend our ears to Asia—and in particular to the popular musics of Asia. Westad argues that we need to heed the Global South if we want to grasp the Cold War, but we were discovering that we also need to head east. In Asia, even the basic parameters of what we know as the Cold War grow hazy. The notion that the Cold War began shortly after World War II, that it ended around 1990 with the collapse of the Soviet bloc, that its front line was the Berlin Wall, and that under its sway the so-called Iron Curtain separated cleanly two distinct global blocs: none of those ideas make much sense from the various perspectives of Asia. The commonly accepted narrative arc and internal periodizations of the Cold War also break down when the era is approached through the perspective of Asian popular music: the "stagnant" 1970s, for example, do not necessarily seem discontinuous from the "turbulent" 1960s. Nor, for that matter, does the Cold War look particularly cold from the perspective of Asia. The Chinese Revolution, the Korean War, the Vietnam War, the Indonesian massacres, the Naxalite insurgency in India and Burma: these Asian wars ran more hot than cold. In place of the notion of the Cold War as a "long peace," Bruce Cumings insists that we think of Asia's Cold Wars primarily in terms of a "balance of terror."[4]

When did the Cold War begin? Scholars often cite 1946, the year Winston Churchill gave his "Iron Curtain" speech, or 1947, the year Walter Lippman's book *The Cold War* was published—but from the perspective of Asia, both dates seem too late. The battle lines between Communism and anti-Communism were clearly already drawn by the late 1920s across China and the Japanese empire (whose indirect rule by puppet state over Manchuria would provide a prescient model for the client state form that would emerge across the region after 1945), clouding any attempt to posit a 1940s start date for the Cold War in the region.

When did the Cold War end? From the perspectives of Asia, the more pertinent question seems to be, did the Cold War ever end? The continued military saber-rattling seen in Korea, Okinawa, and across the Straits of Taiwan calls into question the idea that we are living in a post–Cold War era. Moreover, the Bandung movement as well as socialist and other international fronts crisscrossed the region unevenly, opening up routes for transmission and crossing that sometimes halted at but other times leapt blithely under or over the Iron Curtain.

A number of important recent studies have traced the ways Cold War institutions in the West mobilized modernist art and a concomitant aesthetics centered on notions of freedom and spontaneity.[5] This politically mobilized aesthetic confronted the realism and class-based aesthetics that were the official line of the Soviet bloc. But while the aesthetics of modernism and socialist realism might provide blueprints to help us map out the competing official programs of the Cold War powers, popular music provides in many ways a much better, much messier, and more accurate map of how daily life was lived, with its pleasures and sorrows, across the global in the period. The Cold War in North America or Europe might have seemed an abstract matter of state geopolitics, but in much of Asia, "people had to live the cold war as part of their everyday lives and in their most immediate, intimate domains."[6] In those domains, the soundtrack usually came from the mundane realm of popular song, not high classical or avant-garde jazz.

The many forms of popular music that were performed, recorded, banned, listened to, and danced to across Asia help us map out a less linear Cold War, one in which beginnings, endings, boundaries, and alliances take on more intricate, amorphous structures. Popular music traveled across multiple routes in the era: the network of US military bases and their concomitant apparatuses (including music clubs on and off base, Armed Forces radio networks, and PX stores stocking the latest records from the US and Europe); the international socialist youth festivals that gathered musicians and listeners from around the world; the trafficking in records, films, and television programs on both sides of (and sometimes across) the Iron Curtain, and so on. Songs and styles and performers traveled not only within these various networks but also across them in often unexpected manners.

Accordingly, Asian popular music provides an opportunity for mapping out a different version of the Cold War. We have to be wary, though, in taking this approach, because many of our methodologies and basic assumptions about Asia and popular music are themselves products of the Cold War period. As Lisa Yoneyama and many others have noted, academic area studies fields such as Asian studies are "enduring Cold War knowledge formations" that render certain kinds of information into "facts" while rendering other pasts and historical subjects illegible.[7] As we pursue what is clearly an Asian studies project, we have to remain vigilant of the unspoken presumptions about culture, tradition, nation-states, and modernity, to name just a few, that too often enclose the messy and fluid reality of modern Asia into categories of knowledge in the service of power by producing a version of the past that legitimates existing social and political hierarchies and unevenness. For example, as Yoneyama notes, Cold War Asian studies focused primarily on "the normative development of nation-states and statehood" so that "area studies scholars primarily produced studies of entities that were already constituted as, or were becoming, nation-states."[8] But the activities surrounding popular music often take place through units larger and smaller than the nation-state. When, for example, Thai transgender performers perform cover dances of K-pop songs, they are simultaneously highlighting differences (of gender, sexuality, class, and ethnicity) within the nation of Thailand and mapping themselves onto a cosmopolitan, transnational vision of what Asian modernity might sound and look like.[9] Cold War popular music becomes, as many of the authors here argue, a form of vernacular cosmopolitanism that blurs multiple boundaries. As we rethink the potential of area studies following the critiques of Orientalism and of Cold War ideology, popular music studies potentially provide an entryway for exploring a more fluid approach, one less respectful of the boundaries and periodizations we have inherited from the Cold War era.

Likewise, the academic study of popular music is also part of our Cold War legacy. Many of the professional music associations that would eventually legitimize research on popular music in the academy were shaped in response to Cold War alignments, beginning in 1947 with the International Council for Folk Music (renamed in 1981 as the International Council for Traditional Music [ICTM] in Seoul), followed in 1955 by the Society for Ethnomusicology (SEM). Writing about the complementary work of these organizations, Bruno Nettl recalls how "in the 1960s and 1970s, the cold war and the Iron Curtain played a major but unacknowledged part in defining these roles."[10] Whereas the European-led ICTM emphasized the collection of rural music as the purest form of popular expression in modern socialist and capitalist nation-states, the US-led SEM was more concerned with advancing the holistic study of music cultures through fieldwork, which mostly took place in nonaligned "developing" countries of the Global South. Moreover, much of the funding for American research on non-Western music came from private foundations and the US Department of Education, two influential agents of Cold War–era knowledge formation closely aligned with the national security goals of the US Department of State. For example, in 1952 the Ford Foundation strategically opened its first international field office in New Delhi, India, one of several fronts where the US deployed cultural policy to counter the appeal of Communism in the new global order.[11] Over the same period, national Asian music societies were formed, including the Musicological Society of Japan in 1952 and the Indian Musicological Society in 1970. Founded in the shadows of the Cold War, postwar professional music organizations focused on preserving vernacular traditions that were increasingly competing with popular music for relevance in everyday life.

As rural populations moved to cities in unprecedented numbers after World War II, urban listeners were drawn to the modern aesthetic cosmopolitanism of pop-rock genres. Motti Regev usefully defines this broad category as "music consciously created and produced by using amplification, electric and electronic instruments, sophisticated recording equipment (including samplers), by employing certain techniques of supposed untrained vocal delivery . . . and by filtering all these through sound editing, modification, and manipulation devices."[12] Thus a combination of accelerated urbanization, booming commercial music industries, competing cultural nationalisms (capitalist and socialist), and the priorities of research funding agencies encouraged music scholars to privilege the study of art and vernacular music over electronically mediated, hybridized styles. Popular music was clearly more than a Cold War–era soundtrack; it was the elephant in the room for academic music organizations initially unsympathetic to the idea of including pop-rock as legitimate music in the academy.

The founding of the Centre for Contemporary Cultural Studies in 1964 at the University of Birmingham was a turning point for the academic study of popular music. Established in a climate of polarizing rhetoric and escalating geopolitical tensions in Europe, the Birmingham School of Cultural Studies pioneered the critical analysis of media and working-class cultures at a time of growing American influence in postwar Britain. Whereas Frankfurt School critical theorists such as Theodor Adorno disparaged popular music's use of standardized formulas and repetition to pacify listening publics, early cultural studies drew on the political philosophy of Antonio Gramsci as well as feminist, postcolonial, and poststructural theory to reframe popular culture as an arena of struggle in which both individual agents and structural constraints co-determine social life.[13] As a political and intellectual response to postwar conditions—including postcolonial liberation struggles, the specter of nuclear warfare, the weaponization of media in the cultural Cold War(s), and the inequalities of late capitalism—cultural studies was at its core a movement dedicated to examining the complexity of shifting power relations in highly industrialized capitalist societies.[14] This line of inquiry led to questioning how power operates through sound, including how popular music could be mobilized for domination and/or resistance. Cultural studies thus laid significant theoretical groundwork for the International Association for the Study of Popular Music (IASPM), which was founded by sociologists and musicologists in 1981. While initially limited to the study of music in Western capitalist societies, IASPM gradually expanded its scope to include research on non-Western culture industries by the late 1980s. At last, there was growing realization among music scholars that global popular music was worthy of study, including genres cultivated in Communist societies, where, as Peter Manuel notes in *Popular Musics of the Non-Western World*, star systems were less prominent and musicians faced bureaucratic and ideological challenges more than market pressures.[15]

Meanwhile, the Cold War era also witnessed the growth of sound studies as a separate stream of cross-disciplinary research. A response to the ocular centrism of Western epistemologies and limitations of music-centered disciplines, sound studies coalesced around shared interest in the sensory, ontological, material, and historical dimensions of sound, or as Jonathan Sterne cogently puts it: "what sound does in human worlds and what humans do in sonic worlds."[16]

In addition to expanding the possibilities for using popular music to think about the historical and contemporary dynamics of the Cold War(s), sound studies also introduced more perspectives on how moments of human crisis and conflict shape "sonorous encultured worlds" directly or indirectly.[17] Situated within a broader field of sound studies, the chapters in this volume not only offer a compelling, if inadvertent, response to Western musicology's call to widen the scope of research on Cold War music to include popular and non-Western perspectives.[18] They also contribute to a growing body of literature in Asian sound studies by reaching beyond music genres to approach popular music more nimbly as sonorous worlds embedded in the politics of aurality.[19]

Although the idea of writing popular music histories through a Cold War lens is relatively new, recent work on Latin America, the Caribbean, and Eastern Europe has challenged the Western-centeredness of most research on the cultural Cold War(s).[20] Extending this initiative eastward across multiple Asias, some authors in this volume examine how songwriters and musicians perform Cold War discourses literally. Others take a portal approach to exploring how Cold War forces shaped broader aesthetic and social transformations through case studies of individual careers and creative works. The chapters also implicitly show how the discursive analytical frameworks and professional networks shaping Asian popular music studies themselves stem from "structures of feeling" inherited from the cultural legacies of Asia's Cold War(s). Indeed, whether we adopt a Frankfurt School critical approach to the alienating effects of culture industries, a cultural studies emphasis on limited spontaneity and liberal notions of freedom, or state-sponsored condemnation of decadent yellow music, all are postures rooted in Cold War–era ideological struggles.

The various chapters presented here aim at a rethinking of Asia's Cold War(s) through its popular music—and, simultaneously, a rethinking of Asia's popular music(s) through the Cold War. Working from separate yet overlapping disciplinary backgrounds in places ranging from Maharashtra to the Ryūkyū Islands, they show how historical changes "remotely registered in history books, newspapers, or the pronouncements of politicians can appear in vivid relief and full complexity within products of the popular music industry—if we learn how to read them correctly."[21] In this volume, reading "correctly" involves thinking beyond lyrical analysis to engage the verbal and nonverbal elements of performance as well as the lived histories that illustrate the social life and political force of popular music production, mediation, and reception in Asia's Cold War(s). With this in mind, we have organized the chapters around three interconnected keywords that seem particularly useful in unpacking the complexity of popular musics in Cold War Asia: routes, covers, and fronts. In this introduction, we pick up a few key musical examples from across Asia as a way to begin sketching in the stakes of each of the three concepts.

Routes

The *routes* of popular music traced in the following pages are both material and metaphorical, human and nonhuman: they encompass tangible vehicles, circulation processes, and ephemeral events, and involve media such as sheet music, songbooks, radio, television, and cinema as well as acts of translation, mixing, and appropriation. Performers travel through these routes, but the performers themselves serve as routes. Seen through them, the popular emerges as an effect of (rather than as a precondition for) music's dissemination. There is always something dynamic and impure at the origin of popular music, a dynamism that invites approaches combining rather than contrasting routes and roots: as several of the contributions in this volume make clear, searching for the popular roots of a song often means discovering its previous routes, for "roots are not simply belongings, but re-imaginations and re-narrations of belonging that co-exist with the migrations and displacements of routes."[22]

As Nisha Kommattam shows in her chapter on Kerala cinema, film song in particular can convey a peculiar form of rooted cosmopolitanism, transcending boundaries of class, caste, and communities and serving as a vehicle for aspirations of utopian egalitarianism and social upward mobility. Another example to consider is Jia Zhangke's *Zhantai* (*Platform*, 2000), a film that provides a rich illustration of the diverse musical routes in 1980s China. About twenty minutes into the film, three young men sit in a barely lit room in a Shanxi provincial town. One of them tunes in the radio, and through scratchy sounds, the weather forecast informs, "A cold depression is forming in Ulaanbaatar." One more tiny turn of the knob and Teresa Teng's mellifluous "Coffee and Wine" seeps through, a southern breeze blowing away the chilly draft from the north. Jia has often commented on his teenage love for Teng:

> I was born in 1970, so I was in my formative years in the early eighties when popular music really began to take root in China. I grew up with pop music. Popular music played an enormous role in the lives of people of my generation as we matured and came of age. At first it was all from Hong Kong and Taiwan, and only later did Western music start coming into China. One of the reasons popular music was so important was that before this, China really didn't have any "popular culture" to speak of. The closest thing we had were revolutionary model operas and things

made in that mold. I still remember so clearly the first time I heard the music of Teresa Teng. The experience was exactly as it was portrayed in *Platform*, where the characters listened to illegal shortwave radio broadcasts from Taiwan. At the time, I was quite young and couldn't really say what it was about her voice, but it was so moving—I was utterly hypnotized. There was a special time every day when they would play her songs and I would always tune in.

Later, when I went to college and reflected back on this time, I realized that her music represented a massive change in our cultural landscape.[23]

The director's statement that before the 1980s "China didn't have any 'popular culture' to speak of" urges us to reconsider what might have counted as popular music in Cold War China—an unresolved controversy that Qian Zhang addresses in this volume. The 1930s had seen the emergence of a "hybrid genre of American jazz, Hollywood film music, and Chinese folk music known in Chinese as 'modern songs' (*shidai qu*)" whose creation was attributed to the composer Li Jinhui and which was popularized by such pop music divas as Zhou Xuan.[24] Those tunes were then condemned as "yellow (i.e., pornographic) music" and partly displaced by "a new form of leftwing mass music (*qunzhong yinyue*) expressly designed to counter Li Jinhui's musical idiom in the urban media marketplace of Republican China."[25] From the 1950s to the 1970s, march rhythms, choral singing, and orchestral arrangements often drawn from Soviet models dominated the Chinese musical landscape. Huge state-sponsored efforts went into collecting folk music and folk songs, which were then readapted to fit the current political agenda, combined with new and foreign melodies, and widely disseminated through dance and musical performances, dramas, movies, and songbooks. Lydia Liu has coined the phrase *official popular culture* to emphasize both the role of the state and the broad appeal of such works as the musical film *Liu Sanjie* (*Third Sister Liu*, 1961), but the phrase could also be employed to describe the state-sponsored model works of the 1960s and early 1970s mentioned by Jia.[26]

Encompassing ten operas and four ballets (some of which were made into films), two symphonies, and two piano pieces that drew as much from Western symphonic music as from Chinese folk and traditional tunes, the model works were enjoyed by millions of people and constituted the core of Chinese socialist mass culture, but for Jia they do not qualify as "popular," perhaps due to their ideological content and state sponsorship, and also because by the late 1970s they had been too long in the air and failed to appeal to the youth.[27] In a context in which state media undercut the popular character of mass culture by disseminating it too insistently, what counted as "really popular" was the clandestine music that seeped in through "illegal shortwave radio broadcasts from Taiwan" and captured young people's hearts in an almost secretive manner, generating "a nostalgia for something that was beyond reach."[28]

Popular music's affective power is often enhanced by the fact that it travels through forbidden routes. The Chinese term for popular, *liuxing*, suggests an irresistible wave emerging from an undefined place and expanding everywhere—in the compound *liuxing bing*, it means "epidemic."[29] Jia describes Teng's songs as "moving" and "hypnotizing." Underlying his recollections is a distinction between emotionally compelling sounds, on the one hand, and state-endorsed productions that do not appeal to audiences on the other, between vibes so personal and infective that they enter the body and transport it to some other space and time, and an impersonal voice imposed nationwide that does reach all spaces and yet remains distant, failing even to be heard. The film itself, however, undoes this dichotomy. By interweaving revolutionary songs and sentimental melodies, parodies of official hymns to the Four Modernizations and disco music, *Platform* shows that the infective power of songs is pervasive and not limited to any particular musical source, style, or genre.

Platform memorializes the function of cinema as one of the routes through which music became popular within and across national borders in late Cold War Asia. These routes partly reflected Cold War blocs—but only partly, for they were neither entirely determined by the socialist states nor fully integrated within a capitalist mode of production. As shown by Jennifer Lindsay's chapter in this volume, songs traveled through the biennial World Festivals of Youth and Students organized by the World Federation of Democratic Youth, which gathered delegations from diverse countries, including nonaligned ones, and led to the development of folk regional and national styles informed by those transnational encounters.[30] The festivals functioned as crossroads of musical exchange, laboratories of musical invention, magnets of cosmopolitan aspirations, and grassroots alternatives to state-endorsed cultural diplomacy. Their lingering sounds bespeak desires for nonalignment and solidarity, the unfinished pursuit of a peaceful world unfractured by Cold War rivalries and safe from new nuclear threats. By considering what Lindsay calls the "socialist popular," we discover cultural networks that encompass the then emerging Third World and challenge current definitions of popular music—definitions which are to a large extent still shaped by a Cold War dichotomy of socialist authoritarianism and free-market liberalism.

A focus on the routes of popular music, in other words, allows us to rethink the concept of popular music itself beyond the Cold War frameworks that contrast the mechanisms of capitalist culture industries to those of socialist states. As James Clifford reminds us, "practices of displacement ... [are] *constitutive* of cultural meanings rather than ... their simple transfer or extension."[31] Whether in melody, arrangement, rhythm, tempo, or language, nothing of a song remained the same when it was performed or broadcast elsewhere. Therefore, we treat popular music neither as the reflection of homogeneous nations nor as signifier of a universal global. In most of the cases we examine, songs were reinvented through traveling and at times returned to their place of origin in dramatically muted forms, generating new "cycles of feedback" that transformed the musical cultures of multiple sites.[32] A closer look at the soundtrack of *Platform*—particularly at one song in it, "Good-bye, Friend"—will help illustrate these points.

Titled after a 1987 pop-rock hit about a lonely heart vainly waiting for the train of love, *Platform* focuses on a performing arts troupe as its repertoire of socialist songs is replaced by rock, disco, and breakdance.[33] The soundtrack seems to punctuate the passage from socialism to capitalism, suggesting promises that neither can fulfill. Diegetic songs, however, also do much more. A song can instantly transform the atmosphere of a room, a square, or a street, though often such change turns out to be superficial or inconsequential. When, early in the film, "Awara Hoon" (I am a vagabond) from the Hindi film *Awara* (*The Vagabond*, 1951) bleeds out in the hall of the public movie theater, its boisterous tune seems to make fun of the austere portraits of Vladimir Lenin, Joseph Stalin, and Mao Zedong hanging on the wall, but obviously the structures and legacies of socialism will linger on.[34] Other songs underscore moments of quiet in domestic spaces temporarily sheltered from the violence that still pervades public life, as in the scene when one of the protagonists practices mainland pop hits from a songbook—early 1980s favorites such as "Early Morning at School," "Clear Spring Water at the Frontier," and "Nights in the Navy Ports"—right before a friend drops by to report that someone is being executed a few meters away.[35]

Another troupe member plays a cassette of Taiwanese singer Zhang Di on a tape recorder he has brought back from a trip to Guangzhou, suggesting dreams of social mobility and escape (not unlike those examined in Kommattam's chapter) but also stressing the gap between the southern coastal cities where economic reforms and new forms of popular culture took off in the early 1980s and the inland where these young people are stuck. Songs sometimes define and often blur the boundaries between political and private spheres, cement friendships and romantic relations, offer comfort in separation, accentuate loneliness or keep it at bay. Each of them, Jia recalls, "represents a snapshot of the social reality of the time."³⁶ This is, first and foremost, a reality of new asynchronicities engendered by the economic reforms. Through its complex soundscape, the film shows how cultural change came messily and slowly to the inland rural areas, even though they were initially energized by economic reforms. Some of the change is imported, arriving by fits and starts through unofficial routes from the south coastal urban centers of Guangzhou and Shenzhen, and some is generated locally, amalgamating the familiar and the new. Popular music, then, connotes change that does arrive, eventually, but with noticeable delay.³⁷

There is one song, however, that interrupts the narrative of new expectations and disappointments generated by the passage from socialism to capitalism. It is around 1984: state funding has been cut and the troupe is being privatized. Some performers leave their hometown to go on a tour led by a newly appointed manager, and two of them are breaking up: the male protagonist is leaving with the troupe, while his (ex-)girlfriend stays behind. We first hear the lyrics, seemingly from offscreen, while a still camera shows the male protagonist in profile, sitting on the right of the frame, barely holding his tears; three other performers are viewed from the back. An engine roars. When the truck moves and the camera pans leftward to follow it, we realize that it is the troupe members themselves who are singing the song. The refrain, "A pengyou zaijian, a pengyou zaijian, . . . lalalalala" (Good-bye, friend, good-bye, . . . lalalalala), now accompanied by the strumming of a guitar, continues to resound in the next shot, aligned with the viewpoint of those sitting on the truck looking backward at the streets and walls they are leaving behind. Commenting on the faded slogans on the walls, of which only the Chinese transcription of "Marx" is legible, Michael Berry argues that "this is not just a farewell to Fenyang and the friends and family of their hometown, but a farewell to the ideologies of yesterday."³⁸ The song seems to function as a vehicle transporting these young people away from the socialist past, underscoring separation and change, but the complex history of "A pengyou zaijian" suggests something beyond a linear narrative of separation and change.

"A pengyou zaijian," which literally translates as "Good-bye, friend," is the Chinese version of "Bella ciao," widely considered the most famous song of the Italian resistance movement during World War II. It is a fascinating example of a song that traveled in different guises through many routes. It is often sung with clapping, for instance, but in the Chinese version, the clapping is verbalized with the syllable "ba" following "pengyou zaijian" in the refrain. Tracing "Bella ciao" back in time, one does not find any definite point of origin. In the words of a historian who interviewed Italian partisans on their musical memories of World War II, "the history of 'Bella ciao' is like a novel without an ending, because there is no unique text but several variants that underwent many transformations and interweave with multiple individual and collective stories."³⁹ A hybrid vehicle of diverse sonic and textual materials ranging from rice field labor songs to children's games, it has been translated into thirty languages and continues to be adapted by many protest movements to this day.⁴⁰

In fact, in spite of the widely held assumption that "Bella ciao" was sung by all partisans, during the war its diffusion was limited to central Italy in 1944–45. The brigades fighting in the north mostly sang "Fischia il vento" (The wind whistles), which was based on the melody of the Russian "Katyusha" and whose text included such lyrics as "the sun of tomorrow" and "red flag" that directly referred to socialism.⁴¹ In the early 1960s, "Bella ciao" was retrospectively chosen as the hymn of the resistance because it was a more inclusive song that "focused not on any particular army or brigade, but on a single man, a martyr of that continental tragedy that was Nazi fascism."⁴² Moreover, its growing international fame and dissemination through the media also contributed to its canonization. When "Bella ciao" was performed by a choir of former partisans from Emilia Romagna at the World Festival of Youth and Students in Prague in 1947, in Budapest in 1949, and in Berlin in 1951, thousands of delegates from seventy countries joined in clapping hands and sang along. The Italian Young Pioneers Association, a leftist youth organization for children up to fifteen years old, sang it at their camps and at international youth gatherings. It was sung in both Italian and Russian by Muslim Magomaev, a famous Azerbaijani singer dubbed the "Soviet Sinatra," starting in 1964. In the same year, two differently worded versions, the first originating among rice field workers in northwestern Italy and the second dating back to partisans, were included in the concert "Bella ciao" at the Seventh Festival of Two Worlds in Spoleto (Italy), a controversial event that brought folk songs to the national stage and was broadcast on television.⁴³ Yves Montand's interpretation in 1963 greatly contributed to its fame, paving the way for more recent versions, including those by Manu Chao, Goran Bregovic, and Marc Ribot and Tom Waits.⁴⁴ Over the past few years, it has been translated and adapted for various protest movements, including the 2013 Gezi Park protests in Istanbul.⁴⁵ Thanks to YouTube and other online video sites, the melody of "Bella ciao" continues to galvanize protesters across the globe.

It was the movie *Most* (*The Bridge*, 1969) by Yugoslavian director Hajrudin Krvavac that first served as the conduit for the crossover of "Bella ciao" to China. Along with *Valter Brani Sarajevo* (*Walter Defends Sarajevo*, 1972), also directed by Krvavac, *The Bridge* was one of the most popular films in late-1970s China.⁴⁶ The actor playing the main protagonist in both movies, Velimir "Bata" Zivojinovic, was much beloved by Chinese audiences, who affectionately referred to him by the name of "Walter."⁴⁷ *The Bridge* was dubbed in Chinese in 1973 but was initially distributed only internally, that is, to select audiences of politicians, elite military, and perhaps a few film specialists. It was widely shown in movie theaters and on television only from the late 1970s onward. The film dialogues were in Serbo-Croatian and German and the theme song was in Italian, but when the film was dubbed in Chinese, its multilingual aspect was lost, and many Chinese audiences came to believe that the song was from Yugoslavia. Film scholar Yuan Qingfeng writes:

> There were very few kinds of popular entertainment and consumable cultural goods in 1970s China, and foreign works were even scarcer. Foreign cinema was limited to a handful of socialist countries like the Soviet Union, Eastern Europe, North Korea, and Vietnam, and even nineteenth-century classical music was banned. *The Bridge* not only had a wonderful plot, but the soundtrack was also outstanding. So once it was shown, it strongly reverberated with audiences. For instance, the theme song "Good-bye, Friend" was repeatedly covered by musicians and broadly disseminated. In the late 1970s and early 1980s, the "light music" coming from the west was considered ideologically problematic and was harshly criticized by officials as one of the symbols of capitalist culture. But covers of *The Bridge* theme song were considered safe, because it was a movie from a socialist country.⁴⁸

"Bella ciao," literally meaning "Good-bye, beautiful" and thus suggesting a romantic farewell, was translated as "Good-bye, friend" in Chinese, foregrounding friendship and comradery instead of romantic love. Online Chinese commentators recall that they learned to whistle it and play it on the harmonica, suggesting that what stuck most was the melody and the refrain. From the late 1970s on, notations and text were reprinted in a wide range of songbooks, appearing among folk songs (*minge*) or listed as a popular song (*liuxing ge*). It was generally glossed as the soundtrack of the film, though in some instances its Italian origin was also acknowledged. In one of the earliest songbooks published in 1979, the title is simply "A! Pengyou" (Ah, friend).⁴⁹ A different, partial version, titled "Oh, Farewell, Dear Frends!" (*sic*), however, appears in *Yingyu gequxuan* (Selected songs in English, 1980).⁵⁰ Since the English text is printed above the Chinese, the song appears to be translated from the English, even though it is glossed as "Italian folk song." The book includes

African American folk songs, English versions of Neapolitan folk songs, Franz Schubert's "Ave Maria," and such American classics as "Oh! Susanna" and "This Land Is Your Land." In addition to songbooks, "Good-bye, Friend" was also disseminated through flexi-discs produced by China Records. It was, for instance, included in the 1981 record *Waiguo dianying yinyuehui* (Concert of foreign film music), a collection of a surprising range of film soundtracks, all recorded in the original languages.[51]

Across all these routes, "Bella ciao" reappears alongside songs of different genres, reminding us that the diverse understandings of popular music, encompassing the music of the common people, music that is enjoyed by many, and music promoted by the mass media, are often intertwined. In early 1980s China, it was probably perceived as a song about friendship, heroism, and personal sacrifice. To some it might have suggested national dignity and freedom from oppression, carrying the sound of an alternative transnational left-leaning horizon—the sound of a socialism that was still unknown. In *Platform*, therefore, "A pengyou zaijian" does not simply connote separation but also disturbs the trajectory from socialism to capitalism underscored by the rest of the soundtrack, reminding us of the plural worlds within each of these systems, of the routes that breached their borders, and of routes not taken.

There were other important "routes" across the region, as well. Another group of songs traveled across East Asia, in particular along the networks and relays of American Armed Forces radio and clubs on military bases.[52] US military bases in Japan, Okinawa, South Korea, Taiwan, the Philippines, Vietnam, and elsewhere became nodes of circulation and transference, relaying pop songs from Tin Pan Alley, Nashville, and Southern California into new markets, so that they could be covered by musicians in Tokyo, Taipei, and Seoul (but not Beijing, Pyongyang, or Hanoi). And yet at the same time, as Hyunjoon Shin notes in his chapter here, protest folk music also spread across the region, albeit outside the bases. In South Korea, it was a network of YMCA, YWCA, coffeehouses, and university campuses that opened a space for an avowedly noncommercial counterculture—a movement that began in translated covers of American folk music but that by the 1970s had moved on, as Shin argues, "to construct a distinct music culture for the nation (and its people) rather than merely imitating Western music."

Since the 1990s, moreover, a new network of routes has emerged, some of them carrying on legacies of the Cold Wars directly, others indirectly, and a new imaginary geography of the region is in the process of overwriting the versions that existed across the Cold War. As C. J. W.-L. Wee argues in his chapter, one of the carryovers from the Cold War division of a "security Asia" from an "economic Asia" is the rise in practice and in imagination of a new fictive version of Asia characterized by a kind of "inter-Asian pop." The Cold War practice across much of the region of listening to songs with English lyrics has been coupled with a new practice engaged in by a new middle class: listening to pop songs in non-English foreign languages, whether it is K-pop in Singapore or Tokyo or J-pop in Seoul or Hong Kong. The routes traced by popular music across Cold War Asia continue to reverberate and generate new paths in what Wee calls the "incomplete contemporary."

The tangled, overlapping, and crisscrossing "routes" across Asia during the period were sustained by a particular practice that characterized much of popular music during the Cold War: cover songs. Understanding Cold War popular music in Asia requires an interrogation of the logic of covering, to which we turn next.

Covers

In addition to *routes*, *covers* is another keyword that helps us map out the complex intertwining of popular music with the multiple Cold Wars that were experienced across Asia. As a practice, covers are crucial to popular music: there is an indiscriminate profligacy to the way pop songs allow themselves to be imitated, repeated, and recycled—and through that process to generate overtones that suggest new possible lineages and affiliations. As translated cover versions migrated across the routes crisscrossing Cold War–era Asia, they often evaded ideological disciplining, and as a result provide a remarkable tool for tracing the multiple imagined histories and futures that circulated through popular culture. Mapping out the convoluted pathways of cover versions is one way for us to see that there was not one Cold War in East Asia but several.

Four years after Jia Zhangke released *Platform*, Japanese director Izutsu Kazuyuki released another film that used popular music as a window for reflecting on the history of the Cold War. *Pacchigi!*, known in English as *Break Through!* (or, in another Cold War musical reference, *We Shall Overcome Someday*), achieved considerable critical acclaim, finishing in the top position of the prestigious *Kinema Junpō* Best Ten List of Japanese films in 2005. The movie depicts a Romeo-and-Juliet romance between a Japanese boy who attends high school in Kyoto and a Zainichi (resident Korean) girl who attends a nearby private ethnic high school, all set amid the turbulence of 1968 Japan. The opening scene provides a painstaking re-creation of a rock concert by Group Sounds sensations Ox, and as the narrative unfolds, we discover popular music interwoven into the story in multiple ways.

In particular, the film riffs off a legendary incident from Japanese pop music history: the 1968 cover version of the North Korean song "Rimjingang" (Imjun River) by the Folk Crusaders. That folk-rock trio had unexpectedly become a national sensation when radio stations began playing the novelty song "Kaette kita yopparai" (The drunkard's return), included on its independently released 1967 debut album. Reissued in December 1967 as a single on a major label, "Kaette kita yopparai" soared to the top of Japan's hit charts and sold more than two million copies. "Kaette kita yopparai" subsequently also provided the title for a 1968 film directed by Ōshima Nagisa, known in English as *Three Resurrected Drunkards* and starring the Folk Crusaders—a surreal Cold War narrative in which the band members inadvertently find themselves mistaken for South Korean soldiers who have illegally immigrated to Japan; they end up being shipped off to the battlefields of Vietnam, thereby highlighting the disparate roles South Korea and Japan played under the US security regime for East Asia.

After the success of that debut single, the band's managers chose as the follow-up single a tune the band had been playing in its live set, "Imugin-gawa" (Imjun River), with lyrics by Matsuyama Takeshi. Matsuyama had learned the number as a Korean folk song from Zainichi friends. The band and Matsuyama believed the song to be an old Korean folk song, but in fact it was a propaganda ballad about divided Korea, originally composed in 1957 by Ko Jong-hwan with lyrics by the poet Pak Se-yŏng. The first verse in the cover was a translation of the original Korean lyrics, but the subsequent verses were Matsuyama's own original composition, replacing the more explicitly political content of the North Korean original. The connection to Korea remained clear through the title and contents, but the cover version projected a different historical context, even as it preserved the haunting melody of the original.

The Folk Crusaders' record company announced the new single in February 1968. Immediately, the label found itself flooded with complaints from Zainichi groups affiliated with North Korea, who charged that the Japanese-language version was not a true translation of the Korean lyrics, that the cover was a deliberate deception that aimed to mask the historical reality of Cold War geopolitics and of Japan's own imperial past. Meanwhile, the record label and its parent company also began to fear that South Korean and South Korean–affiliated Zainichi groups would object to the introduction of any North Korean culture into Japan. Since the 1965 accord reestablishing diplomatic relations between Japan and its former colony of South Korea, Japanese corporations had viewed South Korea, rapidly industrializing under the authoritarian developmentalist policies of the Park Chung Hee regime, as a lucrative potential market and were loath to take any action that might limit their access. Faced with objections from both sides of the Iron Curtain, the record company quickly withdrew the record from circulation. This led to the widespread belief that the song had been banned, a prohibition that of course only intensified the desire among young music fans to hear the recording. The phantom cover version became an absent presence, soliciting a forbidden mode of identification among a generation of Japanese music fans.[53]

"Imujin-gawa" provides a telling instance of what Kuan-Hsing Chen has described as the derailed processes of decolonization and deimperialism in Cold War Asia.[54] In this fragmented environment, cover songs could, as with the Folk Crusaders, suggest troubling historical connections and find themselves suppressed. But in another register, Cold War pop music covers also became sites for revitalized modes of (post)colonial mimicry. A figure like Japanese *enka* diva Misora Hibari, for example, provides a striking instance of how in Cold War pop music you could become an original by copying somebody else, how mimicking the foreign other becomes the process by which you acquire a sense of domestic authenticity as well as articulate new lines of affiliation. It was through her covers of "American" boogie-woogie numbers in the late 1940s that Hibari magically emerged as the most Japanese of enka singers, and even later in her career, when she claimed indigenous roots for her music in Japanese blood and critics celebrated her as the embodiment of Japanese cultural tradition, she continued to include brilliant covers of songs like "La Vie en rose" or "Lover Come Back to Me" in her repertoire.[55]

We see this same phenomenon, what Michael Taussig calls the figure-eight form of mimesis, across the region during the Cold War era.[56] The ways in which cover versions of what was supposed to be the same song could generate divergences in identity complicates any attempt to think of the period's musical culture in terms of a simple East versus West, Communist versus capitalist, East/West or North/South divide. Imitation of others becomes a form of both co-optation and resistance, of domination and deviance: "Pulling you this way and that, mimesis plays this trick of dancing between the very same and the very different. An impossible but necessary, indeed an everyday affair, mimesis registers both sameness and difference, of being like, and of being Other. Creating stability from this instability is no small task, yet all identity formation is engaged in this habitually bracing activity in which the issue is not so much staying the same, but maintaining sameness through alterity."[57]

For example, as Hon-Lun Yang argues in her chapter here, cover versions of Anglo-American pop songs in Hong Kong generated a "unique brand of cosmopolitanism," a vernacular cosmopolitanism that signified a local identity, a sense of Hongkongness. Likewise, Anna Schultz demonstrates how traditional songs of religious devotion could be covered in new contexts during the Cold War, translating them to meet shifting cultural and political needs. The musical performances of Sant Tukdoji Maharaj could sing to Gandhian nonviolence, Nehruian nonaligned socialism, international religious conference calls for pacifism, and Indian nationalist resistance to Cold War nuclear threats from neighboring China and Pakistan—sometimes, in the very same performance. As the chapters collected here demonstrate, an alternate history of the multiple Asian Cold Wars can be traced through the networks of mimicry that cover songs generated during the period.

This alternate history of traffic in cover versions complicates our understandings of Asia's Cold War(s). Standard histories of Japan, Taiwan, and South Korea in the era, for example, situate them as allies of the United States and part of the liberal-capitalist bloc that sought to contain Communism in the region. As one would expect from this standard line, South Korean, Taiwanese, and Japanese popular music charts in the 1950s and 1960s were filled with cover versions of American hit songs, often with lyrics partially or wholly translated into Japanese, Mandarin, or Korean. Covering American pop music became one mechanism for drawing lines of affiliation and situating contemporary Japan, Taiwan, and South Korea in a new vision of world history.

But the culture of covering produced unexpected outcomes as well. In Japan, one of the most popular performers of hit covers in the 1960s was the Peanuts, a singing duo composed of twin sisters, Itō Emi (1941–2012) and Itō Yumi (1941–2016). Managed by Watanabe Productions (a major force in Japanese popular music that had its roots in the economy of US military bases), they debuted in 1959 at age eighteen and soon became regulars on the Japanese pop music hit charts with their striking sibling harmonies. The Peanuts released seventy-six singles between 1959 and their retirement in 1975, selling many millions of records along the way. They also became stars on the new medium of television. They made a number of film appearances as well and are best known in the West today for their recurring roles as tiny fairies in the Mothra monster movie series—another popular cultural product through which audiences in Japan and elsewhere tried to make sense of the geopolitical history of the Cold War.[58]

The Peanuts' repertoire consisted of easy-listening mainstream pop songs, including many translated cover versions of Anglo-American hit numbers. These might be (and perhaps were) listened to as aural enactments of modernization theory, a key Cold War ideological framework that positioned Japan and other US allies in the region as pursuing a developmentalist logic of history, in which liberal capitalist states in East Asia were said to be advancing toward modernity (defined as being the contemporary situation of the US and its allies in Western Europe) but always at a time lag and always sidestepping the need for violent historical change. Cover versions, with their appearance at a delay from the original version and with their respectful admiration of that original, provided a striking enactment of the model for modernization theory. The Peanuts' 1970 album *Fīrin Guddo: Pīnattsu no atarashii sekai* (Feeling good: The Peanuts' new world) featured covers of such recent hits as "What the World Needs Now," "Raindrops Keep Fallin' on My Head," "Michelle," "The Look of Love," and "I Say a Little Prayer." The lyrics are kept entirely in English, a sign of faithful covering. It was this stance of loyal imitation, no doubt, that earned the Peanuts their 1966 bookings to appear on *The Ed Sullivan Show* and *The Danny Kaye Show* in the United States.

But while the act of covering a tune opens oneself to be appropriated to a certain "original" and its putative authenticity, it is at the same time an active act of appropriation: a kind of colonial and semicolonial mimicry, along the lines Taussig suggests. Each of the cover songs on the *Feeling Good* album is actively reworked; the original is easily recognizable, but much of the pleasure these cover versions produce comes from the degree to which those originals have been transformed. The vocal parts are rewritten to foreground the Peanuts' signature sibling harmony, and the velvety orchestral backing arrangements are complex, often featuring pronounced syncopation, striking instrumental fills, and other hooks not found on the original recordings. In other words, even as these Japanese covers of American and British pop songs seem to pledge allegiance to the originals, they also simultaneously demonstrate a pronounced degree of originality that opens up a distance through the act of covering.

Moreover, even as they frequently covered Anglo-American hit songs, the Peanuts cultivated an image that was more closely connected with Latin America and continental Europe, especially France, West Germany, and Italy. The Peanuts recorded many cover versions of French, Italian, and German pop songs, often singing lyrics at least partially in the original language. Even the original numbers composed for them by Japanese songwriters often conveyed, in both lyrics and music, a continental European flair: they were meant to sound like covers. The duo's album titles also referred to Europe: for example, their 1971 album, *The Glorious Sound of Frances Lai*, a tribute to the French chanson composer; or their 1965 album, *Hits Parade Vol. 6: Around the Europe*. On their 45 rpm single-record jackets, it was common for song titles to be given in both Japanese and a (non-English) European language, whether the songs were cover versions of foreign numbers or original Japanese compositions. Moreover, the

Peanuts frequently visited Europe to perform concerts, appear on television, and have recording sessions. Their recordings were marketed on the continent and apparently reached a fair degree of popularity, especially in West Germany and Italy, where they performed on concert tours and television specials. Their 1965 recording "Heut' Abend" (released in West Germany under the moniker Die Peanuts) mixes Japanese and German lyrics in a playful manner that embodies the fluid cosmopolitanism of their image.

One of the best-known numbers by the Peanuts is their 1963 smash hit, "Koi no vakansu (Vacance de l'amour)." "Vacance de l'amour" won a Japan Record Award for its composer, Miyagawa Hiroshi (primary producer and arranger for the Peanuts). The lyrics by Iwatani Tokiko are in Japanese, except of course for the keyword *vacance* (French for "vacation") from the title, also used in the chorus refrain. The popularity of the song helped *vacance* become a kind of buzzword in Japan. No doubt this has something to do with 1960s trends in fashion, film, and other domains in which France enjoyed a privileged status. The cosmopolitanism of the Peanuts' cover songs produced a stylish image to their sound, lending an air of cultural sophistication that clearly sold well on the market: it was a kind of commodity branding. Michael Furmanovsky argues that the Peanuts were crucial figures in the introduction of a new Paris-centric upper-middle-class female fashion look in early 1960s Japan.[59]

And yet part of the reason the Peanuts' covers achieved such popularity is that they spoke to real desires that existed in Japan for a certain continental lifestyle, one associated with commodity consumption—but also with relative autonomy within the Cold War global order. The desirability of mimicking French pop music, for example, seems in part linked up with a desire to be more like France, to occupy a less subservient role vis-à-vis the United States in global geopolitics. In 1966, when the Peanuts were at the zenith of their popularity, France withdrew its armed forces from the North Atlantic Treaty Organization (NATO), complicating the Cold War binaries. In other words, this quasi-cover song was drawing alternative lines of affiliation, opening up possibilities for imagining Japan on a different historical trajectory—one not visible from the perspective adopted in more conventional histories of the Cold War period.

As this suggests, cover versions provide one mode for constructing alternative forms of historical consciousness in and of the present moment.[60] After the Peanuts' success in debuting "Vacance de l'amour," it quickly became a standard number in Japan and beyond. A cover version was released in 1963 by the Italian singer Caterina Valente and enjoyed success in Europe. Even more surprising, a Russian-language cover version became a hit in 1965 for

Nina Panteleeva in the Soviet Union. It eventually became a kind of standard number in the Soviet Union. Panteleeva would also record a Russian-language cover of the Peanuts' 1964 hit "Una sera di Tokio," another Miyagawa composition. In these instances, we see a cover song establishing a direct route between Japan and Western Europe and the USSR, tracing out lines of affiliation that do not pass through the United States. In these covers, we see both inside and outside Japan the outlines of an alternative historical consciousness to that which situated Japan simply as a loyal US Cold War partner.

We see this complexity of historical consciousness even more vividly in the Peanuts' many cover versions of South American, Central American, and Caribbean popular hits. If, as Gabriel Solis argues, a cover version is "not a matter of rehashing a song that had done well for a musician operating in some small market, but rather of establishing the credibility and authenticity of the coverer through the established cultural capital of the original," what kinds of tradition were the Peanuts inventing when they turned, as they so often did, to songs identified as Latin?[61] Their 1959 debut LP, for example, included "Aru koi no monogatari," a cover version of the bolero "Historia de un amor" by the Panamanian composer Carlos Eleta Almarán, which quickly achieved global popularity after being featured in a 1956 Mexican film of the same title. In the Peanuts' cover version, the lyrics alternate between Japanese translations and the original Spanish lyrics. The Peanuts would also record covers of, among others, "Quizás, quizás, quizás" (better known in English as "Perhaps, Perhaps, Perhaps"), "La novia," "Magica luna," "Moliendo Café," "¿Quién será?" and many others.

In other words, as cover artists and as covered artists, the Peanuts exist in a seemingly eclectic circulation of songs across the globe, one that opened up new lines of affiliation and new possibilities for imagining Japan's historical situation in the Cold War. Japan was one of the twenty-nine mostly Asian and African countries that sent official delegations to the 1955 conference in Bandung, Indonesia, an early effort to respond to the Cold War division of the world between American and Soviet blocs by creating a third force, the Non-Aligned Movement (NAM). Japan's participation in Bandung was in many ways incoherent. Whereas Bandung was intended to form an alliance among nations undergoing decolonization, Japan participated as a (former) imperial power. As Kristine Dennehy has noted, its delegation included several figures who had played key bureaucratic roles in its pre-1945 empire.[62] But the decision to participate in Bandung suggests the existence of a desire for nonalignment across the political spectrum in Japan, in both the state and civil society. Cover songs became an important means for both soliciting and expressing that desire. It hardly seems coincidental, then, that the Peanuts would sing the theme song for the soundtrack of the 1961 *Mothra* film in Indonesian.

After 1955, under US pressure, the Japanese state backed away from the Bandung movement. But Japanese intellectuals and cultural producers continued to look to the movement, seeking alternate forms of affiliation and cultural tradition. Japanese writers, for example, participated in the 1958 Tashkent meeting of the Afro-Asian Writers Union, despite efforts by the Japanese state to try to prevent them. Japan then hosted a 1961 emergency meeting of the Afro-Asian Writers Union in Tokyo, again in the face of opposition from the Japanese state. This meeting was held in the wake of the massive 1960 Anpo protests in Japan against the renewal of the US/Japan Security Treaty, the primary official apparatus of Cold War alliance between the two states. The participants in the meeting all saw the Anpo protests as a continuation of the Bandung movement. The standard histories of the 1960 Anpo demonstrations frame it within the tense relations of the US/Japan security relationship. But the 1961 Tokyo meeting and—in a quite different register—the cosmopolitan cover songs of the Peanuts suggest that the Anpo demonstrations need to be understood not just for what they opposed but also for what they were in favor of: what was called at the time "neutralism" but would increasingly through the 1960s be called "nonalignment" or "Third Worldism." With the new logic of covers that arose in tandem with rock and roll music, recording a cover song of, say, "Historia de un amor" was a way for the Peanuts to retroactively assert the cultural (and implicitly political) authenticity of the original recording—but also then to associate themselves as Japanese performers with that authenticity, establishing a lineage and a sense of community with the original.[63]

That is, even in the most commodified branches of popular music in Japan and elsewhere across Cold War Asia, we can hear traces of a utopian desire to escape the official binaries of the Cold War. The cosmopolitan cover songs of the Folk Crusaders and the Peanuts represented an attempt to imagine what it might sound like if Japan were not a client state of the US, what Japan might sound like in alternative lineages of musical tradition. To borrow Carol Muller's formulation, their covers of, for example, Korean or Latin songs "enabled an intimate identification between consumers/audiences and their geographically distant, but acoustically real and emotionally centripetal, musical cohorts," and in doing so helped imagine Japan as something other than an American client state.[64] Through cover songs, regardless of their geopolitical spatial location, Asian musicians and their fans could identify themselves with American and English counterparts but also with the nonaligned Bandung spirit and with counterparts within the socialist bloc. The practice of covers as a form of versioning helps us trace out alternative lines of history that necessarily complicate the dominant narratives of Cold War history.

Fronts

Popular songs have shaped contentious political arenas in modern Asia since the mass mediation of recordings began in the early twentieth century.[65] Unlike musical traditions that stay above or out of the fray, the creative agents of popular music, including poets, singers, instrumentalists, songwriters, visual artists, arrangers, and sound engineers, have regularly found themselves on the front lines of ideological and geopolitical struggles. Due to widespread affection for their work and its relative accessibility, popular music artists typically exercise disproportionate influence in political life, either inadvertently or deliberately, and often their vocation involves considerable personal risk where and when dissent is stifled by authorities. A third keyword, *fronts*, thus complements the emphasis on circulation in our discussion of *routes* and *covers*, not least because the martial resonance of the term immediately evokes the specter of human conflict. Violence, threats, hostilities, censorship, persecution, and sacrifice—these themes too figure prominently in our accounts of popular music in Asia's Cold Wars.[66]

Fronts imply competing forces where routes may be blocked or fluid depending on allegiances or which side succeeds at imposing its interests on others. Fronts also hint at alignments, shored-up or contested, as well as alliances, nurtured, broken, or remade anew. Spatially, fronts invoke a field or sphere of competition, but they can equally be social subjects of history themselves, as in revolutions or countercultural movements. If we return to the most literal meaning of the word, however, fronts are foreheads (from the Latin, *frōns*) and faces, markers of visibility and by extension, identity, like when someone claims they "never forget a face." The Hindi word for the recurring catch phrase (refrain) in North Indian film songs is *mukhṛā*, the face or front of the song.[67] As the stylistic and formal feature tasked with establishing a mood, lyrical theme, and stylistic identity, the mukhṛā is the sounded face, the hook or refrain, or catch phrase that listeners remember. But fronts can also be deceptively visible when they conceal more than they reveal, like songs, poems, or images that seem innocuous on the surface while working to stoke radical convictions and intentions for those in the know, those who hear preferred or subliminal messages beneath the face of a song.[68] Indeed, fronts can be covers for subversive actions, like the way tea stalls presented a legitimate front for debating and promoting radical socialist views in India during the 1950s, ideals that found their most compelling expression through street theater and popular song.[69] Moreover, individuals who exude bold confidence in their actions are often said to have a lot of front (nerve), a valence that when braided with the idea of fronts as recognizable identity markers evokes an archetypal figure in global popular music: the charismatic front figure of a band.

These are some of the ways in which "fronts" expand our framework for examining popular music in Asia's Cold Wars. In this section, we introduce the concept of "fronts" through a close reading of a celebrated South Indian songwriting team's classic revolutionary anthem from 1957, "Balikudeerangale" (Monuments of martyrdom). This song is one of the most well known examples of how popular music in the Malayalam-speaking state of Kerala challenged the Republic of India's official policy of nonalignment (see the chapters by Kommattam and Schultz). Its social history complicates any assumption that national forces alone define fronts, thereby bringing into relief interregional frictions and alliances. We choose this song to show how artists in a nascent theater and film music industry created enduring transnational socialist alignments and realignments in response to Cold War politics. Moreover, our example illustrates how a regionally specific front transcended, reimagined, and contested a nonaligned nation from its southern margins.

The song "Balikudeerangale" was written in 1957, two years after the Bandung Conference and the Warsaw Pact. The newly elected state government, led by the Communist Party of India (CPI), asked a songwriting duo to commemorate the martyrs who rose up against the British East India Company in the Indian Rebellion of 1857. The composer, G. Devarajan, and poet Vayalar Ramavarma responded with a bright, upbeat, group song with a catchy refrain and antiphonal verse structure.[70] The song was written only a few days before it was first performed publicly at a prominent traffic circle in Kerala's state capital, Thiruvananthapuram (formerly Trivandrum). The occasion was the inauguration of a martyr's column in the presence of two founding leaders: India's first president, Rajendra Prasad, of the Indian National Congress (the nationalist party of independence); and the first chief minister of Kerala, E. M. S. Namboodiripad, of the Communist Party of India. Four months earlier, the CPI made history as the first state government of the region and as one of the first democratic Communist governments in the world (see Kommattam's chapter). The performers included the popular singer K. S. George and other musicians recruited from the Kerala People's Arts Club (KPAC), a branch of the Indian People's Theatre Association.[71] These activist artists were prominent members of the Communist Party at the time and were therefore committed to a more radical socialist vision than the center-left policies of the Indian National

Congress. Nevertheless, for the inaugural performance at the Martyr's Column, the songwriters emphasized national unity and anticolonial struggle.[72] Shortly after the inauguration, however, the lyrics were swiftly repurposed to express solidarity with international labor and Communism.[73] By changing the color of the flag in the last verse from gold—the color of the Indian Congress party—to red, the songwriters realigned the song with the Soviet Union and the People's Republic of China: "You light the everlasting flames for generations. We now have a new red flag from the soil of Malabar [Northern Kerala], the very battleground where you stood in your armor."[74]

Hence the revised verse honored two revolutionary struggles: the patriotic anticolonialist movement for independence and the anticapitalist front. The example thus builds on our earlier discussion of the many routes taken by the Italian resistance song "Bella ciao" by underlining how popular songs gather multiple, accumulative, and even contradictory meanings. Indeed, Thomas Turino argues that popular music's power to condense sense and experience is the key to understanding its emotional intensity and immediacy, a process he poignantly describes as semantic snowballing.[75] Thus a single word substitution in the last verse immortalized the song for a generation of democratic socialist listeners while also carrying forward the original emphasis on nationalist sentiment.

A year after the memorial performance, Devarajan and Vayalar adapted the song for *Visharikku Kattu Venda* (The fan needs no breeze, 1958), a socialist play by Ponkunnam Varkey. Recognizing the commercial potential, the Gramophone Company of India Limited subsequently produced a recording of the song in Madras (now Chennai) with K. S. George, the same lead singer who performed at the inauguration, along with popular actor-singer Sulochana. This is the song that was widely disseminated through radio and commercial sales under the record label, His Master's Voice (HMV). Thus "Balikudeerangale" did much more than commemorate the centenary of the first war of Indian independence; it also marked the first decade of Indian independence (1947), the election of the first democratic Communist government in Asia, and the birth of an enduring popular anthem in the southwestern corner of a key nonaligned state.

In his book on the political force of music, Barry Shank traces the evolution of anthems from their origins in ritual and religious experience to secular politics, where rulers and nation-states became the primary objects of praise.[76] According to Shank, these are traditional anthems, songs that are sung at formal occasions like rituals at places of worship or nation-building events. As Schultz reveals in her chapter, the devotional repertoire of a singer-saint like

Tukdoji Maharaj might span the gamut of Shank's traditional-popular spectrum.[77] Popular anthems share many of the same musical and social features as traditional anthems, but they also have an ordinary everyday presence in the lives of folks who share an implicit sense of equality. Like traditional anthems, popular anthems create space for reciprocal recognition of belonging, largely because they manage to instill a sense of fairness, which in turn can serve as a base for political action. Such popular anthems avoid engaging in overt political discourse but prepare the ground for widespread collective action around a common sense of purpose in the political public sphere. The role of the urban folk revival and Black congregational singing in the American civil rights movement is a convincing case of how popular anthems harnessed much of the political force of traditional anthems while creating a cultural context for sustained oppositional action.[78] For example, Shin's chapter in this volume demonstrates how the vernacular soundtrack of American resistance in the 1960s and 1970s migrated to South Korea, where Christian churches and singer-songwriters were instrumental in building an ordinary culture of resistance. Shin's account highlights how Korean artists indigenized and adapted the work of leading North American urban folk revivalists by writing original covers and new songs that became anthemic for a youth-led countercultural front that confronted increasingly authoritarian policies in the 1970s. To capture this subtle but significant distinction between traditional and popular anthems, Shank reaches for Lauren Berlant's concept of the juxtapolitical: actions that are neither antipolitical nor explicitly political but are nevertheless constitutive of a ground for collective engagement.[79] He notes that while popular anthems draw on many of the qualities of religious and national anthems, including their accessibility, limited pitch range, antiphonal structure, uncomplicated rhythm, and clear lyrical themes, they differ in one important respect. Namely, they circulate beyond the formal conditions that constrain individual creative agency in highly ritualized (formalized) musical performance. The pop anthem thus "entrains bodies otherwise stifled toward an awareness of the shared, the mutual, the collective that extends beyond the ordinary and the same," and in doing so, they "shift the way the world is heard."[80] Moreover, a song that was originally intended to serve as a traditional anthem—like the commission of "Balikudeerangale" to commemorate anticolonial struggle and sacrifice at an official event—could also later acquire new currency and polysemy as a popular anthem.

In addition to circulating across geographical space, some anthems also transcend their historically specific moment. Drawing on new media and stylistic features, they can be refashioned in ways that appeal to multiple age-based cohorts, thereby fostering the intergenerational solidarity required to shore up artistic fronts in contentious political arenas. The creative process of revitalizing songs several decades after they were originally written is well demonstrated by the recent use of "Balikudeerangale" in the Indian Malayalam film *CIA: Comrade in America* (2017). Directed by filmmaker Amal Neerad, the film tells the story of a young South Indian communist leader, Aji Matthew, whose American-born love interest abruptly returns to Texas when her family finds out about their mutual affection. Determined to reunite with her in Dallas, Aji reveals his plan at the local Communist reading room in a late-night conversation with imaginary comrades: Karl Marx, Vladimir Lenin, and Che Guevara.[81] The next day he flies to Nicaragua, where he can purchase a visa on arrival. With the help of a local Communist party office and a Sri Lankan taxi driver in San Juan del Sur, he travels through Central America and Mexico to the border city of Reynosa, where he joins a group of irregular migrants from Latin America, China, India, and Pakistan. Together they embark on a dangerous journey to cross the US-Mexico border. Along the way, Aji gains firsthand knowledge of the hardships migrants face as they struggle to locate family members, escape the violence of homelands, or find better economic opportunities. As the film unfolds, the narrative moves beyond the romantic plotline to critique the anti-immigration and border security policies of the United States.

Long before the setting shifts from Kerala to Latin America, however, Neerad follows Indian cinematic convention by introducing main characters through the picturization of popular song genres. For example, filmmakers often intensify blossoming romances through "love songs" and amplify protagonists through elaborate "hero introduction songs." Both genres are deployed in the opening scenes of *CIA*, but because of the social realist aspirations of the film, Neerad was especially concerned with the "hero introduction song." It was crucial that the film's protagonist represent more than the average South Indian action hero.[82] Aji would need to embody hypermasculine ideals and the legacy of radical socialism in Kerala as well as contemporary transnational solidarity with working-class people across the Global South. What kind of musical strategies did music director Gopi Sundar mobilize to express these associations?

In a conversation about the soundtrack at his recording studio in Kochi, Sundar recalled how the director insisted on leading with "an anthem type of song." A public supporter of leftist political movements in Kerala, Neerad came up with the idea of reviving "Balikudeerangale."[83] Working in collaboration with lyricist Rafeeq Ahmed, Sundar thus adapted the 1950s-era popular anthem to figure prominently in a new hero introduction song called "Kerala Manninayi" (Out of Kerala soil). The song would provide the non-diegetic soundtrack for an opening dramatic scene depicting a violent confrontation between riot police and Communist protesters led by Aji. According to Sundar, the main challenge was finding a way to pay homage to a beloved Communist anthem for older generations while also capturing the energy and musical tastes of millennial youth.[84]

Sundar deployed three main strategies to boost the song's intergenerational appeal. By rerecording "Balikudeerangale" with crackle effects and midfrequencies only, he created a lo-fi aesthetic to stir feelings of nostalgia among listeners who were familiar with the original. Moreover, instead of inviting a veteran classically trained playback singer to perform the lead vocal part, he recruited Vaikom Vijayalakshmi, a charismatic popular singer known for her unique quality of voice and personal narrative of struggle against ableism in the music industry. As a result, Sundar's reconstruction of the song captured the spirit of the anthem while also functioning more like a sample of the 1957 recording rather than as a cover. Second, in his struggle to "crack the tune," as he put it, Sundar felt the bright tonality of G major and smooth melodic motion in the original song would fall short of capturing the imagination of younger listeners. He decided to use "Balikudeerangale" for the hook and refrain in contrast with a hip-hop aesthetic featuring limited minor key intervals, rhythmic lyrical delivery, and a stronger beat in the verses. One of the musical problems that Sundar had to solve, however, was the task of bridging divergent styles—classic *filmi* group song and contemporary hip-hop—in a way that maintained the coherence of the song overall. He decided to use a clean blues riff on an electric guitar in the relative E minor key, a musical gesture that made it possible to layer and overlap the melodically oriented major refrains and rhythmically driven minor-inflected verses.[85] Finally, Sundar and Neerad felt that a multilingual dimension would capture the outward-looking cosmopolitan aspirations of South Indian youth. Their first idea was to contrast the flow of the Malayalam refrain with rapping in English, but they quickly decided that a "foreign" language associated with British colonization and American imperialism would undermine the patriotic socialist sentiment of the story. So they rejected the more common hip-hop practice of alternating English and local Asian-language lyrics, choosing instead to write the rap verses in Tamil, arguably the most global of South Indian Dravidian languages. For example, Tamil-speaking artists from Malaysia were instrumental in the development of a multilingual hip-hop scene as part of a broader pan-Asian pattern of affinity for Black expressivity and empowerment.[86] Thus to help write and stylize the

Tamil lyrics, Sundar engaged Yogi B—a Kuala Lumpur–based hip-hop artist and founding front figure for the Malaysian hip-hop group Poetic Ammo. The incorporation of the blues guitar riff as well as hip-hop elements, including breaks, syncopation, rhyming, flow, and layering, not only expanded the song's youth cultural resonance as a contemporary vehicle for reviving revolutionary ideals of martyrdom and social justice; it also demonstrated how fusing a reconstructed 1950s Indian anthem with Africanist musical aesthetics in a film about alliance building with Latin America evokes new routes, covers, and fronts. Like the Peanuts' cover versions of Latin American songs in Japan, these routes bypassed the United States. In the process, they realigned Asian, Latin American, and African diasporic interests along a millennial front of socialist solidarity with Latinidad at a time of escalating rhetoric and anxiety over speculation that Asia's "new" Cold War had already begun.[87]

This brief account of the historic and contemporary significance of a South Indian song's passage from traditional anthem to popular anthem anticipates the chapters gathered under *fronts*. Marié Abe's contribution focuses on contemporary Okinawan popular music from the southern Ryūkyū Islands in Japan. She argues that the music of Daiku Tetsuhiro reimagines the spatiality of the archipelago from a highly militarized front in American Cold War strategic policy to a node in a dense transpacific network of relationalities that stretch across time to link multiple forms of difference. Similarly, Anna Schultz's chapter explores how popular music connects people and difference transnationally through a biographical lens. Presenting a North Indian perspective on how popular music can both reinforce and challenge top-down narratives of Cold War fronts, she examines the complex life, art, and politics of Maharashtrian singer-saint Tukdoji Maharaj, including his role as a charismatic public figure in Gandhi's anticolonial struggle, his leadership in the early years of the Hindu nationalist movement, his controversial stance on violence in the Cold War climate of nuclear armament in the region, and his ironic participation in the peaceful front led by the Third World Religion Congress. Schultz's account highlights the many ways in which fluency in local devotional musical styles empowered an Indian spiritual leader to influence the circulation of ideas across various Cold War fault lines. Finally, Qian Zhang examines the role of music criticism in framing and policing popular music as an expression of internal fronts in the People's Republic of China. She shows how critics deployed metaphor and aesthetic discourse to draw clear distinctions between yellow and red musicians as part of the Communist Party of China's media strategy to discredit artists associated with bourgeois values. Just like the substitution of a red flag for a gold one in the lyrics of "Balikudeerangale" and its subsequent revival as a hip-hop anthem in commercial film, Zhang shows how visual imagery, words, media, and the music itself intensify ideologically charged fronts in ways that influence not only how people respond to the political force of popular music but also how and at what cost they align themselves with one side or the other.

Collectively, the chapters in this volume encourage us to listen beyond national fronts, or as Josh Kun argues, to recognize that while music can have roots in a nation and influence national formations, "it always overflows, spills out, sneaks through, reaches an ear on the other side of the border line, on the other side of the sea."[88] Likewise, the authors gathered here invite us to consider how the creative work, circulation, and open or clandestine enjoyment of popular songs call into question the conventional routes, boundaries, and periodizations that throw more shade than light on the cultural complexity of everyday life in Asia's Cold War(s). For example, they invite us to hear covers not as derivative expression of modern yearning but as imaginative acts of mimesis that could amplify homage, subversion, or aspiration, depending on who is performing and listening, where, and when. Regardless of which one of the imbricated themes of routes, covers, or fronts is given more prominence, all the chapters present nuanced accounts of how popular music and Cold War forces mutually shape one another. In that sense, each one unfolds like a cassette playing first the A and then the B side or vice versa. Whereas A sides foreground how sonorous popular music worlds bring uneven, dynamic, and discrepant Cold War alignments into sharper relief, the complementary B sides consider the ways in which human conflict, friction, and territoriality have inspired and provoked some of the most compelling and forceful music of postwar Asia.

NOTES

1. Odd Arne Westad, *The Global Cold War* (New York: Cambridge University Press, 2005).
2. Heonik Kwon, *The Other Cold War* (New York: Columbia University Press, 2010), 8.
3. On the phenomenon of "red restaurants" in contemporary China, see Jennifer Hubbert, "Revolution Is a Dinner Party: Cultural Revolution Restaurants in Contemporary China," *China Review* 5, no. 2 (2005): 123–48; and Claire Conceison, "Eating Red: Performing Maoist Nostalgia in Beijing's Revolution-Themed Restaurants," in *Food and Theatre on the World Stage*, ed. Dorothy Chansky and Ann Folino White (New York: Routledge, 2016), 100–115.
4. Bruce Cumings, *Parallax Visions: Making Sense of American–East Asian Relations at the End of the Century* (Durham, NC: Duke University Press, 1999), 51, 59.
5. See, for example, Daniel Belgrade, *The Culture of Spontaneity: Improvisation and the Arts in Postwar America* (Chicago: University of Chicago Press, 1999); Greg

Barnhisel, *Cold War Modernists: Art, Literature, and American Cultural Diplomacy* (New York: Columbia University Press, 2015); and Eduardo Herrera, *Elite Art Worlds: Philanthropy, Latin Americanism, and Avant-garde Music* (Oxford: Oxford University Press, 2020).

6 Kwon, *The Other Cold War*, 6.
7 Lisa Yoneyama, *Cold War Ruins: Transpacific Critique of American Justice and Japanese War Crimes* (Durham, NC: Duke University Press, 2016), 15.
8 Yoneyama, *Cold War Ruins*, 61.
9 Dredge Byung'chu Käng, "Idols of Development: Transnational Transgender Performance in Thai K-Pop Cover Dance," *TSQ: Transgender Studies Quarterly* 1, no. 4 (November 2014): 559–71.
10 Bruno Nettl, "We're on the Map: Reflections on SEM in 1955 and 2005," *Ethnomusicology* 50, no. 2 (2006): 186.
11 Kathleen D. McCarthy, "From Cold War to Cultural Development: The International Cultural Activities of the Ford Foundation, 1950–1980," *Daedalus* 116, no. 1 (1987): 94. As a newly independent republic under democratic socialist leadership, India was a leading voice in 1955 at the Bandung Conference, where Asian and African nation-states established the groundwork for the Non-Aligned Movement (NAM).
12 Motti Regev, *Pop-Rock Music: Aesthetic Cosmopolitanism in Late Modernity* (Cambridge: Polity, 2013), 17.
13 Theodor W. Adorno, "On Popular Music" (with the assistance of George Simpson), *Studies in Philosophy and Social Science* 9 (1941): 17–18.
14 Lawrence Grossberg, *Cultural Studies in the Future Tense* (Durham, NC: Duke University Press, 2010), 29.
15 Peter Manual, *Popular Musics of the Non-Western World: An Introductory Survey* (Oxford: Oxford University Press, 1988), 15.
16 Jonathan Sterne, "Sonic Imaginations," in *The Sound Studies Reader*, ed. Jonathan Sterne (New York: Routledge, 2012), 2.
17 David W. Samuels, Louis Meintjes, Ana Maria Ochoa, and Thomas Porcello, "Soundscapes: Toward a Sounded Anthropology," *Annual Review of Anthropology* 39 (October 2010): 330.
18 Peter J. Schmelz, "Introduction: Music in the Cold War," *Journal of Musicology* 26, no. 1 (2009): 8.
19 Studies on Asian sound include David Novak, *Japanoise: Music at the Edge of Circulation* (Durham, NC: Duke University Press, 2013); Nicholas Harkness, *Songs of Seoul: An Ethnography of Voice and Voicing in Christian South Korea* (Berkeley: University of California Press, 2014); Noriko Manabe, *The Revolution Will Not Be Televised: Protest Music after Fukushima* (Oxford: Oxford University Press, 2015); Andrew N. Weintraub and Bart Barendregt, eds., *Vamping the Stage: Female Voices of Asian Modernities* (Honolulu: University of Hawai'i Press, 2017); and Andrew F. Jones, *Circuit Listening: Chinese Popular Music in the Global 1960s* (Minneapolis: University of Minnesota Press, 2020).
20 See Jedrek Mularski, *Music, Politics, and Nationalism in Latin America: Chile during the Cold War Era* (Amherst, NY: Cambria Press, 2015); Penny Von Eschen, "Di Ea-

gle and Di Bear: Who Gets to Tell the Story of the Cold War," in *Audible Empire: Music, Global Politics, Critique*, ed. Ronald Rodano and Tejumola Olaniyan (Durham, NC: Duke University Press, 2016), 187–208; and Ewa Mazierska, ed., *Popular Music in Eastern Europe: Breaking the Cold War Paradigm* (London: Palgrave Macmillan, 2016).

21 George Lipsitz, *Footsteps in the Dark: The Hidden Histories of Popular Music* (Minneapolis: University of Minnesota Press, 2007), xv.

22 Peter Wade, "Hybridity Theory and Kinship Thinking," *Cultural Studies* 19, no. 5 (2006): 611.

23 Quoted in Michael Berry, *Speaking in Images: Interviews with Contemporary Chinese Filmmakers* (New York: Columbia University Press, 2005), 190. See also Jia Zhangke, Cheng Qingsong, and Huang Ou, "Jia Zhangke: Zai 'Zhantai' shang dengdai" [Jia Zhangke: Waiting on the *Platform*], in *Wode sheyingji bu sahuang: Xianfeng dianyingren dang'an—shengyu 1961–1970* [My camera doesn't lie: Files on avant-garde directors born in 1961–1970], ed. Cheng Qingsong and Huang Ou (Beijing: Zhongguo youyi chubanshe, 2002), 343; and Jason McGrath, *Postsocialist Modernity: Chinese Cinema, Literature, and Criticism in the Market Age* (Stanford, CA: Stanford University Press, 2008), 149–50. On Teng's arrival in mainland China, see Andrew Jones, *Like a Knife: Ideology and Genre in Contemporary Chinese Popular Music* (Ithaca, NY: Cornell University Press, 1992), 16; Jones, *Circuit Listening*, 169–95; Nimrod Baranovitch, *China's New Voices: Popular Music, Ethnicity, Gender and Politics, 1978–1997* (Berkeley: University of California Press, 2003), 10–13; Marc L. Moskowitz, *Cries of Joy, Songs of Sorrow: Chinese Pop Music and Its Cultural Connotations* (Honolulu: University of Hawai'i Press, 2010), 19–21; and Andrew N. Weintraub and Bart Barendregt, "Re-vamping Asia: Women, Music, and Modernity in Comparative Perspective," in Weintraub and Barendregt, *Vamping the Stage*, 1–2. On the importance of radio and tape recorders for the diffusion of Teng's music in China and on the trend of "copying Deng Lijun," see ChenChing Cheng and George Athanasopoulos, "Teresa Teng (Deng Lijun), the Enlightenment for Democracy in the 1980s and a Case of Collective Nostalgia for an Era That Never Existed," *Lied and populäre Kultur / Song and Popular Culture* 60–61 (2015/16): 41–59.

24 Andrew Jones, *Yellow Music: Media Culture and Colonial Modernity in the Chinese Jazz Age* (Durham, NC: Duke University Press, 2001), 6. On Zhou, see Jean Ma, *Sounding the Modern Woman: The Songstress in Chinese Cinema* (Durham, NC: Duke University Press, 2015); and Yifen Beus, "On Becoming Nora: Transforming the Voice and Place of the Sing-Song Girl through Zhou Xuan," in Weintraub and Barendregt, *Vamping the Stage*, 65–82.

25 Jones, *Yellow Music*, 6.

26 Lydia Liu, "A Folksong Immortal and Official Popular Culture in Twentieth-Century China," in *Writing and Materiality in China: Essays in Honor of Patrick Hanan*, ed. Judith Zeitlin and Lydia Liu (Cambridge, MA: Harvard University Asia Center, 2003), 553–609. Such circular operation of collection, transformation, and dissemination was aimed at retrieving the revolutionary fervor of the people, as reflected in their folk songs, and hence at legitimizing the revolution. See Max

Bohnenkamp, "Turning Ghosts into People: *The White-Haired Girl*, Revolutionary Folklorism, and the Politics of Aesthetics in Modern China" (PhD diss., University of Chicago, 2014), 17–19.

27   Barbara Mittler, "Cultural Revolution Model Works and the Politics of Modernization in China: An Analysis of Taking Tiger Mountain by Strategy," *World of Music* 45, no. 2 (2003): 53–81; Mittler, *A Continuous Revolution: Making Sense of Cultural Revolution Culture* (Cambridge, MA: Harvard University Press, 2012); Paul Clark, *The Chinese Cultural Revolution: A History* (New York: Cambridge University Press, 2008); John Winzenburg, "Musical-Dramatic Experimentation in the *Yangbanxi*: A Case for Precedence in *The Great Wall*," in *Listening to China's Cultural Revolution: Music, Politics, and Cultural Continuities*, ed. Paul Clark, Laikwan Pang, and Tsan Huang-Tsai (New York: Palgrave Macmillan, 2016), 189–212.

28   Cheng and Athanasopoulos, "Teresa Teng," 46.

29   The term *liuxing* is often used interchangeably with *tongsu*. Both characterize a heterogeneous field of musical styles, even though "*tongsu* clearly implies political legitimacy and ideological orthodoxy, while *liuxing* continues to connote 'yellow music,' westernization, and heterodox activity." Jones, *Like a Knife*, 20.

30   The World Federation of Democratic Youth was founded in London in 1945 with the goal of bringing together international youth with a broad antifascist and propeace agenda. With the onset of the Cold War, however, it was accused by the US State Department of being under Soviet control. The first of the World Festivals of Youth and Students took place in Prague in 1947 in commemoration of young Czechs' protests against the Nazi occupation in 1939. Later editions took place in Eastern Europe and in other socialist countries such as Cuba and North Korea, but also in Austria (1959) and Finland (1962).

31   James Clifford, *Routes: Travel and Translation in the Late Twentieth Century* (Cambridge, MA: Harvard University Press, 1997), 3. On the global networks of contemporary music, see Jason Toynbee and Byron Dueck, eds., *Migrating Music* (London: Routledge, 2011).

32   On the concept of feedback, see Novak, *Japanoise*, esp. 17–20.

33   For detailed analyses of the film, see Jason McGrath, "The Independent Cinema of Jia Zhangke: From Postsocialist Realism to a Transnational Aesthetic," in *The Urban Generation: Chinese Cinema and Society at the Turn of the Twenty-First Century*, ed. Zhang Zhen (Durham, NC: Duke University Press, 2007), 81–114; Michael Berry, *Xiao Wu, Platform, Unknown Pleasures: Jia Zhangke's "Hometown Trilogy"* (London: Palgrave Macmillan/BFI, 2009), 50–92; Liu Jin, *Signifying the Local: Media Productions Rendered in Local Languages in Mainland China in the New Millennium* (Leiden: Brill, 2013), 196–201; and Ying Xiao, *China in the Mix: Cinema, Sound, and Popular Culture in the Age of Globalization* (Jackson: University Press of Mississippi, 2017), 118–33. See also the useful appendix "Music and Sound in Jia Zhangke's *Platform*," in Xiao, *China in the Mix*, 239–48.

34   Berry, *Xiao Wu*, 71–74.

35   "Bianjiang quanshui you qing you qun" (Clear spring water at the frontier) was from the soundtrack of the spy movie *Hei san jiao* (Black triangle, 1977). It was the first

hit by the famous singer Li Guyi, "the first mainland singer to use breathing singing after decades in which only . . . Western heroic bel canto singing . . . and artistic folk/national singing . . . were permissible." Baranovitch, *China's New Voices*, 16.

36 Berry, *Speaking in Images*, 191.

37 McGrath notes that the film foregrounds multiple chronologies and sudden, nonlinear changes in fashion (jeans, perms, etc.) that subtly affect the lives of the protagonists. McGrath, "The Independent Cinema of Jia Zhangke," 100.

38 Berry, *Xiao Wu*, 84.

39 Cesare Bermani, *Guerra guerra ai palazzi e alle chiese: Saggi sul canto sociale* [War war to palaces and churches: Essays on the social song] (Rome: Odradek, 2003), 230. All translations are by Iovene unless otherwise noted.

40 One of the earliest attempts at a history of "Bella ciao" is Roberto Leydi e Bruno Pianta, "La possibile storia di una canzone" [The possible story of a song], in *Storia d'Italia*, vol. 5, *I documenti 2* (Turin: Einaudi, 1973). Among other possible affiliations, similarities have been noted with the melody of the Yiddish traditional songs "Koilen" and "Di silberne khasene." Carlo Pestelli, *Bella ciao: La canzone della libertà* [Bella ciao: The song of freedom] (Turin: Add editore, 2016), 84–89.

41 Bermani, *Guerra guerra ai palazzi e alle chiese*, 230–32, 246.

42 Pestelli, *Bella ciao*, 93.

43 Presented by the group Nuovo Canzoniere Italiano, the concert was a milestone in the history of Italian folk revival. See Bermani, *Guerra guerra ai palazzi e alle chiese*, 225; and Pestelli, *Bella ciao*, 60–67.

44 In Montand's version, the last line, "this is the flower of the partisan who died for freedom," is omitted. In the Chinese version, the last verse is omitted as well.

45 Jonathan Sanjeev Withers, "Kurdish Music-Making in Istanbul: Music, Sentiment, and Ideology in a Changing Urban Context" (PhD diss., Harvard University, 2016), 97.

46 Unlike the majority of Yugoslavian partisan films, these two movies focused on an individual character rather than on a group or collective, though they shared with other films in the genre a "strict Manichean narrative structure, pathos-heavy dramaturgy, and film language that is indebted more to classical Hollywood than to European cinematographies." Peter Stankovic, "1970s Partisan Epics as Western Films: The Question of Genre and Myth in Yugoslav Partisan Film," in *Partisans in Yugoslavia: Literature, Film and Visual Culture*, ed. Miranda Jakiša and Nikica Gilić (Bielefeld: Transcript, 2015), 249. On the genre of partisan films, see also Pavle Levi, *Disintegration in Frames: Aesthetics and Ideology in the Yugoslav and Post-Yugoslav Cinema* (Stanford, CA: Stanford University Press, 2007).

47 Yuan Qingfeng, "Nansilafu yingpian yu Zhongguo dalu dianying wenhua yujing de duijie—Yi Beijing dianying zhipianchang 1973 nian yizhi de *Qiao* (1969) wei lie" [The cultural contexts of Yugoslavian movies and mainland Chinese cinema—The case of *The Bridge* (1969), dubbed by Beijing Film Studio in 1973], *Shantou daxue xuebao* 30, no. 2 (2014): 13.

48 Yuan, "Nansilafu yingpian yu Zhongguo dalu dianying wenhua yujing de duijie," 13. China had imported eight Yugoslavian films in the 1950s but none in the 1960s,

for at that time Yugoslavia was considered a revisionist country. Cultural contacts were resumed in the early 1970s, and nineteen Yugoslavian films were imported and dubbed over the decade. The fact that both countries were alienated from the Soviet Union contributed to their rapprochement.

49   Anonymous, *Waiguo gequji* [Collection of foreign melodies] (Chengdu: Sichuan renmin chubanshe, 1979). The volume includes Russian, European, and Indonesian leftist and revolutionary songs. "Ah, Friend" is presented as an Italian folk song and as the soundtrack of *The Bridge*, and its translation is credited to the Beijing Movies Dubbing Group. This version also appears in the collection *Liuxing gequ jianshang*, in which musicologist Xu Shujian offers some background information on the song and a detailed analysis of the melody, emphasizing its power as a war song. Xu Shujian, "Shengming—Meili de hua: 'Ah, Pengyou' xinshang" (Life—A beautiful flower: appreciating "Ah, friend"), in *Liuxing gequ jianshang* [Appreciating popular music], ed. Jiang Chaowen and Zheng Chengwei (Guangzhou: Guangdong gaodeng jiaoyu chubanshe, 1987).

50   *Yingyu gequxuan* [Selected songs in English], ed. Guiyang shifan xueyuan waiyuxi et al. (Guiyang: Zhuankeban yingyuke, 1980), 262–63. This collection must have aimed at teaching English through the greatest hits of world folk songs, as it was issued by the Foreign Language Department of Guiyang Normal University.

51   The record included (1) "Ningen no Shōmei no Tēma," the theme song from *Ningen no Shōmei* (*Proof of the Man*, 1977); (2) "Auld Lang Syne" (theme song from *Waterloo Bridge*, 1940); (3) "Daiya yeh main kahan phasi" (from Bollywood classic *Caravan*, 1971); (4) the theme song from *Future World* (1976); (5) "Bella ciao"; (6) "Merry Unbirthday to You" (from *Alice in Wonderland*, 1951); (7) the theme song from *The Sound of Music* (1965); (8) "Sensei no tsūshinbo" (The teacher's notebook), the theme song from a 1977 Japanese children's movie of the same title; and (9) the theme song from *Walter Defends Sarajevo* (1972).

52   See, for example, Shunya Yoshimi, "'America' as Desire and Violence: Americanization in Postwar Japan and Asia during the Cold War," *Inter-Asia Culture Studies* 4, no. 3 (2003): 433–50; and Andrew Jones, *Circuit Listening*, 109–131.

53   See Maeda Yoshitaka and Hirahara Kōji, eds., *Nihon no fōku & rokku hisutorii 1: 60-nendai fōku no jidai* (Tokyo: Shinkō Music, 1993), 111–15.

54   Kuan-Hsing Chen, *Asia as Method: Toward Deimperialization* (Durham, NC: Duke University Press, 2010).

55   Michael Bourdaghs, *Sayonara Amerika, Sayonara Nippon* (New York: Columbia University Press, 2012). See also Deborah Shamoon, "Recreating Traditional Music in Postwar Japan: A Prehistory of Enka," *Japan Forum* 26, no. 1 (2014): 113–38; and Christine Yano, "Covering Disclosures: Practices of Intimacy, Hierarchy, and Authenticity in a Japanese Popular Music Genre," *Popular Music and Society* 28, no. 2 (2005): 193–205.

56   Michael Taussig, *Mimesis and Alterity: A Particular History of the Senses* (New York: Routledge, 1992), 138.

57   Taussig, *Mimesis and Alterity*, 129.

58 Yoshikuni Igarashi, "Mothra's Gigantic Egg: Consuming the South Pacific in 1960s Japan," in *In Godzilla's Footsteps: Japanese Pop Culture Icons on the Global Stage*, ed. William M. Tsutsui and Michiko Ito (New York: Palgrave Macmillan 2006), 83–102.

59 Michael Furmanovsky, "A Complex Fit: The Remaking of Japanese Femininity and Fashion, 1945–65," *Kokusai bunka kenkyū* 16 (2012): 43–65. This Japanese fascination with "Frenchness" coincided with the golden age of French chanson (i.e., Brel, Brassens, Barbara, as opposed to the American-derived yé-yé music). Some have argued that the ennoblement of a sophisticated poetic song genre was part of a broader French emphasis on cultural and intellectual excellence/leadership in the face of declining international political influence. See Adeline Cordier, *Post-War French Popular Music: Cultural Identity and the Brel-Brassens-Ferré Myth* (Farnham, UK: Ashgate, 2014), 92.

60 John Paul Meyers, "Still Like That Old Time Rock and Roll: Tribute Bands and Historical Consciousness in Popular Music," *Ethnomusicology* 59, no. 1 (Winter 2015): 61–81.

61 Gabriel Solis, "I Did It My Way: Rock and the Logic of Covers," *Popular Music and Society* 33, no. 3 (2010): 300.

62 Kristine Dennehy, "Overcoming Colonialism at Bandung, 1955," in *Pan-Asianism in Modern Japanese History: Colonialism, Regionalism and Borders*, ed. Sven Saaler and J. Victor Koschmann (London: Routledge, 2007), 213–25. See also Kewku Ampiah, *The Political and Moral Imperatives of the Bandung Conference of 1955: The Reactions of the U.S., U.K. and Japan* (Folkestone, Kent, UK: Global Oriental, 2007).

63 Solis, "I Did It My Way."

64 Carol A. Muller, "American Musical Surrogacy: A View from Post–World War II South Africa," *Safundi: The Journal of South African and American Studies* 7, no. 3 (2006): 4.

65 For a recent look at how the circulation of popular music recordings contributed to decolonization movements throughout the Global South, see Michael Denning, *Noise Uprising: The Audiopolitics of a World Musical Revolution* (London: Verso, 2015); and Ronald Radano and Tejumola Olaniyan, eds., *Audible Empire: Music, Global Politics, Critique* (Durham, NC: Duke University Press, 2016).

66 To cite a recent example, Rahile Dawut, the internationally renowned scholar of Uighur expressive culture, disappeared in December 2017. She is widely believed to have been detained by Chinese authorities at a "re-education" facility or prison along with other prominent academics and artists, including popular singer and musician Abdurehim Heyit. Their disappearance appears to be part of a systematic clampdown on prominent figures whose work or voice could be viewed as supportive of Uighur independence or religious extremism. See Chris Buckley and Austin Ramzy, "Star Scholar Disappears as Crackdown Engulfs Western China," *New York Times*, August 10, 2018.

67 Jayson Beaster-Jones, *Bollywood Sounds: The Cosmopolitan Mediations of Hindi Film Song* (Oxford: Oxford University Press, 2015), 33.

68 See Andrew Jones's pathbreaking work on rock, subliminality, subversion, and ideology in the People's Republic of China. Jones, *Like a Knife*.

69   Sumangala Damodaran, *The Radical Impulse: Music in the Tradition of the Indian People's Theatre Association* (New Delhi: Tulika Books, 2017).

70   The original recording of "Balikudeerangale" is available as "Bali Kudeerangale—KPAC Drama Songs," YouTube, accessed October 2020, https://www.youtube.com/watch?v=lAQoOwabJX8.

71   The Indian People's Theatre Association was founded in Mumbai (Bombay) in 1943. The Kerala People's Arts Club was formed in 1951.

72   The Martyr's Column at Palayam Junction in Thiruvananthapuram is also known as the Raktha Sakshi Mandapam.

73   Ravi Menon, personal communication with Kaley Mason, January 5, 2019.

74   "Niṅṅaḷ ninna samarāṅkaṇa bhūvil ninnāṇiñña kavacaṅṅaḷumāyi. Vannu ñaṅṅaḷ malanāṭṭile maṇṇil ninnitā putiya cenkoṭi nēṭi."

75   Thomas Turino, "Signs of Imagination, Identity, and Experience: A Peircian Semiotic Theory for Music," *Ethnomusicology* 43, no. 2 (1999): 242.

76   Barry Shank, *The Political Force of Musical Beauty* (Durham, NC: Duke University Press, 2014), 39.

77   See also Anna Schultz, *Singing a Hindu Nation: Marathi Devotional Performance and Nationalism* (Oxford: Oxford University Press, 2013).

78   See Ron Eyerman and Andrew Jamison, *Music and Social Movements: Mobilizing Traditions in the Twentieth Century* (Cambridge: Cambridge University Press, 1998).

79   Shank, *The Political Force of Musical Beauty*, 48; Lauren Berlant, *The Female Complaint: The Unfinished Business of Sentimentality in American Culture* (Durham, NC: Duke University Press, 2008).

80   Shank, *The Political Force of Musical Beauty*, 40, 69.

81   Conspicuously absent is Mao Zedong. This may simply reflect the director's sense of the spatial and temporal limitations of the scene, or it could also be a commentary on the ambivalent place of China in a new international socialist front. A Chinese character does enter the narrative later on when Aji encounters other irregular migrants in Latin America, but the tech-savvy Akai appears to represent contemporary capitalist China rather than a socialist ally. Special thanks to the EthNoise! workshop participants at the University of Chicago who raised this question in the conversation following Kaley Mason's talk about the film on April 2, 2019.

82   For a more detailed discussion of these song genres in South Indian film, see Amanda Weidman, "Iconic Voices in Post-Millennium Tamil Cinema," in *Music in Contemporary Indian Film: Memory, Voice, Identity*, ed. Jayson Beaster-Jones and Natalie Sarrazin (New York: Routledge, 2017), 120–32.

83   Gopi Sundar, personal communication with Kaley Mason, January 15, 2019.

84   For a trailer for CIA: *Comrade in America* featuring "Kerala Maninnayi," see "Comrade in America (CIA)," YouTube, accessed September 2020, https://www.youtube.com/watch?v=XFrJMiMCgeg. For the entire film with English subtitles, see "CIA Comrade in America with English Subtitle," YouTube, accessed September 2020, https://www.youtube.com/watch?v=x263Eh52cQA. The opening scene begins at 10:34, with the hero introduction song, "Kerala Maninnayi," starting at 12:07.

85 The recurring electric guitar riff in "Kerala Maninnayi" resembles the opening ostinato guitar riff in Jay-Z's and Kanye West's song "No Church in the Wild," the first track on their collaborative album *Watch the Throne* (2011). This riff is in fact a sample from guitarist Phil Manzanera's instrumental piece, "K-Scope" (1978), from the album of the same name. Moreover, Romain Gavras's video for "No Church in the Wild" appears to have inspired the picturization of "Kerala Maninnayi." Both the video and Amal Neerad's hero-introduction scene open with a close-up of a protester lighting a Molotov cocktail before leading a clash with riot police. These intertextual references strengthen CIA: *Comrade in America*'s imagined connection with hip-hop's Africanist aesthetic, global youth cultural appeal, and oppositional vitality.

86 See Hemma Balakrishnan, "Towards an Understanding of the Use of English and Malay in Malaysian-Tamil Hip-Hop Songs," *South Asian Diaspora* 12, no. 1 (2018): 1–15. For a more general discussion of hip-hop culture's transnational youth appeal and the globalization of Black expressivity, see Halifu Osumare, *The Africanist Aesthetic in Global Hip-Hop: Power Moves* (New York: Palgrave Macmillan, 2007).

87 See Jude Woodward, *The US vs China: Asia's New Cold War?* (Manchester, UK: Manchester University Press, 2017).

88 Josh Kun, *Audiotopia: Music, Race, and America* (Berkeley: University of California Press, 2005), 20.

Part I
ROUTES

1. MUSICAL TRAVELS OF THE COCONUT ISLES AND THE SOCIALIST POPULAR

JENNIFER LINDSAY

This is the story of a song—an Indonesian song that traveled abroad during the 1950s; a nationalistic song that linked into the international socialist cultural network of the Cold War and became popular far from Indonesia's shores. It is a story of the travels of that song and how, along the way, it took on a new kind of popular identity both at home and abroad. The story leads to reflection about how the Cold War socialist cultural network popularized certain kinds of music and how this problematizes common understandings of what popular music is.

The song is "Rayuan Pulau Kelapa" (Lure of the Coconut Isles), composed by Indonesia's arguably best-known composer, Ismail Marzuki (1914–1958). Marzuki, who is credited with both the music and lyrics of the song, was born in what is now Jakarta to a relatively well-off family.[1] His father, who owned an automobile repair shop, was wealthy enough to own a gramophone, and so the young Marzuki heard various kinds of popular music in his youth. He attended a Dutch-language junior high school and was fluent in Dutch and English as well as Indonesian (then known as Malay). Upon completing school, he worked selling records on commission for Columbia and Polydor, and so had access to the latest imported music. He joined the band Lief Java, which played light music, including the popular "Hawaiian style" (see figure 1.1).[2]

From 1937 to 1939, Ismail Marzuki worked as a broadcaster for the Nederlandsch-Indische Radio Omroep Maatschappij (NIROM, Dutch East Indies Radio Broadcasting Corporation), as director of the "Western and Indonesian Popular Song" section.[3] In 1940 he formed the radio orchestra for the newly established Perikatan Perkoempoelan Radio Ketimoeran (PPRK,

FIGURE 1.1. Ismail Marzuki (*far left with guitar*) and the Lief Java band in the 1930s. Photo reproduced without attribution in Teguh Esha et al., *Ismail Marzuki* (Jakarta: Pustaka LP3ES, 2005).

Federation of Eastern Radio Associations), which became the Orkes Indonesia Hoso Kyoku Djakarta (Indonesian Orchestra of Jakarta Radio Broadcasting) after the Japanese occupied Indonesia in 1942.[4]

Marzuki began composing when he was in his teens and over his lifetime composed more than two hundred songs, many of which became part of the staple national repertoire, taught in schools over both the revolutionary and Soekarno periods (1945–67) and the military "New Order" (1967–98).

Marzuki composed the music and lyrics for "Rayuan Pulau Kelapa" in 1944 when Indonesia was under Japanese occupation during World War II.[5]

> Tanah airku Indonesia
> Negeri elok amat kucinta
> Tanah tumpah darahku yang mulia
> Yang kupuja s'panjang masa
> Tanah airku aman dan makmur
> Pulau kelapa yang amat subur
> Pulau melati pujaan bangsa sejak dulu kala
> Melambai-lambai, nyiur di pantai
> Berbisik-bisik, Raja K'lana

Memuja pulau, yang indah permai
Tanah airku Indonesia

My native land, Indonesia
Land of beauty that I love so dear
Noble land where my blood is shed
Land I praise until the end of time
My native land safe and prosperous
Coconut isles so very fertile
Jasmine isles praised by their people from time immemorial
Swaying and waving, palms on the shore
Whispering King Klana
Praise the isles of beauty rare
My native land, Indonesia[6]

At the time he composed the song, Marzuki was leading the Hoso Kyoku radio orchestra in Jakarta, but it is unclear whether he would have broadcast this composition of his, at least with these lyrics. The sentiment of the song was problematic. It could be associated with the Indonesian nationalist movement, which the Japanese occupiers in 1944 did not yet support. Marzuki's song is nationalist in the sense of speaking of a homeland called Indonesia where one's (my) blood is spilled, but it is also a nostalgic song with images of beauty, prosperity, and peaceful nature composed at a time when things were far from peaceful or prosperous. It is a song of longing for a place and mood—a song of someone imagining a home, imagining (an) Indonesia from the outside, in space or time.

The history of the song "Rayuan Pulau Kelapa" over the next few years, from Indonesia's proclamation of independence in August 1945 through the years of the republic's fight against the returning Dutch and their allies (1945–49), is unclear. We do not know definitively in what style it was played as there are no extant recordings from this time to tell us. Most likely, though, it was played in *kroncong* (also written as *keroncong*) style, which Philip Yampolsky, who has written the definitive word on the subject, calls "the most prominent type of popular music in the Indies in the first half of the twentieth century." The basic instrumentation of kroncong, as Yampolsky outlines, is "voice, violin, flute, two small plucked lutes (ukulele, mandolin, banjo), guitar, and cello," with the violin, flute and voice carrying a fluid melody over a rapid interlocking accompaniment. The genre, he describes, combines "the basic format of Euro-American popular song: a foregrounded vocal given harmonized accompaniment by an ensemble of European instruments," with some "typical elements of

Javanese and Sundanese music." Yampolsky demonstrates how kroncong was perfectly tailored to fit the 78 rpm recording medium, thus fulfilling one of the often cited defining characteristics of popular music, mediatization.[7]

Marzuki composed many songs in this popular genre, including songs in the late 1940s with more overt nationalistic themes—songs for and about the soldiers fighting for Indonesia's independence, such as "Gugur Bunga di Taman Bakti" (Fallen flowers in the field of service, 1945), and popular favorites such as "Slendang Sutera" (Silk scarf, ca. 1945) and "Sepasang Mata Bola" (A pair of eyes, 1946), with themes of love and longing related to the heroism of the soldiers and the suffering and worry of those left behind.[8]

The earliest extant Indonesian recording of "Rayuan Pulau Kelapa" is listed as kroncong style and dates from 1947 to 1951.[9] The style of performance mixes Western popular dance rhythms like rhumba and tango. It seems reasonable to suppose that this recording is close to the performance style of the song when it was composed in late 1944 and over the early days of the republic (1945–49). The female singer's name is Che Momo, and the recording was made in Singapore, as recording had not yet fully resumed in Indonesia following the revolutionary struggle and independence.[10]

There are no other known recordings of "Rayuan Pulau Kelapa" in Indonesia from the early 1950s. Apart from one kroncong-style recording manufactured in Holland in 1953, the next known recording of the song appears far from Indonesia—namely in Russia (then the USSR) in 1955 with Russian lyrics.[11] The song had traveled there as part of the socialist network of the period via the World Festivals of Youth and Students and taken on a new style along the way.

World Festivals of Youth and Students

The Cold War was a period when culture was at the front line of the ideological battle between the First and Second Worlds. While this "Cultural Cold War" has been well documented, there is still much more to understand about its intersection with the more pressing concerns of the budding Third World, namely cultural identity and nationalism. One arena where these national and international cultural foci overlapped was the biennial World Festivals of Youth and Students (WFYS).

The World Festivals of Youth and Students were organized by the World Federation of Democratic Youth (WFDY), which was established in London in 1945 at the World Youth Conference just after the end of World War II. The WFDY was linked to the International Union of Students (IUS), which was created at the same time and established a headquarters in Paris. (The headquarters moved to Budapest in 1951.)[12] Although the WFDY and the festivals later became dominated by Communist and left-wing organizations, initially few of the WFDY delegates openly represented Communist affiliations. A wide range of religious organizations, socialist and trade union groups, sporting federations, and youth associations made up the majority of the membership. Soon, however, and especially after the Prague Communist takeover in 1948 and the Hungarian uprising of 1956, the WFDY increasingly came under Soviet influence.[13]

The 1947 WFYS held in Prague was the first of the biennial festivals. According to Nils Apeland, the 1947 festival in Prague "was attended by a larger group of non-Communists—both numerically and proportionately—than any of the subsequent festivals."[14] The next four were all hosted in Eastern Europe (Hungary, 1949; East Germany, 1951; Romania, 1953; Poland, 1955), with the fifth and largest festival of the Cold War period held in Moscow in 1957.[15]

The festivals' anti-imperialist mission, socialist orientation, and overt Soviet domination led the US State Department to brand them as tools of Communist propaganda.[16] Leftist, anti-imperialist, and ideologically steered as they undoubtedly were, the biennial festivals were tremendously popular events, with hundreds of thousands of young people traveling from all over the world to participate. They came in groups by boat, bus, and train, meeting up on the journey. Crowds would greet them at harbors, borders, and railway stations on the way. The festivals captured a tremendous sense of excitement about being part of a worldwide youth movement after the horrors of World War II, and for youth of newly independent nations just emerging from colonialism, they provided an international forum for displaying their new national identity (see figure 1.2). Indonesia was an official presence at all the festivals until the last of the Soekarno era, held in Helsinki in 1962.[17]

The festivals featured sports, art exhibitions, performances, film, and literary contests. There were also meetings of delegations organized according to geography and interest, faculty meetings, and trade and professional meetings. Regional meetings were divided into Latin America, Europe, Africa, South East and East Asia, Arab countries, and the Five Big Powers (France, the People's Republic of China, the United Kingdom, the United States, and the USSR).[18] Thematic groupings included "meetings according to religion" and "common interest groups," which (in 1955) included chess, plastic arts, theater and film actors, radio hams, philatelists, esperantists, amateur script writers, amateur photographers, amateur musicians, tourists and campers, folk dancers, choir members, and members of theater groups."[19]

FIGURE 1.2. Opening of the World Festival of Youth and Students in Budapest, 1949. Photo from official pamphlet of that event. Held in the National Library of Australia.

The upper age limit for festival events was thirty-two (in 1959 it was raised to thirty-four). Delegates were paid two dollars per day plus their own travel to and from the festival, and the host country covered local costs. An "international solidarity fund" provided assistance to young people from "colonial countries." According to Apeland, the Soviet bloc also subsidized travel within Communist areas once delegates crossed the borders and in some cases also paid all traveling expenses to the borders of the Soviet bloc.[20]

Competition in the cultural section included fine arts, photography, film, literature, folk art, music, and dance. The music and ballet competitions had separate professional and amateur categories, but the choral category was for amateur choirs only. Singing competition categories included "classical song," in which singers had to perform a compulsory piece plus pieces of their own choice, which had to include "at least one piece of their own national music." Choirs had to perform "folk and classical songs with or without accompaniment." There was a separate category of competition for "folk song," subdivided for male voices, female voices, soloists, and duets.[21]

The first WFYS was initially planned for 1946, and according to Mia Bustam (the first wife of the artist Sudjojono), the Indonesian Republic (which had proclaimed its independence in August the previous year) prepared to send an official delegation.[22] However, the festival was postponed to mid-1947, by which time the beleaguered republic was fighting to defend its independence against the returning Dutch. It is unclear whether Indonesia had any presence at the 1947 festival.

An Indonesian delegation made up of students based in Europe was definitely present at the next WFYS, held in Budapest in August 1949. One of these students was Rose (also known as Ros or Roos) Sumabrata (1930–), who was then studying in Holland. She recalls the Indonesian delegation participating in singing and dance events but not actually competing.[23]

A record of the Indonesian delegation's presence at Budapest in 1949 remains in a songbook for the occasion, printed in Prague. The twelve songs in the book, which are presented with notated melody, lyrics, and a short English explanation, do not include "Rayuan Pulau Kelapa." Apart from the Indonesian national anthem, the songbook includes marches of the Indonesian independence struggle (including "Hello Hello Bandung," which is usually attributed to Marzuki) and songs from Eastern Indonesia, Sumatra, Java, and Bali.[24]

The third WFYS, held in East Berlin in 1951, was the first following the international recognition of Indonesia's independence and transfer of sovereignty in December 1949. Indonesia's official delegation came directly from Indonesia but was supplemented by students studying in Europe. The Indonesian leftist organization for the arts, Lembaga Kesenian Rakyat (LEKRA, Institute of People's Culture), which had been established the previous year (August 1950), sent six artists, including Sudharnoto (also spelled Sudarnoto), who later became head of LEKRA's music branch (Lembaga Musik Indonesia); the singer and conductor Soebronto K. Atmodjo (also spelled Subronto or Soebrongto); and the artist Sudjojono.[25] At the festival, Sudjojono met the woman who was later to become his second wife, Rose Sumabrata, who was attending the WFYS again and competed in the singing events.

Vocal Ensembles and Song

The presentational style of the festivals and their regularity encouraged the development of shared styles between participants, both within and across national delegations. One example was the development of vocal ensembles in Indonesia following the 1951 WFYS in East Berlin.

Apart from Sudharnoto and Soebronto, Indonesia's delegation to East Berlin in 1951 included two other young singers, Titiek Komaria and Bintang

Suradi, who were so impressed by the choral groups they heard at the festival that upon their return to Indonesia, they immediately formed the core of what became the well-known vocal ensemble Gembira.[26] In turn, Gembira inspired the birth of many similar vocal ensembles in Indonesia in the 1950s and early 1960s.[27] These ensembles adapted the WFYS models to the Indonesian situation and their own national concerns, and at the same time molded their own art to fit the international WFYS model.

Choral singing existed in Indonesia prior to this, of course—particularly as a church tradition. Group singing as a secular activity was also popular during the Indonesian Revolution. But during the 1950s and 1960s, new vocal ensembles such as Gembira took choral singing of marches, anthems, and Western-style arrangements of Indonesian songs to a new level of popularity for both performers and consumers. People such as Koesalah Toer (who by his own account was not a good singer) joined these groups as part of the "movement." They toured within Indonesia and regularly broadcast on radio. The Left fostered these new ensembles and their repertoire, and the international WFYS circuit fed into their development.

Ensembles such as Gembira were groups of amateur singers who sang secular songs in Western classical style, with harmony and minimal accompaniment, usually piano or accordion. The singing style was called *seriosa*, a stylistic term referring to the Western classical style of vocal delivery, fitting the "classical song" classification of the WFYS.[28] The "serious" nature of the performance was emphasized with uniforms, posture, and stage presence, which was the required performance style at the singing competitions at the World Youth Festivals (see figure 1.3).

The WFYS also influenced vocal ensembles such as Gembira in the fostering of a particular kind of repertoire of secular serious song. The festival competition included two categories of song: folk songs and national songs. The folk song category particularly resonated with young artists in newly independent Indonesia who were concerned about finding a relevant place in the modernizing nation for subnational, regional, or traditional songs. Gembira and other ensembles like it produced Western harmonized vocal arrangements of Indonesian "folk" songs, meaning songs in regional languages or specifically linked to a certain region, bringing folk tradition into a new "modern" international style. They performed these alongside songs celebrating the Indonesian Revolution or songs with didactic lyrics and slogans composed to promote both leftist ideology and government programs. The "national song" category of the WFYS fitted neatly with songs in Indonesian and worked well with uplifting national themes, like the heroic fight for independence. One of the songs per-

FIGURE 1.3. Gembira performing in Beijing, 1963. Personal collection of Rhoma Dwi Aria Yuliantri.

formed for competition in the national song category in the WFYS had to be a composition by a living composer.

Marzuki's song "Rayuan Pulau Kelapa," in its original style, did not fit either the folk song or national song mold. There was no place on the WFYS stage for commercial, light, popular musical idioms like kroncong. Its lyrics, however, were edifying and national in theme, and its composer was still living. While not a folk song, it could be arranged to fit the more serious WFYS singing style of "a piece of national music." And this is indeed what happened. Marzuki himself might even have assisted in or approved of the new arrangement, for Sudharnoto (the member of the 1951 LEKRA delegation and founding Gembira member) was his friend.[29] "Rayuan Pulau Kelapa" now took on a more solemn anthem-like tone, and from the late 1950s dropped its popular dance-style idiom, so-called kroncong.

Gembira's musical director, Soebronto, had also attended the 1951 WFYS festival as part of the LEKRA group, and he joined the Gembira ensemble in 1952. From 1954 to 1961, he was in charge of Gembira's monthly radio broadcasts.[30] Sometime in 1957 or early 1958, Gembira made a recording of "Rayuan Pulau Kelapa," with Soebronto as conductor.[31] This recording, in solemn harmonized anthem style, was made around the time that Gembira first attended the WFYS as a group at the fifth festival, held in Moscow in 1957. Gembira

Musical Travels of the Coconut Isles · 51

included "Rayuan Pulau Kelapa" on its program and won a bronze medal for the choral category.[32]

"Rayuan Pulau Kelapa" Goes to the USSR

Five years before Gembira recorded "Rayuan Pulau Kelapa," the song had traveled even further abroad and was taking on another life. In 1953, when the fourth WFYS was held in Bucharest, Romania, Indonesia had a huge presence. According to Koesalah Toer, who interviewed members of the Indonesian delegation, the Indonesian group numbered 120 people from 17 organizations and groups—112 of them coming directly from Indonesia and the rest from Europe. Rose Sumabrata was there once again, now as part of the official Indonesian delegation, as she had returned to Indonesia in 1952. She won third place for her solo singing. Gembira members Sudharnoto and Soebronto also attended.[33]

Another member of the Indonesian delegation at Bucharest in 1953 was Gordon Tobing (1925–93), a singer from Medan, North Sumatra, who moved to Jakarta in 1950, initially working in film and radio and later forming his own singing group, Impola. Tobing became famous for his singing of North Sumatran Batak songs and popularized them in the national canon.[34] The trip to Bucharest for the WFYS in 1953 appears to have been his first trip overseas—but he later traveled extensively, representing Indonesia abroad during the Soekarno period singing his Batak songs and what was fast becoming the established repertoire of national songs (see figure 1.4). He joined many of Indonesia's national cultural missions abroad from 1957 and is said to have received the gift of a guitar from Fidel Castro when he toured Cuba.[35]

According to Toer, who has written about Indonesian students in the USSR and studied there himself from 1960 to 1965, Tobing visited Moscow in 1953 after participating at the WFYS in Bucharest. It is not known whether Tobing was invited to Moscow, was sponsored, or was just joining some of the Indonesian students based there who were returning after the festival.[36] Toer, who learned the story from Indonesian students living there at the time, writes that while in Moscow, Tobing made a recording of nine songs, including "Rayuan Pulau Kelapa."[37] I have been unable to trace this recording—if indeed it was ever made. Perhaps Tobing merely broadcast the song. But according to Toer, the song then became popular in the USSR and was translated into Russian. Whether or not it was through Tobing, the song did indeed become popular there—to the extent that its Indonesian authorship became blurred.

FIGURE 1.4. Gordon Tobing (*center with guitar*) at the Cultural Mission curtain call in Prague, 1957. Courtesy of Irawati Durban Ardjo.

Here my tale of the journey of "Rayuan Pulau Kelapa" takes on a personal note. In 2012 I was at the Australia National University in Canberra showing my documentary about the Indonesian national cultural missions abroad, which begins and ends with a 1958 recording of "Rayuan Pulau Kelapa."[38] At the end of the screening, a young Russian woman, Maria Myutel, approached to tell me that she knew this as a Russian song. Maria helped me find the Russian source.[39] It turned out to be the music for a short documentary titled *Around Indonesia*, made by the Central Documentary Film Studio (TsSDF) in 1955 and directed by Kozina E, with production directors Mikosha and Sokolnikov. Mikosha, whose full name was Vladislav Vladislavovish Mikosha, was a renowned photographer. The singer is Tamara Kavtsova, a well-known mezzo-soprano who was recording for Russian labels in the early 1950s, and she sings with a choir and orchestral background. The Russian lyrics are attributed to V. Korchagin (editor of the Central Documentary Film Studio) and the music is attributed to Vitaly Artemyevich Geviksman (1924–2007), a graduate of the Conservatory in Sverdlovsk who worked as music editor at the Central Documentary Film Studio from 1948 and was a well-known composer by the mid-1950s. Over his career, he composed music for documentaries, animated and feature films, and symphonic works and operas.[40]

Was this plagiarism? Or merely loose text explaining the song's provenance? Whatever the explanation, it is clear that by 1955, "Rayuan Pulau Kelapa"—now titled "Indonesia Lubov Moya"—was popular enough in the USSR for a well-known composer there to want his own name associated with it. Following is the Russian version, with a translation by Maria Myutel.

Морями теплыми омытая,
Лесами древними покрытая,
Земля родная Индонезия,
В сердцах любовь к тебе храним.

Тебя лучи ласкают жаркие,
Тебя цветы одели яркие,
И пальмы стройные раскинулись
По берегам твоим.

Песня вдаль течет,
Моряка влечет
В полуденных рек ее края.
И красот полна,
В сердце ты одна,
Индонезия—любовь моя.

Washed by warm oceans,
Covered by woods
My dear land Indonesia
We keep our love for you in our hearts.

You are caressed by hot sun
Dressed in bright flowers.
There are slender palm trees
on your shores

The song flows far away
A sailor is lured by its sound
to the rivers of that land.
You are full of beauty
Only you are in my heart
Indonesia—my love.

The Russian lyrics are close in nostalgic sentiment to the original but with a significant difference. Now there is no "native land" or "shed blood." Without the "native land," the "I" of "Indonesia—*my* love" could be a foreigner (like a lured sailor). It is no longer explicitly a song about Indonesia by an Indonesian. The song has been taken beyond its nation.

Post-1955

While "Rayuan Pulau Kelapa" was entering the socialist cultural network and becoming an icon for Indonesians performing overseas, how was it faring at home? The 1950s was a period of intense debate and discussion in Indonesia about the direction of "national culture." Artists were preoccupied with ideas about how the national could be modern, the modern, national, and where traditional arts fit in all this.[41] A recurring topic in this discourse was the issue of distinctive identity or national "individuality" (the term then used was *kepribadian nasional*). Discussion raged on whether distinctiveness was an essential ingredient of national art, and if so, how Indonesia's national arts could be distinctive.

Topics of debate included the position of Western music compared to Indonesia's own music. Could Western-style art music be considered Indonesian? Could Indonesia's indigenous music be elevated to national status? Could popular forms like kroncong be considered national? Many of these questions had arisen in late colonial times, but now they took on a new urgency in the reality of the nation. Here the discussion moved beyond the issue of distinctiveness into what was considered to be appropriate in terms of seriousness and weight. Light, commercial entertainment was problematic for the serious issue of national identity.

Some Indonesian composers of "serious" Western-style music and national songs considered Marzuki a lightweight and criticized "Rayuan Pulau Kelapa" as unfit for a national song. Writing in 1952, two composers, J. A. Dungga and Liberty Manik, criticized Marzuki.[42] After first dismissing Marzuki's musical abilities as those of an "untrained" composer of "entertainment," they went on to discuss "Rayuan Pulau Kelapa" with stinging words.

> This song, even with its words like "Indonesia, native land, land where my blood is shed, land I praise, that I love," and so forth, is far indeed from our national anthem. . . . It is inspired by the beauty of our country, but the composer goes only as far as beauty, *zonder meer*. . . . Of course Indonesia is a beautiful country, and in times past this beauty was more enjoyed by foreigners who had the opportunity to do so every week with their free weekends spent up in the hills sprinkled with beautiful villas.

But Indonesians themselves, most of whom were among the "have-not's," were lucky if they could sit under a coconut tree on the beach cheering themselves up daydreaming about my native land Indonesia, land of beauty that I love.[43]

The lyrics of "Rayuan Pulau Kelapa," they went on, are "served up in snippets of weak sentimental song with the concept of shallow songs imitating those of similarly cheap films."[44]

While, as far as I know, neither Dungga nor Manik was particularly associated with the Left, their strongest weapon of criticism was to attack "Rayuan Pulau Kelapa" as cheap colonial pap.[45] The venomous tone by two champions of Indonesian art music leads me to suspect that they took this line of attack precisely because the Left was popularizing as a national icon in seriosa style what Dungga and Manik considered a trivial, colonial-sentiment song. Perhaps it was the performances abroad and the adoption of the song by vocal groups such as Gembira who performed it in a reverent style that people like Manik (who composed the patriotic anthem "Satu Nusa, Satu Bangsa") found threatening.[46] "Rayuan Pulau Kelapa" was crossing genres and becoming popular across various groups in Indonesia. The Left facilitated the process of elevating the song from "just" a popular romantic kroncong song to serious national icon, and that angered the likes of Dungga and Manik.

Two years before Dungga and Manik's essay was published, in 1950 a book of ten of Ismail Marzuki's songs with lyrics and notation had been published in Jakarta.[47] The book contained lyrics and notation and included "Rayuan Pulau Kelapa." The idea of making this songbook might well have been inspired by the 1949 songbook prepared for the WFYS in Budapest. Presumably Marzuki had known about the 1949 book (after all, it contained a song attributed to him, "Hello Hello Bandung"). Perhaps his friend Sudharnoto showed it to him. The publisher notes in the preface that the book was made with the full participation of the composer—and that one of the purposes of the book was to ensure that performances of Marzuki's songs used the correct version. Certainly, the idea of printing songbooks that could be used by singing groups was spurred by the World Youth Festivals—and by the need for repertoire to be performed and shared at these occasions.

After the early recording made in kroncong style in Singapore in 1947–51, the next known Indonesian recording of "Rayuan Pulau Kelapa" is by Gembira, conducted by Soebronto. It dates from around 1957–58, two or three years after the Russian version used in the documentary.

In 1958, however, there were three more Indonesian recordings of the song. The first, in kroncong style, was sung by a female vocalist called Netty accompanied by the Orkes Krontjong Mustika, conducted by R. Adikarso; the second (the version that Myutel heard in my documentary) by female vocalist and Radio Republik Indonesia (RRI) Radio Star 1958 competition winner Ratna, accompanied by the Jakarta studio orchestra quintet and recorded in September; and the third, an anthem-like choral version with a combined choir of RRI and Persatuan Pemuda Kristen Indonesia (PPKI, Union of Indonesian Christian Youth) with the Jakarta radio orchestra, directed by R. A. J. Sudjasmin, recorded in October.[48]

Why so many recordings at this time? Gembira's, the first, appears as part of a recording made around the time of their appearance and performance of this song in Moscow in 1957. Then, in May 1958, Ismail Marzuki died. Presumably, the recordings of this song were made in his memory, sung across genres and audiences. The next known Indonesian recording of "Rayuan Pulau Kelapa" is from 1962, a mass choral version performed for the Asian Games in Jakarta.[49]

By the late 1950s, "Rayuan Pulau Kelapa" had become a staple song of gatherings representing Indonesia, both domestically and abroad. It was sung on tours and cultural missions to countries in both the Communist and capitalist blocs of the Cold War. It was also now an iconic song that linked various Indonesian groups, conveying an image of national solidarity. As the final item on the program of the official government cultural missions abroad, performers dressed in different traditional regional dress of Indonesia would stand together and sing "Rayuan Pulau Kelapa." It was performed for visiting foreign dignitaries to Indonesia and was one of the "required national songs" for children to learn at school.

After the coup in Indonesia in 1965, which was blamed on the Indonesian Communist Party and led to a violent purge of communists and sympathizers, secular choral singing went out of fashion, although lately it has had a revival. The small vocal ensembles that had toured villages, the regular broadcasts, and the youth singing groups on campuses that were associated with various youth organizations largely went silent. Many members of groups such as Gembira (some of whom were members of LEKRA) went into hiding. Some were imprisoned. No one dared to sing songs associated, even only stylistically, with leftist ideology or Soekarnoist slogans.

"Rayuan Pulau Kelapa" was not such a song. It was a popular "national song" about the shared revolutionary struggle for independence. But the image of secular choirs and their "serious" style of singing was nonetheless a haunting one. During the Soeharto regime (1966–98), "Rayuan Pulau Kelapa" took on another role: as the closing music every night on the national radio, RRI, but in an instrumental version—no words, fading into the night.

A last word on "Rayuan Pulau Kelapa" is from Marzuki himself. It seems to have been the song of which he was most proud—perhaps precisely because of its popularity domestically and abroad—and its acceptance across genres was a mark of his acceptance as a "real" composer. According to his wife, the singer Eulis, a few months before he died, Marzuki drew an illustration of the song and asked his wife to place this picture on his gravestone. This she did, but the picture later disappeared.[50]

The Socialist Popular

The story of "Rayuan Pulau Kelapa" is a story of just one song that traveled abroad from Indonesia in the early years of the nation, hitching a ride to international popularity on the socialist cultural network. This was a small event in the scheme of things, but it raises questions about cultural circuits and ways we discuss "popular" song. How might we think of "Rayuan Pulau Kelapa" as a popular song?

First, in the most obvious sense, one might say that "Rayuan Pulau Kelapa" is popular because it began in an unabashedly "popular" genre, namely kroncong, as in its early recording. Kroncong, a form of light music and entertainment, was popular in the sense of well liked as a widely accessible and well-loved style of music in Indonesia but also in the narrower sense most musicologists use the word, because it had the characteristics of the broader category of popular music: it was urban, secular, and, as Philip Yampolsky demonstrates, was tailored to the mass media of recording. The production and distribution of this mass media was also linked to market—the other ingredient of popular culture that draws it into the orbit of capitalism.

However, when the song was adopted by singers at the WFYS and also performed on Indonesia's national cultural missions abroad, it entered a different network—one not linked to capitalist mass media. The style was adapted to fit the "popular" (in the sense of well liked) style of singing at these festivals: sung solo in seriosa style with piano accompaniment, or by choirs in a reverent, anthem-like style. While seriosa can be seen, even in its very name, to define itself self-consciously in contradiction to "non-serious" music of light entertainment, it was in fact a type of performance idiom that was enormously popular at the time. It was a style that allowed for easy sharing of repertoire between singers from different countries. Group singing and songbooks provided a kind of road map for sharing both folk and national songs. Furthermore, those promoting the circulation and transmission of these songs and styles were youth, and youth appeal is often cited as one of the defining characteristics of popular music.

The performance style of the socialist youth network was extremely influential in the 1950s. It was promoted by the mass media of the time, namely print (songbooks), and particularly radio. The 1957 WFYS in Moscow, for instance, was covered with daily broadcasts over transmitters on fifteen frequencies and in thirty languages; and Radio Moscow also broadcast features about the festival internationally, including to Indonesia.[51] The performance style was also, of course, carried by the most important media of all—the travelers themselves. A familiar performance vocabulary allowed for easy transfer of repertoire between them, but it also fostered a particular style of performance back home when delegates returned. Indonesian singers and composers looked for folk songs and national songs they could arrange to fit those categories to perform on the international stage, and in Indonesia, on tours and radio broadcasts.

This was particularly important for new multicultural nations such as Indonesia, grappling with ideas about how their myriad cultural forms could be employed to express coherence as a nation. Finding a national place for subnational cultures was seen as a particularly pressing issue. The World Festivals of Youth and Students gave one answer. There was "national music" and there was "folk music." And both, when performed at the WFYS, entered the transnational socialist popular.

But who were the "folk"? In Indonesia, the term *folk* was at this time usually translated as *rakyat* (people), as in *lagu rakyat*, for folk song, or as *daerah* for region.[52] Occasionally, the untranslated term *folk* was also used. Perhaps it is better to see things the other way around, and to say that terms such as *daerah* and *rakyat* (lowercase *r*) were somewhat awkwardly translated into *folk*. For *Rakyat* (with a capital *R*) was also the word used by the Left for the People—the concept of the mass, the proletariat. On the one hand, the *rakyat* of *lagu rakyat* (folk song) was an ethnic subcategory of nation, but on the other hand, the *Rakyat* was a mass, the socialist concept of People beyond the confines of nation. The chairman of the Indonesian Communist Party, D. N. Aidit, for instance, used the term *folklore* (*folklor*) in a 1964 address to the national conference on Revolutionary (with uppercase *R*) literature and arts when explaining how a *rakyat* performance could, with an injection of Revolutionary spirit, be elevated to become revolutionary art of the *Rakyat*.[53]

Slippage around the Indonesian word *rakyat* resonates with the slippage in English around the word *popular*, as both well liked and of, or intended for, the people. To quote Aidit again from the same speech in 1964, the Communist

Party in Indonesia considered that its mission was to develop art forms for the workers that were "popular, simple, and easily understood" (*populer, sederhana dan mudah dimengerti*). There was an urgent need, he repeated, to develop art forms that "were easily accessible to the masses [*massa*]," to reform all kinds of art forms that are "popular and well loved by the People," and to extend further the "market for revolutionary literature and art."[54]

The word *popular* was a potent one in the Cold War period. On the one hand, it could be used derisively to refer to commercially driven entertainment. On the other hand, it could be used to refer to well-liked art of the people (the folk or the rakyat), which could be modernized and whose reach could be extended with an injection of revolutionary spirit. Or it could be art created in simple forms to edify the populace. Raising folk songs to a national level by arranging and performing them in harmonized choral and seriosa style allowed for sharing in the international marketplace of the socialist network. So too with the sharing of national song. Nationally and internationally, there was a market for this material—an "arts market" or "*pasaran seni*," to use Aidit's words.

In any discussion of popular culture, one must attempt to understand its terms in their time and place and not apply them retrospectively to predefine what one is seeking or observing. As the editors of this volume point out in their introduction, the very terms of definition of popular music can also be seen as Cold War legacy. Defined more in cultural, social, and economic terms of production rather than musical characteristics, popular music has always been placed squarely in the First World free-market corner, with descriptive characteristics from a particular context becoming defining criteria for other contexts of place or time. For instance, Peter Manuel's and Craig Lockard's seminal works on popular culture in Asia and the "non-Western world" stress commercially oriented secular music made for mass distribution through forms of mass media, but the concept of mass distribution is limited to the capitalist market system. The same is true of Keith Negus's more general theoretical primer on popular music.[55]

Scholarship on popular culture and popular music avoids discussion of the socialist context by eliminating it at the outset with its focus on markets and capitalism as determining operative criteria of the "popular." Market forces—in the capitalist sense—define a priori what popular culture is and retrospectively what it was. Even Marxist theoretical writing on popular culture has not turned its focus inward to societies and historical periods (like that of the Cold War) where Marxist cultural ideology was being put into practice, to see how alternative "populars" might have operated. We might query, for instance, whether "the popular" is inextricably tied to capitalism. If one removes the market and capitalism from the popular culture equation, there is still print, recording, and broadcast; there are still performance stars and songs that are well liked; there is still mass consumption and an audience or readership, including a distinct youth audience, making choices about what it does and does not like.

"Rayuan Pulau Kelapa" began its life in the late 1940s as a song in the popular genre of light music for entertainment, Indonesian kroncong, a genre inextricably entwined with the recording industry and radio. It went on to become a national icon in another style popularized by the socialist network—the more serious choral song. It became popular in this style both nationally and internationally through its travels via the international circuit of the World Festivals of Youth and Students, a circuit that had its own media of print, broadcast, recording, and most importantly the performers themselves.

The story of "Rayuan Pulau Kelapa" is another example of the importance of reinstating the 1950s and a full picture of the cultural internationalism of that period into any discussion of Indonesia's cultural history, including its music. But the story also shows how an examination of arts in the socialist network in the age of nationalism challenges existing definitions of popular music by teasing apart some of the ways in which popular culture is commonly described and analyzed.

There is a personal postscript to the tale of the journey of "Rayuan Pulau Kelapa." At the meeting in Beijing where I first presented this material, complete with audio examples (which alas this book cannot provide), a Chinese gentleman present came up to me afterward humming the tune. "My grandmother used to sing that tune," he said. Ismail Marzuki's song might well have traces of other manifestations on the socialist circuit yet to be discovered.

NOTES

1 I wish to thank Philip Yampolsky, who helped me with information on Marzuki. See further Firdaus Burhan, *Ismail Marzuki: Hasil karya dan pengabdiannya* (Jakarta: Proyek Inventarisasi dan Dokumentasi Sejarah Nasional, Direktorat Sejarah dan Nilai Tradisional, Departemen Pendidikan dan Kebudayaan, 1983/84). See also Teguh Esha et al., *Ismail Marzuki: Musik, tanah air dan cinta* (Jakarta: Pustaka LP3ES, 2005). The Indonesian magazine *Tempo* had a special supplement on Marzuki in its May 18, 2014, edition (62–71).

2 Hawaiian-style band music was a light jazzy style of music that was popular with the Eurasian community in the Indies in the pre–World War II period. It was similar in instrumentation to kroncong music, but the songs were in English (or sometimes Hawaiian) and usually had some South Seas references. See Philip Yampolsky, "Music and Media in the Dutch East Indies: Gramophone Records and Radio

in the Late Colonial Era, 1903–1942" (PhD diss., University of Washington, 2013), 38.

3   Yampolsky thinks the term *populer* meant songs in Western popular styles (tango, rumba, etc.) but sung in the Indonesian language, and might also include kroncong played in tango/rumba styles (personal communication, March 2014).

4   On the history of radio and recording of this period, see Yampolsky, "Music and Media in the Dutch East Indies." See also Jennifer Lindsay, "Making Waves: Private Radio and Local Identities in Indonesia," *Indonesia*, no. 64 (October 1997): 105–24; and *Sedjarah radio di Indonesia* (Djakarta: Radio Republik Indonesia, 1953).

5   Teguh Esha (*Ismail Marzuki*, 61) says "Rayuan Pulau Kelapa" was composed in October 1944, citing two other sources: Jessy Wenas, "Ismail Marzuki, Bapak Musik Populer Indonesia," *Mutiara* 18 (347), May 22–June 4, 1985; and Ahmad Naroth, "Bang Ma'ing Anak Betawi," *Intisari* 27, Juni 1982.

6   All translations are mine unless otherwise noted.

7   Yampolsky, "Music and Media in the Dutch East Indies," 274, 277–78. See also Philip Yampolsky, "*Kroncong* Revisited: New Evidence from Old Sources," *Archipel* 79 (2011): 7–56.

8   These dates are from the list of Marzuki's songs in *Ismail Marzuki Komponis Pejuang* (Jakarta: Dinas Kebudayaan DKI Jakarta bekerjasama dengan Institut Kesenian Jakarta, 1997), 24–25, 29–30.

9   In writing this chapter, I was assisted by the two world experts on recording in the Dutch East Indies and Indonesia of this time—Philip Yampolsky and Jaap Erkelens. All information on recordings is from them. I express my deep gratitude for their generosity in sharing their incomparable knowledge with me.

10 This recording is HMV P 22939, matrix no. OMJ-190. I am grateful to Erkelens for this information, and for providing me with a copy of the recording. Yampolsky explains that before World War II, most recording companies that issued 78s for Indonesia were based in Europe, a few were based in Batavia, one in Surabaya, one in Bukittinggi, and two in Singapore. This recording of "Rayuan Pulau Kelapa" was made by HMV, which was still based in England. When HMV resumed recording after the war, it did so first in the British colonies of Malaya and Singapore, so this recording was made in Singapore.

11 Thanks yet again to the detective work of Yampolsky, who, as I was writing this chapter, came across a 78 disc manufactured in Holland of "Rayuan Pulau Kelapa" performed by "Krontjong Ensemble 'Bintang Sinar' met zang van Mirjam." Issued on Columbia DH 537, matrix no. BO 93-1.

12 Nils M. Apeland, *World Youth and the Communists: The Facts about Communist Penetration of WFDY and IUS* (London: Phoenix House, 1958), 31, 45.

13 A detailed account of the founding of WFDY and its early years can be found in Apeland, *World Youth and the Communists*. Its own bias is clear from the title.

14 Apeland, *World Youth and the Communists*, 54.

15 After the 1957 WFYS in Moscow, the festivals were as follows: Austria (1959), Finland (1962), Bulgaria (1968), East Germany (1973), Cuba (1978), USSR (1985),

North Korea (1989), Cuba (1997), Algeria (2001), Venezuela (2005), South Africa (2010), Ecuador (2013).

16 See the foreword by Eleanor Roosevelt in Apeland, *World Youth and the Communists*. See also John C. Clews, *Communist Propaganda Techniques* (New York: Praeger, 1964).

17 The festivals were held regularly until 1962, then with less frequency. They continue to this day, held at irregular intervals. See the WFDY website, http://www.wfdy.org/festivals.

18 The plans outlined for the 1957 festival in Moscow list these same regional divisions. It is interesting that although the Asia Africa conference had taken place in Bandung in April 1955, Africa and Asia were kept apart at the WFYS in 1955 and in 1957. This might reflect Soviet rejection of Soekarno's vision of new world power—"Asia Africa" and "Non-Aligned"—both of which locked out the USSR.

19 Information about the WFYS program and costs for delegates is from a booklet (held in the National Library of Australia) titled "World Festivals of Youth and Students" by the World Federation of Democratic Youth, probably from Helsinki 1955 as it summarizes the programs and numbers of entrants for that festival, and also plans for the 1957 festival in Moscow.

20 Apeland, *World Youth and the Communists*, 53.

21 These categories are from the plans for the 1957 festival in Moscow, included in the booklet "World Festivals of Youth and Students."

22 Mia Bustam, *Sudjojono dan Aku* (Jakarta: Pustaka Utan Kayu, 2006), 98.

23 Interview with Rose Sumabrata-Sudjojono-Pandanwangi (now known as Rose Pandanwangi), Jakarta, June 2015.

24 The booklet is titled "Lagu-lagu Indonesia: Disusun oleh utusan Indonesia ke Rajaan Pemuda dan Peladjar Sedunia di Budapest 14–28 Agustus 1949." The twelve songs included are "Indonesia Raya," "Halo-Halo Bandung," "Satu Tudjuh Delapan Empat Lima," "Darah Rakjat," "Salam Alaikum," "Panggajo," "Dedalane," "Ajo Mama," "Djanger," "Tudjuan Kita," "Rege Rege," and "Nusaniwe." The song "Hello Hello Bandung" is usually attributed to Marzuki, but there are also claims it was composed by a soldier named Lumbantobing. According to Yapi Tambayong (aka Remy Silado), who gives no source for his information, in fact the song was already a Dutch popular song (with different Dutch lyrics) in 1923 sung by Willy Derby; so it could be that neither Tobing nor Marzuki composed the song. See "Antara Ismail Marzuki dan Raden Saleh," *Tempo*, May 18, 2014, 70.

25 The others in the LEKRA group were Henk Ngantung, Hendra Gunawan, and Sunardi. This information is from Bustam, *Sudjojono dan Aku*, 169–71, and also my interview in July 2008 with the late Oey Hai Djoen (aka Samandjaja), who was in charge of LEKRA's overseas relations. A sketch by the artist Hendra then in Oey's possession shows Indonesian delegates at Berlin. LEKRA is often described as a Communist organization, although it had no official links to the Indonesian Communist Party, and there was often tension between the two. It pursued leftist ideology in the arts. Many, but certainly not all, of its members were Communists.

26 Interview with Koesalah Toer, August 3, 2008. Koesalah, the younger brother of Indonesia's famous writer Pramoedya Ananta Toer, joined Gembira in 1954. Koesalah

Toer has written his memoirs of his experiences in Gembira in "Ke Langit Biru: Kenangan tentang 'Gembira'" (unpublished manuscript, Jakarta, 1998). Bintang Suradi was of mixed Dutch Indonesian parentage whose original Dutch surname was van der Ster.

27   Rhoma Dwi Aria Yuliantri has written extensively on Gembira and has interviewed members about its early years. See Rhoma Dwi Aria Yuliantri, "LEKRA and Ensembles: Tracing the Indonesian Musical Stage," in *Heirs to World Culture: Being Indonesian, 1950–1965*, ed. Jennifer Lindsay and Maya Liem (Leiden: KITLV, 2012), 421–52.

28   Christopher Miller notes that the term *seriosa* came to be used in Indonesia only in 1951, as one of three categories in the annual Radio Star competition put on by the national radio station, Radio Republik Indonesia (RRI). Christopher J. Miller, "Cosmopolitan, Nativist, Eclectic: Cultural Dynamics in Indonesian Musik Kontemporer" (PhD diss., Wesleyan University, 2014), 140. This is around the same time that Indonesian singers were participating in the WFYS in East Berlin. The use of the term *seriosa* might therefore have been influenced by, or even be a translation of, the WFYS category "classical song," although, as Miller also discusses, composition of art songs in "classical style" in Indonesia had an older history. The term *seriosa* for music and song could also be taken from Dutch *serieuze musiek*, meaning serious music (in distinction to light, popular music). The Nederlandse Omroep Stichting (NOS, Dutch Broadcasting Foundation) used to have a department named *serieuze muziek* whose name was later changed to *klassieke muziek*.

29   *Ismail Marzuki Komponis Pejuang*, 11.

30   Yuliantri, "LEKRA and Ensembles," 437.

31   I am grateful to Erkelens, who gave me information about this recording by Gembira and generously shared the recording with me. "Rajuan Pulau Kelapa," by Paduan Suara Ansambel Gembira and conducted by Soebronto K. Atmodjo, was issued on a 78 rpm disc as Irama, issue no. L 389-96, matrix no. Imco 632.

32   Koesalah Soebagyo Toer, *Kampus Kabelnaya: Menjadi mahasiswa di Uni Soviet* (Jakarta: Kepustakaan Populer Gramedia, 2003), 57. This information is also from my interview with Koesalah Toer and Badhry Djani (another Gembira member), August 2008.

33   Toer, *Kampus*, xi–xii; interview with Rose Sumabrata-Sudjojono-Pandanwangi, May 2015.

34   The song he is most famous for is "Sing Sing So," the composition of which has been variously credited to Boni Siahaan or Siddik Sitompul (aka S.Dis).

35   On Indonesia's national cultural missions abroad at this time, see Jennifer Lindsay, "Performing Indonesia Abroad," in *Heirs to World Culture: Being Indonesian, 1950–1965*, ed. Jennifer Lindsay and Maya Liem (Leiden: KITLV, 2012), 191–222.

36   Participants at the festivals would often travel in groups after the festival itself. Bustam writes that after the 1951 festival, the Indonesian group traveled to Hungary, Romania, Czechoslovakia, the USSR, and the PRC. They also stayed at Tashkent. Sudjojono was away for five months. See Bustam, *Sudjojono dan Aku*, 169–71.

37   Toer, "Ke Langit Biru," 57.

38   The documentary is titled *Menggelar Indonesia: Misi Kesenian ke Manca Negara 1952–1965* (Presenting Indonesia: Indonesian cultural missions abroad 1952–1965), made in 2010. The 1958 recording of "Rayuan Pulau Kepala" in the documentary, which Yampolsky generously provided, is by the Kwintet Orkes Studio Djakarta led by Saleh Suwito. The solo vocal, in an upbeat style reminiscent of the song's kroncong origin, is sung by Ratna, who won the Radio Star competition that year. The Lokananta recording is ARI 012.

39   Archival reference to the Central Documentary Film Studio (TsSDF) documentary "Around Indonesia" can be found at the Russian Net Film website: Net Film. Newsreel. Film Around Indonesia (1955), film document no. 4538, see http://www.net-film.ru/ru/film-4538/, accessed August 2012.

40   This information is taken from the Russian website of On The Embankment Musical Social Network, "A little story of a beautiful song about Indonesia." http://www.tunnel.ru/view/post:260324, accessed August 2012. The same website page has links to an audio recording of the song by Tamara Kavtsova as well as other versions. Geviksman composed music for several films about Asian countries—*Mongolia* (1954), *Indonesia* (1955), *100 Days in Burma* (1957), and *Vietnamese Etudes* (1958)—so it appears this Indonesian documentary was part of a government-sponsored series.

41   I have written about this extensively. See Jennifer Lindsay, "Heirs to World Culture, 1950–1965: An Introduction," in *Heirs to World Culture: Being Indonesian, 1950–1965*, ed. Jennifer Lindsay and Maya Liem (Leiden: KITLV, 2012), 1–30. Other chapters in this volume also discuss these issues.

42   J. A. Dungga and L. Manik, *Musik di Indonesia dan beberapa persoalannja* [Some problems concerning music in Indonesia] (Jakarta: Balai Pustaka, 1952).

43   Teguh Esha, "'Pembersih Kolam Musik' vs 'Gembong Kebudayaan' Kritik terhadap Ismail Marzuki," in *Ismail Marzuki: Musik, tanah air dan cinta*, ed. Teguh Esha et al. (Jakarta: LP3ES, 2005), 81–103, on 99 quoting Dungga and Manik, *Musik di Indonesia*, 26–27. The original text reads: "Lagu ini sekalipun mendemonstratir perkataan-perkataan seperti Indonesia, tanah airku, tanah tumpah darahku, jang kupudja, dan amat kutjinta, sangat djauh letaknja dari lagu kebangsaan kita.... Lagu diatas mengambil inspirasi dari keindahan tanah air kita. Tapi penggubahnja hanja sampai pada keindahan sadja, sonder meer.... Memang Indonesia negeri jang indah, dan diwaktu jang lampau ini lebih dirasakan oleh bangsa asing jang mempunjai kesempatan penuh tiap minggu berweekend dilereng-lereng gunung jang ditaburi dengan villa-villa jang indah. Bangsa Indonesia sendiri jang sebagian besar termasuk golongan have-not boleh ngelamun dibawah pohon njiur melambai ditepi pantai sambil menghibur hatinja: Tanah airku Indonesia, neg'ri elok amat kutjinta." Esha also quotes another prominent composer, Amir Pasaribu (1915–2010), denigrating "Rayuan Pulau Kelapa" and Marzuki.

44   "Dituangkan dalam petakan lagu-lagu lemah meraju dengan konsepsi lagu-lagu dangkal jang diimitir dari film-film jang murah pula." Esha, "'Pembersih Kolam Musik' vs 'Gembong Kebudayaan,'" 99, quoting Dungga and Manik, *Musik di indonesia*, 26–27.

45 Miller discusses the writing of Dungga, Manik, and Amir Pasaribu about Indonesian music in his PhD dissertation, in the context of a fascinating discussion about the position of European art music and its Indonesian composers in the late colonial, revolutionary, and early independent period. See Miller, "Cosmopolitan, Nativist, Eclectic," esp. chapter 2. According to the *Ensiklopedi Tokoh Kebudayaan* (5: 110–11), cited in Miller, Manik lived overseas from 1954 to 1976. See Miller, "Cosmopolitan, Nativist, Eclectic," 119. Junus Adam Dungga, born in Gorontalo in 1922, studied musicology in Amsterdam in 1950. He founded the Akademi Ilmu Musik in Jakarta in 1963, which closed after only one year (from contributor's note in *Budaja Djaja* 2[1]: 128, July 1968). Amir Pasaribu might have had leftist associations. He was fearful enough of recrimination after the 1965 coup that he moved to Suriname in 1968. See Miller, "Cosmopolitan, Nativist, Eclectic," 118–21.

46 Elsewhere, however, Dungga wrote, in an article about the development of Indonesian music, that truly Indonesian music began with kroncong, for it uses the Indonesian language, scales, and instrumentation that were not used before. See J. A. Dungga, "Perkembangan Musik Indonesia," in *Almanak Seni*, ed. Zaini (Djakarta: BMKN, 1957), 107–15.

47 The information here is from Esha, "'Pembersih Kolam Musik' vs 'Gembong Kebudayaan,'" 94. The songbook was *10 Lagu Indonesia* (Jakarta: Humala Pontas, 1950). The other nine songs were "Rinda," "Bandung Selatan di Waktu Malam," "Oh Angin Sampaikan Salamku," "Djauh di Mata di Hati Djangan!," "Mawar di Rindu Melati nan Laji," "Hallo Bandung!," "Gita Malam," and "Indonesia Tanah Pusaka." A second songbook was planned, *Lagu2 Revolusi Perdjoangan*, but it is unclear whether it was published.

48 The kroncong version with vocalist Netty is on the Irama label (Imco 585); the choral version with orchestra directed by Sudjasmin, recorded on October 23, 1958, was published by Lokananta, series ARI 003, and issued on July 11, 1959. The same recording was later released on a 7-inch album, CRE 007 c 1966. Thanks to Erkelens and Yampolsky.

49 This is on the third album in a series of four Lokananta 10-inch LPs, titled *4th Asian Games—Souvenir from Indonesia* (numbered ARI 100, 101, 102, and 103). The recording on ARI 102 is of the Orkes Lokanada under the direction of B. Y. Supardi and was recorded on August 10, 1962. Once again, thanks to Yampolsky.

50 *Ismail Marzuki Komponis Pejuang*, 74.

51 Apeland, *World Youth and the Communists*, 54; Larisa Efimova, "Indonesia's Cultural Traffic Abroad 1950–1965" (unpublished paper on Radio Moscow presented at a workshop held at the Koninklijk Instituut voor Taal-, Land- en Volkenkunde [KITLV, Royal Netherlands Institute for Southeast Asian and Caribbean Studies], Leiden, April 2009).

52 For discussion of the term *rakyat* in a later period and for a different genre of popular music, see Andrew Weintraub, *Dangdut Stories: A Social and Musical History of Indonesia's Most Popular Music* (Oxford: Oxford University Press, 2010), esp. chapter 4.

53 "Dari rombongan folklor, yang karena kekreatifan Rakyat sendiri dan berkat pengaruh gerakan revolusioner, meningkat menjadi drama Rakyat yang mengintegrasikan

diri dengan gerakan revolusioner, seperti misalnya ludruk, ketoprak, reog (Jawa Timur), dan sebagainya. Bersamaan dengan berkembangnya drama Rakyat, berkembang pula cabang-cabang kesenian Rakyat lainnya seperti tari, musik, sastra dan lain-lain." D. N. Aidit, *Seni dan Sastra* (Jakarta: RADJA MINJAK, 2002), 11. Aidit's speech is published in book form. He also said, "Musik daerah kita harus meneruskan tradisi dengan keberanian kreatif dalam mengadakan pembaruan. Mempelajari gerak tari folklor serta musiknya akan sangat memperkaya kemungkinan-kemungkinan mengubah tari baru." Aidit, *Seni dan Sastra*, 42.

54 "Yang paling mendesak untuk [Rakyat pekerja] bukanlah karya-karya yang rumit dan sulit, melainkan karya-karya yang populer, sederhana dan mudah dimengerti ... jenis-jenis kesenian yang mudah mencapai massa" (Aidit, *Seni dan Sastra*, 33); "mengadakan pembaruan segala bentuk kesenian yang populer dan sangat disukai Rakyat" (47); "pasaran seni dan sastra revolusioner" (70).

55 Peter Manuel, *Popular Musics of the Non-Western World: An Introductory Survey* (New York: Oxford University Press, 1988); Craig Lockard, *Dance of Life: Popular Music and Politics in Southeast Asia* (New York: Oxford University Press, 1999); Keith Negus, *Popular Music in Theory: An Introduction* (Cambridge: Polity, 1996).

2. VEHICLES OF PROGRESS

The Kerala Rikshawala at the Intersection of Communism and Cosmopolitanism

NISHA KOMMATTAM

The past two decades have witnessed rich scholarly debates about manifold notions of "cosmopolitanism"—be they "marginal," "rooted," "vernacular," or of any other variety.[1] One fruitful research site that allows us to follow these theoretical trajectories further is the diverse landscape of literary and film productions in the many vernacular languages of South Asia. The South Indian state of Kerala in particular (located on the southwest coast of India), where a unique blend of Communist governance, significant intra- and transnational migration, and rapid development into a global tourist destination have shaped the sociopolitical and cultural landscape of the late twentieth century, constitutes a region in which interesting facets of cosmopolitanisms—both real and imagined—manifest themselves.[2] This chapter examines the iconic trope of the rickshaw puller or autorickshaw driver, generally known as *rikshawala* across South Asia, as represented in two Malayalam movies dating back to the Cold War era.[3] More precisely, I discuss three film songs that illustrate how the "Kerala rikshawala" as a cultural icon is situated at an intersection of vernacular Communist ideologies on the one hand and emerging cosmopolitan aspirations on the other. A close reading of the songs' textual, visual, and sonic structures will expose these intersections as well as lead to larger questions about the uneasy relationship between class, caste, Communism, and cosmopolitanism. My argument here is twofold. First, I argue that the cultural icon of the Kerala rikshawala offers an identificatory trope for many consumers of the mass culture production that is Malayalam cinema. Relatability, ubiquity, and relatively low social stigma (compared to other working-class professions) aid the trope of the rikshawala in serving as an embodiment of the Malayalee audience's aspirations for social justice and upward mobility in the relatively young state. Second, the trope of the Kerala rikshawala can also be read as an embodiment of the postcolonial state of Kerala itself, representing its multifaceted pulls toward larger socioeconomic progress, attempting to provide upward social mobility to its citizens in an increasingly globalizing world. The aspirations and identity outlooks embodied by the Kerala rikshawala as icon can be seen as cosmopolitan at two levels: in its common sense of "transcending the local" and "non-provincial"; and in another sense explored by Magdalena Nowicka and Maria Rovisco, who point to cosmopolitanism as a mode of self-transformation, "which occurs when individuals and groups engage in concrete struggles to protect a common humanity and become more reflexive about their experiences of otherness."[4]

Cinema and Communism in Kerala Culture

Kerala cinema is defined by its linguistic medium, the regional vernacular of Malayalam. Like other Indian cinemas, it can be characterized as "art, entertainment, technology, industry and ideology all at the same time."[5] Its viewership is mostly limited to the South Indian state of Kerala, with diasporic communities in every major city within India, such as Bangalore, Chennai, Mumbai, or New Delhi. The global diaspora of Malayalam speakers spans all continents but is numerically limited to approximately one million people plus their descendants, who may or may not have access to the language of their immigrant parents. Thus, while Bollywood cinema has famously risen from a "formerly national vernacular" cinema to a worldwide phenomenon that came to represent Indian cinema on a global scale in recent years, not all South Indian cinemas have paralleled that development.[6] Malayalam cinema, in comparison, has not quite moved from the "periphery to the center of world cinema" internationally.[7] Nevertheless, it holds a powerful place within the local social imagery and is one of the few unifying cultural practices that transcend boundaries of class, caste, and communities.[8] As in other South Asian cinemas, music features as one of the major components of Kerala's film production and distribution, and the film song is a vital ingredient of Malayalam popular cinema.[9] Gregory Booth has argued for the "unique nature of the relationship between popular film and music production in India" with regard to Hindi film music, and he traces the rise of popular music into both a cultural commodity as well as a lucrative industry, starting as early as in the 1930s.[10] In a similar vein, Joseph Getter and B. Balasubrahmaniam rightly observe: "Of all the music genres in India, film songs of any language possess the largest audience and are the most geographically and culturally widespread," so as to be "ubiquitous in the soundspace (by which we mean all the sounds heard by people in a given place)."[11]

While film songs fulfill important functions at a metadiegetic level within a film, they also acquire a life outside the film in the larger realm of popular music. In fact, it would be appropriate to say that in Kerala, film music has until very recently constituted the bulk of those musical practices we commonly refer to as "popular music."[12] But even beyond that numeric fact, the outreach, impact, and visibility/audibility of the genre are multifaceted. First, we observe the "cross-promotional purpose" of film songs, promoting the movie and aiding in the sales of movie tickets, which, as Jayson Beaster-Jones has argued, is generally overlooked in scholarship. Beaster-Jones rightfully points out that this "promotional angle" has resulted in a very different trajectory for film music and media in India than it has in other parts of the world.[13] This is an important characteristic of not only Hindi but other vernacular film music as well, and, I would argue, has only increased in the early twenty-first century. Film songs nowadays get released weeks before the actual movie comes out, thus advertising the film to the audience and establishing its place within the collective memory of popular culture references, regardless of its subsequent box office success.[14] Second, the prominence given to the sonic aspect of a visual medium may result in reinforcing "escapist" tendencies within this form of entertainment, which, at worst, can inhibit the development of a truly political cinema by diluting the film's underlying ideology.[15] Furthermore, as Alison Arnold has pointed out, the fields of musicology and anthropology "have for the most part focused their attention on Indian classical and folk traditions to the neglect of film song," despite the dual role of the latter.[16] In Arnold's view, too, it serves as film accompaniment on the one hand, yet on the other hand it constitutes a large section of "popular music" on the subcontinent. Kaley Mason then expands that point even further when he colorfully describes the impact of this type of music. Film songs, he writes, "animate the labor of everyday life.... Whether playing on the radio, satellite TV, or mobile phones, film songs provide the soundtrack for daily activities ... amplifying sentiments of love, devotion, innocence, heroism, and pathos for communities at work in coastal Malabar."[17] Similar to Arnold, Mason also attests to the multiple functions of film music, in this case Malayalam film music: "As in other commercial cinemas of South Asia, the prominence given to song-and-dance sequences in film reflects oral storytelling practices that refashion, amplify, synthesize and complement narrative themes and formulae."[18] He thus agrees with the general consensus that "the film song continues to be among the most popular forms of entertainment, as well as an important medium for telling stories that matter to Kerala's listening publics."[19] The role of Malayalam film music in Kerala culture can thus hardly be overestimated, given its pervasive and socially unifying presence within everyday life in Kerala.

This is not to say that the genre as a whole does not face criticism from intellectual quarters. As Peter Manuel has pointed out, popular music in South Asia not only suffers from a form of "self-conscious syncretism" in its presentation and reception; it also monopolized the world of popular entertainment for many decades of the twentieth century.[20] He refers to Indian critics such as Ashok Ranade, who have attributed the huge popularity of film music not so much to its presumed or perceived "authenticity" but to the "lack of public access to other forms of mediated music." This holds true, of course, only until the arrival of cassette technology in the 1980s, which quickly made the field more equal by providing access to recorded classical, devotional, and other types of vernacular music. Manuel goes so far as to speak of a new era that was inaugurated by the media developments of that time.[21] In his classic work, Manuel fleshes out a tension between what he describes as two forces of homogenization and diversification at play in the increase of mass-produced and mass-circulated media: a degree of both homogenization as well as diversification, he claims, can be traced in the aftermath of this expansion. For Manuel, this only testifies to the complexities of multiple, nuanced identities in the postcolonial subject, such as the South Asian listener of the late twentieth century—he does not view that tension as a contradiction per se. This, I find, is a helpful and productive viewpoint for analyzing the Kerala context as well. In contrast to Manuel's productive perspective, other critical attitudes toward Indian popular films, film music, and their massive popularity on the subcontinent figure both popular films and their audiences as vulgar and unsophisticated. Constantine Nakassis and Melanie Dean, in their work on Tamil cinema and youth culture, have rightfully pointed out how familiar and predictable those criticisms appear from today's perspective, given that they are very much in line with the thought of European midcentury critiques by, for example, Theodor Adorno and Max Horkheimer. As Nakassis and Dean point out, though, this dismissive line of criticism has not affected the films' mass popularity in the least.[22] And as the present chapter is meant to demonstrate, it obstructs a productive scholarly engagement with some of India's most important cultural practices.

Insofar as film songs are viewed as political from the perspective I seek to develop in the present chapter, a brief excursion into the political history of postindependent Kerala is required at this point, to contextualize the powerful rhetoric and symbolic imagery encountered in Malayalam films. When Kerala was founded in 1956—almost ten years after India gained independence from British colonial rule—the geographical state boundaries were largely determined by the shared linguistic identity of its inhabitants. The language of Malayalam became the official unifier and regional/cultural foundation of a population that had until then been living in three diverse administrative subdivisions, each a microcosm of its own.[23] Malayalees, the ethnic identity by which the population of the state is still known today, were on the one hand marked by their religious diversity and the comparatively peaceful coexistence of Hindus, Muslims, and Christians, without larger-scale communal riots since the early 1920s. On the other hand, they were simultaneously living in what was arguably one of the most hierarchical, rigid caste systems on the Indian subcontinent.[24] This densely populated state unexpectedly gained international attention when, in 1957, it instated the world's first democratically elected Communist government.[25] In his book *Communism in Kerala*, Thomas Nossiter contextualizes Kerala's relatively marginal status on the global scale by reminding us that "in 1971 its population of twenty-one million was larger than that of several European states including Czechoslovakia, East Germany, and Hungary as well as Chile, Cuba, and what was North Vietnam. More people speak Malayalam ... than speak Bulgarian, Czech, Hungarian, Rumanian, or Serbo-Croat."[26] While Kerala's population today has grown to more than thirty-four million people (post–Census 2011), the relative proportions (especially in relation to some other post-Communist countries) still exist.[27] To put it differently, within the context of South Asia, even perceived marginalities or a minority status can still constitute a demographically impressive research site. Following the framework of this volume's introduction, this chapter aims to disrupt some of the commonly accepted, Euro-American-centric narratives about the Cold War and its reflections in global popular cultures outside North America and Europe.

After its victory in 1957, the Communist Party of India, after various splits and in its multiple manifestations, ruled Kerala (on and off) for the next few decades.[28] Historians, economists, and political scientists have, to varying degrees, credited the Marxist government with the well-known high development markers that the state can boast, such as the highest literacy rate of India, the highest female-to-male sex ratio, the lowest infant mortality, the incorporation of women into the work force, the strength of labor unions, and so forth.[29] The high literacy is among the reasons for a very active political participation on the grassroots level as well as for a vibrant literary scene in the vernacular Malayalam. The escalation of the Cold War during those very decades of Communist rule and influence in Kerala has resulted in at least two phenomena worth scholarly attention. One consists in the fact that Western nations, especially the US and Soviet governments, have in the past kept a close eye on political developments in Kerala, which partially accounts for the study of the regional state and its language in academia. Second, literary and other cultural productions from Kerala have often been closely intertwined with, affected by, or promoted by Communist thought and even party politics. In the sphere of South Indian popular music, Theodore Baskaran has argued that the "hold of cinema and film music on social and political life in Tamil Nadu" has continuously and massively increased since the 1960s.[30] What is true for Tamil Nadu is accurate for the neighboring state of Kerala as well, especially given the latter's affinity for Communist ideologies, which often permeated film music in similar ways. As Baskaran observes in his discussion of Tamil film songs, "some songwriters with leftist leanings who worked in films used songs for political comment and thereby added some substance to them. . . . Often these songs reinforced existing beliefs and value systems of the audience also and one could get an insight into contemporary attitudes by analyzing these songs."[31] That same dynamic can also be observed in the examples I have chosen for this chapter. Sumangala Damodaran's work on the political music of nascent Kerala carefully analyzes various intertwined branches of vernacular art production on the one hand and regional, nationalist, and Communist politics on the other hand.

> The period from the mid-thirties of the twentieth century to the end of the fifties saw the cultural expression of a very wide range of political sentiments and positions around imperialism, fascism, nationalism and social transformation in India. This period, with the years 1936 and 1943 being landmark years that saw the setting up of the Progressive Writers' Association (PWA) and the Indian People's Theatre Association (IPTA) respectively, also happened to coincide with a vibrant radical ethos in many parts of the world where, among numerous political issues, the aesthetics–politics relationship was to be articulated and debated in many unprecedented ways. These organizations, that would formally use literature and culture to express political discontent, came into existence in the crucial transitional phase from colonialism to a postcolonial context, when the leftwing strand of the political movement for national liberation from colonial rule, under the leadership of the Communist Party of India (CPI), had taken a position that contrasted it from the mainstream nationalist movement.[32]

Thus, it is perhaps not surprising that the literary genre or mode of writing referred to as "social realism" has played an important role in the rich and productive sphere of modern Malayalam literature. Starting as early as the 1930s, Malayalam writing witnessed Marxist ideas joining forces with the nascent nationalist and anticaste, egalitarian sentiments of the time.[33] While earlier literature had largely been focused on classicist poetry and the emulation of old genres and styles, the new Western genre of the novel proved to be a fruitful medium for debates about social progress.[34] Focusing on the plight of the "common man," lower castes, Dalits, and women, many of these new works advocated a new and in particular more egalitarian Kerala society.[35] As Damodaran summarizes: "In India, although social issues were being addressed in writing and theatre through the nineteenth and early twentieth century, the anticipations from the possibilities of transformation that characterised the transition period brought a tremendous sense of urgency for artistic expression and by the 1930s, such spontaneous expression was beginning to grow exponentially, even before formal organisation of such activity began."[36]

This "urgency for artistic expression" is highly visible in the literature, music, and visual art of this period, to the extent that Damodaran uses the term *radicalization* when describing the artistic responses to the historical and geopolitical developments in this era. After acknowledging the particular historical conjuncture of the first half of the twentieth century and the emergence of socialist thought after the Bolshevik Revolution, she links these responses to the emergence of radicalized nationalist ideas in colonized societies.

> The radical impulse, signified by a leftward turn in politics and culture, consisted of conceptualising an alternative nationalism and a unique and unprecedented internationalism, both of which were departures from mainstream nationalist positions. In the literary and cultural fields, this radicalisation was prominent, even if the number of people involved were only a small "fraction." This fraction started emerging in different parts of the country from the late 1920s, sometimes initiating, sometimes responding to and sometimes actively participating in mass upsurges and agitations, around which the radical cultural was beginning to be imagined and expressed.[37]

Damodaran's succinct analysis of the proto-nationalist, nationalist/anticolonial, and Communist agendas influencing the musical culture serves as a backdrop for my analysis of Malayalam film songs.

Odayil Ninnu

One particularly successful social realist novel was *Odayil Ninnu* (From the gutter), published in 1942 by P. Kesavadev (1904–1983).[38] Kesavadev, a rebellious self-made author and political agitator, allegedly worked numerous autobiographical experiences into his writing.[39] When director K. S. Sethumadhavan (b. 1931) turned Kesavadev's novel into a film with the same title that was released in March 1965, he followed the novel closely in its plot. A brief synopsis will illustrate the issue of social justice that permeates the story: *Odayil Ninnu* follows the life struggles of a low-class, low-caste rickshaw puller named Pappu, played by Sathyan (Manuel Sathyaneshan Nadar, 1912–1971), who is shown to have a keen sense of justice early on in his life. The film starts with a scene in a boys' classroom, where the strict teacher uses corporal punishment toward all the unruly children but openly spares the local high-caste powerholder's son among them. Pappu stands up against this caste- and class-based discrimination, even though he is just a young boy, by calling the teacher out on his behavior and even trying to incite his classmates to boycott the class. When his timid classmates do not stand up against the teacher like Pappu, he shouts out in anger, "You are dogs, all of you!" and storms out of the school. The prank for which he had been punished—bringing a wild parrot that he caught, tied to a string, into the school—thus ends with the symbolic gesture of Pappu releasing the bird into freedom. He is subsequently thrown out of the house by his own father at the angry decree of his "landlord," whose role in traditional Kerala society is perhaps most aptly described as an oppressive blend of patriarch, landowner, and slaveholder. The Brahmin landlord is simultaneously Pappu's father's employer and the school's owner and thus the teacher's employer. Pappu's passionate, juvenile rebellion has thus endangered his entire family's livelihood, so that his own father feels forced to beat him and drive him out of the house for good. This incident firmly establishes the character of Pappu as a poor but righteous and rebellious member of the downtrodden classes. Kesavadev's biographer, K. P. Sasidharan, has gloriously described Pappu as "a rickshaw puller with a difference, an image of dignity, an upright workman, a rebel, whom people styled the daredevil."[40] The link between his low sociocultural and economic status and his high-spirited moral attitude is starkly contrasted with the immoral, unjust behavior of the high-caste characters that hold power over him. The film first shows how Pappu is forced to earn his living in Kollam (the larger town he escaped to) as a coolie on foot, carrying suitcases and other heavy loads on his head. He forms a friendship with a band of adolescent coolies, igniting rebellious thoughts and demands for fair pay among them. After a violent assault on an exploitative shop owner, he switches labor and is shown manually rolling beedies (small cigarettes), then selling soda. The film then fast-forwards to Pappu's adulthood, where he rises within working-class hierarchies, from being a mill worker to finally becoming a rickshaw puller. In each of these low-skilled, manual labor positions, hotheaded Pappu responds sharply to exploitation and injustices, which results in him having to quit his job—usually after speaking up on behalf of his downtrodden coworkers—and even going to jail. Pappu's final "upgrade" to the profession of rickshaw puller, where he operates a manual two-wheel cart on which passengers are seated, conveys his upward mobility through hard work and innate determination alone. One day, Pappu the rikshawala accidentally runs over Lakshmi, a poor five-year-old girl who was literally standing in the gutter by the road. Even though it was an accident, he is overcome by tremendous guilt. He picks her up, comforts her, and takes her home—only to find that she and her single mother live in abject poverty. Goodhearted and lonely Pappu is touched by what he sees and quasi-adopts the girl, subsequently starts a relationship with the widowed mother, and lovingly raises Lakshmi like a devoted father.

However, over the course of the film, Lakshmi (also the name of the Hindu goddess of prosperity and wealth) grows up to be an arrogant, vain, and materialistic young woman who exploits Pappu for his money but shows him no love or gratitude. Her incessant demands for fancy clothing, jewelry, and the like puts an unbearable strain on aging Pappu, who is still providing for the three of them by manually pulling his rickshaw. Lakshmi is portrayed as a greedy, selfish, superficial, and ungrateful recipient of Pappu's love and care. Only when old Pappu falls ill (and ultimately dies) after eleven years of hardship and physical labor for this girl is Lakshmi, now sixteen, finally stricken by grief and remorse. Thus, Pappu's rescuing of Lakshmi from starvation and her elevation from absolute poverty into a low working-class existence is overshadowed by the young woman's ruthless ambitions toward an imagined space where beauty, wealth, and fame are dangerously conflated, ambitions that are only questioned at the moment of Pappu's death.

The film's utopian, if edgy, from-rags-to-riches tale is of course not without its ambivalences, or even troubling aspects. We note in passing the stylized dichotomy between the generous, selfless, caretaking male protagonist and the undeserving, beautiful, yet heartless female protagonist, which evokes a certain misogyny despite Lakshmi's complete turn of character toward the end, which rather exaggeratedly attempts to restore her as a noble and virtuous, loving woman. Also disturbing is the movie's portrayal of the young girl growing up into an increasingly less innocent seductress, for instance when she engages in semi-flirtatious song and dance with Pappu as a precocious fifth grader in the song "A Tiny Jasmine Bud Has Blossomed...." But audience attention has always focused on the central role of Pappu. If Pappu as the character in Kesavadev's novel has been hailed as the "first working-class hero" in the Malayalam novel, Pappu the film character has only served to cement this notion.[41]

Not only was the novel from 1942 still deemed socially relevant enough to be turned into a film more than two decades later, but the film also went on to become one of the biggest Malayalam film hits of its time. Pappu's character in the film can be said to embody what Nowicka and Rovisco have described as an individual's small-scale moral choice that contributes toward a "more just world order"—a utopia where "every human being is worthy of equal moral concern."[42] Enacting this moral ideal, in their view, constitutes a form of "moral cosmopolitanism" that ascribes great agency to the individual. Furthermore, portraying such moral cosmopolitanism represents, to use Damodaran's formulation, "hitherto unexplored solidarities between the 'real, unrepresented and marginalised people' that went beyond local contexts necessitated [by] the cultural representation of such 'horizontal comradeships' which also allowed for an imagining of a nation as a common identification in a wholly different way."[43] This newly found representation, in turn, would then offer a surface onto which the newly imagined community of "Keralites" (as opposed to the less geographically bound but linguistically defined "Malayalees") could project much-needed narratives of nationalism and internationalism.[44]

In the film's catchy hit song "Oh Rikshawala!," featuring famous playback singer Mehboob (1926–1981) as lead singer, a small group of rikshawalas is bemoaning their plight and the physical strain of their work, culminating in a passionate plea for humane treatment and a demand for respect. The beginning of the song shows a wealthy, overweight man and his heavy suitcase arriving at the rickshaw stand. This scene is immediately legible to local audiences: Here is a North Indian–looking traveler marked by his clearly Northern Indian–style clothes. His relative wealth is symbolized by the circumference of his waistline. Armed with a heavy suitcase, he boards a rickshaw pulled by a thin, wiry rikshawala wearing the typical working-class "uniform" of a checkered lungi (male waistcloth) and a white baniyan (shirt), and a towel wrapped around his head to catch his sweat. The rikshawala's clothes, though they may not be marked as specifically Southern Indian (except for the Madras plaid checkered pattern of the lungi), are not marked as foreign either, unlike the traveler's clothes. During this scene, the singer explains: "A Seth [North Indian businessman] weighing five and a half tons / and the Seth has a suitcase weighing fifty tons." The first, obvious dichotomy of wealth and poverty is thus further polarized by the additional layers of contrasting Northern Indian versus Southern Indian as well as Other versus Local/Regional. The song lyrics then continue to elaborate on the visual scene: "It's really true, it's really true . . . We who roam around when the town is asleep [. . .] when we drag you around, you who weigh as much as ten sacks of rice / please don't lower the fare for this poor rikshawala / It's really true, it's really true / We are not cart oxen, we are definitely no cart oxen! / [...] We are sons of man! Oh rikshawala...." Fittingly, the last scene of the song features a cart, pulled by two oxen, that passes this group of rikshawalas who have just melodiously articulated their human (implied: superior) status in contrast to the working animals. The climax of the song bears a certain dramatic pathos as we witness the musical declaration of a bill of rights of human laborers. This empowerment of the working classes, which was not articulated nearly as concisely in the 1942 novel, became a hit song in 1965 when the film was released. Alternating between the rhythmic stanzas that propel the storyline, accompanied by synchronous clapping reminiscent of local folk traditions and suggestive of unity in community, and the almost shouted chorus line, "Oh rikshawala! Heyya-ho, rikshawala!," this catchy tune has a powerful and memorable effect that continues long beyond the end of the film. It is the transition from novel to film that opens up the metadiegetic space into which revolutionary, passionate pleas for humanitarian treatment of one's fellow citizens like this could be inserted. The sonic rendition of a political agenda is especially possible within the medium of Indian film, where songs and music have always played a central role. Here, the song not only comments on but intensifies the main plot—while taking the liberty to articulate a stronger political agenda than its literary predecessor.

The song "Oh Rikshawala!" can further be read against the political scene at the time of this movie: In the mid-1960s, the Communist Party of India (CPI) had just split off from its more leftist, Marxist branch, the CPI(M), which subsequently found its biggest following in the two states of Kerala and West Bengal. While the CPI(M) had (perhaps pragmatically) shifted its focus of action from ideologically driven, armed revolutions into more tame, parliamentary collaborations, the ignitable momentum of this hit song might be read in terms of its political symbolism: as an inspirational call for empathy with the downtrodden classes, for humanizing the formerly dehumanized, oppressed classes and castes, or even for a unionized course of action toward social equality.

Furthermore, the rikshawala and his labor provide a more accessible identificatory trope to many audiences than some of his fellow working-class contemporaries might have. This is the case, I would argue, for a number of reasons: First, the rikshawala's ubiquitous presence in everyday life and the constant use of rickshaws by the diverse audience members render the rickshaw a site of clashing socioeconomic realities. The ride in a man-pulled rickshaw (as they were almost never pulled by women) was one of the temporary interfaces where those who could afford the ride—a white-collar worker, a businessman, a high-caste landowner, an educated middle-class citizen—engaged in public interaction with a less fortunate, less educated, working-class member.[45] The public and temporary nature of this transaction, I believe, marks this as a different relationship from the one with domestic servants who worked in the privacy of a home, or laborers in visually and geographically removed agricultural settings.[46] The frequency, short duration, and relative intimacy of the rickshaw ride (when compared to, say, train rides) may also play a factor in this relatability.[47] Second, the labor of transportation—though physically grueling for manual rickshaws—could be seen as a relatively "clean" labor. Again, this is mostly a privileged-caste perspective from which this work, unlike many other professions, does not involve direct physical contact with people of different social status, with their bodily fluids, or with other forms of "pollution" like animal carcasses, and so on. In Kerala, where up to that time a rigid quasi-feudal caste system had been regulating every last aspect of daily labor, professional communities, and social hierarchies, the rikshawala was considered "cleaner" than the latrine sweeper, the leather tanner, or other workers. The notion of touchability was certainly present in the minds of audiences at the time *Odayil Ninnu* was released.[48] Third, the un(der)educated rikshawala who passionately articulates the hitherto unspoken, socially sanctioned hardships of his labor while simultaneously displaying pride in his profession and declaring his right to humane treatment in a postfeudal, postindependent society may have hit a nerve in many of the viewers, who must have been very aware of the radical sociopolitical changes of their time.[49] The twentieth century's unprecedented call for social justice—almost unthinkable in a society that for centuries had been dominated by a few privileged communities—had found a memorable outlet in this production of vernacular mass culture. Innocently clad in the form of a catchy tune and sanctioned within a film plot based on an acclaimed work of literary fiction, the song "Oh Rikshawala!" could perhaps most radically be read as a subtle, psychological form of mass mobilization through popular culture.

Aye Auto!

The egalitarian utopia, which I argue is evoked by the "Oh Rikshawala!" song from 1965, finds a more recent manifestation in the movie *Aye Auto* (Hey Auto!—the standard call for an autorickshaw in Malayalam), directed by Venu Nagavally (1949–2010) and released in 1990. The film appeared right after the world—and Communist Kerala—had witnessed the fall of the Soviet Union and the subsequent power shift between previously polarized geopolitical forces. *Aye Auto!* is a tale about a poor yet highly politicized and ambitious autorickshaw driver, played by the megastar actor and audience favorite of many decades Mohanlal (Mohanlal Viswanathan Nair, b. 1960). The film is at the same time a charming declaration of love to the motorized little black-and-yellow three-wheeler, called simply "auto" in Kerala. Lyrics to the title song, "Auto, Auto," are entirely devoted to the praises of the sturdy "little auto that could." The fast-paced song contains brief melodious stanzas about the autorickshaw's talent for maneuvering deep potholes, driving well in extreme rain or heat, and being the rustic, affordable, omnipresent traffic sight that it still is today in India. These stanzas are alternated with the shouted, cheerful chorus line that mimics the typical exclamation used to hail a ride on a busy street: "Auto! Auto! Auto! Auto!" Onomatopoetic lyrics both mimic and narrate a slightly bumpy ride around town, emphasizing the low minimum charge of a mere three rupees. The final stanza climactically extols the brave khaki-clad heart (of the auto driver in his khaki uniform): "Melt, you heart inside a khaki sheath / Danger is your constant companion!" Since these light-built, open-sided vehicles are indeed vulnerable to tremendous damage and injury of passengers when involved in an accident, one could read this line as adding a realistic undertone to the heroism alluded to in these lyrics. The lyrics of this song are accompanied by equally fast-paced visuals: The opening scene shows a large factory hall where hundreds of autorickshaws, some in various states of assembly and disassembly, are shown. The camera angle mimics a view from within another auto, as if driving by. This perspective is maintained for the majority of the song, as the viewer seems to flit by changing landscapes and other autos on the road, peeking inside to catch a view of a gesticulating driver and his passengers. This song not only validates but also glorifies and even romanticizes the mundane profession of the rikshawala—turning his hardships into noble struggles and his dangerous life into a heroic challenge. This resonates with a Kerala audience in particular, because, unlike in other regions of India, Kerala rikshawalas do not have a bad reputation for aggressive behavior and cheating on their fares. This is of course directly correlated to their strong political organization and unionization, which has ensured a certain standard of living for many drivers, which differs from that of their colleagues in other places. Just to give one example of how common the trope of the unionized, politically educated Kerala rikshawala has become over the years: The recent Malayalam movie *My Boss* (2012, dir. Jeethu Joseph) contains a hilarious scene, very much in passing, in which a passenger leaving an auto grumbles at what he perceives to be a high fare, muttering his complaints to himself in a low voice. When the rickshaw driver, feeling provoked, asks him what he is saying, the passenger suddenly startles, stops, rushes to hand over the asked fare, and shouts out, "Lal Salaam!" (the typical Communist greeting, literally "red salute")—all of this in rapid succession of just a few seconds. The comedic value of this hyperbolic moment notwithstanding, the allusion to the cliché of the politically organized, Communist driver is immediately clear to a Kerala audience, even twenty years after *Aye Auto!* The portrayal of an autorickshaw and its driver in an extremely sympathetic light has become a commonplace in Kerala.

Aye Auto! was a commercial success and is still fondly remembered today. Starring Malayalam cinema's superhero of many decades, Mohanlal, in the role of Sudhi—a quasi-orphaned, kindhearted, idealist dreamer who falls in love with an orphaned, English-educated, high-caste college girl—this charming film strikes the viewer as a modern fairy tale. Even though the film was released in 1990, arguably after the end of the Cold War, the Marxist ideology permeating the very fabric of Kerala society is much more pronounced. The opening scene of the movie sets the tone for the whole film: It shows a standoff in a narrow, blocked lane between a white ambassador car with an entitled driver and an autorickshaw. When the car driver snarls, "Hey you, this road does not belong to your father! I have four wheels, you only have three. Think about it!," it is his own passenger who, in an attempt to appease the driver, points out that for people like him, "on a poor government salary, having autorickshaws is a great relief."[50] He thus validates or even idealizes the autorickshaw as the common man's mode of transportation, an affordable alternative to the bourgeois white ambassador, the ubiquitous and dominant car model of Kerala's middle and upper classes at the time. This scene—a rather undisguised metaphor for the clashing of societal classes—exemplifies, in a nutshell, much of the remainder of the film, which is also partly a portrayal of auto driver Sudhi's tender, affectionate relationship with his autorickshaw. Sudhi not only names and decorates his vehicle, which is typical for Kerala, but he gives it the female name Sundari ("beautiful woman"). Sundari being his most prized and expensive possession, numerous scenes show Sudhi lovingly giving his auto a scrub at the riverbank—similar to the way that mahouts bathe their elephants—or talking to her as if she were a live person, even confiding in her. Sudhi's loving banter with Sundari (though of course mostly a monologue), his tender caresses and emotional attachment to her, make it clear that the personified autorickshaw serves here as a narrative placeholder for the other female protagonist, the girl Minu. Moreover, the anthropomorphized vehicle also becomes Sudhi's literal and metaphorical mode of transportation for upward social mobility, as the poor, lovable, and generous working-class hero starts wooing Minu, who happens to be the granddaughter of his own high-caste landlord. This class and caste transgression would normally result in familial and societal intervention and ostracizing.

In their budding, illicit relationship, Sudhi's lack of English education—the medium of choice in Kerala for those who can afford it—is foregrounded several times. After all, Sudhi's daily duties include dropping Minu off at college every morning and picking her up again at the end of the day. When asked by Minu about his English skills, he laughingly replies: "If I knew English, would I be driving this auto? Wouldn't I be flying a plane?" Thus Sudhi sketches out a hierarchy of transportation labor, in which a lowly auto-rickshaw has less value attributed to it than an airplane. Pilot training—which grants access to a highly glamourized profession and bears connotations of a (perhaps imagined) cosmopolitanism as opposed to an auto that cannot transcend the regional—requires English. The emphasis that Malayalee society generally places on English-language education as a means of upward social mobility is thus put into the mouth of an idealistic and smart auto driver who does not have bright future prospects in his professional and social life.[51] I read this as a prime example of the type of cosmopolitan aspirations that Kathryn Hansen has so aptly described: the alluded-to cosmopolitanism here in Sudhi's dream is in and of itself advocating a type of cultural pluralism in the form of (at least) bilingual education.[52] By talking of becoming a pilot, as opposed to a mere rikshawala, Sudhi reveals his dreams of transcending his low societal status, partially in order to improve his marriage prospects. It is noteworthy that the economic reality of Sudhi and his contemporaries had at that point in history already driven tens of thousands of Malayalees into global migration, resulting in Malayalam-speaking diasporic communities on every continent of the world. The girl Minu, in a playful and flirtatious mode, starts teaching Sudhi English, which (of course) results in a song.

This song, "AEIOU," has certain comedic qualities that lighten the mood of the scene. When Minu asks Sudhi to repeat the "vowels," he mistakenly hears the Malayalam word *vauval* (bat) and looks rather confused at encountering a seemingly familiar word or at least a homophone in the foreign language. He then uses the common South Indian exclamation "Ayyo," which she in turn playfully mishears as AEIOU, the sequence of English vowels (phonetically here: "Ah-eh-ee-oh-you," which, spoken fast, does indeed sound a bit like the Malayalam *Ayyo*). However, the underlying desire for knowledge and formal education that is expressed in this song is far from comical. Sudhi goes on to sing "I will grasp this English stuff, even if it takes beatings and repetition, / and I will be a big shot tomorrow, I will become someone, / I will become like an auto pilot [*sic*], B.A., M.A., M.B., B.S."[53] The simple, repetitive melody and hybrid language evoke a playful, almost childish mood. Sudhi is even shown wearing a young boy's school uniform, with shorts, tie, backpack, and a lunch box, which infantilizes and ridicules him, the undereducated working-class adult. This scene where Sudhi finds himself in a childlike position of dependency on Minu for "fancy" English education, which is then undermined and complicated by the highly flirtatious mood, evokes the familiar rhetoric of lower-caste workers attempting to liberate themselves from an oppressive, paternalistic social hierarchy, which infantilizes its dependents.[54] The strong emphasis not only on education but on *English* education is yet another explanation of Kerala's high placement on the human development index. Kerala had by that time surpassed all other Indian states with its educational achievements, yet paradoxically, the lack of economic growth also led to the large-scale mass migration referred to earlier, away from the Marxist state.[55] In the same song, we later see Sudhi, who is usually wearing his khaki rickshaw driver's uniform shirt together with a lungi, in a tank top and a red neckerchief as a symbol of his Marxist orientation. He sings about his rise in education, profession, and society at large, which will then culminate in promising marriage proposals lining up for him, all of which he will reject in a grand manner. This prompts Minu into a daydream in which she sees Sudhi as a college professor, vigorously lecturing on the great European (!) classics. The imagined rise from auto-rickshaw driver to English-speaking college professor is a localized 1990s analogy to the American notion "from dishwasher to millionaire." This career change would mean a significant gain in his social as well as financial standing. The latter becomes apparent in the language of the lyrics: Malayalam, like other languages, differentiates between *kuuli* (wages for manual labor) and *shambalam* (a regular salary, issued by an employer). At the same time, Sudhi's dream of self-improvement reflects the notion of cosmopolitanism-as-self-transformation discussed by Nowicka and Rovisco. Sudhi's relationship with Minu allows him to find in her *otherness* the foundations of a different self. In his ambitions, Sudhi is of course hardly alone but instead functions as a signifier of larger societal aspirations. Sudhi's rhetoric, his social and material dreams, and his open demonstration of party affiliation underline the possibilities and promises of an egalitarian (albeit utopian) Kerala society. With the liberalization of the Indian market on the one hand and the end of Soviet Communism and the Cold War on the other—both occurring around the time of this movie—Kerala society was standing at the threshold of an unprecedented wave of globalization in its economic and cultural spheres. It is safe to assume, then, that the creator of this song, lyricist Bichu Thirumala, was capturing and reflecting a prevailing expectation about the advancement of Malayalee individuals—even if Marxism's exact role in that progress might have been heavily disputed.

There is one further aspect to English education that this film song beautifully illustrates, on both the sonic and the visual level. The song starts and ends with Sudhi's and Minu's mutual English (!) exclamations of "I love you"—shouted loudly across great distances of green fields and flowing waters. It is crucial here that this romantic sentiment is expressed in English—and not in the protagonists' common language, Malayalam, which has multiple ways of expressing romantic love but rarely does so overtly in a film context. The use of English here creates a subtle distance between the provocative message—illicit, class-transcending, premarital love—and the sympathetic characters. Furthermore, the appropriation and use of the English language is what—quite literally—bridges the distance between the two lovers in these scenes. Not only are they physically running toward one another while shouting their I-love-you's, but they are simultaneously using education to bridge previously established, deeply rooted societal gaps between them. Thus, considerable transformative power is ascribed onto the language and onto formal education—if money can't buy you love, as the saying goes, an English education surely can.

Vehicles of Progress?

What links these three different film songs from two popular movies that are decades apart are the tropes of utopian egalitarianism often ascribed to Communist thought and, in more contemporary terms, social upward mobility for the working classes. "Oh Rikshawala!" articulates its resounding plea for the humane treatment of struggling human laborers with a passion both rooted in, and mirroring, the prevailing Marxist ideologies of its time. The narrative strategy of "Auto, Auto" differs slightly. Instead of bemoaning the plight of the rikshawala, the song nobilifies the labor and the whole profession, to the extent of hyperbolic glorification. The song "AEIOU" in the same film, finally, references an almost utopian upward mobility that, at this late point in the twentieth century, the Marxist state had promised its citizens by way of accessible education. Read together, these three songs show how the trope of the rikshawala evolves from a maltreated and dehumanized into a validated, even glorified individual, and finally into a liberated worker and educated, even prosperous citizen. Over the course of the twentieth century, the Kerala rikshawala has been portrayed as "driving under the influence" of Communist rhetoric and ideals as well as cosmopolitan aspirations shared with many other sections of Kerala's population. This historical transformation of the iconic Kerala rikshawala can also be seen in the technological transformation from the manually pulled rickshaws to bicycle rickshaws and finally the motorized autorickshaw portrayed in *Aye Auto!* during the course of the twentieth century. That the evolution of technology has wider social consequences is tragically illustrated in *Odayil Ninnu* when old and sick Pappu loses a passenger to a younger man riding a bicycle rickshaw that is faster and thus preferable to Pappu's hand-pulled vehicle. The rickshaw thus becomes itself a sign of progress, something that audiences in 1965 must have noted when seeing Pappu pulling his rickshaw manually, at a time when more modern rickshaws were already common. As Chris Carlsson remarks: "After the Second World War, hand-pulled rickshaws became an embarrassment to modernizing urban elites in the Third World, and were widely banned, in part because they were symbolic, not of modernity, but of a feudal world of openly marked class distinctions."[56] The motorized autorickshaw triumphed as the vehicle of progress while the khaki uniforms suggested an increased professionalization, and the operation of motor vehicles required a different skill than merely running on one's two feet, which might have then contributed to differing perceptions (again, by those with privilege) of rikshawalas as opposed to other laborers.

There are numerous other scenes in the film *Aye Auto!* that illustrate the complexities of Marxism in Kerala society in 1990, for example, when a gathering of rickshaw drivers turns into a Marxist demonstration, or when a particularly casteist comment by Minu's grandmother evokes old specters of feudalism and high-caste hegemony—perhaps giving us a psychological backdrop to Sudhi's political affiliation. After many twists and turns in the story line and after resistance from family and enemies, Sudhi's and Minu's attempt at a secret marriage results in the abduction of the bride and a violent climax, after which the couple is finally reunited and happily marries with the blessings of the grandparents. We thus find a significant difference in the narrative logic of the two film plots: Pappu, the altruistic, idealistic rikshawala in *Odayil Ninnu*, continues to provide for his increasingly demanding and spoiled foster daughter, even to his own detriment. His demise from tuberculosis is a long and slow process and arguably conveys the message that attempting to save someone else's life, or attempting to transcend one's given social position in life, will result in punishment, suffering, and death. Though Lakshmi is shown to grieve for him and regret her prior actions, the overall mood in the final scenes evokes a pessimistic dystopia. In *Aye Auto!*, by contrast, the fairy-tale-like ascension of Sudhi into marital bliss and high-caste prosperity (with Minu being the sole heiress of her grandfather's and deceased parents' wealth and palatial residence) conveys the idealistic message that one's secret dreams and even seemingly unrealistic ambitions in life can become true—with the right mixture of luck, confidence, charm, handsome looks, righteousness, hard work, and certain political beliefs. Winning Minu's heart and wealth after a long struggle against societal restrictions, I argue, pictures a "concrete utopia" in Ernst Bloch's sense of the word. Pappu has not solved the problem of famine and poverty among girl children in his time, nor has Sudhi changed the overarching oppressive structure of his casteist society, or started a caste-transcending revolution in the realm of romance in Kerala, but both protagonists have operated under what Bloch would have termed the "principle of hope." And it is in these instances of individual hope that we see the nascent cosmopolitanism of self-transformation. In this hope for socioeconomic progress and social mobility, the Kerala rikshawala embodies the postcolonial state of Kerala itself.

Of course, *Odayil Ninnu* and *Aye Auto!* also invite many further questions about Communism in Kerala during the era of the Cold War and beyond. Besides the immediate questions centering around the figure of the rikshawala as both a narrative trope as well as a unionized labor force to be reckoned with, we find many larger, sociopolitical problems referenced in this popular cultural production. But perhaps the most immediate issue is the question of whether the Kerala rikshawala can transform further. In *Aye Auto!* the autorickshaw transported its driver into developed times. Yet the autorickshaw has remained a relatively unchanged vehicle over the past few decades. Is the auto today then more a symbol of stagnation than of growth and development? Will the auto and its driver continue to be meaningful symbols when read against the ever more globalizing and often more neoliberal tendencies in Kerala politics and economics? After all, there are those who, like K. Ramakrishnan, see Kerala today as a "communist vision turned into a consumerist madhouse."[57] In line with the spirit of this volume, I would hold that fictional texts, such as films, novels, and popular music, continue to constitute a valuable ground for investigating Kerala cosmopolitanism in the twentieth and twenty-first centuries. The cultural pervasiveness of, and local accessibility to, both vernacular cinema and vernacular literature provide a useful entry point to this phenomenon. As Michael Bourdaghs, Paola Iovene, and Kaley Mason have stated in the introduction to this volume, the role of popular music in shaping contentious political arenas in modern Asia needs to be highlighted and closely investigated. Further study of cultural texts will reveal more of the complicated intersections of social realism in literature and film on the one hand and recalcitrant socialist ideals within today's post-Marxist cultural-political landscape on the other. For it is in the marginalities, to paraphrase Homi Bhabha's argument, of individual and social realities that cosmopolitanism will continue to be envisaged.[58]

NOTES

I would like to thank conference organizers Michael Bourdaghs, Paola Iovene, and Kaley Mason for their stimulating and invaluable conversations, as well as Xueming Liang and Xia Li for making Beijing feel like home. Thanks are also due to the three anonymous reviewers for their valuable suggestions after reading this chapter.

1. The literature has become very copious. See, for instance, Kwame Anthony Appiah, *Cosmopolitanism: Ethics in a World of Strangers* (New York: Norton, 2010); Sugatha Bose and Kris Manjapra, *Cosmopolitan Thought Zones: South Asia and the Circulation of Global Ideas* (New York: Palgrave Macmillan, 2010); Carol A. Breckenridge, ed., *Cosmopolitanism* (Durham, NC: Duke University Press, 2002); Maria Rovisco and Magdalena Nowicka, eds., *The Ashgate Research Companion to Cosmopolitanism* (Farnham, UK: Ashgate, 2013); and Pnina Werbner, "Vernacular Cosmopolitanism," *Theory, Culture and Society* 23, nos. 2–3 (2006): 496–98.
2. On migration, see Kunniparampil Curien Zachariah and Sebastian Irudaya Rajan, *Migration and Development: The Kerala Experience* (New Delhi: Daanish Books, 2009).
3. Spellings of this term in its anglicized form vary. For convenience, I use here the simplest form, *rikshawala*, and the more common spelling *rickshaw* for the vehicle. Rikshawalas have been a favorite subject of other South Asian cinemas as well. See, e.g., the following films: *Rikshawala* (Hindi, 1938), *Rikshawala* (Bengali, 1955), *Rikshawala* (Hindi, 1960), *Rikshakkaaran* (Tamil, 1971), *Rikshawala* (Telugu, 1989), *Baashha* (Tamil, 1995), *Nirahua Rikshawala* (Bhojpuri, 2012). The Malayalam movie *Odayil Ninnu* discussed here was also remade in Tamil in 1971 with the title *Babu* (dir. A. C. Trilogchander). Unfortunately a comparative study lies beyond the scope of the present chapter.
4. Magdalena Nowicka and Maria Rovisco, "Introduction: Making Sense of Cosmopolitanism," in *Cosmopolitanism in Practice*, ed. Magdalena Nowicka and Maria Rovisco (London: Routledge, 2016), 6.
5. K. Moti Gokulsing and Wimal Dissanayake, "Introduction," in *Routledge Handbook of Indian Cinemas*, ed. K. Moti Gokulsing and Wimal Dissanayake (London: Routledge, 2013), 1.
6. Gokulsing and Dissanayake, *Routledge Handbook of Indian Cinemas*, 2. Of the four main Dravidian vernacular film productions in South India, Tamil currently appears to have the farthest outreach and largest audience, due to extensive diasporic communities of both mainland and Sri Lankan Tamil speakers.
7. Gokulsing and Dissanayake, *Routledge Handbook of Indian Cinemas*, 1. Kerala art films used to be a highly visible and productive strand of Indian regional film production in particular in the 1970s and 1980s. However, I am referring here to mainstream films targeted at large local audiences.
8. For a discussion of audiences in Indian cinema, see Gokulsing and Dissanayake, *Routledge Handbook of Indian Cinemas*, part IV.
9. For a discussion of the role of music in mainstream Indian cinema, see Premendra Mazumder, "Music in Mainstream Indian Cinema," in *Routledge Handbook of Indian*

    Cinemas, ed. K. Moti Gokulsing and Wimal Dissanayake (London: Routledge, 2013), 257–68.
10 Gregory D. Booth, "Preliminary Thoughts on Hindi Popular Music and Film Production: India's 'Culture Industry(ies),' 1970–2000," *South Asian Popular Culture* 9, no. 2 (2001): 215.
11 Joseph Getter and B. Balasubrahmaniam, "Tamil Film Music: Sound and Significance," in *Global Soundtracks: Worlds of Film Music*, ed. Mark Slobin (Middletown, CT: Wesleyan University Press, 2008), 117.
12 Only recently has the field of Malayalam popular music seen an increasing diversification of expanding genres and non-film-based music, such as new devotional music, Christian Dalit music, or the rock band Avial. Also, for much of the twentieth century, Malayalam film music would only become popular after the commercial release of the movie. But from the late twentieth century onward, film companies also began to release the soundtrack of a movie in advance of the actual film release, with the intention to bolster the film's commercial success by increasing anticipation.
13 Jayson Beaster-Jones, "Evergreens to Remixes: Hindi Film Songs and India's Popular Music Heritage," *Ethnomusicology* 53, no. 3 (2009): 425–48.
14 Theodore Baskaran has gone so far as to argue that since the 1990s, many films "succeeded only by the strength of their songs. So much so, that the visual element, the basic quality of cinema, is neglected. . . . It is significant that those films that have won critical acclaim, both in India and in foreign film festivals, are films without songs." S. Theodore Baskaran, "Music for the Masses: Film Songs of Tamil Nadu," *Economic and Political Weekly* 26, nos. 11/12 (March 1991): 758. This is certainly true for Kerala's highly acclaimed art film scene of the 1970s, represented by renowned filmmakers such as Adoor Gopalakrishnan.
15 Baskaran, "Music for the Masses," 758.
16 Alison Arnold, "Popular Film Song in India: A Case of Mass-Market Musical Eclecticism," *Popular Music* 7, no. 2 (1988): 177.
17 Kaley Mason, "On Nightingales and Moonlight: Songcrafting Femininity in Malluwood," in *More than Bollywood: Studies in Indian Popular Music*, ed. Gregory D. Booth and Bradley Shope (New York: Oxford University Press, 2014), 75.
18 Mason, "On Nightingales and Moonlight," 75–76.
19 Mason, "On Nightingales and Moonlight," 76.
20 Peter Manuel, "Popular Music and Media Culture in South Asia: Prefatory Consideration," *Asian Music* 24, no. 1 (1992): 96.
21 Manuel estimates that film music's market share for recorded music fell drastically in the 1980s, from 95 percent to only about 40 percent. This, he argues, points toward a previously undersaturated need or demand for recorded music. Manuel, "Popular Music and Media Culture in South Asia," 93.
22 Constantine Nakassis and Melanie Dean, "Desire, Youth and Realism in Tamil Cinema," *Journal of Linguistic Anthropology* 17, no. 1 (2007): 77–104.
23 See Thomas Nossiter, *Communism in Kerala: A Study in Political Adaptation* (Berkeley: University of California Press, 1982), 13.

24 See Robin Jeffrey, *Politics, Women and Well-Being: How Kerala Became a "Model"* (Houndmills, UK: Macmillan, 1992).
25 As Nossiter observes: "Apart from the tiny Italian principality of San Marino it was the first case of a democratically elected communist government in the world." Nossiter, *Communism in Kerala*, 1.
26 Nossiter, *Communism in Kerala*, 9.
27 "Census of India: Provisional Population Totals India: Paper 1: Census 2011," accessed January 2019, www.censusindia.gov.in.
28 For the history of Communism in Kerala, see Nossiter, *Communism in Kerala*; and E. Balakrishnan, *History of the Communist Movement in Kerala* (Ernakulam: Kurukshethra Prakasan, 1998).
29 See Jeffrey, *Politics, Women and Well-Being*; and Amartya Kumar Sen, *Amartya Sen on Kerala* (New Delhi: Institute of Social Sciences, 2000).
30 Baskaran, "Music for the Masses," 755.
31 Baskaran, "Music for the Masses," 757.
32 Sumangala Damodaran, *Music and Resistance: The Tradition of the Indian People's Theatre Association in the 1940s and 1950s*, NMML Occasional Paper, History and Society, New Series 56 (New Delhi: Nehru Memorial Museum and Library, 2014), 2.
33 Apart from Kesavadev discussed here, the most prominent writers to voice such new social critiques include Thakazhi Sivasankara Pillai (1912–99), Vaikom Muhammad Basheer (1908–94), and Joseph Mundassery (1903–77).
34 On classicist poetry, see Nisha Kommattam, "Malayalam Poetry," in *The Princeton Encyclopedia of Poetry and Poetics*, ed. Roland Greene (Princeton, NJ: Princeton University Press, 2013), 839–40.
35 This is by no means an isolated or unique occurrence, of course; it paralleled powerful global developments. As Damodaran succinctly puts it, "extending from Japan, China, Korea and India in Asia to Mexico and Latin America, nationalist iconographies from below threw up images of exploitative conditions in colonial and feudal societies and the commonalities across such exploitative situations binding people together in imagining the nation." Damodaran, *Music and Resistance*, 8. Damodaran employs terms such as *the people* or *the ordinary person*, whereas I have used the slightly more archaic *common man*, whose figure emerges as a legitimate subject in literature and art.
36 Damodaran, *Music and Resistance*, 4.
37 Damodaran, *Music and Resistance*, 4.
38 The novel is also available in English translation. P. Kesavadev, *From the Gutter*, trans. E. M. J. Venniyoor (New Delhi: Orient Longman, 1978).
39 Kesavadev famously rose from a thirteen-year-old school dropout of Nayar descent to a self-educated writer and Communist activist, who eventually became president of the Kerala Sahitya Akademi, Kerala's state institution for the promotion of literature. After being an ardent Communist during his earlier years, he broke with Communism in his later life and opposed Kerala's Communist government when it came to power in 1957. Throughout his book, Kesavadev's biographer, K. P. Sasidharan, anecdotally recounts the corresponding incidents from the writer's own youth that

inspired the protagonists of his works, in particular the character of Pappu in *Odayil Ninnu*. See K. P. Sasidharan, *Kesava Dev* (New Delhi: Sahitya Akademi, 1990).

40 Sasidharan, *Kesava Dev*, 28.

41 E.g., S. Guptan Nair has used this description, as quoted in Sasidharan, *Kesava Dev*, 27. Sasidharan further describes the readers' reactions to the character of Pappu in the novel as follows: "Many saw in the uncompromising attitude of the hero . . . the manifesto of a programme of regeneration of society. But . . . it was also an expression of the anguish of existence." Sasidharan, *Kesava Dev*, 29. Many critics were outright ecstatic, such as literary scholar K. M. Tharakan, who wrote: "Pappu redeems mankind; he places man on a pinnacle of glory never before attained. He is a saint of our fiction, a great Rishi" (quoted in Sasidharan, *Kesava Dev*, 30). Pappu the film character was thus already imbued with the earlier positive reception of Pappu in the novel.

42 Nowicka and Rovisco, *The Ashgate Research Companion to Cosmopolitanism*, 2.

43 Damodaran, *Music and Resistance*, 8.

44 For a distinction between Tamil-influenced classical traditions such as music theater (sangeeta natakam) and the new "folk idiom" shaping and emphasizing newfound "Malayaleeness," see Damodaran, *Music and Resistance*, 31.

45 In *Odayil Ninnu*, numerous camera shots emphasize the masculine-gendered nature of this labor, by focusing on strong feet; muscular, sculpted calves; sweaty brows; and so on.

46 It is not possible to apply an urban-rural dichotomy when speaking about Kerala, especially in the time period under discussion. To this day the majority of the state is characterized by distinctly fluid rural settlements and infrastructure, and there are few urban centers. Unlike its neighboring states, Kerala does not have a true metropolis like Chennai or Bangalore.

47 Certainly at least in the motorized autorickshaw, the intimate space inside the rickshaw within public space is conducive to political and other small talk.

48 Thus it is probably not a coincidence that many other acclaimed social realist novels of the era, such as Thakazhi Sivasankara Pillai's famous novel *Thottiyude magan* (The scavenger's son, 1947), which depicts the plight of latrine sweepers, were not subsequently made into hit films.

49 It is noteworthy here that the rikshawalas depicted in the film do not own their vehicles. They have to pay a significant share of their earnings plus steep interest as rent to the (usually higher-class, higher-caste) owner of the vehicle or even of the entire fleet. Pappu, however, owns his rickshaw due to a wise and benevolent supporter's financial management of Pappu's own wages.

50 The charming Malayalam expression he uses here is *aashvaasavaahanam*, literally "a vehicle of consolation/comfort."

51 The valorization of English is further exemplified by the significant number of English literary productions in Kerala, which in turn supports Priya Kumar's observation that the very medium of the English language may already signify a certain kind of cosmopolitanism. See Priya Kumar, *Limiting Secularism: The Ethics of Coexistence in Indian Literature and Film* (Minneapolis: University of Minnesota Press, 2008), 177–229.

52   Kathryn Hansen, "Who Wants to Be a Cosmopolitan? Readings from the Composite Culture," *Indian Economic and Social History Review* 47, no. 3 (2010): 291–308.

53   Similarly, in *Odayil Ninnu*, Pappu declares, "I will make her [Lakshmi] into a B.A. holder," at a time when Lakshmi is only five years old and just starting school, thanks to Pappu's financial support. He is determined that his hard work and unskilled labor can and will transform Lakshmi's educational and social status due to the opportunities in Communist Kerala.

54   The theme is reflected in *Odayil Ninnu*, too, when Lakshmi's concerned mother puts it succinctly: "Studying English is not like studying Malayalam. You have to pay fees, buy expensive books, dress up like girls from big [i.e., wealthy] families. How will we pay for all that?" She thus makes explicit some of the invisible class barriers that could still prevent girls like Lakshmi from accessing English-medium education at the time.

55   The phenomenon of Kerala migration, as explored by Zachariah and Rajan in *Migration and Development*, warrants much further research, especially with regard to "cosmopolitan" aspirations. One important step in that direction is Jocelyn Lim Chua, *In Pursuit of the Good Life: Aspiration and Suicide in Globalizing South India* (Berkeley: University of California Press, 2014), whose case studies respond to Nowicka and Rovisco's call for a "focus on the individual" (as opposed to an abstract category) when using cosmopolitanism as an analytical tool. See Nowicka and Rovisco, *The Ashgate Research Companion to Cosmopolitanism*, 1.

56   Chris Carlsson, *Critical Mass: Bicycling's Defiant Celebration* (Oakland, CA: AK Press, 2002), 171.

57   K. Ramakrishnan, review of *History of the Communist Movement in Kerala*, by Dr. E. Balakrishnan, March 7, 2007, https://haindavakeralam.com/history-of-the-communist-hk17069.

58   Homi Bhabha, "Unsatisfied: Notes on Vernacular Cosmopolitanism," in *Text and Nation*, ed. Laura Garcia-Morena and Peter C. Pfeiffer (London: Camden House, 1996), 195–96.

3. EAST ASIAN POP MUSIC AND AN INCOMPLETE REGIONAL CONTEMPORARY

C. J. W.-L. WEE

On September 16, 2011, the still-popular Japanese "boy band" SMAP (Sports, Music Assemble People)—born between 1972 and 1977, and who debuted in 1988—appeared at the Workers' Stadium in Beijing, their first concert outside Japan, before a crowd of some forty thousand.[1] Mundane enough, given the pop-spectacular world we live in, but astonishingly, the band had been invited in May to perform by no less than then Chinese premier Wen Jiabao, after previous attempts by SMAP to appear in China had failed. The band had been scheduled to appear in Shanghai in September 2010, but this was canceled by the mainland Chinese organizers because of the political problem of a Chinese trawler detained by the Japanese coast guard, among the most prominent incidents of ongoing internecine clashes between the two major East Asian states over territorial disputes and contentious Japanese history textbooks.[2] The concert's theme—designed to register Japan's thanks to China for assistance rendered after the disastrous March 11, 2011, Japanese earthquake and tsunami—was "Do Your Best Japan, Thank You China, Asia Is One."[3]

The last phrase, while obviously meant to invoke solidarity between Japan and the now re-emergent power China amid unresolved tensions stretching from before the Second World War to the Cold War, also was provocative in that it was a direct quotation of an (in)famous proclamation by the art historian Okakura Kakuzō (1862–1913), from his English-language book, *The Ideals of the East, with Special Reference to the Art of Japan* (1903).

> Asia is one. The Himalayas divide, only to accentuate, two mighty civilisations, the Chinese with its communism of Confucius, and the Indian with its individualism of the Vedas. But not even the snowy barriers can

interrupt for one moment the broad expanse of love for the Ultimate and the Universal, which is the common thought inheritance of every Asiatic race, ... distinguishing them from those maritime peoples of the Mediterranean and the Baltic, who love to dwell on the Particular, and to search out the means, not the end, of life.[4]

Apart from the fact that Okakura's thinking on "Asia" was later co-opted by the Japanese military to justify colonial expansion in Northeast and Southeast Asia, his high-civilizational ideal of Asian oneness, which opposed thought predicated on commercial-industrial instrumentality, is transformed with breathtaking if unintended irony into a diplomatic placebo linked to a shared inter-Asian commercial pop culture—a form at odds with Okakura's civilizational proclivities.

This chapter examines the emergence of a regionalizing East Asian pop music as at least a partial consequence of 1960s American attempts to bring Cold War Asia back to "normality" through the fostering of regional economic exchange. That economic process would help draw down multiple military structures and take Japanese economic influence back into Northeast and Southeast Asia. The 1980s "East Asian miracle" that resulted in turn supported a regional desire for modern cultural formations that could accompany economic buoyancy. The unexpected spread of Japanese pop culture in East and Southeast Asia in the 1990s and the Korean pop culture that followed in its wake from the late 1990s—both of which were *not* aimed at regional audiences in their origins—follow from a progressive translocal change in cultural subjectivity, even though these pop-cultural phenomena should not be taken as linked in their entirety with the various Asian developmental states' politico-economic agendas. The images in these pop cultures speak of a glossy urban Asia—no cultural essentialisms or exotic Asia here.

Historian Bruce Cumings writes of the cultural incoherence of post-1960s Asia: "The lingering animosities of colonialism and war, combined with the dominance of American mass culture, tend to override ... [any supposedly shared] traditional [Confucian] heritage and to make of northeast Asian popular culture a hodgepodge of national constructions united only by American-style pop songs and videos."[5] Cumings of course is right about traditional culture and the (still-unresolved) colonial-era fractures that came about with the appearance of the first modern Asian nation-state, Japan, in 1868, and the Second Sino-Japanese War beginning in 1937. The animosities are fixed into place by the American postwar settlement, the "loss" of China in 1949, and the Korean War. Nevertheless, we arguably are witnessing the emergence of a putative contemporary cultural sensibility that not only has long since absorbed US pop culture but that now, particularly, can draw new middle-class youth into the multifaceted consumption of various Asian pop-cultural forms more ready to compete with Anglo-American pop culture. The 1960s economic agenda of fostering regional economic exchange has enabled a cultural spectacle that is comfortable with the predispositions of "globalized" capital and in which we see the debordering both of pop music as a medium and of the national linguistic spaces of pop music and culture. The increased circulation and consumption of a regionalizing inter-Asian pop culture signal how existing national social forms have been transformed by economic exchange relations and interdependency. This pop culture has negotiated—though assuredly not overcome—the seemingly oppositional politics of economic regionalism and of postcolonial, not-quite-post–Cold War nationalisms.

If Jennifer Lindsay's chapter examined a *transnational socialist popular* of folk and national songs among postwar youth in the 1940s and 1950s, in which the popular is not tied to capitalism, this chapter inquires how we might think through the contradictions of imagining a capitalist "new Asia" from the 1980s, when tensions with origins ranging from the mid-nineteenth century to the Cold War seem more pronounced than ever. As Wang Hui has acutely noted, the "commonality of Asian imaginaries derives partly from subordinate status under European colonialism, during the Cold War, as well as in the current global order," and the Cold War structure "has to a large extent been preserved and even developed new derivative forms under new historical conditions."[6] No new ideology congruent with the ongoing economic integration has come about, and regionalizing (if not quite regional) pop music is the *cultural expression of the fraught contemporary moment*, in which culture, intertwined as it is with the commitment to economic growth, has engaged with older modernist ideologies in ways not conceivable during the Cold War.

The East Asian Contemporary—and Contemporary Pop Culture?

Can we speak of an "East Asian pop culture" when it is often said that *Asia* is so culturally diverse that it does not truly exist?[7] If this is the case, what then are the means by which this culture is imagined into contemporary existence? Arguably, it is regional economic development fostered during the Cold War that has created the capacity by which emergent forms of East Asian cultural production have been able to materialize, even as old Cold War issues give the region the schizoid makeup of an "Economic Asia" and a "Security Asia," a split identity that indeed has intensified since the Asian financial crisis of 1997–98.

The United States planned for a regional postwar economy driven by a revived Japanese economy with access to markets and raw materials, a goal that complemented its security plan to contain Communist expansion by the USSR. However, the "loss" of China to the Chinese Communist Party in 1949 meant that this hinterland for Japan would have to be Southeast Asia—ironically, given the Pacific War that had recently ended. The mordant fact is that it is the Cold War in the specific manifestation of the Korean War that moves Japan toward its postwar industrial reemergence, as it benefited from "America's wars to lock in an Asian hinterland for Japan and the 'free world' in Korea and Vietnam."[8]

The 1960s saw stronger regional connections come about: under US pressure, Japan–Republic of Korea relations were normalized in 1965, and both Taiwan and South Korea started their export-oriented industrial development, in many cases using obsolescent Japanese technology.[9] In 1985, with the yen revalued after the Plaza Accord, Japanese foreign direct investment (FDI) began to pour into Southeast Asia. Cumings explains yet another irony regarding Japan and the "rise of Asia" and its 1980s "return" to Asia: "Japan never really developed markets or initiated core-periphery linkages in East and Southeast Asia until the 1960s," when US policy pushed it in that direction.[10] In the thirty years that followed 1960, the share of total world exports of the four "mini-dragons" of Hong Kong, Singapore, Taiwan, and South Korea rose from 1.5 to 6.7 percent.[11] While Northeast and Southeast Asian economic development in the 1980s and 1990s was also significantly driven by South Korean, Taiwanese, and so-called overseas Chinese FDI, Japan was the key country providing the "economic force" in the region since the 1960s. Japan also cautiously (and unsuccessfully) argued by the 1980s for the need to channel resources for industrialization so as to develop an internal market for export, going against the dictates of what becomes named as the "Washington consensus"—although it has *not* become the regional political leader for reasons to do with its own unresolved nationalistic tendencies and China's increased regional presence after the Asian financial crisis of 1997.[12]

Despite the changes and developments, "the American cold war military structure still holds down regional security, even as the cold war's abrupt end fades into history."[13] One generally acknowledged result of the US dominance in the postwar settlement is that there were (and are) few multilateral institutions and mechanisms to help settle the nationalistic and increasingly fraught disputes in the region. Outstanding issues over access to and control over parts of the South China Sea by Southeast and Northeast Asian claimants (with China making the largest claim), between South Korea and Japan over the Liancourt Rocks in the Sea of Japan (called Dokdo by the Koreans and Takeshima by the Japanese), and between Japan and China over the Senkaku/Diaoyu Islands have come to demand attention.[14]

The region is at a point at which, as it has been called, "Economic Asia"—"a dynamic, integrated Asia with 53 percent of its trade now being conducted within the region itself, and a [US]$19 trillion regional economy that has become an engine of global growth" that is increasingly dependent on China and the Chinese market—is in conflict with a "Security Asia" inclined to be nationalistic and, despite the integrated economies, "tacking hard toward the United States[, which has decreasing trade with the region,] for their security." "Rampant and competing 19th and 20th-century nationalisms," it is contended, "have moved again to the fore as pathologies that seem frozen in time raise the specter of renewed conflict."[15] The Donald Trump administration has intensified such tensions, for it has increased competition with China, identifying it as a "revisionist power" in late 2017. The result, as one policy paper put it, is that "Southeast Asia has once again become a major arena of Great Power competition."[16]

If a globalized and interconnected world means a world in which there is "the disappearance of History as the fundamental element in which human beings exist, and, not least, the end of an essentially modernist field of political struggle in which the great ideologies still had the force and the great authority of the great religions in recent times," then East Asia functions within an *incomplete contemporary* in which History—one of the "splendors of the modern"—and the great ideology of nationalism have not entirely given way to the blandishments of "the new transnational 'culture-ideology of consumption'" that might be able to conjoin the "different but equally 'present' temporalities or 'times'" in the region.[17] That is, the East Asian contemporary is a present in which modernist ideologies are only partially superseded and, as a result, the processes trying to hold together the region's heterogeneity so that the new religion of Growth Above All can be paramount are still tentative.

Nevertheless, the contemporary pop cultures from Japan and Korea that have crossed national and linguistic boundaries since the 1990s in the region represent what philosopher Peter Osborne describes as a "capitalistic sociality (the grounding of social relations in exchange relations)" that has negotiated the politics of regionalism and nationalism through a combination of regional global dynamics.[18] Indeed, the (often young) middle class seems to have *desired* the coming together of the different times of the region within the parameters of a common pop-cultural world that manifests if not a multicultural New Asia, then at least a more open-minded New Asia possessing multicultures.

The intraregional flow of popular culture was present before the 1990s, after which it increased by leaps and bounds. Collaboration between musicians has certainly existed since the 1930s. By the 1920s, Shanghai was known as a center for jazz. Composer Li Jinhui (1899–1967) had the reputation of Sinicizing jazz in that city. The Japanese were also present in Shanghai, and one of the more important cross-cultural encounters involved Hattori Ryōichi (1907–1993), who first went to Shanghai in 1938 and became impressed by Li's work. Hattori "was one of the first Japanese musicians to attempt to translate Japanese and Asian music genres into the jazz vocabulary."[19] His collaborative work continued into the 1960s, when he composed music for the Shaw Brothers' musical films, including *Qing chun gu wang* (King drummer, 1967), directed by Inoue Umetsugu (1923–2010).

Thereafter, much of the pre-1990s transnational regional cultural circulation was composed of Chinese-language film, televisual, and music productions in Cantonese, Mandarin, and Hokkien Chinese (or *minnan hua*), from Hong Kong and Taiwan, respectively. These circulated primarily to ethnic Chinese communities in Southeast Asia.[20] The Japanese and Korean pop music that arose from the 1990s to a fair extent followed the same routes laid down by various types of Chinese-language pop music in and around the region.[21] The differences between this earlier period and the 1990s is that the later surge of non-Chinese-language products rested on a much broader consumer base than had existed before and, unpredictably, seemed able to more substantially break through ethnic and national linguistic lines. There was what I think of as a preliminary Japanese wave in the 1980s that was linked to the enormously popular television drama *Oshin*, dealing with the travails of a woman born at the start of the twentieth century in Meiji Japan; the male pop duo Chage and Aska; the teen female idol (*aidoru*) singer Matsuda Seiko (b. 1962); and cutting-edge youth fashion from Tokyo.[22] The major Japanese wave starts in the early 1990s, led by televisual dramas and pop music ("J-pop"); and then from the late 1990s, more spectacularly, the Korean wave (Hallyu) developed, led initially by film and television dramas, and, from about 2005, mainly by pop music ("K-pop"), as South Korean political and cultural life was liberalized.[23]

Despite the work that has been done on East Asian pop culture, it remains hard to generalize the conditions that assisted the Japanese and later Korean pop-cultural circulation in a region as diverse as Northeast and Southeast Asia: the easy access, say, to translated song lyrics or fansubbing of television dramas online does not itself account for the cultural resonance of any one national pop product with nonspecialized audiences.[24] It is one thing to speak of a "Pop Culture China," even with three Chinese languages involved, as sociologist

Chua Beng Huat has done, but while it has become normalized for East Asian youth to listen to songs in a foreign language other than English, it was a counterintuitive idea when the practice first developed in the 1990s. Regardless, what is vital is that the formation of the middle classes in East Asia is part of the social bases for regionalization. The first wave of middle-class formation was apparent in Japan in the early 1970s, and the 1980s saw middle-class formation in the four mini-dragons of South Korea, Taiwan, Hong Kong, and Singapore, with Thailand, Malaysia, and Indonesia (to a lesser extent) following suit; the first decade of the twenty-first century saw such class formations in China's cities.[25] As the main consumers of a regional market, they potentially contributed toward new varieties of putative regional cultural commonalities as part of an aspirational lifestyle—the inevitable Americanization is desired but now so is some syncretic version of an East Asian modernity. So, for example, in terms of the success of Japanese cultural products, what is relevant is that regional consumers *appropriate* them as part of their own aspirational desires, and not, for instance, as the result of later (and belated) Japanese government "soft power" attempts to capitalize on that success.[26]

The increasing export and circulation of culture within the region, it can be said, became a part of the means of generating a contemporary Asian way of life that is inextricably linked to consumerism.[27] This is a lifestyle form extensively exported through American media products, but, by the 1990s, there was already a substantial history of pop-cultural production that was no longer simple or simplistic imitations of US content.[28] The following assessment by Fredric Jameson of (the lack of) Japanese cultural power at the height of the bubble economy underlines the central issue here.

> At any rate, it does seem to me that fresh cultural production and innovation—and this means in the area of mass-consumed culture—are the crucial index of the centrality of a given area and not its wealth or productive power.... [Despite] Sony's acquisition of Columbia Pictures [in 1989] and Matsushita's buyout of MCA [in 1990],... the Japanese were unable to master the essentially cultural productivity required to secure the globalization process for any given competitor. Whoever says the production of cultures says the production of everyday life—and without that, your economic system can scarcely continue to expand and implant itself.[29]

Jameson, unsurprisingly, was unaware of the Japanese wave occurring at the time of the publication of his chapter in 1998, and he would have been less likely to know that a television series broadcast by China Central Television

(CCTV) in June 1997, *Sarangi mwŏgillae* (What is love?), produced by Korean broadcaster MBC in 1991–92, became an unexpected hit in China and was broadcast a second time in 1998—this is the televisual production widely held to have initiated the Korean wave.[30] The cultural productivity that supported regionalization in East Asia was emerging, just not within a single national locale—though it naturally did not and could not overtake the US-dominated globalization process.[31]

By the 1960s, the Euro-American West had witnessed the startling outburst of what was then described as *mass culture*, in which cultural commodities exceeded the previous centering in television and Hollywood films. In pop music terms, as Jameson himself noted back in 1979, "the social moment of Elvis or rhythm-and-blues—and behind that Black music—unpredictably develops [after the 1950s into] the 'high modernisms' of the Beatles and the Stones, and thereafter into rock postmodernisms of the most appropriately bewildering kinds."[32] The technological changes in the cultural and creative industries since, with the increasing capital devoted to culture, enabled contemporary pop culture to look like an embodied vision of cultural pluralism rather than the mass culture it once was; and as the Asian miracle economies "take off" (to use a 1960s expression), that "bewildering" vision becomes available for appropriation.[33]

J-Pop as Globo-National Culture, "Equal" to the West

The key contradiction regarding the regional emergence of Japanese popular culture from the 1980s is that, arguably, it was a combination of national pride and a wish for global cultural standards that led, first, to new forms of Japanese pop music for domestic consumption, and second, to J-pop's ability to appeal to a larger regional audience. What has been described as "J-pop nationalism" was thus the startling starting point of debordered pop music going beyond the more predictable boundaries of circulation set by Chinese-language pop music.[34] The term *J-poppu* first appeared in 1988, by which time popular music created within Japan and targeted at a domestic audience had assimilated Anglo-American modalities, rhythms, instrumentation, harmonies, and even language, admittedly used in idiosyncratic ways, leading to new cultural expressions that to its producers and consumers seemed consonant with Japan's more confident presence in international business. The prefix "J" does not refer to the essential(ized) national culture of the nation-state but to a Japanese identity erected upon an "intercultural identity, positioned against a dominant Western [largely American] viewpoint."[35] The exotic and the traditional hailing from some colonial-era modernity were not and are not a notable part of the equation in New Asian cultural fantasies within or without Japan—and why should they be? The invention of a globalized Japanese self for home consumption *separate* from the national sociocultural order that was supposedly a mix of tradition with modernity's mass culture was *also* attractive for a rapidly developing region, despite its (literally) postmodern nationalist origins.

The spread of J-pop was part of a larger diffusion of Japanese popular culture in the region. While it is not possible to articulate a single or singular narrative of the Japanese wave in the region, as different national locales had different contexts (as is the case for the Korean wave), we can say that manga (Japanese comic books) and anime (Japanese animation) were already circulating in the 1970s, but that it was television dramas that led the way in the region from the 1980s, coming to a head in the 1990s and the following decade. One 1995 survey reported that 47.3 percent of Japanese private broadcasters' programming exports went to Asia, compared with 25.7 percent to North America.[36] In 2002 similar figures held: 46.1 percent of television exports went to Asia, with 27.9 percent to Europe and 7.6 percent to the United States.[37] Despite these numbers, Japanese cultural producers were not aggressive in their regional marketing since the domestic market was quite strong on its own and the bigger markets in East Asia (apart from China), Taiwan and South Korea, were both former Japanese colonies that imposed bans on Japanese cultural imports. Those bans, however, were lifted in 1993 for Taiwan, and progressively from 1998 for Korea. The appearance of low-level digital technology in the form of the video compact disc (VCD), though, helped facilitate the widespread illegal distribution of Japanese dramas by the late 1990s in markets such as Hong Kong, China, and Singapore, "largely at the initiative of the Asians on the 'receiving end.'"[38]

Pop music in the 1980s benefited from the television dramas that, increasingly, used pop stars to sing the original soundtracks (OSTs) for the programs. This had a knock-on effect, helping Japanese pop gain prominence in Hong Kong in the mid-1980s, for instance, and the then Crown Colony became at that point the biggest overseas market for Japanese records.[39] By the 1990s, both Taiwan and Hong Kong had become consumption and redistribution centers for television dramas and J-pop content alike, licensed and pirated. A smaller market like Singapore, which tended to be behind the curve in trendy inter-Asian consumption, was a beneficiary of Taiwanese and Hong Kong editions of music album CDs and pop magazines, which retailed at cheaper prices than the Japanese versions. The success of J-pop in Singapore, precisely because it was less a major center of consumption than Taiwan or Hong Kong (or even Bangkok, Thailand), is a testament to J-pop's regional impact.[40] Following Hong Kong, Japanese pop music experienced a smaller and short-lived boom in the city-state in the 1980s, but by 1999, J-pop became visible in a pronounced way, with the third album of the dance-pop girl band Speed (stylized as SPEED), *Moment* (1998), a compilation of all singles to date, becoming the first Japanese album to both break into Singapore's top ten list and take the number 1 spot.[41]

However, though the spread of J-pop throughout the region was part of a larger cultural phenomenon, it could not have occurred without the increased confidence and maturity in Japanese pop sounds that transpired in the 1980s. J-pop does not refer to a single genre of music, though it has been suggested that it applies more to idol singers, whether male or female, individuals or in groups.[42] The term was coined by a Tokyo-based radio station in 1988, J-WAVE 81.3 FM, the first station to use the English "J" to signify a global identity for the Japanese pop music it chose to play, which "often had English and English-like Japanese lyrics, though they were played by Japanese musicians and made in Japan."[43] That musical-linguistic style gained purchase in contemporary J-pop production—and would also influence K-pop production. Initially, J-pop was linked with Shibuya-style (*Shibuya-kei*) music, which originated in the late 1980s from the fashionable youth/young-adult hub of the Shibuya shopping district in Tokyo, which aesthetically defined itself against the then mainstream pop released by the major labels, known as *kayōkyoku* (Western-style pop songs that did not deploy stylized pronunciations based on the English language).

Shibuya-kei music, broadly, can be described as a self-consciously internationalist fusion of jazz, synthpop, bossa nova, and retro-pop that gave rise to what became J-pop.[44] By the 1990s, the Shibuya-kei association was transcended, and the term *J-pop* was applied to a wide range of young people's music, ranging from female and male idol music (especially the latter during the 1990s), to visual-style (*visual-kei*) rock bands such as X-JAPAN and Glay, to female singers Amuro Namie and Hamasaki Ayumi. It has been noted that J-pop is used by the Japanese mass media to distinguish such pop artists from other kinds of *hōgaku* (popular music that is created for a Japanese audience), such as *enka* (popular songs drawing from regionalism and with a sentimental orientation).[45] Arguably, 1988–98 was the golden era for J-pop, when million-seller artists were not uncommon and sales of music albums overseas could reach into the hundreds of thousands.[46] J-pop emerged at a moment when new technologies such as the internet and the mobile phone enabled marketing strategies not available before, and at present the term "is widely used by East Asian audiences to describe music from Japan overseas and has so integrated in a wider East Asian consumer market that this terminology has recently been transferred to describe other Asian pop cultures: '*K-poppu*' ... is another trend [that draws on the term *J-pop*]."⁴⁷ The increasing growth in confidence in the postwar Japanese music industry, combined with forms of transmission not available before the 1990s, played significant roles in the regional emergence of J-pop.

Japan's evolving relationship with the US is one that needs to be taken into this account of cultural change, from the Allied Occupation, which ended in 1952, through the Cold War years to the present. In the years immediately after the Second World War, imported music and Japanese music in the Western modes were predominant, as they (unsurprisingly) signified "modern life."⁴⁸ Cultural sociologist Yoshimi Shunya contends that there is a continuity in the presence of American popular culture in Japan from before the war but that the cultural relationship after the war changed, first, from a "love-hate" nature to one where, by the 1960s, American products were no longer seen as antithetical to Japanese life, and second, by the 1970s, to a relationship in which the US became a "source of information," as American culture was remade in Japan. Increasing postwar prosperity assisted with this change in cultural relations.⁴⁹ In the process, "made in Japan" music became considered music of quality production that both was and was not quite Japanese-sounding at the same time.⁵⁰

In the more confident 1980s, a number of notable socioeconomic transformations occurred that arguably enhanced J-pop's attractiveness. These include the development of idol culture. While J-pop is not a single unified genre per se, some critics associate it with aidoru or idol culture, as earlier noted, for good reason—because of its inextricable link with consumption. Though the first idols appeared in 1971, the 1980s are thought of as "the golden age of idols."⁵¹ That is, the 1980s bubble economy—when Japan could be conceived of as "number 1"—gave rise to new heights of everyday lifestyle consumption that included idol culture, contributing to an alluring image of contemporary Asian lifestyle possibilities.⁵² Idols (still) refer to multifaceted performers who sing and are media celebrities, highly groomed, young (or young-looking), male or female, and who perform across a number of genres and media platforms. They are thus a fitting pop-cultural phenomenon to be associated with the bubble economy, and they also contributed to fortifying domestic pop culture against Anglo-American cultural dominance: "The formation of a pool of local idols and celebrities helped to center the Japanese media on the domestic market. In time, the cult of celebrity came to function as a defense against global media flows[. . . and] indigenized television programming by inviting proximity and familiarity through their regular appearances in a variety of different programming and media outlets."⁵³

Idol music was part of a "Japanese-made" pop music that started to dominate sales in the domestic market, displacing Western pop music.⁵⁴ The 1980s also saw Sony Corporation's buyout of CBS Records in 1988 and Columbia Pictures in 1989, while in 1990 Matsushita purchased MCA/Universal. That decade therefore saw the Japanese creative industry enter the global market, while domestic media companies strengthened their grip on the home market with its own specific tastes.

What of youth attitudes toward the changing cultural production and the valorization of the Anglocentric prefix "J"? If the "old," heavy-duty, modern national identity that drew upon the idea of Nippon depended on traditional and/or serious-minded high culture, along with anchored sociocultural points of reference, a *contemporary* globo-national identity, as it might be described, instead leaned upon lighter, lifestyle culture, a trend that continues into the postbubble 1990s. Drawing upon the work of the postmodern critic Asada Akira and the psychoanalyst Kayama Rika, cultural sociologist Mōri Yoshitaka argues that the move from N (or Nippon) to J is,

> in fact, a side-effect of globalization; it represents young peoples' ambiguous anxiety in the face of a crisis of national identity against globalization. It is an ironical attitude, because they project themselves as a homogeneous and unified entity in a nostalgic or even melancholic fantasy, although they already knew that they will not be able to be the same as in the past: they unconsciously recognize that their society and everyday life has become too fragmented and too destabilized to recover [especially after the bubble economy burst in 1991].... It is a light, small and "petty" nationalism.[55]

J-pop came about at the height of the bubble economy and later became a sort of fix for the deflation that followed and subsequent attempts to liberalize the economy: it provided reassurance that the contemporary Japanese culture that had arrived in the 1980s still had a place in the world in harder times.

What was it about J-pop, then, at its inception that allowed it to generate the possibility of globo-national imaginings? As mentioned, J-pop initially was linked with the appearance of Shibuya-kei music, a term applied to bands that were reshaping accepted conventions in mainstream Japanese pop, such as the duo Flipper's Guitar, with its "happy"-sounding rock-dance music, and Pizzicato Five, with its eclectic synthpop, dance, and retro-style music—artists promoted by the buzzing Shibuya HMV store that opened in 1990.[56] The latter group "was to become the most iconic example of what *Shibuya-kei* was about," and as their music was able to gain international notice, examining this group allows us to see the cultural components that were set in play for J-pop's "petty" nationalism.[57]

Pizzicato Five (P5) was formed in 1985 and was known as Pizzicato V until 1987. Arguably, they came into their own in 1990, when the group consisted of Nomiya Maki (vocals), Konishi Yasuharu, and Takanami Keitarō (whose given name was stylized as "K-taro").[58] In 1991 P5 released the album *This Year's Girl*, which extensively relied on sampling—the use of preexisting music remixed into new forms—as the base for its music. The digital technology that enabled sampling only started developing in the late 1970s, so P5 was innovative in creating a sound that sounded "indie" to Western ears but was actually closer to the commercial mainstream in Japan.

One of the best-known songs from *This Year's Girl* is "Twiggy Twiggy." It is typical of the knowing, ironic, yet light-handed use of 1960s pop-cultural references in the band's compositions, reinforced by clever visuals in the music videos and stage dress. The song was indicative of the cultural possibilities inherent in the rising "J" moment. The lyrics are simple and repetitive:

Sanjikan mo matte ita no yo
Watashi neko to issho ni

Sono toki denwa no beru ga
Watashi neko mitai ni shabetta

Terebi no volume sagete
Watashi uso mitai na koe de

Twiggy no mini skirt de
Twiggy mitai na pose de
Twiggy no mini skirt de
Twiggy mitai ni yassepochi no watashi

I was waiting for about three hours
My cat and I

At the time the phone rang
And I chatted away just like my cat

I turned down the TV and
Talked in a fake voice

In a Twiggy mini-skirt
In a Twiggy-like pose
In a Twiggy mini-skirt
Skinny like Twiggy, that's me[59]

The lyrics say nothing, and that may be part of the point. They reveal to us our reveling in leisure-time activity. As for the music itself, a large portion of it consists fundamentally of a loop dominated by jazzy percussion, with samples from the Ventures' theme for the TV series *Hawaii Five-O* (1968), Burt Bacharach and Hal David's "Another Night" (1966), and Argentinian composer Lalo Schifrin's "The Man from Thrush" (1965) and "The Cat" (1964). "Twiggy Twiggy" is interposed with an Electone-organ-type solo toward the end, and it all concludes with a keyboard solo featuring part of the James Bond theme composed by Monty Norman, first heard in *Dr. No* (1962).

The music video reinforces the subtext that "Japanese" music and its take on leisure activity are now global and that this "arrival" can be taken in a relaxed manner. The dominant image of the video is the three artists doing campy a-go-go dance moves, though executed with restraint and with straight faces. Text is used in the video. The first text that appears proclaims: "inside out with LES PIZZICATO FIVE." The video is largely in black and white, with one color section. We see Nomiya, Konishi, and Takanami performing primarily in a light-colored and airy studio space. Nomiya first appears in a fake fur hat, transparent rain jacket, and dark miniskirt dress with dark leggings, and then, alternatively, in a light, smock-like, miniskirt dress with a dark choker for most of the rest of the video. The next set of texts that appears references the title of the album and shamelessly flags the creativity of everything the viewer sees and hears: "pizzicato five; / the original artform / excerpt from this year's girl / in action."

Later on, "hello America" appears in outline text, with the three colors of the US flag filling in the text. References to pop figures and celebrities from the 1960s and late 1980s/early 1990s are made, in a minimalist, knowing manner: "twiggy [the model] / [author] jackie [Collins?] / cindy [Crawford the model?] / . . . [1960s British singers] sandie [Shaw] and petula [Clark]" are evoked and imposed onto a shot of Nomiya's face, this time in color. A TV set in the room is revealed, with images on it that monitor the three P5 members dancing behind the set, accompanied by the text: "the revolution *is* being televised." As "Twiggy Twiggy" concludes, with the James Bond theme, the last text appears and significantly advises the viewer: "buy japanese."

While "Twiggy, Twiggy" was released the year the bubble economy burst, the sampling, the music assembled and sung, and the video embody the confidence of a creative culture with an edge that rises to French cultural sophistication ("LES PIZZICATO FIVE") and counters American cultural dominance ("hello America") in a (seemingly) casual manner. After all, P5 seem to suggest, we know who "you" are fairly well—you are now part of "us," and the clichéd, Occupation-era binary opposition of the West and the Rest no longer exists. We too can undertake wink-wink, nod-nod ironic approaches to stylish urban pop culture. We can be thin and dress like Twiggy and have fun, with no need to dragoon exotic symbols of Japan for your consumption of otherness. In fact, this is what you should do now: "buy japanese." This cultural transformation, this "revolution," can be broadcast by media everywhere. And herein, perhaps, is revealed at least a slight ambivalence—that the latest version of the new still needs to appeal for a fair hearing, even while advancing its case for equality and cultural quality, albeit in an understated way. If Shibuya-kei must be recognized as part of a "transnational soundscape [in the 1990s that was producing retro-oriented 'lounge music'], an ongoing international co-production involving both Japanese and non-Japanese musics and musicians," this does not mean that the specific Japanese context of its invention is inconsequential: this music is an actively produced *local-yet-metropolitan* variant of a globalizing culture in which the "local is increasingly dissociated from specific social spaces and relations, as it is constituted through the process of commodification."[60] The achievement of this new J-culture continued into the postbubble 1990s but with the "J" getting *repositioned* to represent "young peoples' ambiguous anxiety in the face of a crisis of national identity against globalization."[61]

J-pop's larger impact, it could be said, recedes by about 2004, with the release of Utada Hikaru's English-language album, *Exodus* (2004); this album was her debut in the American market, where it peaked at 160 (for one week) on the *Billboard* 200 chart and only sold some fifty-five thousand units, even as it reached number 1 on Japan's Oricon Weekly Albums chart and sold more than one million units.[62] Utada is significant in J-pop's pantheon because, first, she is a bona fide singer-songwriter (and therefore "creative") rather than an idol singer, and, second, she is bilingual and bicultural, having been born in Manhattan in 1983. These combined traits enabled Utada to be the pop icon who could front the cultural fantasy to "stand shoulder to shoulder" with pop music's origins—which is the "fantasy of globalized Japanese culture."[63] Her compositions and singing style were pop but modified with R&B and house/club music, which gave her an edge; Utada's debut album, *First Love* (1999), sold some nine million copies, mainly in Japan.[64] *Exodus* was a sophisticated, dance-oriented album that experimentally (and adventurously) incorporated a number of electronic genres as well as R&B and hip-hop music; its lyrical content dwelt on matters such as sexual relationships, which complicated Utada's reputation as a clean-cut J-pop star.

In many ways, the cultural urges that fed into J-pop nationalism were what gave J-pop the luster that enabled regional prominence. However, Utada's difficulties in 2004 also indicated that paying too much attention to the US-Japan binary and not enough to the transformation of cultural subjectivity in Japan's regional backyard meant that J-pop could not take full advantage of emergent inter-Asian pop-cultural opportunities. Nor perhaps did it need to, given the size of its domestic market, which, despite the decline in CD sales worldwide, has been the second-largest market for recorded music after the US since the mid-1970s.[65]

K-Pop as Translocal Formation of the Contemporary

It is the expanding South Korean creative industries from the 1990s—first film and particularly television dramas, with pop music coming to the fore from around 2005, "the so-called second stage of [the] Korean wave"—that firmly attempt to take advantage of the debordering of pop-cultural consumption, even while production remains national in origin.[66] Japanese pop culture, though without deliberate effort on its part, made its pre-K-pop cultural presence felt in Korea in the 1980s and 1990s. This new Korean wave's uneven regional advent was surprising, as was the earlier Japanese wave, with specific issues in the Korean market encouraging a more deliberate outward orientation for K-pop when compared to J-pop.

J-pop's "petty" nationalism gave rise to a contradictory regional intake of a putative globo-national culture on offer that ignored its nationalism. K-pop's version of pop-cultural glamor *furthers* that attempt to overcome the underclass status of nonmetropolitan pop-cultural creations that cannot be and is not interested in being labeled as exotic "world music" by leveraging a now existing global sameness in the region that seems tolerant of national/ethnic/linguistic difference. The Korean wave's spectacular stature and keen interest in the actual effectiveness of the Korean state's intervention in the creative industry has generated prodigious scholarship that appears to exceed that on the Japanese wave.[67] I submit that K-pop—as a translocal formation of the contemporary, catering to the "localities" of established and developing urbanized, youth consumerist dreams of the regional middle class, ranging from "advanced" (but postbubble) Japan, to South Korea's own more recently enfranchised "advanced" market status (having joined the Organization for Economic Cooperation and Development [OECD] in 1996), and to "lower-middle-income" Indonesia—builds upon the possibilities that first arose with J-pop in the region. As we know, exchange relations can serve to break down historically formed collective meanings, and K-pop boy and girl "idol" bands are productive imaginative acts that performatively project a fictive identity onto disjunctive spatial standpoints in Northeast and Southeast Asia.

To be sure, *fictive* does not mean "not really there." The region is standardized enough by market integration and social interconnectedness that Korean talent agencies can fulfill consumerist desires with empirical cultural content: capital allows the projection of utopian horizons in the form of a desire for metropolitan culture as a region-wide interconnectedness in the dystopian form of the market. In this regard, K-pop fosters what Peter Osborne calls a "'distributive' unity," in which the different national "stages" of economic development and modernity from which the various pop consumers hail are enfolded into the stasis of the present moment of consumption.[68] The K-pop industry, vitally, works at putting together fandoms.[69] Pop music performance and consumption become enabled as sites for the extraterritoriality of culture to manifest itself, as K-pop groups traverse New Asia for live concerts—and with middle-class youth also crossing borders to attend these concerts. Such consumption indicates how existing national social forms have been transformed by economic exchange but also that the *social* is not necessarily a collective form in any active practical or political sense. Korean pop culture's entanglements with pre–Cold War nationalisms are not surprising, and regionalizing inter-Asian pop's numerous fans are not proof against such entanglements.

Inter-Asian popular music flows did exist with Japan from the 1960s, before K-pop's emergence from the mid-1990s, but the music forms circulating were not mainstream pop. The first relevant music form was enka, which included singers such as Kye Eunsook (b. 1961) and Kim Yonja (b. 1959); Kim moved to Japan in 1977 to further her career. Hyunjoon Shin observes that such singers were "an essential part of a 'postcolonial' networking between Japanese and Korean music industries. Korean *enka* singers stirred nostalgia for older forms of entertainment in Japan and East Asia."[70] This nostalgic orientation placed real limits on the ability to win full recognition for singers such as the versatile rock and pop star Cho Yong-pil (b. 1950), known in Japan only for enka. The second relevant form, folk song (*p'ok'ŭsong*), is examined by Shin in chapter 4 of this volume. Folk song started as adaptations of Western modern folk and included such eclectic influences as Simon and Garfunkel, French *chanson*, and Italian *canzone*. Shin contends in this volume that folk was taken to be people's (or protest) song, raising questions "about the struggle for cultural nonalignment . . . in popular music," with music less commercial than enka. Records by singers such as Kim Min-ki (b. 1951) were distributed in Japan in the late 1970s.

The generally acknowledged point of origin for subsequent pop-music development was the iconic group Seo Taiji and Boys (Sŏ Taejiwa aidŭl), whose rise became conceivable thanks to the end of authoritarian military rule in the form of the Kim Young-sam government that came to power in 1993. As is well known, Kim created the Segyehwa Ch'ujin Wiwŏnhoe (Globalization Promotion Committee) in 1995 to implement structural reforms—and these reforms included a role for culture, especially culture with a less nationally autonomous agenda when compared with that of the 1960s.[71] That process gave the new generation (*sinsidae*) scope to invent and consume new pop-cultural productions in an economy that was benefiting from earlier developmentalist strategies—and development, after the Asian financial crisis in 1997, was transformed into a global rather than national project.[72]

Born Jung Hyun-chul, Seo Taiji formed his group in 1991 with two other young men who also sang and acted as backing dancers. He wrote his own songs and released his first single, "Nan arayo" (I know), a song about heading off a breakup, and first album the following year. The single created a template for later Korean pop music—hip-hop verses with guitars in the bridge, a melodic chorus, a dance orientation, and heightened image consciousness in the assemblage of then unconventional urban, African American–inspired fashion.[73] Seo was an independent figure who dropped out of high school—nonconformism on palpable display—and "contested the [then] hegemonic powers of the broadcasting system with their in-house star system and big band orchestra-centered TV shows."[74] The group helped break the domination of bland pop ballads (*palladŭ kayo*), with their moderate tempos and safe sentimental themes, which had emerged in the 1970s and were deemed unthreatening to the military regime.[75] Seo's lyrics became more edgy as he developed, challenging, for example, the norms of the rigid examination system ("Kyosil idea" [Classroom ideology], 1994) or taking up the topic of national reunification ("Parhae-rŭl kkumkkumyŏ" [Dreaming of Balhae], 1994). The pop-cultural libidinal energies of 1990s Korean youth certainly surfaced in a realm with clear sociopolitical implications, a contrast with that of postbubble 1990s Japanese youth.

If Seo Taiji and Boys' innovations set the stage for the possibilities of expressive popular music, it was H.O.T. (High-Five of Teenagers), assembled by the then new talent agency SM Entertainment, who turned those innovations into a functioning, replicable, and domesticated expressive model for what would be called K-pop across the region. The group was active from 1996 to 2001, almost literally picking up the slack from Seo Taiji and Boys, who disbanded in 1996. Eight hundred thousand copies of H.O.T.'s first album, *We Hate All*

Kinds of Violence (1996), were sold within ten days of its release in South Korea, and the group would go on to record five studio albums before disbanding.[76] H.O.T. sang a range of music, spanning from teen pop to ballads to rock—oftentimes with the genres mixed up and with hip-hop verses thrown into the resulting mix. The band's first hit single, "Candy" (1996), was a piece of bubblegum pop, with lyrics about a boy needing individual space from the girl he loves. The music video, largely set against a merry-go-round in an amusement park, had the members in exaggerated hip-hop fashions using primary colors and oversized, fuzzy mittens, accompanied by deliberately infantilized and "cute," campy choreography. By the time the single "I yah" (Dear child) was released in 1996, we find them offering a critical commentary on a society in which pupils are allowed to be locked in a kindergarten room, with disastrous consequences when a fire occurs. The style was harder-edged rock, and the accompanying music video showed them in slick, all-black Japanese-inspired Goth-cum-sci-fi looks. In 2000 band members appeared in Beijing in front of thirteen thousand fans, launching the export pop music component of the Korean wave, and yet while "China was the big goal, . . . the immediate market was Japan[,] . . . whose music market was twenty times larger than Korea's."[77]

The eclectic musical range and flexible (if not incoherent) dress styles of H.O.T. demonstrate that, like J-pop, K-pop is not a musical genre per se but describes a pop music that is teen-centric, star-centered, and with carefully nurtured performers who are managed by talent agencies. The best known of these are SM Entertainment (the pioneer, started in 1995), YG Entertainment (founded by a former member of Seo Taiji and Boys), and JYP Entertainment. The agencies are organized via an "'in-house' system," which "integrates 'production' and 'management' and all other necessary functions for developing and training talents."[78] This agency system is adapted at least partially from (and in terms of export-orientation, outdoes) the Japanese office (*jimusho*) system—and in particular Johnny and Associates, established in 1962 and the most famous creator of idol boy bands in Japan, including SMAP.[79] K-pop groups, broadly speaking, are marked by being mainly idol bands, by the use of English in the lyrics, by having differentiated roles for each band member (vocalists, rappers, dancers), and in general by being dance-pop and thus performance-oriented, so that the dance routine rather than the melody shapes a song from the start.[80] The end result is a pop-cultural form that simultaneously uses the Korean language and tries to escape looking too "national" as a product.

It is revealing that *K-pop* is not a term of Korean origin, as the more usual South Korean designation for popular song is *kayo* (a term that has historical links to the Japanese term *kayōkyoku*, discussed earlier in the chapter), but was a term first used by the Japanese media and then circulated in the region.[81] This explanation, in effect, makes K-pop into J-pop's successor. And that, in some respects, seems not inaccurate. Shin asks us to think of K-pop as "a combination of heterogeneous elements" that is the result of, apart from the influence of US pop culture, cultural border crossings with South Korea's other, Japan.[82] Japanese popular music—including J-pop—has a historical relationship with pre-K-pop Korea. There was a hidden "presence" of Japanese popular music in South Korea in the years before 1998, when President Kim Dae-jung's administration (1998–2002) launched a gradual lifting of the Cold War–era ban on Japanese culture (film, video, manga, etc.), a process that reached its completion in 2004. Ironically, the banning of Japanese products facilitated the direct unattributed sampling of Japanese music, such as occurred with a song by hip-hop and dance group Roo'ra (Roots of reggae); "Ch'ŏnsang yuae" (Love in heaven, 1996) drew on the song "Omatsuri Ninja" (Ninja festival, 1990) by the Johnny's jimusho boy band Ninja.[83] There were those such as the then president of Line Records, Kim Chang-Hwan, who felt that the lifting of the ban would ultimately be for Korea's good: "Local 'pretty-face' singers who used to copy and plagiarize Japanese pop music will disappear, . . . which will help improve the quality of domestic music."[84] The adaptation of Japanese talent management approaches mentioned in the previous paragraph then became a part of K-pop's translocal and specific inter-Asian formation. K-pop thus is neither a "pure" nor purist cultural production—the latter intentionally so, of course—but exists in interconnection within the longer history of the reinvention of contemporary Northeast Asian culture out of older modern cultural forms dating from the early twentieth century, such as Japanese enka or Korean *yuhaengga* (song in fashion).

To talk about "inter-Asian pop" is not to suggest that any easy multiculturalism has been achieved in East Asia—but the current reality is that K-pop needs East and Southeast Asia, and therefore K-pop needs to be an Asian-global pop, despite the inevitable murkiness that results when any discussion of "Asianness" transpires. Despite an unsurprising postcolonial hope to compete in the homelands of pop music, as witnessed in the JYP Entertainment's star Rain's sold-out concerts in 2006 at Madison Square Garden, the US reviews that followed were withering. With tedious predictability, Asian cultural productions that could not be tagged as ethnically inflected "world music" were taken to be either unoriginal or behind the curve.[85] That is, K-pop finds it hard to be taken as *true* or perhaps *authentic* global contemporary culture in the metropole, though at the same time it is apparent enough that distinct niche (and presumably expandable) cultures now exist for it in various non–East Asian locales.[86] In 2011 music exports to Japan—on the increase for a few years—were worth US$157.9 million (up significantly from US$21.6 million in 2009); to Southeast Asia, US$25.6 million (US$6.4 million in 2009); and to China, with all the challenges its difficult market poses, US$6.8 million (US$2.4 million in 2009).[87] In contrast, exports to Europe were worth US$4.6 million (US$299,000 in 2009); and to North America, a miniscule US$587,000 (US$351,000 in 2009).[88] The 1997 Asian financial crisis saw the domestic music market contract, and export orientation became a necessity for survival for small- and medium-sized companies. The collapse of physical music sales between 2001 and 2005 in South Korea due to the internet and illegal music downloading also spurred the need for overseas expansion. China, given its potential market size, will remain a "point of commercial cultural exchange."[89]

Two well-known and trailblazing cases of the advance into Japan are the SM Entertainment stars Kwon Boa (stage name BoA) and TVXQ. With the opening up of cultural exchange between Korea and Japan in 1998, SM Entertainment's head, Lee Soo-man, arranged for a teen singer with moderate Korean success to move to Japan, where she learned Japanese and he established a partnership with the major Japanese entertainment company Avex Group. The latter's Avex Trax label launched BoA's first Japanese-language album in 2002, *Listen to My Heart*—composed of R&B, dance pop, and ballad tracks written by mainly Japanese composers. It went on to sell more than one million units and the album established, for the first time, that a non-Japanese singer could become a J-pop star.[90] Though her ethnonational identity was not concealed, it was not dwelt upon. BoA thus became a simultaneous K-pop/J-pop star. The strategy of having K-pop stars learn other languages—principally Japanese, Chinese, and English—is now generally practiced. The later five-man boy band TVXQ, which launched in 2003 and signed with Avex in 2004, built upon BoA's success, though it was apparent from their Japanese television appearances that group members were Koreans whose Japanese was improving rapidly.[91] Dance-pop, rock with a heavy urban dance inflection, and R&B mark the overall musical output of TVXQ. The band's effective breakthrough came in 2008, when over the course of the year it had four singles reach the top of the Oricon charts and also had the distinction of being invited to national broadcaster NHK's still-prestigious Kōhaku Uta Gassen, the year-end song festival.[92] But despite such ongoing successes in Japan, Shin rightly observes that inter-Asian pop production is an uneven field: "K-pop is 'localized' for Japan's markets, [but] J-pop is consumed in Korea in its original form, without its contents being altered.... An international imbalance of so-called soft power still persists in this phase of this transnational cultural flow."[93] As K-pop itself is already created with the region in mind (excluding the specific case of Japan), what is seen and heard is the same inside and outside South Korea.

Despite creating and promoting an inter-Asian pop that aimed to affirm a more confident New Asia, nationalist responses occurred as early as 2006. In that year, both Taiwanese and mainland Chinese reacted to the increasing presence of Korean wave TV dramas, with Taipei's Government Information Office and CCTV saying they would restrict the time allocated to such dramas.[94] Similar reactions recurred: 2011 saw Taiwan's National Communications Commission request restraint in airing Korean dramas as well as protests against Korean programs in Japan. The Korean newspaper *Dong-A Ilbo* suggested that "the solution to these problems is for Korea to continue efforts to understand and accept cultures of other countries."[95] Cultural productions may be inter-Asian in production format, but was cultural dialogue adequately emphasized? A particularly notorious anti-Hallyu event took place in Japan with the 2005 publication of *Manga Kenkanryū* (Hating the Korean wave) by the pseudonymous Yamano Sharin; at that point, the Korean presence had been strongly apparent only since 2004, with the second-round broadcast by NHK of the regionally popular KBS drama *Gyeoul Yeonga* (Winter sonata, 2002).[96] Yamano's comic depicts a freshman joining his university's "East Asia Investigation Committee," where he learns the "truth" about historical disputes between Japan and Korea, with pro-Korean Japanese and Korean students' ignorance of this joint history getting exposed in the process.[97] A crude binary of self/other is an inevitable part of the comic's rhetorical strategy. Nearly a decade later, in 2014 the *Korea Times* reported that though "experts and observers in Korea and Japan" said attendance at anti-Korean rallies "reportedly staged every weekend across Japan" were small, Korean culture content exports and even small shops in "Tokyo's Korea Town" "seem[ed] to face grave challenges sparked by right-wing politicians and activists in Japan whose voices against the boom ... resonate widely amid a sluggish economy," as well as unresolved tensions over disputed islands and "comfort women" issues.[98] Political detritus from the Cold War and before made their presence felt in the unending postbubble era.

The various negative reactions to cross-border pop culture do serve to highlight an undeniable change in cultural subjectivity in the region. K-pop, as the more arriviste contemporary pop culture that enjoyed state support, followed and exceeded many of the routes of circulation that J-pop, with its domestic orientation, had unintentionally pioneered. So, we might ask how we can *see* this translocal assortment of pop fans that, in its Japanese "branch," has provoked the right-wing. To do this, we might go back to J-pop as the accidental prototype, because that may reveal to us this translocal "community" as it existed without the additional complexities produced by K-pop's export-oriented glossiness.

We turn to the five-man group Arashi (Storm). The band debuted in 1999 and its members—Ōno Satoshi (the leader), Sakurai Shō, Aiba Masaki, Ninomiya Kazunari, Matsumoto Jun—were born between 1980 and 1983. (The band went into "indefinite hiatus" in January 2021.) Their oeuvre largely consists of upbeat, cheerful pop with a tame hip-hop element, along with some bubblegum pop during the early part of the group's career. A chat session carried out with the audience in a concert at the Taipei Arena in Taiwan on August 17, 2006, is revealing. That is an apposite year, as by that time, the Korean wave (including K-pop) had already started to overtake the 1990s Japanese wave—which meant that the audience present possessed a commitment that continued from the earlier fan-consumption impulses of inter-Asian pop.[99] Even as late as 2016, the Johnny and Associates website directly stated that it did not allow fans not domiciled in Japan to join any of their groups' fan clubs—membership is the only way to receive priority for concert ticket purchases.[100] For a male idol group like Arashi, arguably second in renown in Japan only to SMAP, concert tickets then become nearly impossible to purchase for overseas fans. This situation is compounded by the fact that Johnny's groups rarely tour outside Japan, as there is no need to cater to a larger market, whatever the real demand.

The Taipei concert was part of Arashi's first-ever set of performances overseas. After Taipei, the band traveled to represent Japan at Korea's Third Asia Song Festival in Gwangju—an ongoing, Korean-organized festival that attempts to promote cultural dialogue by inviting singers from across the region and thus fending off the charge of cultural imperialism—and finally to Bangkok, where Arashi headlined a concert commemorating the 120th anniversary of the declaration of amity and commerce between Thailand and Japan.[101] This tour with mixed commercial and semidiplomatic goals was named "Arashi around Asia: Thailand—Taiwan—Korea."[102]

Inter-Asian pop concerts are characterized by a typical pattern that has evolved over the years, including an extended chat session with the audience to enable "bonding" with the fans. The Taipei concert was no exception. In the video of the event, a translator stands on the stage with Arashi facilitating the session. Matsumoto Jun mentions that Arashi started seven years ago and Ninomiya Kazunari apologizes that it has taken band members so long to get to Taiwan, acknowledging that they do know that they have overseas fans. Ninomiya then proceeds to ask if anyone has been to Japan to watch their shows and gets positive shouts in return from the audience, eliciting the response from him, "*Sugoi ne!*" ("amazing" or "wow"). So, it seems "if the mountain won't come to Muhammed,..." Soon after, Sakurai Shō—who notices that sections of the audience had been laughing at their jokes even before the translation to Mandarin Chinese—makes a comment that it appears some in the audience know Japanese. There is again an affirmative audience response, and Ninomiya follows up soon by asking if they learned their Japanese in school or at home. The translator gives them the reply, "by themselves," leaving all of Arashi—surprisingly, given their long careers as pop singers—looking slightly taken aback, as if it is the first time they have heard that overseas audiences learn Japanese to follow the Japanese wave better. (Now, as we know, fans in the region learn Korean to follow the more recent wave.) Sakurai then observes that he sees fans from Hong Kong, Singapore, and Thailand (presumably from the placards that the fans hold up), and Ninomiya edges in, saying that he was confused by a placard that said "Macau" (in Kanji or Chinese characters), thinking that it was a person's name. Aiba Masaki then spots the Macanese contingent and points at them, with Sakurai shouting out, "Hi, Macau!" (in English) at them. Soon after, the recording of the chat ends and the concert resumes. While we can assume that the concertgoers are mainly Taiwanese, clearly youths from other countries are also in attendance and happy to proclaim their identities to the artists on the stage, if they will notice. If Arashi goes "around Asia," Asia is also willing to go to Arashi.

The regional contemporary pop concert becomes a productive imaginative event where a nonnational unity is invoked, perhaps involuntarily, by the multinational audience. It could be said that the artists, their production team, and the audience performatively co-project a fiction of unity, a common (even if internally disjunctive) historical time. The subject of modernity tends to be singular—the nation-state, or national culture, both of which presuppose a "we" with some sort of dialectical unity. In contrast, in Taipei, the concert audience is multiple and multinational, enfolded within an immanently differential contemporary moment in which the desire for urbanized pop culture is fulfilled. Despite the disjunctive spatial and historical relations in the region, the modernity expressed is characterized by the desire for an increasingly regional cultural capital. If art, as it is claimed, is a privileged carrier of the contemporary, as it was of modernity, then pop culture, because it is more quotidian in its claims than high culture, has at least the same capacity to serve as a carrier of the contemporary and to assist in the imagining of a nonsingular subjectivity.

Epilogue

In 2018 the K-pop idol band BTS (Bangtan Sonyeondan [Bulletproof Boy Scouts]), formed in 2013, broke into the metropolitan center of pop music, the United States, in a substantial manner. That year witnessed two of the band's singles, "IDOL" and "Fake Love," reach numbers 11 and 10, respectively, on *Billboard*'s Hot 100 chart, and two of their albums, *Love Yourself: Tear* and *Love Yourself: Answer*, both reached number 1 on *Billboard*'s Independent Albums chart in June and August, respectively, with each remaining in that pole position for two weeks.[103] On October 9, 2018, BTS performed on the American Music Awards show, its first outing on American network television. The band's upbeat hip-hop, inflected with pop and R&B, along with their dynamic, precise, and mesmerizing dance choreography, seem to have propelled its Asian pop beyond the successes of early East Asian pretenders such as Japan's Sakamoto Kyū (1941–85), whose "Sukiyaki" remained at number 1 for three weeks on *Billboard*'s Hot 100 in 1963; K-pop girl band Wonder Girl's "Nobody," which peaked at 76 on *Billboard*'s Hot 100 in 2009; and PSY's "Gangnam Style," which reached number 2 in 2012—the only three notable chart successes before BTS. Is this the moment Asian pop becomes, at last, global pop?

However, in the same year—and in rapid succession—two controversies erupted that took the shine off this potential moment of arrival on the global stage. In September 2019, the boy band's Korean fans reacted negatively to news from the group's management agency, Big Hit Entertainment, that the Japanese producer of the hugely popular Japanese girl band AKB48, Akimoto Yasushi, would be writing a Japanese-language single, "Bird," for BTS. Akimoto had previously used the Rising Flag Sun—which evoked memories of Japanese colonialism—on AKB48's costumes, and he was also accused of using misogynist lyrics in the girl group's songs. Around the same time, images appeared online of a BTS member wearing a T-shirt that had an image of an atomic bomb explosion and the text "Patriotism Our History Liberation Korea" printed repetitively on it. The furor that resulted in Japan led to TV Asahi canceling the scheduled November 9 appearance of BTS on the long-running show, *Music Station*.[104]

The appearance of a postwar global market in cultural commodities had allowed the construction of a world music (even if "experienced as a tide of 'Americanization'"), though that also "enclosed the cultural commons as all sorts of vernacular art forms that had circulated [previously] as common property,... were... copyrighted, and sold as commodities."[105] Partially in reaction to that, as we see in the chapters in this volume, there appeared musical alternatives trying to delink from that market in the socialist and postcolonial world. At the same time, world music becomes more complex as what I elsewhere have described as "the global and cultural dispersal of... the global West" is requisitioned to engender new forms of cultural difference that link various regional identities into a cosmopolitan-contemporary Asianness, though one unable to forswear modern nationalism.[106] The contemporary moment manifests an antagonistic unity within which the great modern ideology of nationalism lives, even if there is a vision of a regional market with a newfound interdependence, where sameness and difference are no longer in an antinomian relationship. Pop culture is now part of a regionally affirmative culture in this inconclusive moment of the contemporary.

NOTES

Thanks to the following for years of engagement with this chapter's content: Mōri Yoshitaka, Anthony Fung, Elizabeth K. Helsinger, Brett de Bary, Chua Beng Huat, Uchino Tadashi, and Hyunjoon Shin. Thanks also to Sun Jung, Shim Doobo, Lee Hyunjung, this volume's editors, and two anonymous reviewers. Conversations with Naoki Sakai also made an impact here. Finally, thanks to the students in my HL4009 and HL7114 classes over a number of years for their thoughts as "native informers"!

1 In the early 1990s, SMAP helped lead a Japanese wave of pop-cultural flows in East and Southeast Asia, including TV dramas and pop music. The most prominent member of the band, arguably, is Kimura Takuya—who is also a well-known television actor—and he was fairly extensively interviewed by China Central Television and other broadcasters such as Phoenix Television (based in Hong Kong) when SMAP went to Beijing. The band's management company made the surprising announcement in August 2016 that the group would break up at the end of the year.
2 In 2010 SMAP had also been scheduled to appear at the Shanghai Expo, but that was canceled because of fears of overcrowding.
3 "Japan Pop Band SMAP in Rare Beijing Concert," BBC News Asia-Pacific, September 16, 2011, www.bbc.co.uk/news/world-asia-pacific-1494563?print=true; "Wen 'Sincerely Welcomes' SMAP's Beijing Concert Fri.," Kyodo News, September 15, 2011, english.kyodonews.jp/news/2011/09/115129.html.
4 Kakuzō Okakura, Ideals of the East: The Spirit of Japanese Art (1904; repr., Mineola, NY: Dover, 2005), 1.
5 Bruce Cumings, Parallax Visions: Making Sense of American–East Asian Relations (Durham, NC: Duke University Press, 1999), 218.
6 Wang Hui, The Politics of Imagining Asia (Cambridge, MA: Harvard University Press, 2011), 62.

7   Naoki Sakai, "'You Asians': On the Historical Role of the West and Asia Binary," *South Atlantic Quarterly* 99, no. 4 (Fall 2000): 789–818.
8   Cumings, *Parallax Visions*, 213. See also John W. Dower, *Empire and Aftermath: Yoshida Shigeru and the Japanese Experience, 1878–1954* (Cambridge, MA: Council on East Asian Studies, Harvard University, 1979).
9   Jung-en Woo, *Race to the Swift: State and Finance in Korean Industrialization* (New York: Columbia University Press, 1991).
10 Cumings, *Parallax Visions*, 213.
11 World Bank, *The East Asian Miracle: Economic Growth and Public Policy* (New York: Oxford University Press, 1993), 38.
12 For an account of some Japanese attempts to open up non-neoliberal paths to development, see Vijay Prashad, "Tokyo's Road to Nowhere," in *The Poorer Nations: A Possible History of the Global South* (London: Verso, 2012), 145–58.
13 Cumings, *Parallax Visions*, 216. According to Takashi Shiraishi, "The United States remained hegemonic [in East, including Southeast, Asia], casting a long shadow over the regional architecture. This is especially evident in security, and to a lesser extent in finance and trade." Takashi Shiraishi, "The Third Wave: Southeast Asia and Middle-Class Formation in the Making of a Region," in *Beyond Japan: The Dynamics of East Asian Regionalism*, ed. Peter J. Katzenstein and Takashi Shiraishi (Ithaca, NY: Cornell University Press, 2006), 238.
14 Bonnie Glaser explains: "The risk of conflict in the South China Sea is significant. China, Taiwan, Vietnam, Malaysia, Brunei, and the Philippines have competing territorial and jurisdictional claims, particularly over rights to exploit the region's possibly extensive reserves of oil and gas. Freedom of navigation in the region is also a contentious issue, especially between the United States and China over the right of US military vessels to operate in China's two-hundred-mile exclusive economic zone (EEZ). These tensions are shaping—and being shaped by—rising apprehensions about the growth of China's military power and its regional intentions." Bonnie S. Glaser, "Armed Clash in the South China Sea: Contingency Planning Memorandum No. 14," Council on Foreign Relations, April 11, 2012, www.cfr.org/report/armed-clash-south-china-sea. China's claim is based on its "nine-dash line" map published by the Republican Chinese Ministry of the Interior in 1947: "The map served as the basis for the Declaration on China's Territorial Sea, which was made by the Chinese Government in 1958 and laid territorial claim to a majority of the islands in the South China Sea. Additionally, in 2009 China submitted a diplomatic note to the United Nations Secretary-General, asserting its sovereignty over islands in the South China Sea which was presented with a map of the 'nine-dash line.' The legality of the nine-dash line map, which China charges is based on historical evidence, is disputed by other South China Sea territorial claimants and under the UNCLOS [United Nations Convention on the Law of the Sea] Treaty. This situation continues in 2014, with China's new map of mid-2014 showing a controversial ten-dash line encompassing the South China Sea and Taiwan." "South China Sea: Conflicting Claims and Tensions," Lowry Institute for International Policy, accessed September 19, 2015, http://www.lowyinstitute.org/issues/south-china-sea. The Association of Southeast Asian Nations (ASEAN) has tried to take the

lead in a relatively neutral fashion to mediate the disputes but thus far has been unsuccessful.

15   Evan A. Feigenbaum and Robert A. Manning, "A Tale of Two Asias," *Foreign Policy*, October 31, 2012, foreignpolicy.com/2012/10/31/a-tale-of-two-asias/.

16   Ian Storey and Malcolm Cook, "The Trump Administration and Southeast Asia: America's Asia Policy Crystalizes," *ISEAS Perspective*, no. 77 (November 29, 2018): 6, www.iseas.edu.sg/images/pdf/ISEAS_Perspective_2018_77@50.pdf.

17   Fredric Jameson, "Notes on Globalization as a Philosophical Issue," in *The Cultures of Globalization*, ed. Fredric Jameson and Masao Miyoshi (Durham, NC: Duke University Press, 1998), 55, 69; Peter Osborne, *Anywhere or Not at All: Philosophy of Contemporary Art* (London: Verso, 2013), 17.

18   Osborne, *Anywhere or Not at All*, 194.

19   Michael K. Bourdaghs, *Sayonara Amerika, Sayonara Nippon: A Geopolitical Prehistory of J-Pop* (New York: Columbia University Press, 2012), 128.

20   Sheldon Hsiao-peng Lu, *Transnational Chinese Cinemas: Identity, Nationhood, Gender* (Honolulu: University of Hawai'i Press, 1997).

21   According to Chua Beng Huat, "Without the massive and well-established Pop Culture China market and its audience that receives the Japanese and Korean pop cultures via different Chinese languages, flows and exchanges between Japan, Korea and other particular East Asian locations would be merely bilateral rather than regional." Chua Beng Huat, *Structure, Audience and Soft Power in East Asian Pop Culture* (Hong Kong: Hong Kong University Press, 2012), 5. If this circulation represents "Chineseness," then such an identity is already non-monolithic as it is not linked to a "homeland."

22   The series *Oshin* originally aired on Nippon Hōsō Kyōkai (NHK, Japan Broadcasting Corporation), the national broadcaster, from April 4, 1983, to March 31, 1984. Fifty-three countries broadcasted *Oshin*, fourteen of them in Northeast and Southeast Asia—Singapore was the first in 1984. Kant Udornpim and Arvind Singhal, "*Oshin*, a Pro-Social Role Model, in Thailand," *Keio Communication Review*, no. 21 (1999): 3–21.

23   On televisual dramas, see Koichi Iwabuchi, *Recentering Globalization: Popular Culture and Japanese Transnationalism* (Durham, NC: Duke University Press, 2002); and Koichi Iwabuchi, ed., *Feeling Asian Modernities: Transnational Consumption of Japanese TV Dramas* (Hong Kong: Hong Kong University Press, 2004). On pop music, see David Leheny, "A Narrow Place to Cross Swords: 'Soft Power' and the Politics of Japanese Popular Culture in East Asia," in *Beyond Japan: The Dynamics of East Asian Regionalism*, ed. Peter J. Katzenstein and Takashi Shiraishi (Ithaca, NY: Cornell University Press, 2006), 212–13. For possibly the earliest assessment of the Japanese Wave, see Honda Shiro, "The Spreading of Japan's Popular Culture in East Asia," *Japan Echo* 21, no. 4 (1994): 75–79. For an early critique, see C. J. W.-L. Wee, "Is Consumption-Oriented Popular Culture in Singapore Being 'Japanized'?" [in Japanese translation], *Gaiko Forum* 74 (November 1994): 66–68, in which this writer (wrongly) dismissed the strength of this wave in Singapore. On the emergence of the Korean wave, see Mark James Russell, *POP Goes Korea: Behind the Revolu-*

tion in Movies, Music, and the Internet Culture (Berkeley, CA: Stone Bridge, 2008); Dooba Shim, *Waxing the Korean Wave*, ARI Working Paper 158 (Singapore: Asia Research Institute, National University of Singapore, 2011); and Chua Beng Huat and Koichi Iwabuchi, eds., *East Asian Pop Culture: Analysing the Korean Wave* (Hong Kong: Hong Kong University Press, 2008). The term *Hallyu* was used beginning in the 1990s. There are different accounts as to the origins of the term—either mainland China or Taiwan are cited as sites of its emergence.

24 Revealingly, despite his pioneering work on transnational Japanese pop culture, Koichi Iwabuchi concedes that *how exactly* translation (subtitling of dramas or pop songs incorporating more than one language) or how "cultural translation" (when the viewer feels that there is "cultural proximity" between the television program she is watching and her own urban context) lead to the creation of regional cultural "resonance" is not apparent. Koichi Iwabuchi, "Pop Culture's *Lingua Franca*: Language and Regional Popular Cultural Flows in East Asia," in *Babel or Behemoth: Language Trends in Asia*, ed. Jennifer Lindsay and Tan Ying Ying (Singapore: Asia Research Institute, National University of Singapore, 2003), 171–72.

25 Shiraishi, "The Third Wave."

26 Leheny, "A Narrow Place to Cross Swords." See also Yoshiko Nakano, "Who Initiates a Global Flow? Japanese Popular Culture in Asia," *Visual Communication* 1, no. 2 (2002): 229–53; and Hiro Katsumata, "Japanese Popular Culture in East Asia: A New Insight into Regional Community Building," *International Relations of the Asia-Pacific* 12, no. 1 (2011): 133–60.

27 See Hiroshi Aoyagi, "The Spread of Idol Performances in New Industrial Economies," in *Island of Eight Million Smiles: Idol Performers and Symbolic Production in Contemporary Japan* (Cambridge, MA: Harvard University Asia Center, 2005), 232–58.

28 Shunya Yoshimi, "'America' as Desire and Violence: Americanization in Postwar Japan and Asia during the Cold War," trans. David Buist, *Inter-Asia Cultural Studies* 4, no. 3 (December 2003): 433–50; Carolyn S. Stevens, *Japanese Popular Music: Culture, Authority, and Power* (Abingdon, UK: Routledge, 2008); Bourdaghs, *Sayonara Amerika*.

29 Jameson, "Notes on Globalization," 67.

30 Korean Culture and Information Service, *The Korean Wave: A New Pop Culture Phenomenon* (Seoul: Korean Culture and Information Service, Ministry of Culture, Sports, and Tourism, 2011), 20. The series' audience share was 16.6 percent. Sun Jung, *Korean Masculinities and Transcultural Consumption: Yonsama, Rain, Oldboy, K-Pop Idols* (Hong Kong: Hong Kong University Press, 2011), 1.

31 Cho Hae-Joang argues of Korean pop culture that "it appeals to a certain global middle and lower middle class by presenting upscale hyper-modern lifestyles. In a way, the Korean Wave plays a significant role in accelerating the transformation of global residents into neoliberal subjects in an era where all types of communities are being disintegrated and atomized." Cho Hae-Joang, "Reading the 'Korean Wave' as a Sign of Global Shift," *Korea Journal* 45, no. 4 (2005): 176.

32 Fredric Jameson, "Reification and Utopia in Mass Culture (1979)," in *Signatures of the Visible* (New York: Routledge, 1990), 156.
33 Michael Denning, *Culture in the Age of Three Worlds* (London: Verso, 2004), 102–3.
34 Yoshitaka Mōri, "J-pop: From the Ideology of Creativity to DiY Music Culture," *Inter-Asia Cultural Studies* 10, no. 4 (2009): 479.
35 Stevens, *Japanese Popular Music*, 10.
36 Japan Ministry of Posts and Telecomunications, "White Paper: Communications in Japan 1997," accessed June 8, 2001, http://www.mpt.go.jp/eng/Resources/top.html.
37 Katsumata, "Japanese Popular Culture," 138.
38 Nakano, "Who Initiates a Global Flow?," 231. See also the essays in Iwabuchi, *Feeling Asian Modernities*.
39 Masashi Ogawa, "Japanese Popular Music in Hong Kong: what does TK present?" in *Refashioning Pop Music in Asia: Cosmopolitan Flows, Political Tempos, and Aesthetic Industries*, ed. Allen Chun, Ned Rossiter, and Brian Shoesmith (London: RoutledgeCurzon, 2004), 146–47; Nakano, "Who Initiates a Global Flow?," 236–37.
40 On Bangkok, see Ubonrat Siriyusavak, "Popular Culture and Youth Consumption: Modernity, Identity and Social Transformation," in *Feeling Asian Modernities: Transnational Consumption of Japanese TV Dramas*, ed. Koichi Iwabuchi (Hong Kong: Hong Kong University Press, 2004), 177–202.
41 Benjamin Wai-ming Ng, "Japanese Popular Music in Singapore and the Hybridization of Asian Music," *Asian Music* 34, no. 1 (Fall/Winter 2002/3): 4–5, 2–3. Speed was a teenaged, four-girl group from Okinawa that had its label debut in 1996; it disbanded in 2000 and reformed as a group in 2008. In the first three years of its existence, it racked up sales of more than twenty million units. Jon Herskovitz, "Top Japanese Girl Group Speed Coming to a Halt," *Variety*, October 11, 1999.
42 Bonnie C. Wade, *Music in Japan: Experiencing Music, Expressing Culture* (Oxford: Oxford University Press, 2005).
43 Mōri, "J-pop," 476. See also Stevens, *Japanese Popular Music*, 16, 106–7. Mōri and Stevens both draw from Ugaya Hiromichi, *J-Poppu to wa nani ka* [What is J-pop?] (Tokyo: Iwanami Shoten, 2005), in their accounts of J-WAVE and the appearance of "J-pop." For a detailed examination of "English and English-like Japanese lyrics," see Stevens, "Translations: 'Internationalizing' Language and Music," in *Japanese Popular Music*, 132–55.
44 Martin Roberts, "'A New Stereophonic Sound Spectacular': *Shibuya-kei* as Transnational Soundscape," *Popular Music* 32, no. 1 (2013): 111–23. See also Mōri, "J-pop," 476.
45 Stevens, *Japanese Popular Music*, 16.
46 For example, the eighth album of pop trio Dreams Come True, *Love Unlimited* (1996), sold more than 200,000 units in Taiwan. Steve McClure, *Nippon Pop* (Tokyo: Charles E. Tuttle, 1998), 153.
47 Stevens, *Japanese Popular Music*, 16–17.

48. Wade, *Music in Japan*, 134.
49. Yoshimi, "'America' as Desire and Violence," 434–44. See also Shunya Yoshimi, "Consuming 'America': From Symbol to System," in *Consumption in Asia: Lifestyles and Identities*, ed. Chua Beng Huat (London: Routledge, 2000), 202–24.
50. As Iwabuchi argues: "Japanese cultural products themselves have come to hold a certain symbolic appeal to other Asian nations—which can be conceived neither as merely 'odorless' [that is, without any marked 'Japanese' identity], nor as nonderivative of American cultural power, nor as comparable to the Americanization paradigm—in the context of the proliferation of non-Western indigenized modernities." Iwabuchi, *Recentering Globalization*, 47.
51. Shin Sannin Musume (literally, Three New Young Girls) is considered the first idol group.
52. Ezra F. Vogel, *Japan as Number One: Lessons for America* (Cambridge, MA: Harvard University Press, 1979).
53. Patrick W. Galbraith and Jason G. Karlin, "Introduction: The Mirror of Idols and Celebrity," in *Idols and Celebrity in Japanese Media Culture*, ed. Patrick W. Galbraith and Jason G. Karlin (Houndmills, UK: Palgrave Macmillan, 2012), 4. See also Stevens, *Japanese Popular Music*, 49–51.
54. According to Mōri: "Looking back to the age of the analogue record in the mid 1980s, Japanese audiences listened to western music much more than they do [around 2009]." Mōri, "J-pop," 477.
55. Mōri, "J-pop," 477. For a critique of Asada, see Tomiko Yoda, "A Roadmap to Millennial Japan," *South Atlantic Quarterly* 99, no. 4 (Fall 2000): 659–62.
56. David Marx writes: "The shop's real innovation . . . was the corner where the staff curated a selection of more interesting contemporary Japanese bands—ones that had strayed far from classic *kayōkyoku* conventions to sound like Japanese-language versions of modern Western music. At first, this focused around Flipper's Guitar, Love Tambourines, Pizzicato Five, and Scha Dara Parr." W. David Marx, "R.I.P. Shibuya HMV," *Néojaponisme*, August 25, 2010, neojaponisme.com/2010/08/25/r-i-p-shibuya-hmv/.
57. Roberts, "'A New Stereophonic Sound Spectacular,'" 113.
58. Takanami remained with the group until 1994.
59. "Twiggy Twiggy Lyrics," *AllTheLyrics.com*, accessed January 11, 2016, www.allthelyrics.com/lyrics/pizzicato_five/twiggy_twiggy-lyrics-227513.html#ixzz3wre0s3wA.
60. Roberts, "'A New Stereophonic Sound Spectacular,'" 112; Yoda, "A Roadmap," 661.
61. Mōri, "J-pop," 478.
62. "Hikaru Utada: Chart History," *Billboard*, accessed 13 January 2016, www.billboard.com/artist/303512/hikaru-utada/chart; Lars Brandle, "Utada's 'Exodus' Breaks Record in Japan," *BillboardBiz*, September 10, 2004, www.billboard.com/biz/articles/news/1428984/utadas-exodus-breaks-record-in-japan.
63. Stevens, *Japanese Popular Music*, 146 (quoting Ugaya Hiromichi's critique of J-pop); Mōri, "J-pop," 478.

64 "Hikaru Utada—Biography," *Billboard*, accessed January 13, 2016, www.billboard .com/artist/303512/hikaru-utada/biography.

65 Kawabata Shigeru, "The Japanese Record Industry," *Popular Music* 10, no. 3 (October 1991): 327.

66 Ubonrat Siriyuvasak and Shin Hyunjoon, "Asianizing K-pop: Production, Consumption and Identification Patterns among Thai Youth," *Inter-Asian Cultural Studies* 8, no. 1 (2007): 128n13.

67 Keith Negus, *The South Korean Music Industry: A Literature Review*, CREATe (Centre for Copyright and New Business Models in the Creative Economy) Working Paper Series (Glasgow: CREATe, 2015).

68 Osborne, *Anywhere or Not at All*, 25.

69 Haekyung Um, *K-pop on the Global Platform: European Audience Reception and Contexts* (Seoul: KOFICE [Korean Foundation for International Cultural Exchange], 2014).

70 Hyunjoon Shin, "Reconsidering Transnational Cultural Flows of Popular Music in East Asia: Transbordering Musicians in Japan and Korea Searching for 'Asia,'" *Korean Studies* 33 (2009): 109.

71 Michael Fuhr, *Globalization and Popular Music in South Korea: Sounding Out K-Pop* (New York: Routledge, 2016), 133–49; Gi-Wook Shin and Joon Nak Choi, "Paradox or Paradigm? Making Sense of Korean Globalization," in *Korea Confronts Globalization*, ed. Chang Yun-Shik, Hyun-Ho Seok, and Donald L. Baker (London: Routledge, 2009), 250–72; Jung-Yup Lee, "Managing the Transnational, Governing the National: Cultural Policy and the Politics of 'the Cultural Archetype Project in South Korea,'" in *Popular Culture and the State in East and Southeast Asia*, ed. Nissim Otmazgin and Eyal Ben-Ari (London: Routledge, 2011), 123–43; Seung-Ho Kwon and Joseph Kim, "The Cultural Industry Policies of the Korean Government and the Korean Wave," *International Journal of Cultural Policy* 20, no. 4 (2014): 422–39.

72 Youna Kim, "Introduction: Korean Media in a Digital Cosmopolitan World," in *The Korean Wave: Korean Media Go Global*, ed. Youna Kim (Abingdon, UK: Routledge, 2013).

73 On melodic chorus, see Eun-Young Jung, "Transnational Cultural Traffic in Northeast Asia: The 'Presence' of Japan in Korea's Popular Music Culture" (PhD diss., University of Pittsburgh, 2007), 70–73. See also Fuhr, *Globalization*, 52–54; and Russell, *Pop Goes Korea*, 143–47.

74 Fuhr, *Globalization*, 53–54.

75 Eun-Young Jung, "The Place of Sentimental Song in Contemporary Korean Musical Life," *Korean Studies* 35 (2011): 71–92.

76 The album sold 1.5 million units. Keith Howard, "Exploding Ballads: The Transformation of Korean Pop Music," in *Global Goes Local: Popular Culture in Asia*, ed. Timothy J. Craig and Richard King (Honolulu: University of Hawai'i Press, 2002), 80–95.

77 Russell, *Pop Goes Korea*, 156. See also Fuhr, *Globalization*, 75–76. Japanese pop music, as a point of comparison, began to have a notable presence in China from the

early 1990s; for example, in 1992 the pop-rock band Southern All Stars had the first concert of any foreign group in China at the Beijing Capital Gymnasium. Amuse Inc., "Corporate History," accessed June 27, 2016, ir.amuse.co.jp/english/company/history.html; Jung, *Transnational Cultural Traffic*, 238.

78 Hyunjoon Shin, "Have You Ever Seen the Rain? And Who'll Stop the Rain? The Globalizing Project of Korean Pop (K-Pop)," *Inter-Asian Cultural Studies* 10, no. 4 (2009): 510. Shin continues: "Although it would be controversial to say that this system has 'East Asian' characteristics, it is true that it cannot be easily found outside the [East Asia] region" (510).

79 Natsuko Fukue, "Johnny's: So You Wanna be a Johnny," *Japan Times*, April 14, 2009; W. David Marx, "The *Jimusho* System: Understanding the Production Logic of the Japanese Entertainment Industry," in *Idols and Celebrity in Japanese Media Culture*, ed. Patrick W. Galbraith and Jason G. Karlin (Houndmills, UK: Palgrave Macmillan, 2012), 35–55.

80 Dal Yong Jin and Woongjae Ryoo, "Critical Interpretation of Hybrid K-Pop: The Global-Local Paradigm of English Mixing in Lyrics," *Popular Music and Society* 37, no. 2 (2014): 113–31; Fuhr, *Globalization*, 59–124.

81 It has also been reported that a former journalist, Cho Hyun-jin, was the inventor of the term *K-pop*, when he wrote for *Billboard* from 1999 to 2002. Kim Hyung-eun, "Bringing U.S. Music History to Korea," *Korea Joongang Daily*, December 29, 2015, koreajoongangdaily.joins.com/news/article/article.aspx?aid=3013294.

82 Shin, "Reconsidering Transnational Cultural Flows," 107. See also Oliver Boyd-Barrett, "Reconfiguring Media and Empire," in *The Korean Wave: Korean Media Go Global*, ed. Youna Kim (Abingdon, UK: Routledge, 2013).

83 Jung, *Transnational Cultural Traffic*, esp. 121–23; Keith Howard, "Coming of Age: Korean Pop in the 1990s," in *Korean Pop Music: Riding the Wave*, ed. Keith Howard (Folkestone, Kent, UK: Global Orient, 2006), 96. Ninja's song was an update of "Omatsuri Mambo" (1952) by Misora Hibari (1937–1989), the famous postwar enka singer, whom some accused to be *zainichi*, a Japanese of Korean descent. Bourdaghs, *Sayonara Amerika*, 79–83. An unintended echo of fraught, historically imbricated debates occurs here.

84 Quoted in Cho Hyun-jin, "S. Korea Braces for Japanese Pop: Lifting of Culture Ban Will Allow Imports for First Time," *Billboard*, July 25, 1998, 59.

85 Shin, "Have You Ever Seen the Rain?"; Jeroen de Kloet and Jaap Kooijman, "Karaoke Americanism Gangnam Styl [*sic*]: K-pop, Wonder Girls, and the Asian Unpopular," in *Unpopular Culture*, ed. Martin Lüthe and Sascha Pöhlmann (Amsterdam: Amsterdam University Press, 2016), 113–28; Jeongmee Kim and Basil Glynn, "'Oppa'-tunity Knocks: PSY, 'Gangnam Style' and the Press Reception of K-Pop in Britain," *Situations: Cultural Studies in the Asian Context* 7, no. 1 (Winter 2013/14): 1–20.

86 Christian Oliver, "South Korea's K-pop Takes Off in the West," *Financial Times*, February 10, 2012, www.ft.com/cms/s/0/ddf11662-53c7-11e1-9eac-00144feabdc0.html#axzz4DY5wwcc8.

87 On exports to Japan, see Patrick St. Michel, "How Korean Pop Conquered Japan," *Atlantic*, September 13, 2011.
88 Fuhr, *Globalization*, 142. The figures in this paragraph are from Korean Creative Content Agency (KOCCA) publications.
89 Negus, *The South Korean Music Industry*, 13.
90 This is certainly Carolyn Stevens's view of the matter. See Stevens, *Japanese Popular Music*, 32–33.
91 At the start, SM had China as one of its overseas target markets for TVXQ. This resulted in a version of its first Korean album, *Tri-Angle* (2004), being released in China under the title *Dongfang Shenqi*, the group's Chinese name, by the CRC (China Record Corporation) label. This version had three of the songs appear twice, in Korean and in (slightly strained) Mandarin Chinese. In Korea, TVXQ is known as Dong Bang Shin Ki, and in Mandarin Chinese as Dongfang Shenqi, both meaning "gods rising in the east." They later appeared in Japan under the name Tōhōshinki, which has the same meaning as the Korean and Chinese names. Despite its Japanese success, all activities by TVXQ in Korea ceased at the end of 2009, owing to contractual challenges from three of the singers. The revamped boy band that reappeared in 2010 contained only two of the original five members.
92 "NHK Sees Ratings for 'Kōhaku' Music Show Sink to Lowest Ever," *Japan Times*, January 2, 2016.
93 Shin, "Reconsidering Transnational Cultural Flows," 108.
94 "Taiwan, China United in Backlash against Korean Wave," *Chosun Ilbo*, January 11, 2006, english.chosun.com/site/data/html_dir/2006/01/11/2006011161009.html.
95 Hong Chan-sik, "Korean Wave Backlash in Taiwan," *Dong-A Ilbo*, January 2, 2012, english.donga.com/List/3/all/26/402867/1.
96 Yoshitaka Mōri, "*Winter Sonata* and Cultural Practices of Active Fans in Japan: Considering Middle-Aged Women as Cultural Agents," in *East Asian Pop Culture: Analysing the Korean Wave*, ed. Chua Beng Huat and Koichi Iwabuchi (Hong Kong: Hong Kong University Press, 2008), 127–42.
97 Nicola Liscutin, "Surfing the Neo-Nationalist Wave: A Case Study of *Manga Kenkanryū*," in *Cultural Studies and Cultural Industries in Northeast Asia: What a Difference a Region Makes*, ed. Chris Berry, Nicola Liscutin, and Jonathan D. Mackintosh (Hong Kong: Hong Kong University Press, 2009), 171–89; Rumi Sakamoto and Matthew Allen, "'Hating "The Korean Wave"' Comic Books: A Sign of New Nationalism in Japan?" *Asia Pacific Journal / Japan Focus* 5, no. 10 (October 1, 2007), apjjf.org/-Rumi-SAKAMOTO/2535/article.html.
98 Park Si-soo, "Anti-Hallyu Voices Growing in Japan," *Korea Times*, February 21, 2014.
99 The K-pop artists that might be mentioned as outstanding around 2005 in Southeast Asia include R&B singers Rain and Se7en (pronounced "Seven"), along with dance-pop girl band Baby V.O.X.
100 Johnny's Net, "Family Club," accessed July 4, 2016, www.johnnys-net.jp/page?id=jfcJoin&lang=en_us.

101 The festival is organized by the Korean Foundation for International Cultural Exchange (KOFICE). See Fuhr, *Globalization*, 143–49; and Gunjoo Jang and Won K. Paik, "Korean Wave as Tool for Korea's New Cultural Diplomacy," *Advances in Applied Sociology* 2, no. 3 (2012): 196–202.

102 A two- and three-DVD concert selection was released in 2007 by J Storm, Johnny's in-house music label. The fan-chat session is on the first disc of the three-DVD "limited" edition (JABA-5020~5022).

103 "BTS: Chart History: Hot 100," *Billboard*, accessed February 16, 2019, www.billboard.com/music/bts; "BTS: Chart History: Independent Albums," *Billboard*, accessed February 16, 2019, www.billboard.com/music/bts/chart-history/independent-albums.

104 Kwak Yeon-soo, "K-pop Boy Band BTS Agency under Fire for Working with Japanese Producer Yasushi Akimoto," *South China Morning Post*, September 18, 2018, www.scmp.com/magazines/style/people-events/article/2164649/k-pop-boy-band-bts-agency-under-fire-working-japanese; "BTS T-Shirt: Japanese TV Show Cancels BTS Appearance over Atomic Bomb Shirt," *BBC News*, November 9, 2018, www.bbc.com/news/world-asia-46147777.

105 Denning, *Culture in the Age*, 30–31.

106 C. J. W.-L. Wee, "Staging the Asian Modern: Cultural Fragments, the Singaporean Eunuch, and the Asian *Lear*," *Critical Inquiry* 30, no. 4 (summer 2004): 772.

Part II
COVERS

4. SEARCHING FOR YOUTH, THE PEOPLE (*MINJUNG*), AND "ANOTHER" WEST WHILE LIVING THROUGH ANTI-COMMUNIST COLD WAR POLITICS

South Korean "Folk Song" in the 1970s

HYUNJOON SHIN

Pak Ch'an-uk's film *JSA* (*Joint Security Area*, 2000) is arguably one of the high-water marks of South Korean New Wave cinema. Located at P'anmunjŏm, a small town in the Midwest of the Korean peninsula, JSA is the point within the Demilitarized Zone (DMZ) where North and South Korean forces confront each other face to face. The film revolves around an unlikely friendship between two pairs of North Korean and South Korean soldiers, which ends up in a tragic shootout due to the unyielding military standoff between the two Koreas. The ensuing investigation reveals that a missing bullet was stuck in a cassette tape player and discarded by one of the North Korean soldiers in an attempt to protect the South Koreans from the suspicion of befriending the "enemy."

The South Korean popular songs on that bullet-ridden cassette tape are played in the film soundtrack. In particular, two songs by Han Tae-su (b. 1948) and two by the late Kim Kwang-sŏk (1964–1996) stand out. Han's "Haruppam" (One night, 1974) and "Haruach'im" (One morning, 1989) are heard in the scenes depicting their befriending, while Kim sings "Idŭngbyŏng ŭi p'yŏnji" (The letter from a private, 1994) and "Puch'iji anhŭn p'yŏnji" (The unmailed letter, 1996) during the breakup of the highly risky friendship.[1] All these songs fall under the umbrella category of folk song (*p'ok'ŭ song*), folk music, or simply folk—a distinct popular music genre in South Korea. Even though Han's and Kim's songs set contrasting moods in the movie, musically they are not that far apart. Actually, during his heyday in the late 1980s and early 1990s, Kim was often regarded as the rightful successor of Han, who had been a true pioneer of the genre until his career was put on hold in the mid-1970s. To North Korean ears, Han's free-spirited songs probably still sound painfully foreign, unlike Kim's—a sorrowful ballad about a new young conscript in the Cold War South Korean army that may well strike a chord with military-age males in both Koreas.

Perhaps we should not dwell too much on the plausibility of fictional North Korean soldiers appreciating South Korean folk songs. The point is that quite a few South Koreans exhibited a sincere desire to touch on the issues of Korean reunification and to have their songs heard in the other half of the divided nation. In particular, some folk song artists provided a voice for the young generation, most of whom were university students longing for a democratic South Korea and a peacefully reunified nation that had transcended the Cold War confrontation. That being the case, what is the "folk song"?

Making Sense of the "South Korean Folk Song"

When he discusses Japanese folk music of the 1960–1970s, Michael Bourdaghs argues that folk has "a broad range of meanings." It runs from "campus folk" through "indigenous genres of popular song" to "protest folk."[2] The South Korean case is not so different from the Japanese one despite the differences in terms of routes, trajectories, and effects. Before returning to a discussion of the differences across Asia, this chapter deals with the evolution of "South Korean folk song" as a genre first associated with the young generation (hereafter "youth") of the 1970s. In Korea, just like anywhere else in the world at the time, the most important medium in forming the identity of youth and the discourse on youth culture was popular music. In other words, the folk song genre was a major component of the identity, communication, and everyday life of youth in the period.

Yet it should be noted that the terms *folk song* or *folk*, widely used in this chapter, should be differentiated from *traditional folk song* (*chŏnt'ong minyo*) or *new folk song* (*sinminyo*) as used in pre- and early modern Korea.[3] The folk song in South Korea is "a developed form of pop music imported from America and Europe," which started as covers or adaptations of mostly American modern folk and other Western popular songs, followed by the creation of a national-popular style.[4] Since the genre is typically accompanied by acoustic guitar, it acquired the vernacular name acoustic guitar music (*t'onggit'a ŭmak*). Instead of Romanizing such Koreanized terms as *p'ok'ŭ song* or *t'onggit'a ŭmak*, I will simply refer to this genre of music as the South Korean folk song in order to denote its connection with Western, mostly US, modern folk music, at least in its early period of development.

Needless to say, the political context and cultural contestation surrounding modern folk music were diverse across the globe, and the South Korean folk song took a different historical trajectory from the rest of the world. Put simply, the folk song was thrown into the politics of the Cold War regardless of the wills of musicians and listeners. All genres and styles of popular music were affected by Cold War politics to varying degrees, but the folk song was arguably the most sensitive and, as a result, most vulnerable genre, causing it to sustain a dramatic history. Christian institutions, which were not free from American cultural imperialism, were one important hotbed of folk song. However, in a complicated route of evolution, the folk song invented its own version of South Korean nationalism. This irony would not have taken place if the South Korean folk song was not entangled in the global Cold War at the local and regional levels.

Before investigating the trajectory of the folk song, a brief overview of the historical background is in order. The 1970s is generally known as the détente period in global Cold War history. The Korean peninsula saw very little easing of tension until a glimmer of hope was delivered by the surprising Nambuk Kongdong Sŏngmyŏng (North-South Joint Statement) on July 4, 1972. Just three months later, however, the situation was dramatically reversed as South Korean president Park Chung Hee declared the infamous Siwŏl Yusin (October Innovation) to perpetuate his dictatorial reign, which rolled inter-Korea relations back to a high degree of tension. The ideology of anti-Communism was instrumental in suppressing opposition movements until the assassination of Park in 1979. That is why the 1970s, rather than the preceeding or succeeding decades are remembered as the culmination of Cold War politics by South Koreans.

The Age of Innocence (?–1970): The Importation and Adaptation of Western Modern Folk

Those familiar with the turbulent politics surrounding the Korean peninsula during the early Cold War period would likely take the "Americanization" of South Korean popular music and culture for granted. Since the consolidation of national division in the aftermath of the bloody Korean War (1950–53), South Korea has been an anti-Communist bulwark in Northeast Asia with the Eighth US Army stationed in South Korea on a quasi-permanent basis. The presence of US military bases explains the Americanization of South Korea, in terms of not only politics and economy but also culture and ideology. In the realm of popular music, a particularly important role was played by the Eighth

US Army show, popularly known as the "camp show," which featured Korean musicians and entertainers.

However, as I have argued elsewhere, Americanization has not always been a smooth operation meeting little resistance.[5] Furthermore, its modus operandi has been uneven across different parts of Asia. In Japan, Shunya Yoshimi argues that "America" has become internalized since the 1960s, when "American military facilities became more and more invisible in the urban areas of the Japanese mainland" and the consumption of America was transformed "from symbol to system."[6] According to Yoshimi, the internalization of America is closely associated with the invisibility of US military facilities. The same cannot be said of South Korea, where US military bases are visible almost everywhere, including the Eighth US Army headquarters, still located in the heart of Seoul.

Nevertheless, an internalization of America did take place to some extent in South Korea as well. A case in point is the American modern folk music that resonated with middle-class youth, especially university students, in the 1960s–1970s. Before the arrival of folk, rock music had enjoyed wide popularity in the mid to late 1960s thanks to the bands—colloquially referred to as "group sounds"—who transitioned from performing for US military camp shows to domestic audiences.[7] However, not all university students welcomed rock in this early period. For some, rock was merely a tool for entertaining the US servicemen, just like other American pop genres such as jazz, soul, and country. America might have been an object of envy and the source of cosmopolitan imagination, but in South Korea the US military base was associated with unpleasant experiences and memories.

The South Korean folk song arrived along a different route, which makes it stand out among other genres imported from the West. One of the important points of entry in that route was Christian church-based organizations. A prominent example was the YMCA in Chongno, located in the heart of downtown Seoul, which offered Singalong Y, a "recreational" program in which instructors taught choral singing with "folk songs of the world" (*segye ŭi minyo*) (see figure 4.1). The YMCA venue became a communal, alternative gathering place for youth to enjoy new musical experiences. Since its introduction at this time, group singing has been considered an important aesthetic standard and cultural value for the folk community. As seen in figure 4.2, instructors with acoustic guitars taught participants how to sing the songs collectively, and some of them became popular icons in their own right. Other Christian organizations such as the YWCA also provided the space for sing-along meetings.

If Christian organizations constituted a noncommercial entry point for folk song, venues such as music coffeehouses (*ŭmak tabang*), music listening halls

FIGURES 4.1 AND 4.2. Sing-along at YMCA (*top*) and at YWCA (*bottom*) in the mid- to late 1960s and early 1970s respectively. Courtesy of Seoul YMCA and YWCA.

(*ŭmak kamsangsil*), and live music bars (*saeng'ŭmak sarong*) offered a commercial entry point, as they catered to young music lovers hanging around the downtowns of Seoul and other major cities. C'est Si Bon, one of the music listening halls located in Mugyo-dong, was widely recognized as the birthplace of the folk song due to its various programs, including sing-alongs, which fostered a communal and sociable atmosphere. C'est Si Bon and other similar venues also played a significant role in grooming amateur folk musicians into mainstream pop stars by providing a space that allowed them to connect with other pop music genres.

Covers or adaptations of foreign tunes (*oegukkok*) into the Korean language took place on a massive scale during the formative period of the folk song.[8] Until around 1970, such American folk-pop acts as the Brothers Four; the Kingston Trio; Peter, Paul and Mary; and Simon and Garfunkel held a very strong influence on Korean folk. French chanson and Italian canzone were also particularly influential around the same time. Foreign-adapted songs from a wide variety of origins all over the "free world" became classical art songs (*kagok*), Christian hymns (*sŏngga*), ethnic folk (*minyo*), and modern pop. These were deemed to represent "another" America or "another" West, different from that represented by the US camp show entertainment.[9]

Thus foreign-adapted Korean folk songs achieved a kind of highbrow cosmopolitanism that helped folk singers distance themselves from the professional showbusiness world that had emerged from the US military camp shows. Granted, some of them already had professional experience appearing in the camp shows. And yet the folk singers were largely successful at creating a public image of innocent amateur artists who were tainted with the image of "lowly entertainers" associated with camp show performers. This ideology of innocence, which matched the intellectual identity of university students who were living through the early, soft phase of Park Chung Hee's authoritarian rule, provided an excuse to privilege folk over other imported genres from America.

The adapted folk songs became a minor pop sensation between the late 1960s and early 1970s, catering to the rapidly growing youth-oriented popular culture. In particular, Twin Folio (Yun Hyŏngju and Song Ch'ang-sik) and Toi et Moi (Yi P'il-wŏn and Pak In-hŭi) turned into cult figures among the university crowd thanks to their repertoires of mostly foreign adaptations. With its surging popularity, folk soon became synonymous with the emerging youth culture (*ch'ŏngnyŏn munhwa*), eclipsing the soul and psychedelic rock that still struggled with a public reputation of being noisy, alien music. Moreover, folk implied stronger sociability because of its softer sound and far less aggressive image in comparison to rock. Thus, folk functioned as a means of affective communication among students.

The development of folk did not stop at adaptation. The acoustic guitar, by providing cheap, easy, and convenient instrumental accompaniment, ushered in a creative revolution that mobilized hundreds of thousands of aspiring young amateur musicians. Soon there emerged a group of singer-songwriters who wrote their own songs in Korean and welcomed the ethos of protest folk. They established an ideal of do-it-yourself (DIY) songwriting and performance (*chajak chayŏn*) as the norm for the genre; their songs were communal as well as personal. Furthermore, the unusual, growling voice of the DIY folk pioneer Han Tae-su, who had spent significant time in New York before returning to Seoul in 1968, carried a countercultural ethos embedded in his original songs.

It should be noted, however, that folk was not necessarily associated with counterculture or protest before 1971. The aforementioned sing-along movement was very much compatible with the cultural policy of the authoritarian regime that promoted "wholesome songs" (*kŏnjŏn kayo*). Folk songs were even contrasted with "mass songs" (*taejung kayo*), trot (*t'ŭrot'ŭ*), and other genres that were considered commercial, vulgar, and decadent, and it was expected to offer a genuine alternative to the stale mainstream popular music of the time. Despite their early influence from the West, the newly created folk songs were often dubbed as "our song" (*uri norae*) as well as "beautiful song" (*koun norae*) and "bright song" (*palgŭn norae*) (see figures 4.3, 4.4, and 4.5).

At least in its early stage, the ideology of innocence—folk music as an authentic expression of everyday life of youth—did not pose a threat to the official ideology of cultural wholesomeness. This all changed after 1971, however, as Park Chung Hee's reign began facing a serious challenge from Kim Dae Jung, the major opposition party's candidate for the upcoming presidential election.

Contested, Confronted, and Divided (1971–1975): "Radical" and/or "Decadent"

It was in the autumn of 1971 that Kim Min-ki, a student majoring in fine arts at Seoul National University, released two albums of his songs, including the anthemic "Ach'im isŭl" (Morning dew). The first album featured female singer Yang Hŭi-ŭn and the second his own voice. At the age of twenty, he showed amazing poetic prowess in his Korean lyrics, particularly in his creative use of metaphors. After leading a sing-along session during the freshman orientation at his school, he was taken to a police station and his records were confiscated. According to Kim's own recollection, his songs and performances were deemed radical or

FIGURES 4.3, 4.4, AND 4.5. Covers of the first albums by Yang Hŭi-ŭn (*opposite page, top*) and Kim Min-ki (*opposite page, bottom*), both released in 1971, plus a live recording *Milestone* (*Maettol*) of several folk singers including Yang and Kim from 1972. The phrases *beautiful song* (*koun norae*) and *bright song* (*palgŭn norae*) appear on the Yang and *Milestone* record covers, respectively.

rebellious (*puron*) by the authorities.[10] This incident marked the beginning of his hardships that lasted until the democratization of South Korean society in 1987.

The story of Kim Min-ki further highlights the role that Christian youth organizations played in the birth of the "protest" branch of South Korean folk. Kim and Yang Hŭi-ŭn frequented the Ch'ŏnggaeguri (Blue Frog) Hall, a singalong venue at the YWCA building in downtown Myŏng-dong, which opened in 1970. In 1973 another singalong venue, Haebaragi (Sunflower) Hall, opened at the Catholic School Girls Center, also located in Myŏng-dong.[11] These singalong venues became a hotbed of creative collaborations among amateur singer-songwriters and their audiences. The fact that not all participants were devoted Christians did not deter them from making use of the Christian organizations' facilities. For example, Yang's legendary 1971 concert backed by Kim's acoustic guitar took place in the YMCA auditorium.

The same YMCA building was home to Kidokkyobangsong, the Christian Broadcasting Station (CBS), a radio network whose contribution to folk went beyond simply delivering a wider audience to the music. The staff (producers and DJs) of CBS worked as powerful intermediaries between the musicians and the music industry, sometimes taking the roles of talent manager and/or executive producer. They encouraged young folk singers to write songs expressing national sentiments.[12] Thus, it is not a coincidence that some songs of the South Korean folk canon by Kim Min-ki and others sound like Christian hymns while conveying patriotic messages.[13] As one commentator put it, Korean Christianity was a "religious movement that arose out of American imperialism" and then "became the center of Korean nationalism."[14] This same kind of irony is apparent in South Korean folk music. And yet it is clear that South Korean folk invented and established its own version of popular nationalism in the early 1970s.

In general, the students who revered the folk singer-songwriters as iconic figures were strongly nationalist and averse to foreign popular culture. In this regard, the most notable among those figures is again Kim Min-ki. The Catholic-based cultural movement he was involved in contributed to the revival of pre-modern Korean performance traditions such as open-air theater (*madanggŭk*) and mask dance (*t'alch'um*), which would become a crucial element of the people (*minjung*) protest culture in later years.[15] Under the influence of the renowned protest poet Kim Chi-ha and other cultural activists, Kim Min-ki experimented with *minyo* and *kugak*, both traditional forms of Korean music, writing such songs as "Kamum" (Draught) and "Kohyang kanŭn kil" (The road to hometown) during the mid-1970s. In this regard, Kim's songs may well deserve the designation of genuine "Korean modern folk." To university students and university-educated youth, his creativity not only went beyond covering foreign songs but actually did away with foreignness altogether. And just like the traditional folk songs in olden days, his songs circulated by word of mouth since he was officially banned from recording, not to mention performing or broadcasting. In addition to resorting to oral tradition, his student followers also spread Kim's music by transcribing it and circulating copies of the scores.

However, Kim was an exception rather than the rule in the folk community at the time. The strong bond that formed within the community did not prevent its members from taking divergent paths according to their own desires, which led to extremely successful transitions from folk to rock and other popular styles. In particular, Yi Chang-hŭi made a successful turn from folk to country and rock-oriented pop with the major hit song "Kŭgŏn nŏ" (It's you) in 1973. The very next year, another of Yi's songs, "Hanjanŭi ch'uŏk" (The memory of drinking a shot), was featured in the blockbuster movie *Pyŏltŭl ŭi kohyang* (Heavenly homecoming to stars), directed by Yi Chang-ho.

This partnership between countercultural filmmakers and folk singers continued with Ha Kil-chong's movie *Pabodŭl ŭi Haengjin* (March of fools) and Song Ch'ang-sik's youth culture anthems, "Wae pullŏ?" (Why do you call me?) and "Korae Sanyang" (Whale hunting), all from 1974. Formerly half of the male duo Twin Folio, Song Ch'ang-sik had built a solid reputation as a singer-

FIGURES 4.6, 4.7, AND 4.8. Canonical albums by rebellious folk rock singer-songwriters Yi Chang-hŭi (*previous page, top*), Han Tae-su (*previous page, bottom*), and Yang Pyŏg-chip. The first was released in 1973, and the other two in 1974.

songwriter. Not unlike Bob Dylan, who "went electric" in 1965, Korean folk artists increasingly turned toward rock and other genres of pop music by the mid-1970s, following the lead of Yi and Song. As folk music no longer sounded innocent, its genuinely countercultural side became much more apparent during this period in such creative and canonical works as the recordings of Han Tae-su, Yang Pyŏg-chip, and Yi Chŏng-sŏn.[16] The impassive, refracted, and cynical faces in their record covers show their anger, frustration, and rebelliousness (see figures 4.6, 4.7, and 4.8).

The marriage between youth culture and folk music suddenly grabbed the attention of daily newspapers and monthly magazines, and a heated debate ensued in the mainstream media through the spring and summer of 1974.[17] The debate looks almost silly by today's standards since the youth culture then symbolized by acoustic guitar (*t'onggit'a*), blue jeans (*purujin*), and draft beer (*saengmaektchu*) was demonized as consumerist hedonism not only by adult cultural elitists but also by student political activists.[18] The activists' criticism is understandable if we consider what happened in April 1974: a crackdown on the National League of Democratic College Students (Minch'ŏnghangnyŏn), which rounded up 253 suspected "communist revolutionaries" in order to suppress political activism on college campuses and in civil society in general. Furthermore, the term *youth* carried a specific meaning in Korea's historical context. In the long tradition of social protest and political resistance, youth occupied a special position as the agent of change and reform for a better future for the nation. Youth culture as it appeared in the 1970s might have been a cultural rebellion, but it was still far from constituting actual political protest.

A final decision on youth culture was made by the government. In December 1975, the increasingly paranoid Park regime launched a full-force assault on the thriving youth culture, and folk music was one of its main targets. As the "popular music purge campaign" and the "marijuana clampdown" went on a rampage against "rebellious" and/or "decadent" music, the flourishing folk music scene was wiped out overnight.[19] While the student activists did not welcome this brutal assault on "decadent" folk, they did not voice any serious objections either when singers and musicians were arrested or when public performance spaces were shut down. Was this because of an implicit "agreement" between the authoritarian regime and the student movement that the decadent culture had to go? Possibly, but the answer is blowing in the wind. We also have to remember that the South Korean popular mood at the time was a product of the national anxieties resulting from the "Fall of Saigon" in the spring of 1975.

Thus the year 1975 signaled the death of youth culture. To say that it died of political repression would be too simplistic, for it reflected an internalization of Cold War politics that was shared by both the official and popular nationalist fronts in South Korea. This cultural death led to a division within youth between the "radical" (*puron*) and the "decadent" (*t'oep'ye*) factions, if we borrow the terminology of the authoritarian regime. It took a very long time for the public to realize that this was a result of the authoritarian regime's strategy of "divide-and-rule."

The Consolidation of Division (1976–): "Campus Song" versus "Minjung kayo"

After 1975, popular music came under routine surveillance and control by the state. Precensorship on recording and postcensorship on broadcasting combined to produce a formidable control mechanism for recorded music. At the same time, laws regulating public performance, fire services, and food sanitation were put in place to restrict live music. Due to strict enforcement of these laws, the number of public places available for folk songs and other popular music activities declined rapidly. Folk became underground music in a literal sense. This is the main reason why the late 1970s are often dismissed as the dark age of Korean popular music history. This assessment is unfair, though, because both survivors and newcomers went on to create new songs and sounds. In what follows, I discuss two diverging instances of the survival and renewal of folk song in the latter half of the 1970s.

The first is the campus song (*taehakkayo*), a genre that transcended the scope suggested by the literal meaning of its name. Songs written and performed by amateur musicians from university campuses came to public attention thanks to the unexpected success of the Campus Song Festival in 1977 hosted by the Munhwa Broadcasting Corporation (MBC) as well as to the continued popularity of similar song contests throughout the 1970s and beyond.[20] The typical campus song was a brand of folk song characterized by simple melodies and innocent lyrics conveyed in a sincere if not overly competent fashion. To a certain extent, the boom in campus songs was a product of its time. After the expulsion of the folk song from the cultural landscape, young people were suddenly deprived of music they could relate to. Although the campus song was not as musically sophisticated as its predecessor, it was nonetheless enthusiastically embraced by young audiences who eagerly awaited the reemergence of "our song." At least initially, the diffusion of the campus song constituted a second age of innocence.

However, the limitations of media-organized musical events soon became apparent when the artists from the Campus Song Festival and other similar song contests were heavily exploited by the media as well as by the music industry. The ratings-seeking drive of the media combined with the performers' own naiveté to lead many campus musicians to chase pop stardom. Television shows cashed in on the popularity of the campus song and propelled some of these amateur singers to immediate stardom. In so doing, however, the media transformed them into instant stars rather than promoting them as serious musicians. Although some artists managed to survive this short-termism, this ill-advised strategy was responsible for the short careers of many promising campus singers.

As soon as campus singers turned professional, they were incorporated into the pop mainstream. In other words, their careers were organized according to the formula of the media industry, especially TV, which started color broadcasting in 1980. They were advised to abandon their folk roots and sing politically safe pop songs written by professional songwriters, to appear continuously on television, and to perform in commercial venues. After military officer Chun Doo Hwan rose to power in 1980, these artists were asked to take part in various state-sponsored events, promoting government policies and celebrating its achievements. Wittingly or not, they became deeply involved in state propaganda.

In this respect, Meari, the student song club at Seoul National University, took quite a different road. Established in 1977, the club was a typical amateur sing-along club specializing in campus song. However, at the invitation of Kim Min-ki, some of its members took part in the recording of the song-drama (*noraegŭk*) or song-exorcism (*noraegut*) *Kongjang ŭi pulbit* (The light of the factory). This work, which chronicled the oppression and struggle of workers attempting to organize a trade union, was recorded on "illegal" cassettes clandestinely distributed by the Urban Industrial Mission (Tosisanŏpsŏn'gyohoe) located in Yŏngdŭngp'o, a working-class district in southwest Seoul. After this experience, these club members quickly became politicized and went on to produce three cassette tapes consisting of music produced by themselves and by others during 1979–80. In short, the release of these illegal cassette tapes proved to be a pivotal moment in the club's political progress.

Two years after *Kongjang ŭi pulbit*, another landmark release appeared. This recording came not from Seoul but from Gwangju, a year after the bloody suppression of the democratic movement in May 1980. *Nŏkp'uri pich'ŭi kyŏrhonsik* (Repose of souls: The wedding of the light) was an illegal cassette recording of the eponymous song-exorcism that contained what was arguably the most famous protest anthem arising from the Gwangju Uprising, "Nimŭl wihan haengjin'gok" (The march for the beloved). The work portrayed a marriage of souls between the spokesperson for the civil army during the Gwangju democratic movement and a labor movement activist. It was directed by the novelist Hwang Sŏk-yŏng, who at the time ran the drama troupe Kwangdae (Clown) in Gwangju, and was recorded by a collective of local amateur musicians. Illegal copies of the cassette tapes were clandestinely distributed outside Gwangju starting in 1982.

This defiant practice of producing and distributing illegal tapes marked the beginning of radical politicization of the university song clubs in the 1980s. University campuses rapidly became the main space of progressive politics and student activism. The clubs acquired a clear political orientation, not only collecting existing folk songs but also writing new protest songs themselves. In addition, their performances also transformed from being simple musical concerts to full-fledged musical dramas designed to convey certain political narratives. These practices soon spread to universities throughout the country. Song clubs built ties with other organized social movements. In these circumstances, the university clubs began to sing a very different repertoire of songs. At first, these new songs were spread by word of mouth or songbooks, and then later by concerts and cassette recordings. Singing became a strategy used by the university song clubs in order to spread political consciousness effectively. In the process, the adapted term *folk song* was replaced with the indigenized term *people's song* (*minjung kayo*). While still based on the practice of sing-alongs, in terms of political orientation and cultural disposition, it became the exact opposite of the early folk song of the 1960s.

The division of folk song into campus song and minjung kayo did not become clear-cut until 1980. In fact, some of those who became activists in the minjung kayo movement participated in campus song festivals before 1980. Thus it can be said that the division was the inevitable effect of political crisis, especially the bloody Gwangju massacre in 1980. It only became clear much later that there had existed a gray zone between the black and the white (i.e., "mass" and "people") and that not a small part of minjung kayo was short-lived due to its close "alignment" with progressive political and social movements in the 1980s. What is certain is that the songs that would enjoy a tenacious hold on Korean public life are ones ranging from pre-minjung singer-songwriter Han Tae-su to post-minjung singer Kim Kwang-sŏk, who were not aligned with any kind of politics. Could this perhaps be an example of sonic nonalignment in the microcosm of a divided and closed nation?

AS PREVIOUS STUDIES have shown, imported folk music took different life paths in different parts of East and Southeast Asia during the 1970s.[21] It was transformed into a genre of political song aligned with revolutionary movements in Thailand, while it evolved into a popular genre (as "new music") in Japan. What is specific to the South Korean case is that it was neither aligned with a political movement, nor did it become established as a popular genre in the same period. Yet it would be an exaggeration to say that 1970s South Korean folk represented sonic nonalignment. As a rigidly anti-Communist nation, South Korea never took part in the political Non-Aligned Movement, and most Korean folk artists were actually pro-West in their cultural attitudes.

Nonetheless, the independent ethos of 1970s South Korean folk song, at least in its protest branch, show that it tried to construct a distinct music culture for the nation (and its people) rather than merely imitating Western music. At the same time, they imagined "another" West in music, not the version that was portrayed in popular entertainment and state propaganda—the rich, strong, and free world—but another version characterized by conscience, principles, and integrity. This chapter has explored the ironic situation in which the music culture that stemmed from what was essentially a Western, mostly US imperialist institution (the Christian church) became a central means of expression for an alternative form of nationalism in South Korea in the context of the Cold War.

However, it is also unfortunately true that a division emerged within the folk community, one overdetermined by the Cold War politics of an authoritarian regime. If decadent (t'oep'ye) was a serious misnomer for cosmopolitan desires emerging in a claustrophobic society, rebellious (puron) was likewise a serious misnomer for nationalist aspirations arising under conditions of national division. The two were disconnected as the 1970s passed, and the division was consolidated during the 1980s. Indeed, the partition of the folk community is not unrelated to the tension between pro- and anti-US stances that still pervades Korean society. As a result, this history still raises pertinent questions about the struggle for cultural nonalignment not only in popular music but also in Korean culture at large.

Let me return to the movie *JSA* (*Joint Security Area*). What triggers the tragic shooting in the film is the sound of an electric guitar riff played through a malfunctioning cassette player. In the ending, the orchestral sound of a Russian traditional folk song ("The Rush Light") is played when an American official talks with the North Korean soldiers. In between these two scenes, the sad melody of the aforementioned South Korean folk song "Puch'iji anhŭn p'yŏnji" (The unmailed letter) is played as background music. Can the message in the letter be sent to North Korea as well as to the USA and USSR?

IT MIGHT NOT be out of place here to introduce Lee Sooman (aka Yi Su-man), the most successful impresario of so-called K-pop and the founder of SM Entertainment—a company that has with semiautomatic regularity produced idols of the genre. It might surprise readers to find out that he was a 1970s folksinger. Starting out as half of the folk-rock duo Sawŏl kwa owŏl (April and May) in the early 1970s, and following that with a career as a solo singer with minor success in the mid to late 1970s, he definitely belonged to the folk song community. Although labeling him "a product of the campus-led 'song movement'" is misleading and unpersuasive, his name does appear in the handwritten acknowledgments included by Yang Hŭi-ŭn on her second full-length album (1972), which deserves its status as a seminal protest folk record (see figure 4.9).[22]

The story of K-pop, idols, and SM Entertainment deserves a lengthy description, elaborate theorization, and critical evaluation beyond the scope of this chapter. Yet it would be safe to say that K-pop has become an essential part of South Korea's "new nationalism," which was recently conceptualized as "globalized cultural nationalism." According to Emma Campbell, this "new nationalism" is different from old forms, both official and popular, in terms of its reluctant, even negative, attitude toward reunification and the notion of "one Korea."[23] Setting aside the relevance of the risky qualifier "new," the current popular sentiments of the young generation in South Korea are different from those of previous generations, which directly or indirectly touched on the issue of reunification as a national agenda.[24]

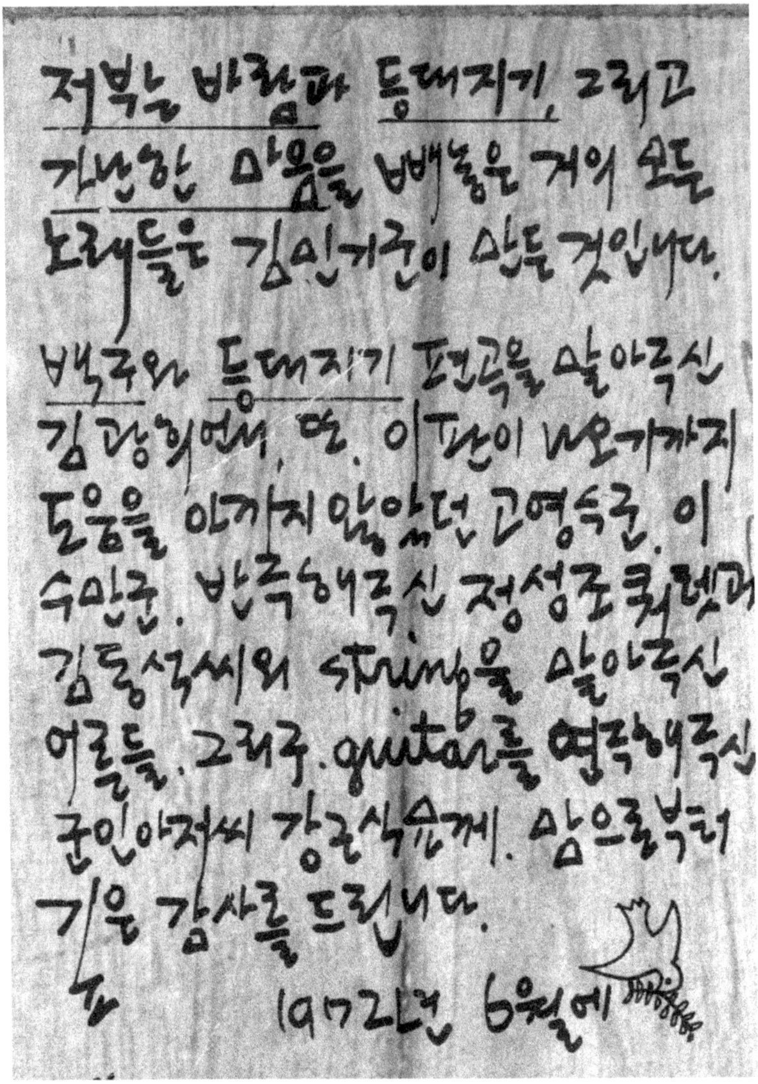

저희는 바람과 등대지기, 그리고
가난한 마음을 배불은 거의 모든
노래들은 김민기군이 만든 것입니다.

백구와 등대지기 편곡을 맡아주신
김광희언니, 또, 이판이 나오기까지
도움을 아끼지 않았던 고영수군, 이
수만군. 반주해주신 정성조쿼텟과
김동성씨의 string을 맡아주신
어른들. 그리고. guitar를 연주해주신
군인아저씨 강근식유께. 맘으로부터
기운 감사를 드립니다.

1972년 6월에

FIGURE 4.9. A rare moment when Kim Min-ki, the pioneer of people's song, and Lee Soo-man, the industry mogul, are mentioned together on the back cover of a record.

Rather than enumerating the relation between K-pop and the new nationalism embraced by South Korean youth, I would like to share a scene from the documentary *I Am* (2012) that chronicles the global advance of SM Entertainment's products. In this scene, Lee prays sincerely with his eyes closed, together with a group of entertainers about to go on stage: "We are gathered here, representing the Republic of Korea and its people." It is clear that this prayer ritual is close to a Christian one. One of the roots of South Korean popular music in general, and of the folk song in particular, was still lingering in his mind in spite of the complicated and divergent routes that music took through several decades. The irony pointed out throughout this chapter still persists. However, what remains is not a critical reflexivity but an inverted recursivity.

NOTES

Korean and East Asian personal names begin with the family name (usually one syllable), followed by the given name (usually two syllables). This chapter respects this order in transcribing Korean and East Asian names. However, in the cases of Korean names, it adds a hyphen (-) between the two syllables of the given name in order to avoid prolonged sounds, although this is not used in Korean writing. This method of transcription also corresponds with the McCune-Reischauer Romanization System, which has been standard in international Korean Studies. It is also applied consistently to Korean words other than personal names. Exceptions to the McCune-Reischauer Romanization System are those Korean authors who have published in English using a different spelling in their publications and internationally known names. For instance, "Park Chung Hee" would be rendered Pak Chŏng-hŭi according to the McCune-Reischauer Romanization System but the former has been used. The same principle applies to geographical designations. For instance, "Gwangju" is used instead of "Kwangju." This work was supported by the Ministry of Education of the Republic of Korea and the National Research Foundation of Korea (nrf-2018s1a6a3a01080743).

1 Han Tae-su is undoubtedly the first folk singer-songwriter in South Korea, but he could not release a record until 1974. "Haruachi'm" (One morning) was supposed to be included in his first album but was not expected to pass censorship. It was finally released when the record was reissued in 1989. It was also rerecorded for his third album, which marked his comeback after sojourning in the US for more than a decade.
2 Michael K. Bourdaghs, *Sayonara Amerika, Sayonara Nippon: A Geopolitical Prehistory of J-Pop* (New York: Columbia University Press, 2012), 159–60.
3 *Sinminyo* or *shin minyo* is a style of popular music whose origin is traced back to the colonial period and that continued to enjoy popularity until the 1960s. See Hilary Finchum-Sung, "New Folksongs: Shin Minyo of the 1930s," in *Korean Pop Music: Riding the Wave*, ed. Keith Howard (Folkstone, Kent, UK: Global Oriental, 2006), 10–20. Not surprisingly, a genre named with the same Chinese characters and a similar pronunciation existed in Japan, too.

4   Ae-kyung Park, "Modern Folksong and People's Song (*Minjung Kayo*)," in *Made in Korea: Studies in Popular Music*, ed. Hyunjoon Shin and Seung-ah Lee (New York: Routledge, 2017), 92. Adaptation is a type of covering, including in most cases a Korean translation of English lyrics with the original melody left untouched. Though "cover" has no equivalent Korean word, "adaptation" is called *pŏnan*, which is still used in journalistic and academic discourses. As one interviewee insightfully argued, the naming of folk as a music genre itself as well as its cultural practices are works of adaptation. Interview with singer-songwriter Song Ch'ang-sik, October 19, 2002.

5   Hyunjoon Shin and Tung-hung Ho, "Translation of 'America' during the Early Cold War Period: A Comparative Study on the History of Popular Music in South Korea and Taiwan," *Inter-Asia Cultural Studies* 10, no. 1 (2009): 83–102.

6   Shunya Yoshimi, "'America' as Desire and Violence: Americanization in Postwar Japan and Asia in the Cold War," trans. David Bust, *Inter-Asia Culture Studies* 4, no. 3 (2003): 443.

7   Pil Ho Kim and Hyunjoon Shin, "The Birth of 'Rok': Cultural Imperialism, Nationalism, and the Glocalization of Rock Music in South Korea, 1964–1975," *Positions: East Asia Cultures Critique* 18 (2010): 199–230.

8   A survey of 170 albums (including 1,773 songs) released by folk singers between 1970 and 1976 found there were 513 cover songs. They comprise 28.9 percent of the total songs recorded. The percentage was higher in the early period: 65.9 percent (58 out of 88 songs) in 1970 and 61 percent (125 out of 205 songs) in 1971. Key-young Park, "Isik kŭrigo tongnip: Han'guk modŏn p'ok'ŭ ŭmak ŭi sŏngnip kwajŏng 1968nyŏn–1975nyŏn [Plantation and independence: Development and completion of Korean modern folk music 1968–1975]" (master's thesis, Dankook University, 2003). On the case of the song "Sŏul Hanŭl" (Seoul sky, 1974) by Yang Pyŏng-chip, a Korean adaptation of Woody Guthrie's "New York Town" (1961/89), which is in turn a cover of Blind Lemon Jefferson's "One Dime Blues" (1927), see Rosaleen Rhee, "The Shifting Censorship and Emergent Politics of South Korean P'ok'ŭ music in the 1970s" (paper presented at the Association for Asian Studies [AAS] Annual Conference, Denver, CO, March 21–24, 2019). In the actual presentation, the title was revised to "Tracing Songs of Urban Plight from American Blues to Korean P'ok'ŭ."

9   The adaptation of chanson and canzone can be heard in the recordings of Ch'oe Yang-suk and Yi Yong-pok, respectively, though they were lumped together into the category of folk. The attraction to continental Europe is reflected in the names of listening halls such as C'est Si Bon, Die Schöne, and Renaissance. The adaptations included tunes from Mexico ("La Golondrina"), Israel ("Hatikva"), New Zealand ("Pokarekare Ana"), and South Africa ("Mbube"). In many cases, South Koreans do not know the origins of the songs, even while they can sing them with Korean lyrics.

10   On Kim's memories about receiving the label of puron, see Kim Min-ki, transcribed by Yi To-sŏng, "Kim Min-ki: Sidae ka naŭn kiin kasu" [Kim Min-ki: Eccentric singer of our time], *Dong-A Ilbo*, May 23, 1993.

11   Haebaragi was a vital location for another strand of singer-songwriters such as Yi Chŏng-sŏn and Kim Ŭi-chŏl.

12   In 1972 a series of concerts called Maettol (Milestone) were held, where newly created songs were performed and one of the concerts was released as a live record

also titled *Maettol*. These songs brought together lyrics written by poets and novelists and music composed by young folk singers. In 1972 another compilation record, called *Uuridŭl* (We), was released, sharing a similar ethos with that of *Maettol*.

13   Kim Min-ki wrote the Christian hymn-style songs "Ach'im Isŭl" (Morning dew, 1971) and "Sangnoksu" (Evergreen tree, 1977) that were popularized by the recording and performance by Yang Hŭi-ŭn. For more details about Kim's legacy, see Ch'ang-nam Kim, ed., *Kim Min-ki* (Seoul: Hanul, 1986); and Okon Hwang, "Kim Min-ki and the Making of a Legend," in *Made in Korea: Studies in Popular Music*, ed. Hyunjoon Shin and Seung-ah Lee (New York: Routledge, 2017), 133–41. Hwang's assertion that "the defining factor that established Kim Min-ki . . . as the legend was, ironically, the autocratic regime of Park Chung Hee" (140), however, seems to understate the complexity of the situation.

14   Publicity material for Chung-Shin Park, quoted in *Protestantism and Politics in Korea* (Seattle: University of Washington Press, 2003). On Protestant Christianity during the 1960–1980s, which "expanded at a rate unparalleled in the annals of church history," see Yong-Shin Park, "Protestant Christianity and Its Place in a Changing Korea," *Social Compass* 47, no. 4 (2000): 507. As these authors demonstrate, it should be noted that the mainstream Protestant Christianity was largely pro–authoritarian regime and anti–North Korea, with the exception of some small liberal and progressive factions.

15   On theories and practices of *minjung*, see Nancy Abelman, "Minjung Theory and Practice," in *Cultural Nationalism in East Asia: Representation and Identity*, ed. Harumi Befu (Berkeley: University of California Press, 1993), 139–68; and Namhee Lee, *The Making of Minjung: Democracy and the Politics of Representation in South Korea* (Ithaca, NY: Cornell University Press, 2007). As the title of the edited Lee volume suggests, *minjung* is invested with "cultural nationalism."

16   Most of the canonical records by the folk singers were produced by Orient, an independent record company run by legendary producer Na Hyŏn-ku. In these records, Tongbang ŭi bit (Light of the East), the band led by guitarist Kang Kŭn-sik, produced a creative and experimental sound. Its status can be compared to that of the Caramel Mama/Tin Pan Alley studio musician group in Japan during the same period. One difference is that Kang's band was forced to disband due to the marijuana incident mentioned later. On Caramel Mama/Tin Pan Alley, see Bourdaghs, *Sayonara Amerika, Sayonara Nippon*, 178–86.

17   The beginning, evolution, and conclusion of the debate are well summarized in Song Ŭn-yŏng, "Taejung munhwa hyŏnsang ŭrosŏ ŭi Ch'oe In-ho sosŏl: 1970nyŏndae ch'ŏngnyŏn munhwa/munhak ŭi sŭt'ail kwa sobi p'ungsok" [Choi Inho's novel as a phenomenon of mass culture: The style and consumption of youth culture/literature in 1970s Korea], *Sanghŏhakpo* 15 (2005): 419–45; and Hŏ Su, "1970 nyŏndae ch'ŏngnyŏnmunhwaron" [The discourse on 1970s youth culture], in *Nonjaeng ŭro pon han'guk sahoe 100 nyŏn* [100 years of Korean society seen from debates], ed. Yŏksabip'yŏng p'yŏnjip wiwŏnhoe (Seoul: Yŏksabip'yŏngsa, 2011), 318–24. Here I would like to address one point: the reluctant attitude shown by vanguard student movements as represented in university newspapers. What is striking is that the movement was suspicious of, or even hostile to, "the discourse on youth culture"

that was championed by literary critic Kim Pyŏng-ik. Kim wrote a short newspaper article, "Onŭllal ŭi chŏlmŭn usangdŭl" (These days' young icons), *Dong-A Ilbo*, March 29, 1974, which ignited much social discussion. What the students resented most is the fact that the supporters of youth culture celebrated singers such as Yi Chang-hŭi and Yang Hŭi-ŭn. One of the students who intervened in the debate regarded the singers as *ttanttara*, which is a derisive word for pop entertainers. Those who were celebrated as icons of youth culture by Kim were condemned as symbols of "decadent" (*t'oep'yejŏk*) and "cosmopolitan" (*k'osŭmop'ollit'an*) culture, which were seen as being polar opposites of the "progressive" (*chinch'wijŏk*) and "nationalist" (*minjokchuŭija*), as can be seen in "Chigŭm ŭn chinjŏnghan moksori ka tŭllyŏya hal ttaeda" (Now it is the time that the true voice should be heard), an article published in *Taehaksinmun* (*Seoul National University News*), June 3, 1974. In all seriousness, other participants in the debate suggested that the model for youth culture in Korea should not be that kind of pop culture but *hwarangdo*, a troupe of elite youth from the ancient Shilla dynasty!

18 On the discussion of youth culture in mainstream media, see No Chae-bong, Yi Ŏ-ryŏng, Ch'oe In-ho, and Han Wan-sang, "T'oron: Yuhaeng inya panhang inya" [Discussion: Fashion or rebellion], *Sindonga*, July 1974.

19 For a more detailed and quantitative account of the popular music purge campaign and the marijuana incident, see Sin Hyŏn-chun, Yi Yong-u, and Ch'oe Chi-sŏn, *Hanguk pap ŭi kogohak 1970* [The archaeology of 1970s Korean pop] (Seoul: Hangil Art, 2005), 180–215.

20 On the Campus Song Festival and the invention of campus song, see Hyunjoon Shin and Pil Ho Kim, "Birth, Death, and Resurrection of Group Sound Rock," in *The Korean Popular Culture Reader*, ed. Kyung Hyun Kim and Youngmin Choe (Durham, NC: Duke University Press, 2014), 275–95.

21 On the different routes, paths, and meanings that folk music took in Thailand, Japan, and Taiwan, see Pamela A. Myers-Moro, "Songs for Life: Leftist Thai Popular Music in the 1970s," *Journal of Popular Culture* 20 (1986): 93–113; Yasuko Sato, "Retorosupekutivu na kakumei: 70-nendai fōku-songu" [Retrospective revolution: Folk songs in the 1970s], in *Sengo seron no media shakaigaku* [The sociology of media on postwar popular opinion], ed. Takumi Sato (Tokyo: Kashiwa shobo, 2003), 167–92; and Tung-hung Ho, "The Social Formation of Mandarin Popular Music Industry in Taiwan" (PhD diss., Lancaster University, 2003).

22 Keith Howard, "Exploding Ballads: The Transformation of Korean Pop Music," in *Global Goes Local: Popular Culture in Asia*, ed. Timothy J. Craig and Richard King (Vancouver: University of British Columbia Press, 2002), 93.

23 Emma Campbell, *South Korea's New Nationalism: The End of "One Korea"?* (Boulder, CO: First Forum, 2016), 3.

24 For an agreeable but debatable interpretation of the South Korean nationalism associated with K-pop, see chapter 3 in this volume.

5. COSMOPOLITANISM, VERNACULAR COSMOPOLITANISM, AND SOUND ALIGNMENTS

Covers and Cantonese Cover Songs in 1960s Hong Kong

HON-LUN YANG

Though thousands of miles away from the center of the Cold War, British Hong Kong was not spared from its impact. In fact, in the 1950s and 1960s, the tension of the two ideological camps was channeled into two conflicting political forces locally, the left wing associated with the People's Republic of China (PRC) and the right with nationalist Taiwan and the West.[1] The cultural arena in Hong Kong, among an array of other establishments, was picked as an ideological and political battleground. The local film industry, for instance, was marked by a clear left-right divide in funding sources and the types of films produced.[2] The genre "youth movie musical," which emerged in the second half of the 1960s, was connected to the right—it was indebted to Western influences not only in the genre's origin but also in the films' themes and music.[3] For instance, many of the songs used in this genre's films were covers of Western hits—in the sense that their melodies were adapted to newly written Cantonese lyrics and sung by the film's actors and actresses.[4]

As has been pointed out in this volume's introduction, "covers"—the act of resinging and recomposing Western hits—was a common phenomenon in Asia during the Cold War.[5] How do we interpret this phenomenon of "covers" in Asia? Aside from treating it as a sign of ideological and sound alignments to the West, what other meanings did the act of covering and the production of cover songs convey, particularly when the covers not only involved resinging but also entailed a recomposing of the original?

Dredge Käng points out in his study of Thai K-pop cover dances that covering presents "an aspiration for development and the instantiation of participation in a new cosmopolitan Asia."[6] The act of covering is indeed a cosmopolitan endeavor, a form of cross-cultural participation. In addition, I would also like to propose that covering in the form of recomposing, particularly in the case of cover songs, is a form of "vernacular cosmopolitanism." The process of remaking and reconsuming Western songs in Hong Kong movie musicals, I want to emphasize, inevitably turned these songs into something else, something that reflected the local context—local traditions, aesthetic aspirations, musical practices, and people's sociocultural experiences. I show in this chapter that some of the songs I have studied displayed antagonism toward the West in their newly composed lyrics, while others conveyed localness in their musical adaptations that embodied the complex relationships between Asia and the West.

As has been pointed out in a number of recent Cold War studies, Asia's relationship with the two ideological camps was far from straightforward.[7] While the impacts of the Cold War were far reaching in Asia's nation-building process and economic development, local factors also played a role in shaping each locale's developmental trajectory, particularly in the cultural front. Thus there is a need to examine/reexamine Asia's recent development from a more Asian-centered perspective—to try "to de–cold war" as a possible approach.[8] My study in this chapter, in a way, exemplifies this attempt to "de–cold war." I do not deny the importance of the Cold War in shaping Asian culture in the past half a century, but I want to emphasize the local forces at play by focusing on the interaction of contrasting ideologies, values, and cultural traditions in the formation of local cultural forms such as the cover songs in Hong Kong. While part of this chapter examines the cultural context that led to the covering of Western hits and their adaptation in local cover songs in movie musicals, my objective is to unravel the complexities and localities embedded in these cover songs beyond the notion of sound alignment to the West.

Cosmopolitanism, the Cold War, and Sound Alignments

To understand the act of covering in Hong Kong, it is necessary to understand the city's colonial history, which bred the city's unique brand of cosmopolitanism and contrasts with the cosmopolitanism seen in trendsetting megacities such as New York and Paris, shaped by immigration and the emergence of diasporic culture(s).[9] As pointed out by various scholars, cosmopolitanism is an elusive concept as it is not a known entity, nor is it a clearly established practice.[10] Cosmopolitanism, which originated in the Greek words *cosmo* and *polis*, meaning "world city," or Diogenes's idea of the "citizen of the world," suggests a city culture defined by worldliness as a result of its residents' sense of openness that transcends local and city-state affiliations in favor of universal identification.[11]

Hong Kong as an Asian metropolis and cosmopolitan city was intricately connected to the Cold War. Once referred to as one of Asia's four tigers or dragons, Hong Kong, together with South Korea, Singapore, and Taiwan, enjoyed a period of rapid economic growth during the Cold War era, which was credited by some to the neoliberal policies implemented as a result of the colonial government's political alignment with the West.[12] Naturally, the hundreds of thousands of Chinese émigrés who fled from Communist China to Hong Kong in the early 1950s—bringing along skills and capitals essential for the colony's development—played a part in constructing Hong Kong's "cosmoscape," which, in addition to "constituting the architecture of global flows," offers "a performative frame for commodities, transforming things through a variety of practices, discourses, and images into cosmopolitan objects."[13]

In this sense, the widespread transmission of Western popular music in Hong Kong in the 1960s was a mark of its "cosmoscape"—it testified to Hong Kong's position as a node in the geopolitical network of the West as well as to its transnational popular music industry, distinguishing the city from the PRC, where popular music was banned.[14] The popularity of Western music in Hong Kong at the time was due to a number of reasons. First, as a colony, Hong Kong had always been more receptive toward Western culture than other Chinese cities, with the exception perhaps of pre-1949 Shanghai. The openness of Hong Kong's younger generation toward Western culture, both pop and serious, stood for Hong Kong's cosmopolitan outlook and the colonized Hongkongers' aspiration toward the culture of the colonizer. Second, this phase of Hong Kong's cultural development coincided with the maturation of a new generation of youngsters whose parents came to Hong Kong in the early 1950s, and who were brought up in Hong Kong's Western education system. Third, the diffusion of popular music represented a democratization process that began to burgeon in Hong Kong at the time. Unlike its classical music counterpart, which was largely associated with the social elite in the colony, popular music was transmitted largely through the media—such as radio stations and the consumption of music products such as LPs—and was accessible to a much broader public, particularly to those with less monetary means.

During the 1960s, Western superstars such as the Rolling Stones, Cliff Richard, and the Beatles were extremely popular among Hong Kong's teenagers.

The Beatles' 1964 visit was reported to have created something close to a riot, as did the Searchers' 1966 visit.[15] Just as in the West and many other parts of Asia, Beatlemania left its marks on Hong Kong's soundscape, evident in the proliferation of local bands after 1964. Notable ones included Fabulous Echoes, Teddy Robin and the Playboys, and the Lotus, all of which covered (resang) Beatles' songs as well as the songs of other rock and roll groups. Pop singers such as Irene Ryder, Teresa Carpio, and Frances Yip thrived in covering Western pop.[16] For instance, the local singer Joe Junior, nicknamed "Hong Kong's Golden Boy," admitted his admiration of the British singer Cliff Richard in a recent interview.[17] His 1968 album *Tribute* was a salute to his idol that entailed his covering/resinging Richard's songs.[18] In a concert held on August 15, 2014, he also covered Cliff Richard's "The Minute You're Gone," "When the Girl in Your Arms," and "Visions."[19]

The six-CD box set *Legend of the Super Voices 101: Hong Kong's Muzikland of the 60/70s*, released in 2012 by Universal-Pathé, documented this unique phase of Hong Kong's popular music soundscape, locally referred to as "Hong Kong–style Western pop" 港式西洋風. As pointed out in the preface to the album's accompanying booklet, the act of covering/resinging Western songs was a process of self-learning that paved the way for the development of Cantopop, a genre that emerged after the mid-1970s and was recognized as an emblem of local identity: "At the time, without the internet or music downloads, as many of the singers of the older generation remember, it took them a long time and much effort to notate the lyrics, the melody, as well as the accompaniment. That is, to cover a song also requires a great deal of effort.... Most important of all, this phase of 'Hong Kong–Style Western Pop' was a cradle that nurtured the first generation of local musicians and movie makers."[20]

Hong Kong singers of this period were indeed "cosmopolites," "someone in possession and command of the cultural knowledge and skill to discern, appreciate and use the field of cultural difference."[21] Through mastering the music and lyrics of Western songs, these local musicians became the city's own superstars, enjoying unprecedented success as local idols, and played a part in transforming the city's soundscape. While cosmopolites are often criticized as urban elites, Hong Kong musicians both conformed to this perception as well as challenged it, because even as local cosmopolites, many of them did not come from privileged social backgrounds but instead grew up as children of immigrants or as first-generation immigrants themselves.[22] The cosmopolitan zeitgeist and their ability to grasp the opportunities of the moment were what brought them to popular music.

Cover Songs as Empty Containers of New Meanings

The boom in Hong Kong musicians covering/resinging Western pop songs was short-lived. Local singers turned to Cantopop after the early 1970s. Western popular music's decline in Hong Kong was a result of the emergence of a local identity, which was better captured in Cantonese cover songs that had Cantonese lyrics set to Western hit tunes. This form of "covering"—fitting lyrics to preexisting melodies—was a well-established practice locally. For instance, in traditional theatrical forms, the practice was known as *diaoji*/diuhgei 調寄, the term literally meaning attaching [words] to a tune. While the original melody served as a creative framework, the re-creativity was what defined the aesthetic value of the new product, in part because in traditional Chinese music practice, the performance is often valued more than the original composition and is expected to entail a degree of re-creation.[23]

The first notable and indeed extremely successful example was "Fei go dit lok hang keui" 飛哥跌落坑渠 (Teddy boy in the gutter), which appeared in the 1958 Cantonese-language movie *Leung so yau dei yuk* 兩傻遊地獄 (*Two Fools in Hell*), its tune based on the theme song of the film *Three Coins in the Fountain* (1954).[24] According to the actor-producer Tang Kee-Chan 鄧寄塵 of *Two Fools in Hell*, the idea of covering, fitting Cantonese lyrics to a Western song, arose as part of his aim to refashion the movie industry's practice of merely using Cantonese ditties, which he considered a bit stale.[25]

The way Hong Kong musicians saw Western hits coincides with various scholars' views that commodity can be looked at as objectified containers of meanings; that is, the commodities can be taken as holding no meanings of their own, or their original meanings can be stripped away entirely to be reconstructed and reinterpreted by those who want to engage with them.[26] Popular music, which has long been seen as a form of commodity and which is often marketed to places beyond its source of production, is inevitably appropriated in an array of ways, such being the nature of music consumption. Covering, the act of both resinging and recomposing Western hits, is a case in point. The resulting product shows how a song's original sonic quality, its intended meaning, and its targeted audience group can be totally reconstructed.

The lyrics of "Teddy Boy in the Gutter," which are written in Cantonese slang to poke fun at the mores of society, provide a good example of "meaning reconstruction" in the process of re-creation. Through this process, what was originally a love song was turned into a satirical local ditty. The term *teddy boy* alludes to those who sold out to Western cultural influences, such as listening to Western popular music or dressing in Western outfits, which were deemed rebellious traits of teddy boys and teddy girls. In the lyrics, the teddy boys' and girls' wearing cologne or perfume is compared to the smell of ammonia and their dance steps to that of a toad, and youngsters are warned to keep a distance from these "bad influences," as their excessive dancing will end in breaking their noses or tumbling down:

飛哥跌落坑渠 飛女睇見流淚
似醬鴨臭腥攻鼻 飛女夾硬扶住佢
飛哥跌落坑渠 飛女心痛流淚
臭夾壓果 d 滋味 飛女索著唔順氣
索野索著 ammonia 跳舞好似隻彭其
應該跌落坑渠 百厭終歸會跌
猛咁跳盞僕猛
咁跳盞僕崩鼻一交撞直唔順氣難下

Teddy boy falls in the gutter, teddy girl cries at the sight
Stinks his duck-like stench, reluctantly, teddy girl supports him
Teddy boy falls in the gutter, teddy girl cries brokenheartedly
Terrible is his rotten stench, unwillingly, teddy girl smells it
He smells like ammonia and dances like a toad
He should fall into the gutter, if he continues to be annoying
He should fall into the gutter, if he continues to be annoying
He dances too much, he will hurt his nose tumbling down, he would be so upset, and so upset

The popularity of the song is evidenced by the issuing of an LP named after the movie in 1959.[27] The film's sequel, *Leung so yau tin tong* 兩傻遊天堂 (*Two Fools in Heaven*), reuses "Teddy Boy in the Gutter" and also includes a cover version of Harry Belafonte's "Banana Boat Song" retitled as "Yat san ngaih" 一身蟻 (Ants all over the body), its lyrics poking fun at the swinging body movement of Western dances, which are said to look as though the dancer was bitten by ants.[28]

唉唷唉唷 週身郁蹄得一身都蟻
拮得猶如用利錐拮入格肋底
拮一拮拮得郁身郁勢
拮得痕痕癢癢真犀利似錐仔
拮幾拮拮得西身西勢
西下西下 西幾西西甩呢一身蟻
郁下郁下 心急急急得擺手擺勢
蟻咬暗暗抵咯 詐詐諦諦 (重複)

Aiya, aiya, the body moves as ants all over
Pinch the armpit as by an awl
Pinch and pinch, pinch the body moves
Itchy when it pinches as though by an awl
Pinch and pinch, pinch the body swings
Swing and swing to get rid of the ants
Swing and swing to get rid of the ants
Move and move so anxiously that move the hands
Ant bites, putting it up, masquerading [repeat]

It is interesting to note that not every cover song from the period was antagonistic toward the West. The tone of the lyrics was dependent upon the producers' ideological outlook. For instance, another cover of the "Banana Boat Song," titled "Gou go hei mouh" 高歌起舞 (Sing and dance), released in 1959, revealed a different attitude as is evident in the following passage, which shows a strong alignment with the West—praising the dancing body and its youthful vitality, regarding them as signs of "progress": "Sing loud and start dance / Let's dance a calypso / Throw away the troubles / Dance calypso daily.... You see times do make progress and never get old / So new things you have to know."[29]

Comparing cover songs from the late 1950s to those of the late 1960s, we clearly see a change in attitude toward Western culture. This can be taken as a sign of the colony's heightened cosmopolitan outlook as a result of the Cold War. The satirical tone in the earlier songs was replaced by one that embraced Western culture with enthusiasm. The three cover songs included in the film *Fei chaak gam si maau* 飛賊金絲貓 (*The Golden Cat*) (1967) provide good examples. The song "Git buhn yauh cheun" 結伴遊春 (Spring outing), a cover of Cliff Richard's "Summer Holiday," is a case in point. Written in a style less slangy than its earlier counterparts and depicting the happiness of an outing in spring, the song accompanies an outing sequence in the film and is semi-integrated into the film narrative. The audience first hears it as nondiegetic music that backs the sequence but then is led to see that it is perhaps sung by the two protagonists during their outing. The lighthearted mood and feel of the original song with its celebration of the joyfulness of summer holiday fits its adapted screen soundscape well, conveying the two protagonists' youthful happiness. Even though the lyrics of the cover are not a direct translation of the original, they do share its sentiments of youthfulness: "The cold breeze blowing and the flowers blooming / Dragonflies and butterflies around the flowers / The meadows and hills / Green mountains and clear streams / Scenes of spring we take into our eyes." Nonetheless, the Cantonese lyrics also convey a didactic message—an exhortation to youth not to waste their time: "Youths should not be lagging / Should be motivated / Hard work should not be put aside / Happy youth full of laughter / Youth is full of dreams / Singing hearts embracing loving faces / Songs of happiness everywhere." This seems to contradict the carefree attitude conveyed in the original song about going on holiday and skipping work for a couple of weeks.

When one scrutinizes the emergence of cover songs, particularly in movie musicals, it becomes clear that this "mapping process" was what the film producers and songwriters tapped into. As suggested by Michael Bourdaghs, the process of music consumption is a mapping process in that the experience of the music also affords us an imagination of the place and culture from which it originated.[30] Those who were familiar with these cover songs' origins could readily relate them to where the songs originated and thus took extra pleasure in their newly rendered localness. But to those who had not heard the originals, these cover songs would appear as genuinely local, their lyrics articulating local sentiments and values. In this regard, the notion of "cosmopolitanism" falls short as an explication for the complexities in Hong Kong cover songs, which can be better unraveled through the more nuanced concept of "vernacular cosmopolitanism."

Vernacular Cosmopolitanism, Cover Songs, and Youth Movie Musicals

"Vernacular cosmopolitanism," as argued by Pnina Werbner, is a family of concepts that address some of the contradictions within the notion of "cosmopolitanism" as it arises in colonial and postcolonial societies—"cosmopolitan patriotism, rooted cosmopolitanism, cosmopolitan ethnicity, working-class cosmopolitanism, discrepant cosmopolitanism," to name just a few.[31] Homi Bhabha, who envisages colonial societies as at the margin of a global cosmopolitan community, coined the term to describe the various cosmopolitan-vernacular related contradictions that emerge in border zones such as Hong Kong.[32] Sheldon Pollock used the phrase *cosmopolitan vernacular* to describe the emergence of vernacular literatures in various parts of Southeast Asia from 1000 to 1500 amid the widespread dominance of Sanskrit, the cosmopolitan language of the time.[33] What Bhabha and Pollock noticed was the interplay of the cosmopolitan and the vernacular in many artifacts of postcolonial societies, entailing universal ideals recognizable as cosmopolitan versus place-specific features that are noticeably vernacular, which would be better accounted for with the concept of vernacular cosmopolitanism. The application of the concept to the analyses of border zones, I gather, should result in a much more nuanced reading of local features, allowing analysts to address controversial and contradictory issues pertinent to "cosmopolitanism."

For example, some of the contradictions embodied in the genre "youth movie musical" and the Cantonese cover songs mentioned above can be unraveled by applying the concept of vernacular cosmopolitanism. One readily available instance is the film *Colorful Youth*, released in 1966. Aside from the film's genre as an adaptation of the Western musical, the film's name also capitalized on the popularity of the British musical *Summer Holiday*.[34] When *Summer Holiday* was shown in Hong Kong in August 1963, its translated title was Choi sik ching cheun 彩色青春 (*Colorful Youth*).[35] Like its Western counterpart, *Colorful Youth* showcased a number of song and dance sequences. The two most popular hits from *Summer Holiday*, namely "Summer Holiday" and "La La La Song," though not covered in *Colorful Youth*, were covered in another movie, *The Golden Cat*. Nonetheless, the film's intended audience was not "cosmopolites," and the "cosmopolitanism" embedded in it did not represent genuine cultural values but instead a fabricated "utopia" intended for working-class young women.

Wong Yiu 黃堯, the director of *Colorful Youth*, made the film during the low tide of his career. As Wong explained, when he ran into a large number of young female factory workers in the district where he lived, he thought he could make films that would appeal to them.[36] Thanks to the Cold War, the number of factories in Hong Kong saw a six-fold increase from the early 1950s to the mid-1960s due to the global demand for cheap Asian products. This intense industrialization led to a spike in employment opportunities for young women to work in factories. The success of the genre in a way rescued Wong as well as the local Cantonese movie industry at a time when local mass culture was being challenged by the massive inflow of Western products.[37]

Wong was a "cosmopolite" who was not only very familiar with Western musicals but also was able to translate the Western form for local use, thereby creating a local version of the genre. The "cosmopolitan" outlook in the original films, with their glorification of youthfulness, universal values, and middle-class lifestyles, was particularly appealing to Asian elites. When these "cosmopolitan" phenomena were repackaged to fit the local context, rewritten into local narratives and conveyed in the local language, they could reach to even a working-class audience, the factory girls who were not meant to be "cosmopolites" but could still embrace certain "cosmopolitan" values and lifestyle traits. They thus became "working-class cosmopolites," an identity that was in contradiction to the original notion of "cosmopolites."

In *Colorful Youth* as well as in Wong's other movie musicals, the zeitgeist of the 1960s—the youth movement, the glorification of rock and roll, and the emergence of a middle-class lifestyle—were adapted to the local context. These were all cosmopolitan traits but did not necessarily suggest the locals' engagement with cosmopolitan values. Borrowing a rather clichéd notion, the screen world was a form of utopia that Wong constructed for his targeted audience, the female factory workers, to provide an escape from the mundaneness of life and even the social unrest of Hong Kong at the time.[38]

While the Beatles and the Searchers were teen idols for those young people receiving a Western/English education, two onscreen local teen idols—Connie Chan 陳寶珠 and Josephine Siao 蕭芳芳—were intended for young female factory workers. Through the characters they played in the movies, Chan and Siao became the embodiment of a projected cosmopolitan/middle-class persona. While growing up as child actresses in Kungfu movies during the previous decade, both Chan and Siao were able to reinvent themselves to ride the high tide of the zeitgeist created by the Cold War. Unlike female characters in previous movies who were generally victims of poverty and family abuse and who won spectators' sympathy rather than admiration, the new roles they played in these 1960s films were marked by "cosmopolitan" attributes, partaking of middle-class activities such as singing and dancing, going on outings, bowling, cycling, and partying—all lifestyles imported from the West. Such sequences were accompanied by the cover songs in the movies. While spectators could only vicariously experience these film characters' cosmopolitan experiences onscreen, many young women in Hong Kong at the time found their aspirations materialized in the roles played by Chan and Siao.[39] On- and off-screen, Chan and Siao gave their spectators the experience of a middle-class/cosmopolitan life they could only dream about. This aspirational lifestyle was conveyed through the characters they portrayed, such as student, clerk, private tutor, movie star, singer, dancer, flight attendant, reporter, and factory worker, to name but a few of the roles in these movie musicals. From a political perspective, these films conveyed the ideologies of the right, extolling the glamorized lifestyle of the capitalist world to a group of working-class laborers who were themselves victims of the former.

The fact that the female protagonists were embodiments of ideological alignment and that their singing and dancing were deployed as signifiers of a Western-inspired cosmopolitanism is worth pondering. Indeed, the two actresses were made to perform the "role of body," as icons of both cosmopolitan modernity and contemporary womanhood, which was no doubt commercially motivated to appeal to the genre's targeted audience.[40] Even though female protagonists in these films appeared to perform new gender roles of womanhood, the grip of patriarchy and its values are detectable in the films' narratives as well as the ways they use cover songs.

The song and dance sequences, for instance, were often written into the film narrative as a form of social critique. Josephine Siao's performance in *The Golden Cat* of the song "Fa giu bat chih yuhk yahn meih" 花嬌不似玉人媚 (The flower is not as pretty as the girl), a cover of the Searchers' "Love Potion No. 9," is a case in point.[41] In the film, she is disguised as a teddy girl and frequents night clubs, which gives her the opportunity to sing the song with lyrics that glorify dancing: "Let's sing songs pleasing to our ears / Twist our waist as swaying in spring breezes / Bright eyes and flushed cheeks are such beauties / Young girls in their magical dance movements." But in the movie narrative, she is mistaken for a "bad girl" and warned by her future lover that the night club is not a suitable place for her since it is frequented by bad people.

The contradictory messages in these movie musicals—on the one hand using cover songs to convey a sense of cosmopolitan modernity but on the other hand critiquing the occasions in which such modernity was delivered—are baffling. Such a contradiction could well be gender based. That is, while the female protagonists were deployed to be cosmopolitan and modern on screen through singing and dancing, they were also scripted to conform to traditionally expected gender roles, to be "good girls" in the narrative.[42] Such irony, in a way, is inevitable. After all, vernacular cosmopolitanism is complex, just as was the Cold War's impact on and relationship with Asia. Ingrained into Hong Kong's cultural psyche was a need to constantly negotiate and reposition itself in relationship to the two very different cultures it inherited from its motherland and the West. What is perhaps most cosmopolitan about Hong Kong lies in its ability to generate new cultural forms adapted from the West, such as the youth movie musicals and cover songs that express its unique vernacular cultural position.

THE YEAR 1974 WAS special for Hong Kong's popular music industry. It was marked by the release of *Gwai mah seung sing* 鬼馬雙星 (Games gamblers), the first Cantonese album by Sam Hui 許冠傑, showcasing authentic Cantonese rock and roll songs. The year was also marked by the popularity of Cantopop songs such as "Taih siu yan yuhn" 啼笑姻緣 (Unhappy marriage) by the composer Joseph Koo 顧嘉煇. The success of Hui and Koo marked the beginning of a new phase of popular music development in Hong Kong that can be regarded as constituting an "aesthetic cosmopolitanism." Songs from this era succeeded in fusing Cantonese lyrics to original melodies written by local composers in a style that showed an affinity for Western rock and pop. According to Motti Regev, with its aspiration to seemingly "universal" musical features, Cantopop, like other pop and rock genres from outside the West, is an example of aesthetic cosmopolitanism in that its songs share "wide common grounds in their aesthetic perceptions, expressive forms, and cultural practices."[43] It is important to note that both Hui and Koo were strongly influenced by American popular music styles. In fact, Hui had "covered" many Western hits with his band Lotus in the late 1960s before he became a Cantopop star, and he also fitted new lyrics to songs by Elvis Presley and the Beatles. Koo was a band leader who specialized in Mandopop prior to his studying at the Berklee College of Music in the 1960s. They both turned to Cantopop only in the 1970s when Western popular music and Mandopop faded in popularity.

Whether Cantopop is a manifestation of aesthetic cosmopolitanism and thus a sign of alignment with the West is up for debate. After all, its trajectory veers far away from cosmopolitan ideals and its relationship with the Cold War is far from straightforward. While the music might appear as familiar to Western ears in sonority, its success lies in its "localness." What defines its localness and gives it a strong local identity are its Cantonese lyrics and the local singing style that inevitably point to various contradictions in terms of Cold War sound alignment. Most of all, its localness has also prevented it from reaching out to a larger market, thus lessening its opportunity to become genuinely cosmopolitan by being consumed beyond the local space. The truth of Hong Kong's popular music scene, which has been dominated by Cantopop since the 1970s, is that the city's residents are perhaps the least cosmopolitan in the region in terms of their listening habits in the realm of popular music. In that regard, it is perhaps necessary to revisit the validity of "aesthetic cosmopolitanism" as a theoretical framework for examining popular music outside the West. At the same time, I would suggest "vernacular cosmopolitanism" as a better alternative to examine hybrid cultural forms in border zones such as Hong Kong since this type of frame affords a much higher degree of local-centeredness, as seen in my reading of Cantonese cover songs. Likewise, it is also necessary to reexamine the impact of the Cold War in Asia's musical fronts, especially regarding the issue of cultural homogeneity. But without a doubt, the presence of covers and cover songs in Hong Kong in the 1960s testified to a very special moment in world history as well as in Hong Kong's development. While Hong Kong singers' covering Western hits was an instantiation of local participation in the transnational musical soundscape, the articulation of a strong local identity in Cantonese cover songs pointed to the many contradictions in Cold War sound alignments that this volume unveils.

NOTES

1. In this chapter, song and film titles in the main text are transliterated using the Yale Cantonese romanization system to reflect actual pronunciation in Cantonese. Proper names are presented according to their local Hong Kong transliteration and/or in their English rendition. In the notes, all Chinese titles and publication venues are rendered in pinyin, with the exception of sources written in Cantonese for which the Yale romanization system is used.

2. For scholarship on Hong Kong's left wing, see Stephan Chiu 趙永佳, Lui Tai-Lok 呂大樂, and Yung Sai-Shing 容世誠, eds., *Xionghuai zuguo: Xianggang aiguo zuopai yundong* 胸懷祖國：香港「愛國左派」運動 [Passion for the country: Hong Kong "patriotic leftist" movement] (Hong Kong: Oxford University Press, 2014).

3. See Wong Ain-ling 黃愛玲 and Lee Pui-tak 李培德, eds., *Lengzhan yu xianggang dianying* 冷戰與香港電影 [The Cold War and Hong Kong cinema] (Hong Kong: Hong Kong Film Archive, 2009).

4. "Youth movie musical" is a film genre identified by the Hong Kong Film Archive. The archive catalog lists the genre as lasting from 1965 to 1969. Ng Yuet Wah's study identifies the genre as starting in 1966. See Ng Yuet-Wah 吳月華, "Geying paihe: Yueyu qingchun gewupian gequ yu dianying de guanxi (1966–1969)" 歌影拍和：粵語青春歌舞片歌曲與電影的關係 (1966-1969) [Songs in tune with movies: The relationship of movie songs and Cantonese youth musicals in 1966–1969] (MPhil diss., Hong Kong Baptist University, 2006). Yung Sai-Shing notes that "youthfulness" as a subject matter had been explored by Cantonese films produced by the Shaw Brothers in the late 1950s to early 1960s. See Yung Sai-Shing 容世誠, "Huanle qingchun: Xianggang zhizao" 歡樂青春：香港製造 [Happy youth: made in Hong Kong] (unpublished manuscript, posted on a Cantopop blog), http://www.hkmemory.org/jameswong/text/index.php?p=home&catId=121&photoNo=0. My understanding of the difference between the films identified by Yung and those identified as movie musicals lies in the incorporation of nondiegetic song and dance sequences in the latter.

5. Cantonese is a regional dialect spoken in Hong Kong and southern China. It is a tonal language in that the same syllables can be rendered in different tones written with different Chinese characters carrying different meanings. Many of the words used in dialect could not be properly rendered in Mandarin, the official Chinese language. Some scholars see Cantonese as a language of symbolic contention between Hong Kong and the People's Republic of China. See, for instance, Bryce T. McIntyre, Christine Cheng W. Sum, and Weiyu Zhang, "Cantopop: The Voice of Hong Kong," *Journal of Asian Pacific Communication* 12, no. 2 (2002): 217–43; and Matthew M. Chew, "The Subversive Sociocultural Meanings of Cantopop Electronic Dance Music," *Chinese Sociology and Anthropology* 42, no. 2 (2010): 76–93.

6 Dredge Byung'Chu Käng, "Idols of Development: Transnational Transgender Performance in Thai K-Pop Cover Dance," *Transgender Studies Quarterly* 1, no. 4 (2014): 560.

7 See, for instance, Beng Huat Chua, "Southeast Asia in Postcolonial Studies: An Introduction," *Postcolonial Studies* 11, no. 3 (2008): 231–40; Kuan-Hsing Chen, *Asia as Method: Toward Deimperialization* (Durham, NC: Duke University Press, 2010), particularly chapter 3, "De–Cold War: The Im/possibility of 'Great Reconciliation,'" 115–59; and Tuong Vu, "Cold War Studies and the Cultural Cold War in Asia," in *Dynamics of the Cold War in Asia: Ideology, Identity, and Culture*, ed. Tuong Vu and Wasana Wongsurawat (New York: Palgrave Macmillan, 2009), 1–16.

8 All the above studies propose a more Asian-centered approach. "To de–cold war" is a term used in Chen's monograph. As he explains, "it means to mark out a space in which unspoken stories and histories may be told, and to recognize and map the historically constituted cultural and political effects of the cold war." Chen, *Asia as Method*, 120.

9 Ackbar Abbas, "Cosmopolitan De-scriptions: Shanghai and Hong Kong," in *Cosmopolitanism*, ed. Carol A. Breckenridge, Sheldon Pollock, Homi K. Bhabha, and Dipesh Chakrabarty (Durham, NC: Duke University Press, 2002), 212.

10 See, for instance, Sheldon Pollock, Homi K. Bhabha, Carol Breckenridge, and Dipesh Chakrabarty, "Cosmopolitanisms," *Public Culture* 12, no. 3 (2000): 577–89.

11 Brian Hu, "Worldly Desires: Cosmopolitanism and Cinema in Hong Kong and Taiwan" (PhD diss., University of California, Los Angeles, 2011), 7.

12 See, for instance, the discussion in Chua, "Southeast Asia in Postcolonial Studies," 233–34.

13 Gavin Kendall, Ian Woodward, and Zlatko Skrbis, *The Sociology of Cosmopolitanism* (London: Palgrave Macmillan, 2009), 128.

14 In the PRC, Western popular music was regarded as "yellow music" and "music of the imperialist." For more information on the PRC's music aesthetics and ideology, see my articles "People's Music in the People's Republic of China: A Semiotic Reading of Socialist Musical Culture from the Mid to Late 1950s," in *Music, Meaning and Media*, ed. Erkki Pekkilä, David Neumeyer, and Richard Littlefield (Helsinki: International Semiotics Institute, University of Helsinki, 2006), 195–208; and "Socialist Realism and Chinese Music," in *Socialist Realism and Music*, Colloquium Musicologicum Brunense 36, ed. Mikuláš Bek, Geoffrey Chew, and Petr Macek (Prague: Bärenreiter-Verlag, 2004), 135–44. See also Qian Zhang's chapter in this volume.

15 "The Beatles Due Here Tomorrow," *South China Sunday Post-Herald*, June 7, 1964, 5. It was reported that the group's visit brought with them Beatlemania that affected many people from different walks of life in the colony. "An Afternoon with the Beatles: Liverpool Boys Win Another Fan," *South China Sunday Post-Herald*, June 14, 1964, 7. The Searchers' visit was reported to have caused almost a riot at the performance venue, and later scores of teenagers were reported to have waited at the airport in order to get a glimpse of their idols on the day of the group's departure, forcing the band members to stay in a closely guarded VIP room to avoid the chaos. "The Searchers Leave for Manila," *South China Morning Post*, January 28, 1966, 7.

16. A 2016 volume is the only published study of this phase of Hong Kong's popular music. See Stephen Li 李信佳, *Gangshi xiyangfeng: liushi niandai xianggang yuedui chaoliu* 港式西洋風: 六十年代香港樂隊潮流 [Hong Kong–style Western music: Hong Kong 1960s band trends] (Hong Kong: Zhonghua Book Company, 2016), 14–23.

17. "68 seui Joe Junior biu meih wuih huhng gwo nihn siu gaap Band sih" 68 歲 Joe Junior 標尾會紅過年少夾Band時 [68-year-old Joe Junior is at the height of his career, more famous now than when he was a young band player], *Mingpao Online*, May 17, 2014, https://news.mingpao.com/pns/%E5%89%AF%E5%88%8A/article/20140517/s00005/1400262826845/68%E6%AD%B2joe-junior-%E6%A8%99%E5%B0%BE%E6%9C%83.

18. The songs covered included A side: "Congratulations"/"Outsider"/"All My Love"/"La La Song"/"Do You Want to Dance?"; B side: "Look Homeward Angel"/"Bachelor Boy"/"Its All in the Game"/"Catch Me"/"Don't Talk to Him." The above information is gleaned from the exchange among bloggers on a local website on Hong Kong's musical oldies run by local blogger Muzikland, accessed August 11, 2014, http://blog.roodo.com/muzikland/archives/1804176.html. The platform provider for the blog is no longer in service as of April 1, 2019. The LP was released in 1968 by Diamond Records, LP-1041.

19. Joe Junior's performance covering these songs is posted online. "Joe Junior Concert at QE Hall 15 Aug 2014—3 x Cliff Richard Songs," YouTube, September 9, 2014, https://www.youtube.com/watch?v=Ozvu58rTsf4.

20. The preface was written by the local blogger Muzikland, who was the initiator of this project.

21. Kendall, Woodward, and Skrbis, *The Sociology of Cosmopolitanism*, 109.

22. On the classification as urban elites, see Siby K. George, "The Cosmopolitan Self and the Fetishism of Identity," in *Questioning Cosmopolitanism*, ed. Stan van Hooft and Wim Vandekerckhove (New York: Springer, 2010), 66.

23. See Bell Yung, *Cantonese Opera: Performance as Creative Process* (Cambridge: Cambridge University Press, 1989).

24. The song "Fei go dit lok hang keui" 飛哥跌落坑渠 is posted online, https://www.youtube.com/watch?v=6rtDC1g_8_Q. The film was produced by the Sixi Film Production Company. Information about the film is compiled by the Hong Kong Film Archive, https://ipac.hkfa.lcsd.gov.hk/ipac/cclib/search/showBib.jsp?f=e&id=65537998656005. The song's lyrics were fitted by the renowned local composer/lyricist Hu Wensen 胡文森. For more information on him, see Wong Chi-Wah 黃志華, *Qu ci shuang jue: Hu Wensen zuopin yanjiu* 曲詞雙絕: 胡文森作品研究 [Music and lyrics: Study on the works of Hu Wen-sen] (Hong Kong: Joint Publishing, 2008).

25. Mentioned in the online Film Archive catalog.

26. Indebted to Arjun Appadurai's view of commodity exchange as being susceptible to paths and diversions, Kendall, Woodward, and Skribs regarded the commodity network as an important part of the cosmoscape as "objects which flow through societies via commodity exchange . . . [are] objectified containers of meanings amenable to reconstruction and reinterpretation by groups." Gavin Kendell, Ian Woodward,

and Zlatko Skribs, *The Sociology of Cosmopolitanism* (London: Palgrave Macmillan, 2009), 129.

27 All songs from the film were collected on the 1959 album *Leung so yau dei yuk din ying chaap kuk* 兩傻遊地獄電影插曲 (Film songs in *Two Fools in Hell*), issued by Yule changpian 娛樂唱片 (Entertainment Records).

28 For information about the movie *Leung so yau dei yuk* 兩傻遊地獄, consult the catalog entry in the Hong Kong Film Archive, https://ipac.hkfa.lcsd.gov.hk/ipac/cclib/search/showBib.jsp?f=e&id=6553752940805. The lyrics to "Yat san ngaih" 一身蟻 are also by Hu Wensen.

29 "Gou go hei mouh" was included on the album *Do do fuk* 多多福 [More blessing], released by Hesheng changpian gongsi 和聲唱片公司 (Harmony Records). The lyrics of "Sing and Dance" were adapted by Chow Chung 周聰. Information about the LP was obtained from the Muzikland blog, accessed July 30, 2016, http://blog.roodo.com/muzikland/archives/3920133.html. Chow was regarded as the founder of Cantopop by the Chinese scholar Yung Sai-Shing in his unpublished article "Huanle qingchun: Xianggang zhizao."

30 Michael Bourdaghs, *Sayonara Amerika, Sayonara Nippon: A Geopolitical Prehistory of J-Pop* (New York: Columbia University Press, 2012), 49.

31 Pnina Webner, "Vernacular Cosmopolitanism," *Theory, Culture and Society* 23, nos. 2–3 (2006): 406.

32 See Homi Bhabha, "Unsatisfied: Notes on Vernacular Cosmopolitanism," in *Text and Nation*, ed. Laura Garcia-Morena and Peter C. Pfeifer (London: Camden House), 191–207.

33 Sheldon Pollock, "The Cosmopolitan Vernacular," *Journal of Asian Studies* 57, no. 1 (1998): 6–37.

34 The film was eagerly anticipated by the public. An eye-catching photo of Cliff Richard and Ethne Milne in a dance routine along with an advertisement for the film were published in a local English newspaper. "Most Popular Film Star," *South China Morning Post and the Hongkong Telegraph*, January 8, 1963, 14. The film's lasting popularity is evident in its many reruns. A rerun was advertised on October 9, 1963, allegedly due to audience demand. Yearly advertisements for reruns were published in *South China Morning Post*; one such ad can be found on September 8, 1967, the year *The Golden Cat* was released.

35 *Summer Holiday* was shown in Hoover and Gala, two of the local cinemas devoted to Western films in Hong Kong in August 1963, as reported in Jean Gordon's article "Plenty for Youthful Tastes," *South China Morning Post and the Hongkong Telegraph*, August 3, 1963, 4.

36 Interview notes with Wong Yiu, interview conducted by Law Kar 羅卡 on August 20, 2001, and notes transcribed by May Ng 吳君如, quoted in *Xianggang yingren koushu lishi congshu zhiwu: Modeng secai xianggang—maijin 1960 niandai* 香港影人口述歷史叢書之五：摩登色彩——邁進1960年代 [Oral history series (5): An emerging modernity: Hong Kong cinema of the 1960s], ed. Kwok Ching-Ling 郭靜寧 and Au-Yeung Fung-Ki 歐陽鳳琪 (Hong Kong: Hong Kong Film Archive, 2008), 184–85.

37 Challenges included inadequate supply of movies for the increasing number of cinemas and the lack of innovations in most of the produced works. Chung Po-Yin 鐘寶賢, *Xianggang yingshiye bainian* 香港影視業百年 [A hundred years of the Hong Kong film industry] (Hong Kong: Joint Publishing, 2004), 158–67.

38 For example, the "Double 10 Riot" in 1956, triggered by the government's order to remove the nationalist flag on Taiwan's national day, was orchestrated by pronationalist rioters, using the opportunity to unleash their anger by attacking the properties of Communist supporters. Subsequently, the infamous "67 Riot" that took place in 1967 began as a series of labor disputes led by left-wing union workers, but the demonstrations escalated to uncontrollable violence, including terrorist attacks and bomb raids led by pro-Communist rioters who used militia support from the PRC.

39 One film critic wrote about his attending a movie in 1966: "One evening, I went to see a rerun of the film *Gu neuhng sahp baat yat deu fa* 姑娘十八一朵花 (*Girls Are Flowers*). It was a full house. I got a ticket at the last minute. In the movie theater, I felt that I was too old as I was surrounded by a big crowd of teenagers. They were anxious as well as excited, as though expecting something. When Connie Chan's name appeared on the screen, they screamed. They must have watched the film many times based on the way they chit-chat nonstop the entire time. I was so moved and wished that I were one of them. To be able to love [one's idol] wholeheartedly is a blessing." Originally published in *Zhongguo xuesheng zhoubao* 中國學生週報 [*Chinese Youth Weekly*] 16, no. 12 (1966): 11.

40 "Role of body" is a notion I borrow from Michael Bourdaghs's reading of the performance of the Japanese singer Shizuko Kasagi in that the singer was presented as simultaneously attractive and threatening, "an icon of bodily pleasure and material consumption." Bourdaghs, *Sayonara Amerika, Sayonara Nippon*, 42.

41 The three songs in the film were collected in Siao's album *Fei chaak gam si maau* 飛賊金絲貓 (*The Golden Cat*), issued by Pathe. See RTHK Top Ten Chinese Gold Songs Committee, ed., *Xianggang Yueyu Changpian Shoucang Zhinan: Yueyu Liuxin Qu 50s–80s* 香港粵語唱片收藏指南 [Hong Kong Cantopop Records collection guide: Cantopop 50s–80s] (Hong Kong: Joint Publishing, 1998), 330.

42 Hon-Lun Yang, "Gendering '1968': Womanhood in Model Works of the People's Republic of China and Movie Musicals of Hong Kong," in *Music and Protest in 1968*, ed. Beate Kutschke and Barley Norton (Cambridge: Cambridge University Press, 2013), 232.

43 Motti Regev, *Pop-Rock Music: Aesthetic Cosmopolitanism in Late Modernity* (Cambridge, UK: Polity, 2003), 3.

Part III
FRONTS

6. SONIC IMAGINARIES OF OKINAWA

Daiku Tetsuhiro's Cosmopolitan "Paradise"

MARIÉ ABE

After a short prelude with light strumming on the ukulele and an accordion phrase, the prominent Okinawan traditional singer Daiku Tetsuhiro's relaxed voice enters—no vibrato, and with open vowels.

> Puzzled by the flowers blooming in the heart
> Searching for the path toward the future?
> You cannot go alone, you cannot go alone
> The faraway country named happiness
> [chorus]
> I want to go, I want to go, to the place where heart is at peace
> I want to go, I want to go, it must surely exist[1]

The moderate tempo and sparse texture of the ukulele and laid-back vocal delivery conjure up a tropical feel, appropriately evoking the utopian place invoked in the lyrics. An ensemble of the tuba, drums, mandolin, xylophone, and accordion join on the second verse, providing a jubilant and lighthearted, if not humorous, accompaniment to Daiku, who continues to sing about a paradise situated far away both in distance and in time. It is not until the last chorus that the distinct sound of the Okinawan three-stringed lute (*sanshin*) comes in, as if to clue the listener in on the origin of Daiku's distinct vocal timbre and ornamentation. But it would be only a careful listener who would be able to identify the Okinawan reference; for most, the sound world of the song "Hātorando (Heartland)"—written by Kyoto-based singer-songwriter Okuno Osamu—remains anonymously tropical and paradisiacal.

The opening track of Daiku's 2003 album, "Hātorando (Heartland)" sets the tone for the album title that thematically holds together the thirty tracks contained in the double-CD album: *Hōraikō: Exo-Pai Patirohma*. The Japanese word *Hōrai* has multiple meanings, including the name of one of the three sacred mountains in Chinese mythology called *Penglai*, or an otherworld believed to exist near sacred mountains; and *kō* means to travel. *Penglai* refers to a Chinese utopian myth, the legendary, idyllic land free of pain or sorrow and abundant with rice and wine. Believed to exist somewhere in the ocean to the east of China, this paradisiacal land surfaces in variant myths across the East China Sea. The album subtitle, "Exo-Pai Patirohma," is one example. Meaning "the southernmost coral reef island," Pai Patirohma is in the dialect of the Yaeyama Islands—the southernmost cluster of islands in the Ryūkyū Islands archipelago where Daiku is originally from—and refers to a fabled paradise further south of Yaeyama. A historical record of the Yaeyama Islands from 1648 describes dozens of Hateruma islanders fleeing the heavy taxation in search of Pai Patirohma. Similar utopian myths and historical accounts of islanders who sought to evade oppressive regimes by embarking on journeys to the paradise abound among the hundreds of islands within the Ryūkyū archipelago. Some speculate that the imaginary paradise in question referred to Taiwan, or small islands south of Taiwan, or perhaps the Philippines; but Hōrai has always remained a placeless place that held significance for the islanders in the region, a geographical imaginary that has circulated across the circum–East China Sea region in stories and songs. The reference to this imaginary paradise in the album title—evoking an alternative mapping of the region—is especially suggestive, considering the geopolitical schisms, tensions, and violence that have pervaded the area during World War II and the Cold War.

Aside from the unusual fact that the esteemed Okinawan folk singer Daiku Tetsuhiro chose to release an album that hardly contains any music from the standard folk song repertoire, the geographical imagination that the album presents, both aurally and visually, painted a radically different picture of Okinawa from the popular representations and perceptions of the island in Japan. Take, for instance, the cartographic representation of Okinawa with which I was most familiar: the map of Japan widely used in most official textbooks and popular publications (see map 6.1). Okinawa Island is drawn in the bottom-right corner of the map, separated by a line that obscures the physical relationship and distance between Okinawa Island and mainland Japan. The separating line invokes otherness and peripheral positionality. Okinawa can only be included at the mercy of the line, which renders its location invisible while accentuating its small landmass and distance. Furthermore, the bottom-right corner only represents the island of Okinawa, after which the prefecture is named, while omitting from view more than one hundred other Ryūkyū Islands

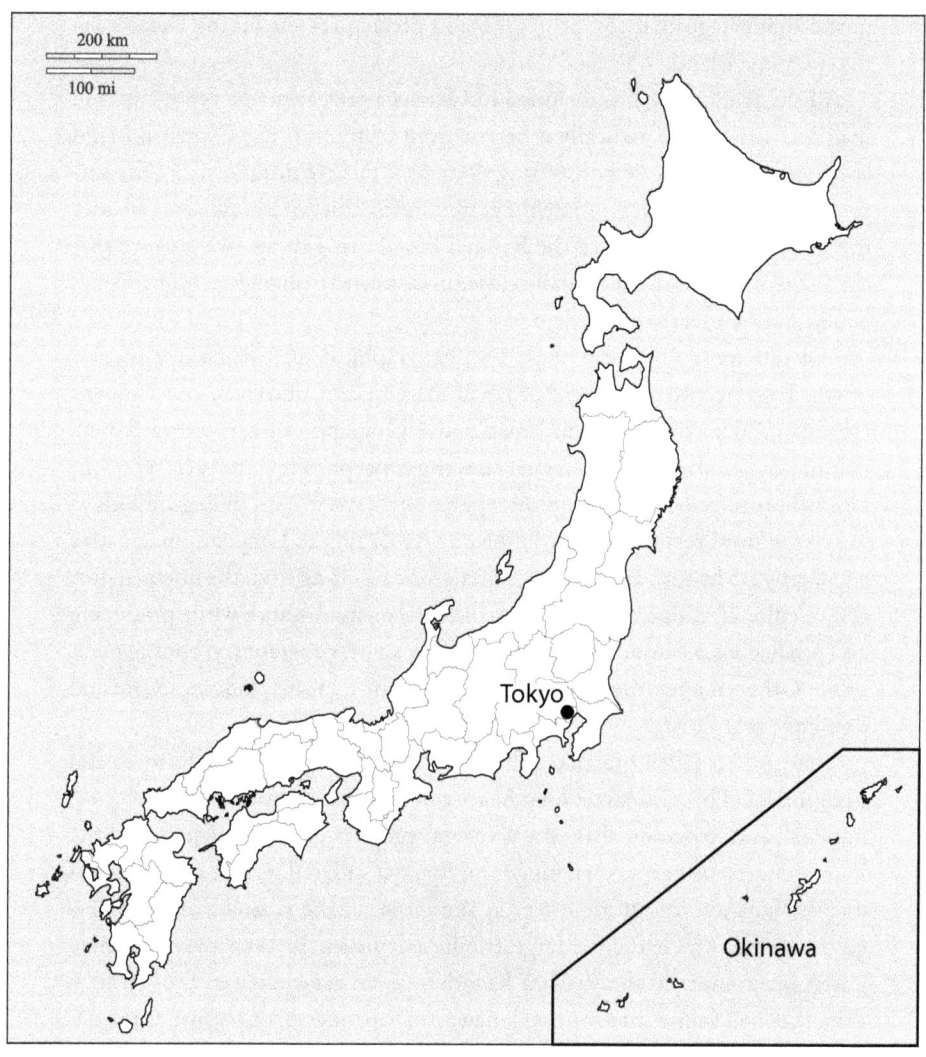

MAP 6.1. Common map of Japan, with Okinawa in the corner. Source: Allie Scholten, University of Chicago Visual Resources Center.

in the archipelago that comprise Okinawa prefecture—including Daikū's native Yaeyama Islands.

All the Ryūkyū Islands included in Okinawa prefecture are represented in map 6.2. This map is radically different from map 6.1; it has Okinawa Island at the center, thereby demonstrating Okinawa's relative distance from the surrounding areas. It renders visible the extreme proximity of the Yaeyema Islands, the most southern cluster of the Ryūkyū Islands, to Taiwan. We also see that the Okinawan Islands are actually closer in distance to Shanghai, Hong Kong, Seoul, and Manila than to Tokyo.

The differences between these two geographical representations suggest how a Tokyo-centric discourse of Japan marginalizes, abstracts, and conceals Okinawa. Borrowing the term "imaginative geographies" from Edward Said, cultural geographer Derek Gregory uses the concept to refer to such representational processes whereby physical separation allows for distancing and othering of the lived realities of a given place.[2] According to Gregory, imaginative geography is a historically constructed rhetoric resulting from the unequal process of colonial contacts, which folds difference into distance while producing and privileging the dominant power itself. In short, geographical confinement of the Other in a representational process can be a means to domesticate and dominate that Other.

These power-laden practices of imaginative geography have informed, and been inflected by, Okinawa's long history of subjugation to multiple colonial, imperial, and neocolonial (Cold War–era) projects of China, Japan, and the United States.[3] Once its own kingdom, Ryūkyū suffered its first experience of dual subjugation to outside forces in 1609, that of the Japanese and Chinese governments, which excised large tribute payments. In 1879 the new Meiji government annexed the Ryūkyū Kingdom in an act known as the "Ryūkyū dispensation," thus establishing Okinawa as a Japanese territory just as the nation was launching a course of imperial expansion. Within the context of the following imperial incursions to Taiwan, Korea, Manchuria, Northern China, Southeast Asia, and the Pacific, Michael Molasky suggests that "Okinawa might thus be understood as modern Japan's first foreign colony."[4] These colonial projects of imperial Japan in and through Okinawa have paved the way for an even more complex, double subjugation to Japan and the US in the post–World War II era.

Famously dubbed a "cold war island" by Chalmers Johnson, Okinawa, with its violent histories of the catastrophic battle between Japan and the US (1945), the postwar US military occupation (1945–72), and the troubled present as the host site of the majority of US military bases in Japan, reminds us that the

MAP 6.2. Map with Okinawa at the center, demonstrating relative distance to surrounding cities. Source: Allie Scholten, University of Chicago Visual Resources Center.

Cold War is not quite over.[5] During the last stages of World War II, Okinawa Island became the only site of ground battle fought on Japanese territory. The Battle of Okinawa turned into the bloodiest battle fought in the Pacific Theater; nearly one-third of the prewar civilian population on the island was killed, not only by the US army but also by Japanese soldiers. With the San Francisco Peace Treaty in 1952, Okinawa came under direct US military occupation for the following twenty years, rendering Okinawans a stateless people who were neither Japanese nor American citizens. Considered a strategic military foothold in Asia during the Korean and Vietnam Wars, Okinawa was a particularly crucial site for the US during the Cold War period. Even after its "reversion" to Japan in 1972, a massive American military presence remained in Okinawa on an indefinite basis. The everyday life of Okinawa residents continues to be impinged upon by the consequences and conflicts stemming from the arrangements that directly resulted from the Cold War geopolitical dynamics that made Okinawa a crucial military site for the US in its campaign against the perceived threat of Communism in Asia.

I posit that by listening to Daiku's album *Hōraikō*, we begin to hear how power-laden imaginative geographies that abstract, contain, and exploit Okinawa's difference can be contested through musical sounds—through sonic imaginaries.[6] How did Daiku, who has become well known as a voice of Okinawa (and more specifically of the Yaeyama Islands), come to create this rather peculiar album about a placeless place, a site of utopian myths from across the circum–East China Sea? What kinds of Okinawa do we hear in this multifaceted musical framework, if at all? What kind of "paradise" is being sounded on this album, and how might we sift through the imaginative and the real that have been woven together within its musical renderings? How might we understand the politics of such musical geographies?

In this chapter, I explore the distinct spatiality that emerges from listening to Daiku Tetsuhiro's musical sounds on the album *Hōraikō: Exo-Pai Patirohma*. By listening to what Jocelyne Guilbault calls the "audible entanglements" of social relations, cultural expressions, and political formations that are assembled in this particular album as a case study, this chapter reframes the neo–Cold War present of Okinawa, the southernmost prefecture of Japan consisting of hundreds of the Ryūkyū Islands archipelago.[7] I suggest that Daiku's musical practices urge us to reconceive the prevalent view that confines the island within the Cold War histories of US-Japan relations by presenting a locally grounded geographical imagination that situates Okinawa as part of a cosmopolitan "paradise" in peripheral Asia. Combining interviews and musical analysis, I highlight how his "paradise" reveals not only the contradictory practices that silence

Okinawa's difference on the one hand, and render Okinawa as a racialized internal Other on the other, but also the uneven relations existing within the region of the Ryūkyū archipelago and the transnational affective alliances between Okinawa and locales in East and Southeast Asia. I argue that Daiku's "paradise" offers alternative designations of time and space that are capable of asserting historical subjectivity and forging transnational connections, thereby exposing the limitations of the resistance-dominance framework that pits Okinawa against the US military regime and the Japanese government's complicity therein.

Daiku Tetsuhiro

The biography of Daiku Tetsuhiro, a Yaeyama native born in 1948 on Ishigaki Island at the periphery of the Ryūkyū archipelago, affords the artist a vantage point from which to critique US hegemony, Japan's colonialist past, and the Okinawa-centric discourse that elides differences within the archipelago. Daiku is a chief voice of the local traditional music—folk songs (*min'yō*) (see figure 6.1). Having won numerous competitions, Daiku holds licenses to teach traditional songs from both Okinawa and Yaeyama Islands and has been awarded the intangible cultural heritage award by Okinawa prefecture. Now living on Okinawa Island, Daiku frequently travels to teach at twenty-three Okinawan music schools that he founded across Japan while also touring abroad as the musical ambassador of Okinawa. Since 2015 he has been appointed as the honorary president of the Association of Ryūkyū Folk Music and a representative of the nine folk music associations in Okinawa.

Daiku won his reputation as a maverick in 1994, when he broke away from the expectation of traditional singers to sing exclusively Okinawan folk songs and instead released an album titled *Okinawa Jinta*, which mostly contained songs from mainland Japan with tunes stretching from the 1870s to the 1960s. On this album, alongside songs from the Ryūkyū archipelago such as "Asadoya Yunta" (Asadoya song) and "Amami Kouta" (Amami song) as well as Yaeyama-specific tunes, the listener encounters an eclectic assemblage of tunes, ranging from the 1915 socialist satirical song "Rappa bushi" (Trumpet song) to "Tokyo Bushi" (Tokyo song) and "Kago no Tori" (Bird in a cage), big hits that were widely popular in mainland Japan in the 1910s and 1920s; a 1936 military song about Manchukuo, "Manshū Omoeba" (Remembering Manchukuo); and "Makuramu Dōro" (McCullum Road), a 1947 Yaeyama song dedicated to a US lieutenant colonel who helped build a road on Ishigaki Island during the occupation.

FIGURE 6.1. Daiku Tetsuhiro in April 2019. Photo by the author.

Commenting on how he came to select tunes for this album, Daiku told me in an interview that it was not so much an arbitrary selection of songs as it was remembering songs he grew up listening to his grandfather sing in Yaeyama.[8] These old Japanese songs traveled all the way to Yaeyama and became part of Daiku's childhood soundscape, continuing to live in his memory even as the songs lost their currency in mainland Japan, where they originated. These are the sounds through which he came to know the world, his place in Yaeyama, and his view of mainland Japan.

While Daiku took a rather nonchalant attitude toward reworking the songs he grew up with in Yaeyama—not only the folk songs but also the Japanese popular tunes that circulated all the way to the islands—he politicized the process of recording these songs in 1994 by admitting that this album was driven by a longtime grudge he had held against mainland Japan. At age twenty-two, he had won a nationally televised regional traditional folk song competition eight weeks in a row. Just two weeks before the final round, in which the winner would land a major record deal, he was booted from the competition by the judges, who criticized and humiliated him for his "incomprehensible" Okinawan accent. Daiku explained that decades of living with the anger following this incident lay behind his releasing of this record: "Japanese listeners, listen to me sing Japanese songs that you don't even remember."[9] These older popular songs, largely forgotten in Japan, carry historical traces of Japanese colonialism, the US occupation, and the cultural hegemony of mainland Japanese popular culture. Claiming such old Japanese songs as his own, Daiku challenged the difference ascribed to Okinawa not only geographically and historically but also sonically. Rendered through the sonic markers of "Okinawan difference" audible in the Okinawan traditional songs, the distinct vocal ornamentations, and his Okinawan accent, the juxtaposition of the wide array of songs on *Okinawa Jinta* reactivated the dormant histories of violence and local struggle, and the uneven dynamics between the Ryūkyū Islands and mainland Japan that constitutively produced the very "difference" of Okinawa. Although not all songs on the album are from Okinawa, it is precisely the locality of Yaeyama that enabled Daiku to sing these tunes as a way of revealing both the wide reach of mainland Japanese popular culture and the political oppression Okinawa has endured.

Inspired by Daiku's 1994 album, various musicians in mainland Japan followed suit, revisiting older social satirical songs or popular songs reflecting colonial and imperial ideologies in order to rearticulate these inequalities with contemporary struggles.[10] Daiku's musical work thus had the unexpected consequence of giving rise to a new musical trend among mainland Japanese musicians and listeners alike of revisiting older popular songs. In fact, *Okinawa Jinta* still remains the best-selling album, of more than one hundred albums released by the label, Off Note, to this day. Daiku has cemented his status as both the chief voice of Yaeyama and Okinawan folk music and as a trendsetter who has given new life to older Japanese popular songs as if to reawaken the memories of metropole-colony relations.[11]

Ten years, eight albums, and six international tours after he began performing, in 2003 Daiku released his ambitious double album *Hōraikō: Exo-Pai Patirohma*, including disc 1, "Taihei Ongaku EXOTICA—The Birth of Pan-Pacifican Music," and disc 2, "Hōraikō EODUS—Pai Patirohma" (see figure 6.2). Unlike his previous albums, the music on *Hōraikō* stretches outward to locations beyond Japan. The album contains a diverse array of tunes varied in their geographical and historical backgrounds—from traditional Okinawan songs to Japanese popular songs from the 1930s, songs from Hawai'i and Taiwan, and even a Brazilian popular song. Daiku explained that his life as a Yaeyama native living on Okinawa Island informed his musical geography on *Hōraikō*: "Geographically, [Okinawa Island] is a place that allows me to see so many areas. I can see the mainland, China, other Okinawa Islands—they all start to appear equidistant. That's attractive to me."[12]

FIGURE 6.2. Cover of the *Hōraikō* album, released in 2003.

This double album has thirty songs in total, all performed by Daiku Tetsuhiro and fellow Okinawan artists as well as Tokyo musicians who played various non-Okinawan instruments and arranged most of the songs. All the tunes are reworked through creative arrangements to evoke a sense of continuity and coherence despite the variety of musical styles included. A review of the album effectively summarizes this aspect.

> It is difficult to explain simply what this album is like, as it holds not only the traditional Okinawan folk songs but a wide range of songs from various genres. Of course it does contain traditional Okinawan folk songs, but it also has commercial popular songs, state-sponsored songs, and anonymous songs sung by the common people. However, for each song, we can see a thread that is connected to Okinawa. This thread is connected not only to Okinawa but to Asia and Hawaii. Once you start to imagine the emigration history of Okinawa, the history of politics, and the problems of establishing identity, the imagination becomes endless, making us feel as though many pieces of threads were all tangled up. This album is decidedly excellent, whether you listen to it while thinking about the meaning of the lyrics and the historical background of the tunes, or you listen to it to appreciate the sanshin sound and the voice of Daiku Tetsuhiro.[13]

Although undeniably an "Okinawan" album because of Daiku's renown, his unmistakable vocal inflections typical of Okinawan folk songs, the sound of the sanshin, the selection of tunes, and the musical arrangements on this album encourage listeners to sift through multiple layers of spatial and temporal sonic imaginaries. The resultant sense of space that emerges from them is what Doreen Massey calls an "extroverted" sense of space. Instead of the widely held conception of space as a static and passive physical container in which history, geography, and people are held in a homologous relationship, Massey puts forward an alternative conceptualization of space: space is actively produced through power relations and negotiations—and not delineated by physical boundaries. Space, for Massey, is a "geographical stretching-out of social relations" that in itself is an "extroverted," dynamic process without geographic borders.[14]

In what follows, I describe three ways in which the sonic imaginaries on this album make audible a number of geographical possibilities. Through the constellation of various tunes and musical arrangements, *Exo-Pai Patirohma* simultaneously makes audible mainland Okinawa relations, the diversity within the Ryūkyū Islands, and Okinawan diasporic formations. As I tease out these spaces and histories, I argue that the music calls for listeners to reimagine Okinawa's spatiality as dynamic, multiple, and extroverted, reworking the pervasive Cold War narrative that reduces Okinawa to the status of being occupied, colonized, and marginalized by both the US and Japanese governments.

The Production of Okinawan Difference

The mainland Japanese connection and disconnection are evident in numerous songs on the album. On the one hand, selections of tunes such as "Otomi San" (Ms. Otomi), "Romance Kōro" (Romance ship line), "Jyūku no Haru" (Spring at age 19), and "Dōtonbori Kōshinkyoku" (Dōtonbori march) attest to how mainland Japanese popular tunes circulated through the Ryūkyū Islands and became indigenized in the process. Dating from the 1920s through the 1950s, these songs show long and ongoing metropole-colony relations. On the other hand, Daiku makes explicit the oppression of Japanese imperial rule through the inclusion of Japanese popular or propaganda songs such as "Hyōjungo Reikō no Uta" (Standard Japanese encouragement song). Daiku's selection of this propaganda tune, which he learned from Iruma Kazumasa of Yonaguni Island, seems to remember, lament, and satirize the mainland's attempt at cultural erasure in Okinawa. Between 1895 and 1945, the Japanese state attempted to forcibly erase Okinawa's difference through a rigorous cultural assimilation policy.[15] Imposition of the Japanese language and a banning of the Okinawan language were at the core of the policy. The tune, written for Okinawan elementary school students in the 1930s, is here accompanied by the somewhat stiff, if not slightly awkward, sound of the piano—as if to invoke a schoolteacher playing the piano in a classroom—and the humorous sound of a musical saw. The lyrics depict the fervent attempt at implementing prefecture-wide assimilationist policies that mandated the use of standard Japanese on school grounds and prohibited Okinawan dialects.

> "Hyōjungo Reikō no Uta"
> Tides of epoch / To the Southern Island / Simply abandon the old customs
> You, me, and this town / Everyone speaks the fun standard Japanese
> Strong body and beautiful language / Beautiful language
> Proper person
> Go happy people / in Okinawa / Everyone speaks the fun standard Japanese
> It is Showa Era / Wind of Reconstruction of Asia / We are cheerful Children of Japan
> Smiley and merry every day / Sprightly Language
> Standard Japanese

In his humorous and ironic rendition of this song, Daiku not only awakens his own memory of being punished for speaking dialect in the classroom but also reasserts the history of Japanese oppression of Okinawa that is forgotten by most Japanese and is certainly elided from the national historical narrative. Although Daiku's diction is in perfectly fine standard Japanese, his Yaeyama folk vocal technique audible in ornamentations and the use of the musical saw draw our ears to the unassimilable difference of Okinawa and denaturalize the assimilation efforts of imperial Japan, as if to reclaim its own historical subjectivity while also uncovering the history of oppression by the Japanese state.

Contrary to the widely accepted conception of Okinawa as being simply another part of Japan, like any other prefecture, the Japanese government used racialized difference of Okinawa to justify military brutality during the first half of the twentieth century, including massacres and abuse—notably, the order for local residents to commit compulsory group suicide during the Battle of Okinawa—or as a bargaining chip in diplomatic exchanges to achieve its own independence from US military occupation on the mainland in 1952.[16] Paradoxically, then, Okinawa's rendition of the propaganda song that touts assimilationist efforts highlights the exoticization of Okinawa as internal Other.

Michael Molasky notes: "In the eyes of mainland Japanese, Okinawa and its people appeared not only different but exotic.... The Japanese, replicating a colonial stance well established by Europe and the United States, assumed the position of the advanced, 'northern culture' and looked with both longing and disdain to its exotic and less developed territory to the south."[17]

The unassimilable difference of Okinawans is registered and polarized in the spatial terms of north versus south as well as in the temporal terms of "advanced" versus "backward." This backwardness of the south was articulated in the register of race.[18] Japan's display of Okinawans as exotic specimens along with other "racial" groups at the 1903 Osaka Exhibition is a case in point. Laura Hein and Mark Selden put Japanese racialization of modernity in the context of European colonialism: "Indeed, modern scientific racial prejudice developed in Japan at roughly the same time as it did in Europe and North America, and it was clearly influenced by international racial 'science' and Western colonial practices."[19]

Both the Japanese and the US capitalized on this spatialized, temporalized, racialized difference of Okinawa: "In 1947 General McArthur proposed that the occupation of Japan be brought to an end..., yet he insisted that the United States maintain control over Okinawa, claiming that Okinawans are not Japanese."[20] The American authorities also enforced a "Ryūkyū-ization" cultural policy that aimed to indoctrinate local residents with a sense of the ethnic and cultural distinctness of the Okinawans in order to undo the Japanese cultural assimilation policy and thereby legitimize prolonging the American military occupation. In this light, Okinawa can be described as a doubly racialized subject. The Cold War policies of the US occupation and its military presence—justified as a critical countermeasure against the perceived Communist threat in Asia—were rationalized and enforced by both Japanese and American authorities as a necessary project of modernizing the backward, ethnically distinct, southern islanders of Okinawa.[21]

Looking at how Okinawa's difference has been produced and naturalized in spatial, temporal, and racial terms helps explain the ambivalence and contradictions in the mainland Japanese attitude toward Okinawa's difference today. On the one hand, the Japanese government insists on pursuing homogeneity in line with its claim of racial and ethnic purity, which was enforced through the cultural assimilation policy. On the other hand, it produces Okinawa as a racialized Other, folding difference into both time and space. This spatialized difference has not only discursive but also material repercussions, resulting in cultural, economic, and political marginalization; military violence against the Okinawans; and dispossession of land.

Dispossession of Land and Okinawan Indigeneity

With a view of the East China Sea in the front
There is our land we've lived on
This land is our life
A treasure passed on from our ancestors

We shall no longer be deceived
On the palm of our aging hands
Are scars from farm work
We shall hand over not even one tsubo [3.3 square meters of land]

Today, again, black murder machines
Fly to shoot friends in Vietnam
We shall not disgrace again
This sky that connects the world

The song "Hitotsubo Taritomo Watasumai" (We shall give up not even one *tsubo*) was written in 1967 during the land struggle in Konbu, a neighborhood in Gushikawa City, Okinawa. In 1965 the US military ordered the villagers of Konbu to effectively give up their land, with no compensation. Already having had a significant amount of their land confiscated by the US military for weapons storage, Konbu locals opposed this plan by staging sit-in protests over the following five years. In 1970 the military conceded and canceled the plan.

Contrary to the intensity of the lyrics in this protest song, the musical arrangement on *Hōraikō: Exo-Pai Patirohma* is disarmingly sweet. The track starts with a wind chime, recorders, melodica, and toy piano outlining the chord progression of the song. The bass and drum come in after the first verse, shifting the groove to a faux-reggae feel. These sonorities and groove, seemingly incongruent with the lyrics and context of the song, achieve the effect of covering up the militant tone of the original. Many of the protest songs in the 1960s followed the formulaic style of military marching songs, and this tune was no exception.

While the innocence evoked through toy instruments and the relaxed, pop feel of reggae groove effectively displace the combative and masculine tone of the original, Daiku's strident voice cuts across and over the accompaniment, firmly asserting the voices of local opposition to land dispossession by the US military and against the US military at large (the third verse). The updated arrangement of a song specific to the 1967 moment hints at the continued struggles of Okinawans whose land and sea remain under threat of appropriation by the US military—including Henoko and Takae, two contested sites for new military base construction plans.

Land expropriation is an issue that acutely highlights the uneven development and disconnection between Okinawa, Japan, and the US in the Cold War arrangement of power.[22] Okinawans' struggle against land dispossession by both Japan and the US has been a long ongoing process: "In Okinawa, private land ownership was legalized in 1903 following a Japanese government land survey. Before then, all land was collectively owned, managed, and used by village communities [*jiwarisei*]."[23] On April 1, 1945, American occupation began with the dislocation and detention of 300,000 Okinawans (the great majority of surviving local residents) in twelve POW internment camps, which were established throughout the main island of Okinawa. Most of the land from which Okinawans were evicted was requisitioned by the military, forcing the residents to resettle elsewhere.[24]

Uneven development between Okinawa and mainland Japan is acutely evident in the imbalanced sharing of the burden of hosting US military bases: "Approximately 75% of the land occupied by U.S. military installations in Japan remains concentrated on the island of Okinawa, which constitutes a mere 0.6% of the nation's land mass and is home to only 1% of its population."[25] While the number of US troops stationed on mainland Japan has steadily diminished since 1945, the US presence on Okinawa grew. In 2001 there were eighty thousand Americans in Okinawa, including thirty thousand active duty personnel. In contrast, there were fewer than twenty thousand in the rest of Japan combined.[26] Additionally, Okinawa has single-handedly absorbed ecological and environmental risks posed by the US military, which used Okinawa as a nuclear arsenal throughout the postwar era, both before and after reversion.

Such disparities between Okinawa and mainland Japan make the "reversion" of Okinawa from the US to Japan in 1972 a contested issue. For many Okinawans, the question of to whom Okinawa should be reverted was not to be taken for granted. Daiku Tetsuhiro tackled precisely this question by releasing a controversial recording of the song "Okinawa o Kaese" (Return Okinawa) in 1997. Originally written by two mainland Japanese, the tune was composed as a protest song calling for the return of Okinawa to Japanese control.

"*Okinawa o Kaese*"
Japanese
Kataki Tsuchi o Yaburite
Minzokuno ikarini moyuru shima Okinawa yo

Warera to warerno sosen ga chi to ase o mote

Mamori sodateto Okinawa yo
Warera wa sakebu Okinawa yo

Warera no monoda Okinawa wa
Okinawa o kaese
Okinawa o kaese

Breaking through the solid land
Island burning the rage of the people, Oh Okinawa
With the blood and sweat of ourselves and our ancestors
protected and nurtured, Okinawa
We cry out, Okinawa
It is ours, Okinawa
Return Okinawa
Return Okinawa

The struggle over land appropriation did not end with Okinawa's reversion to Japanese sovereignty in 1972. The Japanese government treated the formerly privately owned land as public land belonging to the state in accordance with the terms of the Land Acquisition Law, a long-standing measure for forced lease or sale of land for public purposes. The government then transferred this land to the US for extended use under the terms of a newly enacted Special Measures Law for Land Used by the American Forces.[27] The Japanese government in effect forcibly leased the land and paid the owners rent, then sublet the land to the US forces in Japan but with the Japanese government actually footing the bill.

One particular historical moment that captured these complex power relations over claims to land between Okinawa, Japan, and the US was the "in-lieu signing" incident in 1995. Since Okinawa's reversion to Japanese rule, a number of landowners and their local mayors refused to sign the land-lease documents transferring their land to the Japanese government. As a result, between 1972 and 1995, the prefectural governor always signed the lease renewal every five years as an in-lieu signer. However, in 1995, shortly after the islands erupted in massive protest in response to a gang-rape incident involving an elementary school girl, then governor Ōta Masahide refused to perform the in-lieu signing, thereby precipitating a major crisis for the state. Ōta was sued by the prime minister of Japan. Immediately following this incident, the government passed a revision of the Special Measures Law for Land Required by the U.S. Military Bases, transferring the power to sign forced leases from the prefectural governor to the central government—highlighting what Giorgio Agamben calls the "state of exception" where law suspends itself to privilege the state.[28]

Following this event, Daiku Tetsuhiro released a recording of "Okinawa o Kaese" on a compilation album titled *Chibariyo Uchinā* (Fight! Okinawa) in 1997.[29] The song is the opening track of the album, and instrumentation is minimal—sanshin and traditional drum (*taiko*), the traditional instrumentation typical of Okinawan folk songs. The controversy arose over a slight lyrical change he made. Instead of singing "Okinawa *o* Kaese" twice in the refrain, Daiku sings "Okinawa *o* Kaese, Okinawa *e* Kaese," changing the proposition "o" modifying the direct object (Okinawa) into "e," referring to the indirect object and indicating to whom/what Okinawa is being returned.[30]

This change of a vowel in the lyrics raises a critical question about historical subjectivity; Daiku is asking who "we" are in the song. In the original version, "we" refers to the collective "Japanese," as it was written by Japanese people in the Japanese language, calling for Okinawa's reversion to Japan. In Daiku's 1997 version, however, with the "o" changed into "e," the refrain changes from "Return Okinawa, Return Okinawa" into "Return Okinawa, *to* Okinawa," thus redefining the subject as exclusively Okinawans. Suddenly, such words as *ancestors* and *blood* become signifiers of Okinawa's self-assertion as a distinct ethnic group, as indigenous inhabitants of the land. In light of the particular histories of oppression by Japan and the US, reclaiming Okinawan indigenous identity is intimately tied with claims to their land that has been doubly exploited by the Japanese government and the US military.

The song also exposes the contradiction within the Japanese attitude toward Okinawa: land expropriation was justified under the terms of a unified nation-state, yet there has been a long history of political, economic, and human exploitation of Okinawans justified in the name of race. Making audible this contradiction, Daiku's recording shows how histories of dispossession are intimately tied to the production of difference in terms of race and space, and how the struggle over land is simultaneously a struggle over the meaning of nationality, indigeneity, and ethnicity.

Considering the histories of uneven power relations between mainland Japan and Okinawa that have produced the spatialized difference of Okinawa, which has in turn enabled appropriation and dispossession of the physical geography itself, one might expect the paradise evoked in the title "Hōraikō" to reflect an escapist desire to run away from the colonial projects of imperial Japan. But a close listen to other tracks on the album presents a complex and nuanced sound world of Okinawa, which cannot be captured by the simplistic geographical framework of metropole-colony. The imaginary map of Okinawa that is stimulated by Daiku's sonic imaginaries expands to the micropolitics among peripheral islands within the Ryūkyū archipelago as well as to Okinawan diasporic formations beyond Asia.

Circum–East China Sea Micropolitics and Diasporic Formations

As a Yaeyama native, Daiku also highlighted the distinct histories and differences of other Ryūkyū Islands that are often elided under the monolithic notion of "Okinawa prefecture," including three songs from or about peripheral islands within the Ryūkyū archipelago. "Yonaguni Kouta" is a pastoral praise song for Yonaguni Island, the archipelago's southernmost island, which is closer to Taiwan (only 100 km away) than to Okinawa. A pastoral image and sense of "praise song" are evoked by the unlikely pairing of the Okinawan sanshin with the ethereal sounds of a church organ and tropical sounds of Caribbean steel pans and African kalimba. The peacefulness evoked by this instrumentation holds double layers of irony: it highlights the contrast between Okinawa Island, now burdened with the US military bases, and Okinawa Island's historically dominant position among the other islands from the fifteenth through the nineteenth centuries.

"Yusakuya" is a traditional song from Yaeyama in which the producer Kamiya presents his hypothesis about the suffering experienced by coal miners in Iriomote Island. The laborers were not only locals but also underclass mainlanders, North Koreans, and Taiwanese. "Toganisuza" is a creatively arranged instrumental rendition of a traditional tune originating from Miyako Island, which later spread to other Ryūkyū Islands, including Yaeyama. The inclusion of these tunes not only signals the diversity and internal differences among the Ryūkyū Islands of Okinawa but also displaces the metropole-colony axis through which most historiography of Okinawa has been written. Instead, these tunes elucidate the interconnections and micropolitics among places within, and beyond, the Ryūkyū archipelago.

Hōraikō: Exo-Pai Patirohma reveals not only the internal differences within the Ryūkyū archipelago but also external relations produced through its distinct history and geography. Several songs on the album are tunes steeped in the histories of emigration from Okinawa: "Between 1899 and 1935, about 15% of the Okinawan population emigrated either to the mainland or overseas due to extreme poverty and famine. The largest number of emigrants went to Hawai'i, Brazil, the Philippines, and Peru, mainly as agricultural laborers. By 1945, about 332,000 Okinawans (some born overseas) were living abroad."[31] About 4,000 more were labeled Communist and forcibly sent to Bolivia by the American military between 1945 and 1965, some of whom were displaced by the building of military bases on the island.³² There continues to be a large and extensive network of Okinawan emigrants and their descendants living abroad today.

Numerous songs on the album stem from these transnational connections. For example, there are three songs related to Hawai'i. "Hore Hore Bushi" (*Hore hore* song) is a work song of Okinawan emigrants in Hawai'i. The hard labor of sugarcane harvesting was accompanied by singing this song, which depicts the harshness of life and labor as well as nostalgia for the homeland. In contrast to the solemn lyrics and austere sonorities of "Hore Hore Bushi," "Japanese Rumba," released in 1951 from Nippon Columbia in Japan, offers commentary in a lighthearted and humorous tone on colonial ambivalence between the US and Japan as mediated by the Okinawan diasporic formation in Hawai'i. "Japanese Rumba" was written by J. Miller; arranged by Itsuro Raymond Hattori, who is a Japanese national; and sung by the Japanese Hawaiian singers George Shimabukuro and Nobuo Nishimoto, who were all stationed in Japan (Shimabukuro is of Okinawan descent). The song is written in pidgin Japanese or so-called Bamboo English, caricaturing the awkward attempts by US GIs to flirt with Japanese women while also serving as a form of studying Japanese for the stationed GIs who wanted to "get together with" Japanese women.³³ In his incisive analysis of the mainland Japanese star Hosono Haruomi's cover of the same song, musicologist Hosokawa Shūhei shows how the original recording demonstrates Japanese American singers' complicity with US imperialism in the country of their ancestry on the one hand and mockery of their fellow GIs' linguistic incompetence on the other.³⁴ Daiku's rendition of this song, sung as a native Yaeyaman/Okinawan, doubles down on this and cuts through the colonial ambivalence enfolded within the song. Having struggled with discrimination and been mocked for his thick Okinawan accent in the past, Daiku singing in pidgin Japanese accentuates his Otherness, highlighting the continuity of Japanese colonial oppression, stretching from the prewar assimilationist policy to insidious discrimination against Okinawans today. At the same time, Daiku's voice covering the Okinawan Hawaiian George Shimabukuro can also be heard as a bridge across historical and geographical distance, elucidating diasporic connections. Some Okinawans immigrated across the Pacific to Hawai'i and beyond under the US suppression of dissidents labeled Communist, leading to the formation of the Okinawan diaspora—which then produced the feedback loop of returning diasporic Okinawans, partaking in the US military occupation of Okinawa during the Cold War. This ironic twist of fate is amplified by the sound of the Cuban "rumba" rhythm of the song—the sound of a Cold War adversary of the US providing the comical, "exotic" musical background.

This ambiguous humor of the original song is retained, if not exaggerated, in Daiku's version through the relaxed and humorous instrumentation reminiscent of New Orleans brass bands, which conjures up the exotic "island" feel of the rumba rhythm. In Daiku's cover, the Otherness audible in the sound of pidgin Japanese and the Cuban rhythm is realigned with Okinawan difference mediated through diasporic formations—poignantly contesting not simply Japanese colonial mimicry of the West but also the active role Japan has played in the colonial oppression of Okinawa, the ironies of the Cold War, and the pervasiveness of US imperialism.[35]

The third Hawai'i-related song on the album is "Hiyamikachi Bushi" (Cheer up! in Okinawan), one of the most beloved Okinawan folk songs performed by sanshin players and singers. The original lyrics were written by Taira Shinsuke, an Okinawan activist who participated in the civil rights movement in the 1880s and 1890s. Taira immigrated to Hawai'i and eventually to California in 1901, where he was detained in an internment camp during World War II. Upon returning to Okinawa in 1953, Taira wrote the lyrics in the Okinawan language to express hope for fast reconstruction and to cheer up Okinawans who faced a devastated homeland after the war. A musical maverick as well as an Okinawan émigré who spent time in Brazil before returning to Okinawa later in his life, Yamanouchi Seihin wrote additional verses and set them to a tune he composed in a style that pushes the envelope of traditional sanshin technical skills. Taira's and Yamanouchi's desire to "make our island Okinawa known to the world" (lyrics) reflects their cosmopolitan view of the island, which was informed by their immigration experiences and strong connection to Okinawa despite the displacement and internment camp trauma.

While these narratives of migration to Hawai'i and the Americas prevail within discourses of Okinawan diaspora, Daiku also highlights the lesser-known and yet strong relations between Taiwan and Okinawa. Among the four Taiwan-related songs on the album is "Taiwan Yuki Kazoe Uta" (Going to Taiwan song). Sung in turn between Daiku and his wife, Daiku Naeko, the traditional folk song chronicles the life of a Taketomi girl who steals money from her parents to buy tickets and travel to Taiwan in search of new opportunities. While it captures her longing for her home island, it ends with the girl becoming pregnant and her parents leaving Taketomi Island to claim a new "home island" in Taiwan together as a family. The song reflects the trend from the 1930s for many Taketomi Island girls to immigrate to colonial Taiwan to work as nannies to support their families back home.

The album also includes several Taiwanese popular songs that make audible the colonial traces of Japan. The album includes two songs from the time of the Japanese occupation of Taiwan during the 1930s; such Taiwanese popular songs written in Mandarin were quite rare at the time, especially as a result of the strict imposition of Japanese as the official language. Written and composed by Taiwanese musicians, "Bou Shun Pū" (Hope in spring wind) is sung in both Mandarin and Japanese, while "Getsu Ya Shū" (Melancholy on a moonlit night) is sung in Japanese instead of the original lyrics in Taiwanese, indicative of the cultural policy of imperial Japan. Furthermore, there are three songs from 1960s Taiwan that are considered folk songs from the mountains (*sanchi minyō*). Sanchi minyō are recordings by, and for, the indigenous people of Taiwan, and in the Japanese language—illustrating the deep reach of the Japanese colonial assimilationist project as well as the ambivalent attitude among Taiwanese toward the memories of Japanese colonialism.

These three songs—"Ai Ai Jō de Kanpai" (Toasting Ai Ai Jo), "Osake Kouta" (Drinking song), and "Kawaii Sūchan" (Pretty Ms. Su)—are all lighthearted, humorous songs about drinking and women. Finally, "Irinu Miruku" is a traditional song from Yaeyama, but the title has been hypothetically linked to a village on Ranyū Island, located southeast of Taiwan and home to the Tao tribe. The name of the village in the indigenous language sounds the same as "Miroku of the West" in Yaeyama dialect; it reinforces the paradisiacal imaginations that circulated among the circum–East China Sea islands. Incorporating Okinawan instruments, steel pans, and percussion that evoke an "island" sound, with reed instruments playing the melody, this arrangement invites an imagination of cultural and historical continuity between the small indigenous Taiwanese island and the southern islands of Ryūkyū. Furthermore, these imaginative evocations of historical and cultural continuity put into relief the historical resonances between Taiwan and Okinawa, both of which are former Japanese colonies caught suspended in impossible tensions under Cold War geopolitics.

As the album review I quoted earlier states, the seemingly disconnected constellation of tunes on *Hōraikō: Exo-Pai Patirohma* articulates entangled threads of transnational relations and histories—from the distinct histories of peripheral islands within the Ryūkyū archipelago to Ryūkyū-Taiwan connections, Okinawan migration to Hawai'i and beyond, Japanese colonialism in Taiwan, and the indigenous presence in Taiwan. Hein and Selden characterize these entanglements as a source of the distinctly Okinawan sense of cosmopolitanism: this "history of emigration, and resultant diasporic Okinawan community, is often cited by Okinawans as evidence of a distinctive level of Okinawan cosmopolitanism in contrast to an allegedly homogeneous Japan."[36] Okinawa's locality and particularity is defined precisely through its dynamic relations with locales beyond the islands; the kind of geography that emerges from listening to this dynamic constellation of tunes together is at once "both-cosmopolitan-and-vernacular."[37]

Conceptualizing Okinawa as space conscious of its links with the wider world, Daiku expressed to me his geographical perspective, saying: "Sure, the Philippines were different. But for me, Manila, Tokyo, and Osaka are foreign cities anyway."[38] Daiku's geographical sensitivity, however, is far from apathetic or relativist. For example, the destinations on his 2002 international tour suggest that he goes out of his way to cultivate affective alliances with formerly colonized places, including the Solomon Islands, Myanmar, and Papua New Guinea, to name a few—places that share the memories of violence by the Japanese imperial army.

By drawing out these often covert, forgotten, or silenced connections and sentiments archived within these songs that relate Okinawan Islands and the destinations of Okinawan immigrants, Daiku simultaneously distinguishes Okinawa from Japan, makes audible Japanese colonial projects not only in Okinawa but also in Taiwan, and reminds listeners of both the forced and voluntary migration of Okinawans across the Pacific and to the Americas—thereby building transnational alliances grounded in the politics of indigeneity, the language of self-determination, and postcolonial alliances reminiscent of the "Bandung spirit."[39]

Paradise as Extroverted Geographies

In this chapter, following Kuan-Hsing Chen's invitation to "de–cold war" Asia by "mark[ing] out a space in which unspoken stories and histories may be told, and to recognize and map the historically constituted cultural and political effects of the cold war," I have shown how Daiku's 2003 album, *Hōraikō: Exo-Pai Patirohma*, makes audible the multiple, overlapping, and sometimes contradictory geographies and histories of Okinawa.[40] Daiku's distinct positionality as a Yaeyama native, his extensive collaboration with a mainland record label and musicians, his international perspective, and his genealogical attempts to render anew the forgotten songs and histories embedded therein enable him to produce a musical geography of Okinawa that cannot be contained within an absolutist notion of space or a Cartesian notion of geography.

As if to show the limitations of such understanding of space as an enclosed site upon which differences are mapped, Daiku's music instead compels us to reimagine geography as an extroverted space—space that is conscious of external relations, produced by multiple social relations and histories, and not defined by geographical boundaries. This reimagined geography urges us to understand how the narratives of purportedly homogeneous Japan are in fact inextricably produced through the silenced production of ethnic/racial difference while reconceptualizing Okinawa's geography in ways that stimulate new cultural expressions and redefine parameters of citizenship, ethnic identity, and historical memory in Japan. In other words, Daiku's sonic imaginaries on the album produce a new spatial configuration of East Asia while troubling the standard maps on which the Cold War narrative of Okinawa—positioned between Japan, Taiwan, and China and occupied by the US until 1972—is built.

Noting the prevalent discourse of Okinawa as a cosmopolitan place contrasted to allegedly homogeneous Japan, Hein and Selden warn us about the danger of casting Okinawa's difference within a global framework as being utopian, naive, and highly romantic.[41] It is important to think through this caution, especially because Daiku's musical geography of Okinawa is indeed presented in the trope of a mythical utopian island of "Hōrai" or "Paipatirohma." Is Daiku's *Hōraikō* then merely a romanticized notion of Okinawa's difference simply repackaged in the notion of cosmopolitanism, an imaginary geography of escapism?

I suggest that Daiku's musical geography of Okinawa is not simply celebrating cultural particularities of Japan's "internal Other" or engaging in an oppositional politics against Japan. Rather, it calls into question the underlying assumption of both Okinawa and Japan as exclusive, static, and bounded spatial units enclosing specific territories and a unilateral history, from which Okinawa is marginalized at the same time as it is forcibly internalized to it. The "paradise" that his album makes audible is not simply a reversal or rebuttal of hegemonic histories and geographies, but a reimagination of geography outside the narrative deeply inflected by the Cold War arrangements of power relations. The utopian Paipatirohma is not simply a mythical place in our fantasies but a call for imaginatively reconceptualizing the spatiality of Okinawa itself; as the word *exo* in the title indicates, it is in the "going" rather than the destination itself where we hear Daiku's sonic imaginaries of the paradise.

The efficacy of such cultural politics is subject to critique. Who listens to Daiku's sonic imaginaries, and what tangible consequences might they have produced? While Daiku's first album, which displayed the mutual construction of subjectivity between Okinawa and Japan, was popularly embraced and led to spinoff projects by other musicians, *Hōraikō*, which urged a radical reconceptualization of both Okinawa and Japan, has fallen short in making a similar social impact. Despite Daiku's active engagement with mainland Japan and transnational communities through both his musical imaginations and his touring and teaching engagements, the extroverted geography of Okinawa seemed not as easy to hear for the mainland Japanese's ears; the mythical island seemed too far away from Tokyoites to hear.

As if to acknowledge this difficulty of engaging mainland listeners in a mutual reimagining of Okinawa's geography, Daiku jokingly told me he found his Hōrai in Bali, Indonesia. In 2010 he released a new album recorded in Bali, where he sang Yaeyama folk songs with a Balinese gamelan ensemble—continuing to expand his creative imaginings of the transnational, postcolonial affective alliances, as if to refuse the pervasive narratives of an Okinawan daily life that is inescapably defined by US military base politics. Daiku's search for his internal, imaginative countergeography continues through a process of looking outward. It is telling that the album *Hōraikō* concludes with a tune by Brazilian pop star Milton Nascimento, "Travessia" (Bridge). The selection of this tune is not only a nod to the large waves of Okinawan immigration to Brazil but also the recapitulation of the even more globally expanded longing for a utopian paradise—or rather, the extroverted reimagination of spatiality itself. The historically imagined paradise within the circum–East China Sea has now circulated, through the layers of Cold War geopolitical dynamics and relations of the twentieth century, across the Pacific Ocean into the Americas.

> Is it an illusion? The faraway country of dreams
> The ship departs, gathering the longings and yearnings
> If you build a long bridge across the ocean during a high tide
> You are close to Corcovado.

NOTES

1. Lyrics from the album booklet, *Hōraikō: Exo-Paipatirohma* (released 2003, Off Note ON-43). All translations are mine unless otherwise noted.
2. Edward Soja, *Postmodern Geographies: The Reassertion of Space in Critical Social Theory* (London: Verso, 1989); Edward W. Said, *Culture and Imperialism* (New York: Vintage Books, 1993); Edward W. Said, *Reflections on Exile and Other Essays* (Cambridge, MA: Harvard University Press, 2000); Derek Gregory, "Imaginative Geographies," *Progress in Human Geography* 19, no. 4 (1995): 447–85; Derek Gregory, *The Colonial Present: Afghanistan, Palestine, Iraq* (Malden, MA: Blackwell, 2004).
3. This historical progression of modern Okinawa—beginning with Japanese neocolonial control in the prewar era, followed by Japanese military control during the war, which in turn succumbs to American military occupation and lasts until Okinawa's "reversion" to Japan in 1972—"is encapsulated in Okinawan dialect as 'Yamatu-yu kara Amerika-yu, Amerika-yu kara Yamatu-yu' (From Japanese rule to American rule, from American rule back to Japanese rule)." Michael S. Molasky, *The American*

Occupation of Japan and Okinawa: Literature and Memory, 2nd ed. (New York: Routledge, 2005), 21.
4   Molasky, *The American Occupation of Japan and Okinawa*, 13.
5   Chalmers Johnson lists four "great betrayals" Okinawa experienced at the hands of the Japanese and Americans during the twentieth century. The first was February 1945, when "even though Emperor Hirohito knew that the war was lost, he ordered one last great battle not fought on the Japanese mainland so as to buy time to negotiate better surrender terms for the Imperial institution." The second great betrayal occurred in 1952, when Japan won an early peace from the United States but with a price attached: the indefinite US military occupation of Okinawa. The third betrayal was the "reversion" of Okinawa to Japan. "Instead of being an American military colony directly ruled by the Pentagon, after 1972 Okinawa became an American military colony superficially legitimized by the Japanese-American Security Treaty. But nothing changed." The fourth was the Clinton-Hashimoto summit of April 1996, in which the US and Japan pretended to offer Okinawa relief, but no substantial change occurred in the policies that caused difficulties. Chalmers Johnson, "Foreword," in *Okinawa: Cold War Island*, ed. Chalmers Johnson (Cardiff, CA: Japan Policy Research Institute, 1999), 7–8.
6   Here, I am expanding on Allen Chun and Ned Rossiter's discussion of cultural imaginaries and popular music in Asia. By sonic imaginaries, I highlight how sound is inextricably integral to the formulation of the imaginary: "an imaginary construction signals that there can be no essence, but multiple imaginary terrains that contest, support or ignore one another. Each imaginary formation is articulated with a series of material preconditions. A genealogy of any imaginary formation would involve examining the constellation of material forms and practices and symbolic dimensions that distinguish one imaginary formation from another. So the imaginary does not forgo the possibility of the real, but actively inculcates the real or non-discursive entity as a necessary condition of its own formation." Allen Chun and Ned Rossiter, "Introduction: Cultural Imaginaries, Musical Communities, Reflexive Practices," in *Refashioning Pop Music in Asia: Cosmopolitan Flows, Political Tempos and Aesthetic Industries*, ed. Allen Chun, Ned Rossiter, and Brian Shoesmith (London: Routledge, 2000), 3.
7   Jocelyne Guilbault, "Audible Entanglements: Nation and Diasporas in Trinidad's Calypso Music Scene," *Small Axe* 9, no. 1 (2005): 40–63.
8   Daiku Tetsuhiro, interview, December 10, 2007.
9   Daiku Tetsuhiro, interview, December 10, 2007.
10 Most notably, the band Soul Flower Mononoke Summit attributes its acoustic outfit that frequented disaster-affected areas after the 1995 Kobe Hanshin Earthquake to Daiku's album.
11 Ann Laura Stoler and Frederick Cooper, "Between Metropole and Colony," in *Tension of Empire: Colonial Cultures in a Late Bourgeois World*, ed. Frederick Cooper and Ann Laura Stoler (Berkeley: University of California Press, 1997), 1–36.
12 Daiku Tetsuhiro, communication, December 24, 2018.
13 "Daiku Tetsuhiro Tokushū," Takara Records, accessed June 29, 2019, http://www.takara-r.com/takarahp/text/daiku-cd.html.

14 Doreen Massey, *Space, Place, and Gender* (Minneapolis: University of Minnesota Press, 1994), 147.
15 Despite the cultural assimilation efforts, Okinawa's otherness remained problematic to mainland Japan; the Japanese considered Okinawans second-class citizens but nonetheless perceived them as being "more Japanese" than were the Taiwanese, Koreans, or other occupied peoples. In this way, Okinawa can be described as a doubly racialized subject. Its occupation and the subsequent American military presence were rationalized and enforced both by Japanese and American authorities as a necessary project of modernizing the "backward," ethnic, southern islanders of Okinawa.
16 Based on cultural, linguistic, and racial differences, soldiers of the Imperial Japanese Army turned on the Okinawan civilians they were sworn to protect, sometimes ordering them to commit "compulsory group suicide" rather than surrender to the enemy. For example, on Tokashiki Island, 329 islanders died by their own hands; mostly family members killed each other. The Japanese soldiers "sometimes callously killed Okinawans—men, women, and children—in order to claim safe shelter for themselves." Many villagers obeyed orders to kill themselves and family members, while military units on the island avoided combat and many soldiers survived. Laura Hein and Mark Selden, "Culture, Power, and Identity in Contemporary Okinawa," in *Islands of Discontent: Okinawan Responses to Japanese and American Power*, ed. Laura Hein and Mark Selden (Oxford: Rowman and Littlefield, 2003), 14. It is reported that in 1945 Emperor Hirohito privately indicated to the Supreme Commander for the Allied Powers (SCAP) that he was willing to have Okinawa remain under American military authority. Hein and Selden, "Culture, Power, and Identity in Contemporary Okinawa," 19; Molasky, *The American Occupation of Japan and Okinawa*, 20. Taira Kōji notes the significance of this event: "By this act, the emperor became a symbol of the 'disunity' of the people, although perhaps in the emperor's view, Okinawans were never part of the Japanese people whose unity he symbolized. This opens up the issue of the ethnicity or nationality of Okinawans." Taira Kōji, "Okinawa's Choice: Independence or Subordination," in *Okinawa: Cold War Island*, ed. Chalmers Johnson (Cardiff, CA: Japan Policy Research Institute, 1999), 174.
17 Molasky, *The American Occupation of Japan and Okinawa*, 13.
18 Another rather idealistic way in which Okinawa was temporalized was through the imposition of Japanese folk authenticity onto Okinawa. Mainland ethnologist Yanagita Kunio asserted that Okinawa was the source of a "pure Japanese culture" that had "regrettably disappeared in the cultural mishmash of modern Japan." Quoted in Steve Rabson, "Assimilation Policy in Okinawa: Promotion, Resistance, and 'Reconstruction,'" in *Okinawa: Cold War Island*, ed. Chalmers Johnson (Cardiff, CA: Japan Policy Research Institute, 1999), 143.
19 Hein and Selden, "Culture, Power, and Identity in Contemporary Okinawa," 3.
20 Molasky, *The American Occupation of Japan and Okinawa*, 20.
21 Although it lies beyond the scope of this chapter, I would also argue that Okinawa is doubly feminized, by American soldiers' sexual violence toward local women and by the dominant discourse against military violence, which portrays Okinawa as a "daughter" in need of paternal help from masculine Japan.

22 In addition to the issue of land, the disconnection and uneven dynamics between the centralized Japanese authority and Okinawa is well portrayed in Ōta Masahide's comparative analysis of Japanese and American military plans in the Battle of Okinawa. Ōta points to the miscommunication and the lack of understanding between the overly centralized mainland and Okinawa, claiming that the self-defeating incidents taking place during the battle "appear almost inevitable as a result of the lopsided relationship between the central power and the remote backwater prefecture," especially combined with a lack of understanding of Okinawa's particular political and cultural conditions. Masahide Ōta, "Re-Examining the History of the Battle of Okinawa," in *Okinawa: Cold War Island*, ed. Chalmers Johnson (Cardiff, CA: Japan Policy Research Institute, 1999), 17.

23 Eiko Asato, "Okinawan Identity and Resistance to Militarization and Maldevelopment," in *Islands of Discontent: Okinawan Responses to Japanese and American Power*, ed. Laura Hein and Mark Selden (Oxford: Rowman and Littlefield, 2003), 239.

24 Asato, "Okinawan Identity and Resistance," 230.

25 Molasky, *The American Occupation of Japan and Okinawa*, 23.

26 Hein and Selden, "Culture, Power, and Identity in Contemporary Okinawa," 22.

27 Johnson adds: "Those provisions of the Land Acquisition Law that stipulate that public seizure of land be justified in terms of the public's welfare were simply ignored." Chalmers Johnson, "The 1995 Rape Incident and the Rekindling of Okinawan Protest against the American Bases," in *Okinawa: Cold War Island*, ed. Chalmers Johnson (Cardiff, CA: Japan Policy Research Institute, 1999), 111.

28 Giorgio Agamben, *State of Exception* (Chicago: University of Chicago Press, 2005). On this revision, Johnson makes the observation that "it is inconceivable that the Japanese Diet would have agreed to such a law if it had affected mainland Japanese." Johnson, "1995 Rape Incident and the Rekindling of Okinawan Protest," 113.

29 Prior to this recording, on October 21, 1995, Daiku performed this version at the mass rally of eighty-five thousand people protesting against the rape of the schoolgirl and calling for an end of the US military presence in Okinawa.

30 For a more detailed discussion of the song and a particularly insightful analysis of the politics of place in Okinawan popular music, see James Roberson, "Uchina Pop: Place and Identity in Contemporary Okinawan Popular Music," in *Islands of Discontent: Okinawan Responses to Japanese and American Power*, ed. Laura Hein and Mark Selden (Oxford: Rowman and Littlefield, 2003), 192–227.

31 Hein and Selden, "Culture, Power, and Identity in Contemporary Okinawa," 5.

32 Kozy K. Amemiya, "The Bolivian Connection: U.S. Bases and Okinawan Emigration," in *Okinawa: Cold War Island*, ed. Chalmers Johnson (Cardiff, CA: Japan Policy Research Institute, 1999), 55; Taku Suzuki, *Embodying Belonging: Racializing Okinawan Diaspora in Bolivia and Japan* (Honolulu: University of Hawai'i Press, 2010), 29–34.

33 Shūhei Hosokawa, "Soy Sauce Music: Haruomi Hosono and Japanese Self-Orientalism," in *Widening the Horizon: Exoticism in Post-war Popular Music*, ed. Philip Hayward (Sydney, Australia: John Libbey, 1999), 127; Shin Aoki, "Singing Exoticism: A Historical Anthropology of the G.I. Songs 'China Night' and 'Japanese Rumba,'" *Journal of American History* 13, no. 4 (2017): 950.

34 Hosokawa's analysis of Hosono Haruomi's imaginary circumnavigation in his "Soy Sauce Trilogy" shows remarkable parallels with Daiku's musical endeavors on *Hōraikō*. See Hosokawa, "Soy Sauce Music." Both artists use musical detours and retours through sonic imaginaries of different locations around the world to reveal colonial memories, employing ambiguity and humor at the core of their aesthetic stylings. However, the positionality of the two artists—Hosono as a mainland Japanese and Daiku as a Yaeyama native—leads to a stark contrast in the cultural politics their music performs. For instance, while Hosono's music critiques Japan's self-orientalism and collective amnesia in its attempt to assimilate into the West, Daiku points to the dual subjugation Okinawa has endured by both Japan and the "West." Hosono's music attempts to recover the colonial memory of American occupation, while Daiku's Okinawa never "forgot" the occupation—Okinawa is in a permanent (neo)colonial state, where the American military is an ongoing presence. I thank Michael Bourdaghs for pointing out this parallel to me.
35 On Japanese colonial mimicry, see Hosokawa, "Soy Sauce Music."
36 Hein and Selden, "Culture, Power, and Identity in Contemporary Okinawa," 18.
37 Sheldon Pollock, Homi Bhabha, Carol Breckenridge, and Dipesh Chakrabarty, "Cosmopolitanisms," *Public Culture* 12, no 3 (2000): 588.
38 Daiku Tetsuhiro, interview, August 10, 2013.
39 S. J. Wardaya and T. Baskara, "Global Solidarity against Unilateralism," *Inter-Asia Cultural Studies* 6, no. 4 (2005): 476–86. Conceptualizing Okinawa as a space conscious of its links with the wider world has also led to forging connections with other minorities and indigenous groups, creating a sense of solidarity in the struggle against land dispossession, economic marginalization, and military violence. For instance, some Okinawans have forged political links with Japan's other major ethnic minority, the Ainu of the northern island Hokkaido, as well as with indigenous peoples in other parts of the world, including Native Americans and Australian Aborigines. The world tour "White Ship Tour 1998" of Kina Shokichi, a politically active Okinawan musician and former parliament member, is one example of Okinawan cultural outreach in solidarity with other indigenous peoples' struggles. His tour included stops at the Ute and Pine Ridge Reservations and ended at the Onondaga Iroquois Nation. Such interconnections with indigenous groups have provided Okinawans with a globalized language of minority and human rights, concepts of ethnic identity, political pluralism, and multiculturalism that animate various social movements worldwide. This is evident in the March 2001 Okinawan Appeal to the United Nations, which claimed that "the people of Okinawa possess their own history and culture. As such, their rights are those of indigenous people, including the right to self-determination." Hein and Selden, "Culture, Power, and Identity in Contemporary Okinawa," 35.
40 Kuan-Hsing Chen, *Asia as Method: Toward Deimperialization* (Durham, NC: Duke University Press, 2010), 120.
41 Hein and Selden, "Culture, Power, and Identity in Contemporary Okinawa," 31.

7. COSMAHARAJA
Popular Songs of Socialist Cosmpolitanism in Cold War India

ANNA SCHULTZ

Throughout the Cold War, India maintained a policy of nonalignment, first in relation to China and later in relation to the US and the USSR. This policy allowed India to receive support from both superpowers during the Cold War and bolstered Jawaharlal Nehru's efforts to craft a secular nation that would modernize rapidly along socialist lines. In reality, this was a fraught and contradictory process: India worked with nonaligned partners to find a peaceful alternative to the threat of massive nuclear destruction, even as violent, bipolar conflicts—residues of the "peaceful" standoff between the US and the USSR—erupted at its Pakistani and Chinese fronts. Moreover, myriad versions of socialism in regional contexts pulled at the seams of Nehru's dream, particularly in the rural areas he sought to modernize through dams, irrigation projects, and infrastructural development. The socialist ideas that reached village India were refracted through the interpretations of state politicians whose ideas were in turn translated by regional religious teachers.

This chapter asks how the power of personality, bolstered by music and religion, performed political work that had eluded middle-class nationalists in the period leading up to and during South Asia's Cold War. I explore the margins of the Cold War through the work of Sant Tukdoji Maharaj (1909–1968), a rural Indian singer-saint whose influence was local, national, and international. Tukdoji was many things to many people: a devotional singer, a Gandhian, a champion of progressive land reform, an international spokesperson for world peace, and a supporter of nuclear defense at the Chinese and Pakistani fronts. These seemingly unreconcilable tensions in Tukdoji's oeuvre mirror the ambivalences of a "cold" war marked by "hot" antagonisms, even as they reveal the struggle of a rural devotional singer translating between disparate worldviews.

But why devote a chapter to a holy man who is unknown beyond India? Even within India, he is barely remembered outside Maharashtra, but at critical historical moments Tukdoji met regularly with India's political elite and his activities were covered by major newspapers. To say that he rubbed elbows with Mahatma Gandhi and Jawaharlal Nehru, however, does not do justice to the power and reach of his individual influence. As a singer, he was moving and exuberant—a sonic presence that exceeded the capabilities of the nation's primary architects. Indeed, he was important to the middle-class political elite precisely *because* he was a singer and beloved leader in his own right. As such, he garnered their respect as well as their fear of how he might use this power to inspire emotion.

Tukdoji was known in his time as *rashtrasant*, indexing both his commitment to the nation (*rashtra*) and his affiliation with the Hindu saint or holy person (*sant*) tradition.[1] To be a sant is to be a singer, poet, and spiritual guide on the path of devotion (*bhakti*). Between the sixth and seventeenth centuries, bhakti sants used regional vernaculars to sing of the pure emotional connection that could draw singers and listeners into proximity with the divine. John Stratton Hawley's eloquent description of bhakti religion seems particularly apt for the present discussion of the Cold/Hot War.

> Bhakti is heart religion, sometimes cool and quiescent but sometimes hot—the religion of participation, community, enthusiasm, song, and often of personal challenge. . . . It evokes the idea of a widely shared religiosity for which institutional superstructures weren't all that relevant, and which, once activated, could be historically contagious—a glorious disease of the collective heart. It implies direct divine encounter, experienced in the lives of individual people. These people, moved by that encounter, turn to poetry, which is the natural vehicle of bhakti, and poetry expresses itself just as naturally in song.[2]

As this excerpt asserts, poetry, song, and community experience are at the core of bhakti traditions. In Marathi-speaking areas now encompassed by the postcolonial state of Maharashtra, the regional bhakti tradition known as the *varkari* movement is rooted in the songs and hagiographies of sants who lived between the twelfth and seventeenth centuries, from Sant Jnaneshvar through Sant Tukaram.[3] And while bhakti is not typically associated with politics, Tukdoji and others recognized the potential of this "sometimes hot" religion to inspire people toward collective, nationalist action.[4]

It is in this context of rural, religious performance that we need to position the meanings of "popular music" relevant to Tukdoji Maharaj. In his genealogy of popular music, Richard Middleton notes that the term *popular* has always had something to do with "the [common] people," and that it dropped its formerly negative associations of vulgarity to reemerge as a positive, quantitative, class-inflected concept in the eighteenth century. By the early nineteenth century, "popular music" had come to be associated with "'peasant,' 'national' and 'traditional' songs."[5] These latter meanings were largely offloaded in the late nineteenth century to "folk" music, leaving "popular music" to Tin Pan Alley and other mass-mediated/marketed songs. As Middleton argues, these understandings of "popular music"—music of the common people and peasants, music that is liked by many, and music made for the mass media—continue to coexist in the twentieth century, being drawn to the center depending on the scholarly and political frames of the author. This chapter shuttles between all three meanings in ways that mirror Tukdoji's own flexibility with regard to style and audience. He was beloved by masses of (mostly rural) people for the religious folk songs he performed live, but he also recorded Bollywood-inflected versions of his compositions for a mass-media market that spanned class boundaries.

South Asian politics of resistance have been sounded musically as much as they have been read or spoken, and subaltern histories must engage with song *as* song. Devotional song is not simply a means for illiterate people to communicate texts—through its participatory nature and capacity for repetition between performance contexts, it brings poetry into the bodies and memories of listeners. Tukdoji's life as a singer-saint corresponded with the emergence of recording and radio in India, and he alternately used and ignored these media to fashion multiple, shifting identities. The challenge of this chapter is to approach an understanding of the presence of Tukdoji's song in performance, though all we have are residues left in recordings, third-person accounts, and Tukdoji's own didactic reflections on the importance of devotional song. That said, bhakti performance continues to thrive in today's India, and we can learn from ethnographic work in this milieu. Linda Hess, in her book on North Indian Kabir (a fifteenth-century sant) song, demonstrates how singers shape interpretation and create community in performance, and Sukanya Sarbhadikary's ethnography of Bengali Radha-Krishna poetry attends to the bodily experience of devotional song, arguing beautifully that Krishnaite landscapes and stories are resounded in the body.[6] My own ethnographic work with Marathi nationalist devotional song conducted between 1998 and 2012 explores how singers generate heightened experience by playing with musical intertextuality and guiding listeners on participatory journeys that promote sensations of blurred distinctions between the self and the divine.[7]

This chapter also reconsiders trajectories of cosmopolitan sound and thought in India's Cold Wars. Recent work in anthropology has complicated earlier understandings of the Cold War as bipolar, Eurocentric, and state-centric. Heonik Kwon argues that although the Cold War was a truly global phenomenon, the idea of a "long peace" does not reflect the experience of postcolonial nation-states ridden with pervasive violent conflict throughout this era.[8] My project contributes to this decentering of the bipolar Cold War and is inspired by ethnographic research on the conflict's cultural reverberations by Kwon, Susan Bayly, Akhil Gupta, and Magnus Marsden.[9] By looking at the political through the popular, we find discrepant circulations that confront and bypass the fronts established by the Cold War and that map connections different from those officialized via the Non-Aligned Movement.

I am particularly interested in how the Cold War made certain forms of cosmopolitanism available to Tukdoji and other rural leaders during the transition from anticolonial nationalism to postcolonial socialism. Bayly's work in India and Vietnam demonstrates that Cold War–era "Asian moderns" used socialism to articulate identities that were cosmopolitan and modern while also being anti-American and anti-imperialist.[10] This was equally true for Tukdoji, but unlike the educated "Asian moderns" described by Bayly, he did not carry markers of Westernized cosmopolitanism in dress, language, reading choices, and so on.[11] He was neither educated nor urban, and he lived his entire life in and around Yawali, a village in Amravati district in rural eastern Maharashtra state.[12] He was more akin to what Vinay Gidwani and K. Sivaramakrishnan describe as a "rural cosmopolitan," that is, one whose cosmopolitan sensibilities were shaped by movement between rural and urban spaces within the nation-state. Indeed, by all accounts he was almost perpetually on the move, encountering, assimilating, and responding to a range of ideas and practices.[13]

Tukdoji not only absorbed cosmopolitan political ideas; he also projected his voice outward beyond Marathi-speaking areas and even beyond India. One might imagine that he would have foregrounded music that *sounded* cosmopolitan to reach beyond Maharashtra, and to some extent that was true, but he also—strategically—sang without the bells and whistles of the studio in Delhi and in Shimizu, Japan. In *Singing a Hindu Nation*, I wrote of noncosmopolitan devotional singers and storytellers (*kirtankars*) from the Indian state of Maharashtra who translated nationalism and generated devotion to the nation from the late nineteenth century. The nationalist kirtankars I wrote about in that book had contact with middle-class nationalist leaders, but for the most part, their travels and idioms were limited to Maharashtra and Marathi.[14] Tukdoji forged routes of a different order—he sang in both Marathi and Hindi in a style of devotional song that was intelligible and moving for people from all parts of India, and even for listeners from outside India. His musical, political, and religious pathways intersect and provide clues to one another, but they are not the same thing. I begin this story in the 1930s, when Tukdoji developed his social and political voice and came to the attention of Mahatma Gandhi, but focus on the increasing ambivalence of that voice after independence from Britain and the onset of the Cold War in 1947.

Becoming Tukdoji: Saint, Singer, and Gandhian

Sant Tukdoji was born Manik Ingle in 1909 to a family of Hindu devotional hymn (*bhajan*) singers. The term *bhajan* means different things in different parts of India, but in all cases it refers to bhakti songs, that is, songs that musically and poetically help the singer or listener feel the emotion of devotion. Like most North Indian bhajans, Tukdoji's songs are in a vernacular rich in metaphor and spiritual lessons, with a final line that includes the name of the poet. From a tender age, Manik showed great facility in composing and singing bhajans and playing the tambourine (*khanjiri*). Also from a young age, he evinced a desire for spiritual growth that led him to become a disciple of the famed spiritual teacher Aadkoji Maharaj and to spend years in the forest in meditation and study. He was a child when he first met Aadkoji Maharaj, who purportedly gave him the nickname Tukadya while feeding him a piece (*tukada*) of sorghum flatbread.[15] Almost as soon as he emerged from isolation, Manik came to be revered as Sant Tukdoji Maharaj and developed a large following of people who gathered to hear his spiritual insights and enchanting bhajans in Hindi and Marathi.[16] Tukdoji communicated with his followers not only through recorded and live song performance but also through lectures, sermons, and open letters to his followers and a versified treatise on rural development in Marathi called *Gramgita* (Village song). Though he was illiterate, Tukdoji dictated sixty-five books in prose and verse.[17]

By the age of twenty, Tukdoji was singing bhajans about national determination, and by 1936 Gandhi had received news of Tukdoji's popularity and invited him to his religious hermitage, Sevagram, which was just 100 kilometers from Tukdoji's own ashram (hermitage) called Gurukunj in Mozari. Indeed, it seems that Tukdoji became nationally known through his association with Gandhi, which was in turn a result of the close proximity between the two men's ashrams. Gandhi was the single most influential ideological force in Tukdoji's life and work, and although the influence ran primarily in one direction,

Tukdoji's poetry and song also took hold in Gandhi's heart. Gandhi earned a law degree in London and served as a lawyer in South Africa before returning to his native India, and though the Mahatma adapted what he learned abroad to Indian contexts, someone like Tukdoji could more firmly plant his cosmopolitan ideas in Maharashtrian soil. Tukdoji stayed with Gandhi for a month, delighting the Mahatma with his bhajans and learning about satyagraha ("truth force," Gandhi's mode of political resistance), ahimsa (nonviolence), anti-untouchability, and swaraj (self-rule, self-reliance).[18] During his stay at Sevagram, Tukdoji stayed in Gandhi's small 29 × 14 foot room, with Tukdoji in one corner, Gandhi in another, and one of Gandhi's coworkers in the third. In these close quarters, Gandhi witnessed Tukdoji's followers "stream in all day," and Tukdoji learned about Gandhian philosophy by being drawn into conversation with the latter's visitors.[19] Tukdoji was particularly interested in learning about the finer points of spinning cotton, which Gandhi had transformed into a symbol of national self-reliance and a gesture of resistance to British control of the Indian textile industry.[20]

Clearly Gandhi was fascinated with the power of Tukdoji's songs; in a letter to Amrit Kaur soon after Tukdoji arrived at Sevagram, Gandhi referred to Tukdoji as "a great singer of *bhajani.*"[21] Denigrating his own oratory vis-à-vis Tukdoji's songs, Gandhi said to a group of students in a village workers' training school, "[Tukdoji Maharaj] does not talk like me; he simply sings bhajans and preaches and teaches through them. I must need [*sic*] talk as I can neither compose nor sing."[22] One Tukdoji bhajan in particular—about how the loss of family, friends, health, and money are actually a blessing, leaving one's mind free to concentrate on the divine—made a lasting impression on Gandhi. In 1947 he invoked it in a speech as a comfort for the pain and loss of the Partition of India and Pakistan, and the next year, just three weeks before his assassination, he quoted the entire bhajan to console a dear friend who had lost a sum of money during Partition.[23]

Tukdoji's commitment to Gandhi lasted long past India's independence in 1947 and the Mahatma's death in 1948. Even as the postcolonial socialist state was moving away from Gandhian models of decentralized governance and toward state-sponsored modernization and mechanization, Tukdoji continued to promote Gandhian ideals through his songs, speeches, actions, and his association with Acharya (teacher) Vinoba Bhave. Inspired by Gandhi, Tukdoji founded the Seva Mandal (Service Collective) at Gurukunj in 1943 to provide social services, unify sects, and improve the condition of villages, writing, "all these dreams, those noble ideals, those spiritual ways chalked out by Pujya Mahatma Gandhi have been adopted."[24] Tukdoji's *Gramgita*, composed in 1953 and published in 1955, can be seen as a distillation of the ideology that fed the Seva Mandal and as a translation of Gandhian thought for Maharashtrian villagers.[25] Written entirely in the *ovi* meter (an ancient genre associated with both women's song and sant poetry) and using illustrative examples drawn from village life, Tukdoji's magnum opus advocates religious tolerance, collective decision-making through the Panchayat system, village economic independence, voluntary service (*seva*), gender equality in education, land sharing, health, hygiene, and simplicity of dress, and it argues against untouchability, caste, dowry, and lavish weddings.[26] A thematic thread of the book is the notion that unity, cooperation, and the minimization of religious, caste, gender, wealth, and sectarian differences benefit both village and nation. All this resonates with Gandhian philosophy but is couched in a rural Maharashtrian idiom that would have been only vaguely familiar to Gandhi.[27] Tukdoji, then, enhanced the intelligibility and emotional resonance of Gandhian ideas for Marathi-speaking audiences.

Vinoba Bhave was a close associate and spiritual successor of Gandhi, devoting his life to rural empowerment through the postcolonial uplift of all (*sarvodaya*) and land gift (*bhoodan*) movements. The term *sarvodaya* was adopted from Gandhi's loose Gujarati translation of *Unto This Last*, an exegesis on social justice and a critique of capitalism by John Ruskin, a Victorian-era artist, art critic, and social commentator. The concept of sarvodaya became thoroughly localized in Gandhi's ashram, which was run according to the movement's ideals of the dignity of labor and equitable distribution of wealth.[28] Sarvodaya shaped the course of rural development throughout India—Maharashtra in particular—and influenced Tukdoji, who promoted national self-reliance and valorized physical labor to resist an Indian social order that denigrated low-caste occupations.[29]

Born of the same egalitarian impulses as sarvodaya, the bhoodan movement sought to equalize land ownership in rural areas by convincing wealthy landowners to donate a portion of their land to farmers who could not afford land.[30] Tukdoji was a leading activist in the bhoodan movement—appointed to the Bhoodan Yagna (Offering) Board by Bhave in 1953, he spent that entire year traveling through Maharashtra convincing people to donate land.[31] Indeed, he was one of Maharashtra's most successful bhoodan activists, collecting 11,500 acres during a ten-day tour of Yeotmal (now Yavatmal) District in eastern Maharashtra.[32] Song was at the center of Tukdoji's efforts: Joseph Jean Lanza del Vasto, a European pacifist who traveled with Bhave in the 1950s, reported that Tukdoji wrote new hymns in honor of Bhave and sang songs that inspired people to donate land for the common good.[33]

Tukdoji's involvement with bhoodan was covered widely in national and regional newspapers, framed not as the work of a marginal radical but as a viable national strategy of postcolonial rural development. According to an English-language *Times of India* article, the chief minister of Madhya Pradesh, Pandit Ravi Shankar Shukla, said that bhoodan would "Indianise socialism," solve India's economic crisis, and drive out communism. In the same article, the journalist paraphrased Tukdoji's speech: "Sant Tukdoji described 'bhoodan' as a movement of love and peace. He said it could not progress without the willing co-operation of the landlords. It would bring real swaraj to the kisans [farmers], freeing them from the clutches of patels [landowners, village leaders] and patwaris [village accountants], he said."[34] Tukdoji—whom the author referred to as the "leader of the movement"—expressed the importance of bhoodan by grounding it in a rural central Indian imaginary of local castes and the Gandhian concept of swaraj. In these two statements by Shukla and Tukdoji, paraphrased one after another, we see the translation from cosmopolitan political ideologies to concepts and identities familiar to Indian farmers in a particular region.

The Rural Cosmopolitics of Tukdoji's Marathi Bhajans

The throngs of people who came to see Tukdoji wanted to hear him sing—it was in song that his imposing physical presence became palpable, his ideas shone brightly, and his devotees felt the emotional power of his words. Song was at the core of Tukdoji's identity and it was the primary means through which he gained not just listeners but devotees. With that in mind, it is instructive to consider how his songs' lyrical meanings were enhanced by musical and religious intertextualities and by the participatory mode in which he performed. Some of Tukdoji's recorded songs also evoked cosmopolitan imaginaries that reached beyond local audiences, providing a counterpoint to the rural, religious socialism of his poetry.

A glimpse into Tukdoji's live performance style can be heard on a concert recording from 1968, the last year of his life. He was probably already sick with cancer by that time, but he spoke and sang with verve and began the concert by engaging audience members of successive age groups in spirited exclamations of praise (*jayjaykar*).[35] This manner of engaging audience members is pronounced in this performance but is common to bhakti music from all regions of India. By singing together, devotees not only collaborate to generate a heightened emotional/devotional state but also articulate the accessibility of pure devotion. Gandhi's disciple, Balvantsinha, reported that the hundreds of people who attended prayers at Gandhi's ashram to hear Tukdoji's bhajans were left "spellbound," and Professor Ram Ghode recalled a childhood memory of hearing Tukdoji's "echoing, powerful voice" as he sang nationalist bhajans.[36] The most vibrant account, though, comes from Lanza del Vasto, who heard Tukdoji perform during the bhoodan campaign.

> Then Tukdo made ready to sing the way a big gourmet makes ready to eat: he straightened up and settled himself on his seat, rolled his eyes, licked his chops and drew his dishes and pots—his instruments I mean—towards him, blew on his tambourines and rubbed them with the palm of his hand to warm them, stretched his kettle-drums, tried their liquid sound, and gathered his young pupils round him. At last he gave them the signal by a shake of the shoulders—for he conducted with his back and the slight shaking of the little mat on the nape of his neck—and threw himself back, with dilated nostrils, giving vent to a magnificent hullaballoo. His mouth, whose teeth jutted out in all directions, was like the mouth of a trombone. The melody weeps, the rhythm laughs and the singer wears himself into a frazzle and is lulled into a slumber in the midst of his own uproar. At one time his voice lifts its trembling notes sky-high, at another time it comes down rumbling to join the confused fury of the drums. But his eye, impassive and far-away, hovers like an eagle over a vast landscape.[37]

In his *Gramgita*, Tukdoji himself echoed the notion that bhajan should thrill its listeners: "One's heart should be overflowing with reverence / It should be overcome by emotion // The hair on one's body should stand on end / Because of bhajan // 74 //."[38] He continued, though, that this devotional excess should be moderated by a vocal manner that is "gentle" (*komal*), "plain/straight" (*saral*), "pious/virtuous" (*sattvik*), and "sweet" (*goda*).[39] All this can be heard in his bhajans. With this backdrop of performance in mind, we begin our close readings with "Mani Nahi Bhav" (If you pray without faith), Tukdoji's most popular and beloved bhajan.

मनी नाही भाव म्हणे देवा मला पाव
देव अशानं भेटायचा नाही रे
देव बाजारचा भाजीपाला नाही रे

दगडाचा देव त्याला वडराचं भेव
लाकडाचा देव त्याला अग्निचं भेव
मातीचा देव त्याला पाण्याचं भेव
सोन्याचांदीचा देव त्याला चोरांचं भेव
देव बाजारचा भाजीपाला नाही रे

देवाचं देवत्व नाही दगडात
देवाचं देवत्व नाही लाकडात
सोन्याचांदीत नाही देवाची मात
देव बाजारचा भाजीपाला नाही रे

भाव तिथं देव ही संतांची वाणी
आचारावाचून पाहिला का कोणी
शब्दाच्या बोलानं शांती नाही मनी
देव बाजारचा भाजीपाला नाही रे

If you say without faith, "God, answer my prayer,"
You won't be able to meet God, *re*
God is not some vegetable from the market, *re*!

A stone god fears a mason
A wooden god fears fire
A clay god fears water
A gold and silver god fears thieves
God is not some vegetable from the market, *re*!

God's divinity is not in stone
God's divinity is not in wood
God cannot be appraised like gold and silver
God is not some vegetable from the market, *re*!

The saints say, God lives where there is true devotion.
Has anyone seen Him without proper conduct?
Mere words cannot give peace of mind
God is not some vegetable from the market, *re*!

God's divinity is all around,
Duality cannot be experienced without death
Tukdya Das says, listen to this:
God is not some vegetable from the market, *re*![40]

In most respects, this bhajan exemplifies the speech and musical patterning of rural Maharashtra state. It is in modern, conversational Marathi and is peppered throughout with the word *re*, a term of intimacy used to address a close male friend or family member. It conveys the message—through the ever-effective list form—that objects can be counted ad infinitum but that God is neither material nor enumerable. This song is clearly Tukdoji's—the playful chastising of false beliefs and the use of *re* characterize his style, as does his poetic signature, "Tukdya Das says…" (Tukdya the servant says). The use of the signature line itself, though, positions this song within the world of bhakti poetry, as does its ovi meter. Typically, an ovi is composed of four lines: three rhyming lines of six to fifteen syllables and a fourth, often shorter, nonrhyming line.[41] In "Mani Nahi Bhav," each stanza consists of three twelve-syllable rhyming lines, followed by the twelve-syllable refrain, "God is not some vegetable from the market, *re*!"[42] It is truly in Tukdoji's singular voice despite his use of a common varkari genre—typically the fourth line will be distinct in each stanza of an ovi, but in Tukdoji's ovi, the fourth line is a catchy refrain of equal length to the other three lines. He also enthusiastically adds an extra line in the second stanza. In addition to these formal features, Tukdoji drew on the topoi of bhakti poetry, which eschew ritual knowledge and scripture in favor of the more accessible devotional methods of collective song and pilgrimage.[43] More specifically, this song's acerbic, colorful rhetoric evokes the seventeenth-century abhanga (a varkari rhymed couplet form) poetry of Tukaram, the most beloved of Marathi sants, who criticized the hypocrisy of Brahmins and preachers.[44] And like Kabir, the fifteenth-century North Indian saint whose deeply moving songs addressed a formless divine, Tukdoji decried the worship of material idols.[45] This antimaterialist stance—expressed most pointedly with the line "God cannot be appraised like gold and silver"—was similarly consonant with Gandhian swadeshi and the austerities of Nehruvian socialism.[46]

Musically, "Mani Nahi Bhav" is in Tukdoji's own style but is evocative of songs performed on the annual varkari pilgrimage to Lord Vitthala's temple in Pandharpur.[47] It also promotes the type of embodied participation characteristic of varkari song; one can easily imagine listeners clapping along and joining in on the refrain. It is in the eight-beat meter called bhajani theka and is accompanied by a double-headed drum (*pakhwaj*), which is the case for nearly all varkari songs. Like most varkari melodies, this one has a descending contour and employs a flat third and flat seventh (there is also some use of the natural third and flat sixth). That said, just as Tukdoji's personality informed his poetry, he also brought a unique flair to performance. He sang in a grainy voice that indexes rurality throughout South Asia, but in his own, particularly forceful (for bhajan) style, and he employs an unusually fast tempo enhanced by his virtuosic playing of a small tambourine called khanjiri; the overall effect is of incredible intensity and energy.[48] Linguistic intimacy and khanjiri playing mark this bhajan as unique to Tukdoji, but other aspects of music and poetry position him within the Marathi varkari bhakti tradition.

In South Asian genre terms, bhajans by Tukdoji Maharaj would generally be considered "Marathi folk" or "devotional," but if we listen in a new way to "Mani Nahi Bhav," we also hear hints of a popular cosmopolitan aesthetic characteristic of the breadth of his experience. Indeed, Tukdoji himself extolled musical "modernization" in the *Gramgita*: "We can set [bhajans] to modern tunes / to fix people's attention on what we say // Let us show what the saints have done / in the language of this time // 57//."[49] In "Mani Nahi Bhav," his voice is accompanied not only by the double-headed barrel drum (*pakhawaj*), khanjiri, and concave hand cymbals (*tal*) of Marathi rural devotional idioms but also by the clarinet, violins, and *bulbul tarang* of pan-Indian film music.[50] Most film songs from the 1940s through the 1980s began with an instrumental introduction showcasing contrasting timbres, textures, and melodic themes, with instrumentalists returning to the foreground to trade precomposed solos during interludes between verses.[51] Despite having a *filmi* ensemble, though, "Mani Nahi Bhav" approaches neither the introduction nor the interludes in a particularly filmi way.[52] Tukdoji sings an unmetered melody in a strong voice characteristic of folk music before the instruments join him, and his interludes are filled by a small chorus singing the refrain while rhythm instruments—dominated by Tukdoji's khanjiri—come to the foreground. The melodic instruments are doubling the voice rather than playing consecutive solos in a prearranged manner. While the timbres of the instruments index Hindi film song, they adapt to Tukdoji's style and the performance practice of rural Marathi song. Even the clarinet performs the role of a traditional chorus by answering Tukdoji's calls with a response.[53]

Other recordings by Tukdoji trade more explicitly in the vocabulary of pan-Indian popular song. His bhajan "Ghadi ghadi," (Every single moment), for example, uses the same instrumentation (plus piano) as "Mani Nahi Bhav" but to a different effect. [54] The chorus translates as: "Every single moment, I want to recite your name in my heart / To behold your feet with a calm mind, *re*." This abhanga is about the peacefulness of chanting God's names and the impermanence and meaninglessness of life, accompanied almost ironically by a Latin dance rhythm. The rhumba rhythm of the carefully arranged introduction is paired with Western harmonies and the rhythmic and textural contrasts of Hindi film song. The recording starts with the entire ensemble playing a dramatic, tightly synchronized tonic to dominant chord progression, followed by a clarinet-driven filmi melody repeated four times as a descending sequence. When Tukdoji Maharaj begins singing, an eight-beat Maharashtrian folk rhythm that shares an affinity with the Latin rhythm redirects the performance from Bollywood stylistics back to a Marathi song. Though he was accompanied by an ensemble of musicians trained in Bollywood aesthetics, and even though they start out with a rhumba bang, the force of Tukdoji's musical personality transformed this aesthetic into something grounded in Maharashtrian rural practice. Ultimately, sounds that conflict with the formal structure, rhythms, and textures of rural Marathi devotional music do not make their way into the final translation.

घडी घडी मनीं तुझे नाम जपावे ।
चित्त स्थीरवोनि चरण पहावे रे ॥धृ॥

कोणा आवडतो संसार सारा । घरदार सारे मोह पसारा ॥
परी दुःख वाटे अंतरी बघावे रे । अनुभव घ्यावे ॥१॥

सगुण साकार रूप ते निर्मळ । ध्यान ठेवितांची पळे कळिकाळ ।
संत देती साक्ष ग्रंथासी बघावे । अनुभव घ्यावे ॥२॥

आम्हां साधकासी हाची मार्ग सोपा । जन्म मरणाच्या चुकवाव्या खेपा ।
तुकड्या म्हणे क्षण फुका न गमावे रे । अनुभव घ्यावे ॥३॥

Every single moment, I want to recite your name in my heart
To behold your feet with a calm mind, *re*

Some people enjoy worldly existence
House and home and all the allures of worldly goods
But they lead to inner sorrow, *re*,
Learn from [this] experience

The pure and virtuous form [of God]
If we focus on it, grief will disappear
The saints and scriptures attest to this
Learn from [their] experience

This is the simple path for us devotees
It will free us from the cycle of birth and death.
Tukadya says, don't waste a single moment, *re*
Learn from [my] experience//[55]

Modernization, Nehruvian Socialism, and the Bharat Sadhu Samaj

After independence and at the onset of the Cold War, Jawaharlal Nehru, India's first prime minister, developed a system of rural development that diverged significantly from that of Gandhi. Gandhi hoped that postcolonial India would be a loose network of locally governed, socially progressive, philosophically Hindu panchayats, but Nehru imagined India as a modern, highly centralized socialist state. Tukdoji sanguinely attempted to find a common ground between the two—though he embraced the Gandhian ideals of sarvodaya and bhoodan and encouraged each village to independently find its own route to progress, he was equally enthusiastic about Nehru's plans to modernize India.[56] Gandhian reform, based as it was in Hindu ideals and local governance, synchronized easily with Tukdoji's religious persona and popularity in Maharashtrian and North Indian villages, but the greater translational work needed for Tukdoji to adapt Nehru's internationalist socialism did not deter the sant. Tukdoji met with the prime minister on more than one occasion and performed at events featuring Nehru, and Nehru was reportedly as captivated by Tukdoji's bhajans as Gandhi had been.[57] When Nehru was criticized by Dwarka Prasad Mishra, chief minister of Madhya Pradesh, Tukdoji stepped up to serve as the featured performer for a rally in support of the prime minister.[58] Despite Tukdoji's efforts to contribute to Nehru's new Indian nation, the prime minister's enthusiasm for Tukdoji's songs was tempered by a mistrust of holy men. Indeed, Nehru's skepticism exposed a fault line between Tukdoji's Hindu-tinged nationalism and the internationalist, nonreligious socialism that he enthusiastically embraced.

During the anticolonial struggle, socialist members of the Indian National Congress disagreed about whether they should align with the mainstream members of Congress or insist on a complete socialist revolution outside the auspices of Congress. Nehru had become an avowed socialist in 1929, following 1927 trips to Brussels for a meeting of the League Against Imperialism (a unit of the Communist International) and to Moscow, but he considered Gandhi a close ally and realized that the real work of socialism could only happen after independence.[59] Moreover, he was convinced that no "-ism" could be adopted wholesale, and that India should instead use whatever means were best suited to transform it into a nation-state wherein all members of society could thrive equally. When debuting his five-year plans, a scheme of planned development inspired by the Soviet Union, he downplayed the plans' socialist orientation and relied on local leaders like Tukdoji to translate and popularize them in their regions. The first two five-year plans (1951 and 1956) prioritized agrarian modernization, allocating state funds to support dam and irrigation projects while pledging other funds for transportation, industry, communications, and social services.[60]

In the first decades following independence, Maharashtra became a model of Nehruvian rural development, in part because Maharashtra's first chief minister, Yashwantrao Chavan, had been able to convince farmers to adopt a decentralized form of government, and in part because the sugar industry had adopted a successful cooperative model and used its wealth to promote rural education and modernization in alliance with state and local Congress leadership.[61] Marathi religious leaders and singers played an additional important role in interpreting international political ideas, national initiatives, and state programs for constituents. In the 1950s and 1960s, as the new India was becoming manifest, politicians understood the power of singer-saints to not only attract voters but also promote understanding and acceptance of government initiatives. Of these sants, which also included the much-revered Gadge Maharaj and Kaikadi Maharaj, only Tukdoji earned the honorific of *rashtrasant* (national/ist saint) from President Rajendra Prasad in 1949, indexing not only the nationalist content of some of his bhajans but also his nationwide appeal cultivated through relentless travel.[62] Prasad praised Tukdoji's social work in a 1961 letter to the governor of Maharashtra, noting that Tukdoji had thousands of volunteers at his ashram and that his work had "a background of culture based on our old religious ideas and traditions."[63] That said, Tukdoji was not content to stay at his ashram. He often traveled to Madhya Pradesh, even singing at the election rallies of Ravishankar Shukla, chief minister of the state between 1950 and 1956.[64]

In February 1956, at the first meeting of the Bharat Sadhu Samaj (BSS, Indian Society of Ascetics), Tukdoji Maharaj became the Samaj's president and lent his support for a resolution from Indian Planning Commissioner Guzarilal Nanda to assist Nehru in implementing the second five-year plan by donating one million hours of volunteer work (*shramdan*).[65] *Sadhus* are Hindu ascetics of various sects who have renounced family life to focus on spiritual pursuits. The Bharat Sadhu Samaj was created in association with the Congress party to unify Hindu religious sects and use spirituality to serve the "all-round development of the country and . . . the betterment of the world on the basis of truth, non-violence, fearlessness, equality and unity."[66] Nanda's proposal to the Sadhu Samaj was framed as a response to Nehru's repeated statements that India's holy men contributed nothing to the nation, were plagued by corruption, and had become a national liability.

Nanda convinced the one hundred sadhus assembled for the meeting to rally their oratorical power and massive audiences to build bridges, irrigation canals, and roads, and the second of the two parts of the BSS constitution is a list of organizational "objects" (objectives) almost entirely dedicated to instilling Indian citizens with a commitment to social progress.[67] The more specific "functions" of the BSS included projects such as bhoodan, wealth-giving (*sampattidan*), and shramdan.[68] Tukdoji promoted Nehruvian rural development through sermons, social work, and songs like "Cala apulya gavala" (Let's go back to our village) and "Shetakaryano, gramkaryano, samajak shikshan gheyu" (Farmers and villagers, let's become socially educated).[69] He was considered by top Indian brass to be a model for how sadhus could serve the nation and promote planned development. Finance minister C. D. Deshmukh—in his speech unveiling the second five-year plan—praised Tukdoji's rural activism and the model villages he had founded in Madhya Pradesh and Hyderabad, an initiative he hoped the government would adopt.[70] The Samaj requested government funding to support its promotion of the five-year plans, but Nehru ultimately decided in 1959 not to award funding, reiterating that some sadhus had misused people's trust and finances.[71]

Between Violence and Nonviolence

The side of Tukdoji that promoted Gandhian reform and Nehruvian socialist development among rural audiences through devotional song does not represent the complete picture. In the heat of the Cold War, Tukdoji sang and preached of peace while advocating violence at the Pakistani and Chinese fronts, and in 1963 he became a founding member of the Hindu nationalist Vishwa Hindu Parishad (VHP, World Hindu Council). His involvement with the VHP may seem out of character with the Gandhian Tukdoji, but he was brought into the VHP in part because he represented an older model of saintliness. Moreover, the aggressively nationalist side of Tukdoji's persona actually dates back at least to 1942, when he allegedly incited villagers to use violence in resisting colonial injustice.[72] As he moved more firmly into national and international arenas through his Cold War political work, Tukdoji increasingly found himself singing for audiences that responded viscerally to his songs even when they could not understand the words.

The VHP was founded in reaction to Pope Paul VI's declaration in August 1964 that the International Eucharist Council would be held in Bombay, and as a response to the Report of the 1955 Niyogi Committee on the Christian conversion of marginalized Hindus in Madhya Pradesh. A fear that Christianity, Islam, and Communism were spreading in India motivated VHP efforts to unify, strengthen, and nationalize Hinduism.[73] Positioning itself as a cultural and religious organization rather than a political one, the VHP rallied sants and sadhus from various sects who had already been involved in nationalizing Hinduism. As rashtrasant, Tukdoji was a natural choice. According to Christophe Jaffrelot, Tukdoji represented the "Hindu traditionalist line" because he had served as past president of the Bharat Sadhu Samaj.[74] In an open letter to his followers, Tukdoji explained that he became an adviser to the VHP because

Hindus could no longer count on the stability formerly afforded by caste and needed the guidance of holy men and ascetics to prevent religious disorder. He stressed that he supported the good aspects of all religions but decried any attempt to shatter a person's faith in religion, presumably a veiled admonition against religious conversion.[75] At the first International Hindu Conference in 1966, Tukdoji chaired a session on "Unity in Diversity in Society" and was one of six Hindu luminaries chosen to create a "religious code suited to the needs of the time." He also gave a speech urging his colleagues to help reverse religious dissolution in India and reminded listeners of his own part in creating the Bharat Sadhu Samaj: "I feel so glad seeing how successfully the Vishwa Hindu Parishad has been exerting to translate the ideas, which inspired the setting up of the Sadhu Samaj."[76] Tukdoji regarded the VHP as a "translation" of the work he had been doing with the Bharat Sadhu Samaj, even though the BSS was bound to Nehruvian socialism while the VHP was developed in opposition to state secularism.[77] Tukdoji was not involved with the VHP for very long—he passed away in 1968, which was before the organization came to be dominated by the aggressive, militant yatras and Ram Janmabhumi campaign of the 1980s.[78] That said, his involvement in the VHP hints at a Hindu-centric fractiousness at odds with his writings on national unity.

During his short tenure with the VHP, Tukdoji expressed some support for its Hindu chauvinist agenda, but there are no indications that he used this platform to advocate violence. His aggressive strand surfaced earlier and was directed against the British rather than against Indian minorities. On August 16, 1942, a week after Gandhi's famous Quit India speech prompted the immediate arrest of almost all Indian National Congress leadership, people across India rose up in resistance against the colonial state and the imprisonment of their leaders. In the Vidarbha (now a region in eastern Maharashtra) villages of Chimur and Ashti, initially peaceful protesters were arrested and rushed by police, who fired until their ammunition had been exhausted. In retaliation, protesters attacked police stations in Ashti and Chimur, killing five policemen in Ashti and three policemen and two magistrates in Chimur. The government responded to this by sending in the military on August 19, forcing their way into homes, arresting 120 people, and raping women.[79] This tension between the violent and nonviolent in the Quit India movement was not unique to Chimur and Ashti. Gandhi provided the movement's spirit of resistance, but non-Gandhian eruptions of violence were common in Maharashtra as well as in Eastern Uttar Pradesh and Bihar.[80]

Tukdoji was among those arrested in Chimur, having been accused of inflaming the residents of Chimur and Ashti and prompting them toward violent revolution. The accusations against him were not entirely unfounded. Just after the arrest of Gandhi and other nationalist leaders, Tukdoji went to Ashti, where he met with members of his prayer circle (*arti mandal*), told them of Gandhi's arrest, and exhorted them to follow Gandhiji's "do or die" message.[81] From there, he went to Chimur to perform his inspiring bhajans—indeed, he held a bhajan session the night before the bloody protest, and many of those who were arrested claimed that Tukdoji had incited their action.[82] After Tukdoji's August 28 arrest, politician N. B. Khare pled with the police to release him, but they initially refused, reporting that the sant had incited the violent crowds by saying, "When necessary, stones could become bombs and sticks could become guns."[83] Eventually, Khare succeeded in convincing them that Tukdoji was just a "religious propagandist" rather than a politician, and he was released on December 4.[84]

The tension in Tukdoji's career between Gandhian nonviolence and nationalist violence moved onto an international stage in the 1950s. During this period, he paradoxically engaged in international dialogues on peace while advocating nuclear armament during the wars with China and Pakistan. As Tukdoji's spheres of influence expanded, so did his need to translate sociopolitical ideas to different constituents in different ways. With his reputation across India firmly established through three decades of public work, Tukdoji went to Japan as a Hindu representative at the Fifth World Religion Congress in 1955.[85] The World Religion Congress was founded in 1953 in the aftermath of the American atomic bombings of Hiroshima and Nagasaki with the hope of finding a collective path toward interreligious, international peace.[86] Shin Negami, president of Ananai-Kyo, the Shinto sect sponsoring the conference, wrote in the invitation to the approximately one hundred delegates from around the world, "The humanbeing [sic] is now on the brim of life and death being threatened by the appearance of horrible weapons of absolute force, and we feel keenly it needs to realize the conclusion of the successional world religion congress without a minute's delaying."[87]

Tukdoji graced the proceedings of the Fifth Congress with bhajans and addressed the council with a speech on the need for love and tolerance between members of different religious communities.[88] Although he had an interpreter, only his speeches were translated into English and Japanese; his songs were untranslated or minimally translated from Indian languages.[89] According to *The Report on the Fifth World Religion Congress*, "The words [of his songs] could not be understood, for it was Hindoo, but these tunes and skillful beating of the khanjiri were very charming. It made a scene float before our eyes of his pilgrim in Indian rural districts shouting to many thousands peoples [sic]."[90]

Given the conference theme, it is likely that they hoped for what Deborah Kapchan calls "the promise of sonic translation—premised on the belief that music can translate across cultural and linguistic divides."[91] Tukdoji's charisma and physical presence also seemed to translate across barriers of language and culture. An unnamed Japanese attendee described Tukdoji as "a giant with seal-like moustache and eagle-eyes, but [with] total features [that] are very gentle and affectionate, and seemed having something that commands respect."[92] In the only photos I can find of his participation, Tukdoji is on stage without accompanists—only his khanjiri—so people would *not* have been connecting with the cosmopolitan sounds of the multi-instrumentalist recordings discussed previously.[93] Though the description of audience response to his bhajans in the conference proceedings was minimal, Shriman Narayan described Tukdoji's bhajan singing for a similarly international, pacifist audience five years earlier during the World Pacifist Conference at Sevagram. According to Narayan, they were surprised to know that a local "saint-worker" attracted such a crowd of thousands of people and were pleased by the performance, framing Tukdoji as a "man of the people."[94] Paradoxically, in both Japan and Sevagram, his localness and partial incomprehensibility may have been part of the appeal for international listeners.

What did he say to those assembled at the World Religion Congress? How did he connect with a much more international audience than he ordinarily encountered in India? According to a letter that Tukdoji wrote to his followers about the event:

> In my speech for that occasion, I said that we welcome the many national representatives to the council. But in this country, we would never allow the World Religion Congress to permit religious conversion in the name of religion. In our country and in all countries, people of all religions should be treated with brotherhood. . . . Every religion represented at the WRC should have love and tolerance for every other religion in the world, that is all we need to accomplish. And we need to stop one religion from casting aspersions on another religion. If not, people will think that this congress is only related to politics. . . . Countries, soldiers, and governments need to do this.[95]

In his reporting about this event, Tukdoji depicts himself as a tough opponent to religious conversion and religious hatred, even asserting that these values should be protected by the state and the military. By referencing religious brotherhood using militaristic language, he found a way to connect with the international conference's mission of peace while appealing to Indian nationalist sentiment during a moment of mounting tension with China and Pakistan. In Tukdoji's English contribution to the Third World Religion Correspondence Congress (also in Japan in 1955), he made the same points he made in the Marathi letter to his followers, but in the English statement he did not go as far as to condone violence in support of peace. Instead, he wrote that every religion has people who do good work and people who do bad work, and that we should support those who labor for peace, equality, and justice. His conclusion was directed toward a Japanese audience and articulated connections between his Gandhian lineage and Japanese Buddhism:

> I thank the Third World Religion Congress from the bottom of my heart for its inspiration to struggle for the World Peace and protection of human-being. India has been a pioneer in this field. Her perpetual light has been kindled and kept burning by Gautama Buddha and Mahatma Gandhi has further rekindled it even to this day. This tree has further been made to grow and expand itself by "Shri Gurudeva Mandal" and this has been further accelerated by Acharya Vinoba, who through his movement of Grant of Land to the landless has tried to bring about a change of heart as the way for peace of the world. I am also on the way of that ideal. You should extend your cooperation and be a partner in the problem of World Peace.[96]

An irony of his participation in this Japanese conference is that he supported violence and even nuclear defense to maintain peace.[97] That stance seems to have been a later development—in *Gleams of New Age* (1956), a collection of Tukdoji's speeches and writings translated by S. M. Chitre, he sadly observes that talk of peace had increased while countries were developing increasingly more destructive weaponry.[98] Nine years later, during the India-Pakistan War of 1965, he said, "If we only sit around talking about nonviolence, we will be defeated. We need to develop our military strength. If people build hydrogen bombs, then we need to acquire that bomb in order to face them."[99] During this era of upheaval, Tukdoji was on the front lines, advocating for a defensive stance and singing nationalist bhajans for soldiers at the borders of China and Pakistan in 1962 and 1965.[100] One such Hindi bhajan that he sang on the Chinese front began with the line "Aao Chinio maidan me, dekho Hind ka haath" (Come to the fields of China; see the hand of India).[101] Throughout India, those who knew little about international politics were inspired by Tukdoji's Hindi and Marathi *deshbhakti* (devotion to the nation) songs like "Shaandaar ho mera Bharata" (Spectacular be my India).[102]

During this time period, tensions between India and Pakistan mirrored and were entrenched in the Cold War between the US and the USSR. When Pakistan became dissatisfied by the level of support it was receiving from the US and India became disillusioned with the depth of its alliance with the USSR, they sought other sources to negotiate their subcontinental Cold War, leading toward a parallel nuclear weapons race between India, Pakistan, and China. Pakistan began a nuclear weapons program secretly in 1972, but discussions of the possibility of developing atomic weapons date back to 1965, when Pakistan's foreign minister Zulfikar Ali Bhutto began pushing publicly for a nuclear defense program in the face of defeat in the war with India and skepticism about India's nuclear intentions.[103] In 1968 Pakistan took India's refusal to sign the Nonproliferation Treaty as a cue and similarly decided not to sign.[104] India had been secretive about its nuclear weapons program since the 1950s but began openly debating nuclear armament even earlier than Pakistan did.[105] The issue was brought before Parliament for the first time after India's defeat in the China-India War of 1962.[106]

At the time of these conflicts, Tukdoji deviated most from his promise to Gandhi to spread the word of ahimsa. Though it is not clear what inspired this transformation, it was very much in step with South Asian Cold War political discourse. In a speech he made in 1965, Tukdoji obliquely criticized Gandhian ideals as impractical and attempted to ameliorate discomfort with his own ideological change by reframing violent *resistance* as the brave and necessary removal of something bad.

> If people are going to build hydrogen bombs, then if we are to confront them in a conflict, we will also need to acquire that bomb. If violence is resisted violently, only then can there be no violence. Harm is a part of life. A doctor cuts out the bad part when he does an operation. But no one calls the doctor violent. In the same way, there is also no point in calling the firm resistance to an attack "violence." . . .
>
> Many people consider nonviolence to be the ideal. I am not much of one for ideals. I am much more practical. . . . As long as there is hate along with love in people's hearts, I know that war is unavoidable. Therefore we cannot expect to live without weapons. If the enemy takes massive guns and tanks to attack us and if we resist them with mortar and pestles in our hands, people will say we are completely ridiculous. To attack is cruel, but to resist is brave.[107]

Despite this aggressive thread in his prose writings, it is primarily through bhajans that Tukdoji's legacy lives on today, and most of his nationalist bhajans performed by devotees and posted on YouTube advocate for an inclusive, socially just nation. In "Aamuca Desh Sukhaci Khan" (Our nation is a wellspring of happiness), he sang, "Increase faith in true non-violence" (*vadho satya ahimsa man*) and pleaded for listeners to honor "the life and soul of all religions" (*sagalya dharmaca jivapran*). These sentiments were echoed in "Come, let us live in India with everlasting brotherhood" (*Ya bharatat bandubhaav nitya vasu de*) which ends with the couplet "Whether Hindu, Christian or Muslim, / let everyone enjoy the pleasure of freedom" (*Mag Hindu aso Christian va ho Islami / Swatantrya-sukha ya sakalamaji vasu de*).[108]

As a singer-saint on the boundary of religious pedagogy and political action whose influence was local, national, and international, Sant Tukdoji Maharaj is a perfect figure through whom to chart the translational exertions of postcolonial, Cold War rhetoric. By noting Tukdoji's engagement with Gandhian social programs, peace activism, and nationalist military posturing, I do not intend for these "unsettling ironies of experience" to serve as indications of his insincerity.[109] Instead, they emerge from an ever-changing philosophy and from translations that were sensitively honed toward particular contexts. These ironies were also expressive of contradictions inherent in the subcontinental Cold War—India maintained an international nonaligned status even while engaging in a nuclear arms race against Pakistan that mirrored and was buttressed by the bipolar Cold War.

In the words of translator Chana Bloch, "to translate is literally to 'carry across,' from the Latin *trans + ferre*—that is, to carry something across the borders of language and culture that separate us from an unknown country on the other side."[110] The "unknown countr[ies]" of Tukdoji's cultural translations were not China or Pakistan but the Cold War fronts themselves. He amplified those fronts by singing at and of them, widening their reach by translating them into devotional songs that resounded into India's interiors. In Maharashtrian villages and cities, these songs mingled with socialist, Gandhian, and local religious imaginaries to transform Tukdoji into a sant. And it was only as Sant Tukdoji that he could transcend the impermeable border of the fronts to access a different, distant "unknown country."

Even as religion provided a frame through which Tukdoji could be understood locally, religion also provided a context for his circulation beyond the local. Other chapters in this volume attend to the cosmopolitan networks activated by socialist song cultures and the circulation of recorded media. Tukdoji participated in similar routes through his socialist songs and filmi studio techniques, but his main pathway to an audience beyond India was—somewhat ironically—a very regional form of religious performance. When he arrived in

Japan in 1955 for the World Religion Congress, it was just three months after the Bandung Conference, which Japan had joined despite its official alliance with the United States. Both conferences participated in Cold War "peace diplomacy," a pillar of post-1952 Japanese foreign policy.[111] The World Religion Congress sought "universal truth" directed toward world peace through an epistemology of religious difference.[112] In this context, the "universal truth[s]" of Tukdoji's songs were paradoxically amplified by the *particularity* of his style, religion, and language.

Tukdoji understood that music could be used to localize cosmopolitan ideas and in turn to project particularized cosmopolitanisms outward. In his *Gramgita*, Tukdoji emphasized that any utterance should be adapted to its unique conditions of time, audience, and place: "The conditions of the world are changing / Today they are one way, tomorrow another // What we say and to whom we speak / When we are saying it should be understood // 22 //."[113] Lanza del Vasto reported that Tukdoji "asked me how, not knowing Marathi, I could say that his songs were good. I replied that music is a common language."[114] Lanza's sense that he could appreciate Tukdoji's songs without understanding their words was mirrored by international audiences in Japan, but the notion of a "common language" does not do justice to Tukdoji's skill in actively *making* music resonate across cultural boundaries.

NOTES

I thank the editors of this volume, the anonymous reviewers of an earlier version of this chapter published in *History and Anthropology* 28, no. 1 (2017), and Ronit Ghosh for their enormously helpful feedback.

1. For a further elaboration of the South Asian concept of "sant," see Karin Schomer and W. H. McLeod, *The Sants: Studies in a Devotional Tradition of India* (Berkeley: Berkeley Religious Studies Series, 1987), 2–3; and John Stratton Hawley, *Saints and Virtues* (Berkeley: University of California Press, 1987), 57.
2. John Stratton Hawley, *A Storm of Songs: India and the Idea of the Bhakti Movement* (Cambridge, MA: Harvard University Press, 2015), 2.
3. Although modern sants like Tukdoji have occasionally emerged, and although they may be inspired by the varkari sants, they are not themselves considered varkari sants.
4. See Anna Schultz, *Singing a Hindu Nation: Marathi Devotional Music and Nationalism* (New York: Oxford University Press, 2013).
5. Richard Middleton, *Studying Popular Music* (Milton Keynes, PA: Open University Press, 1990), 3–4.
6. Linda Hess, *Bodies of Song: Kabir Oral Traditions and Performative Worlds in North India* (New York: Oxford University Press, 2015); Sukanya Sarbhadhikary, *The Place*

of Devotion: Siting and Experiencing Divinity in Bengal-Vaishnavism (Oakland: University of California Press, 2015).
7 Schultz, *Singing a Hindu Nation*.
8 Heonik Kwon, *The Other Cold War* (New York: Columbia University Press, 2010), 121–41.
9 Susan Bayly, *Asian Voices in a Postcolonial Age: Vietnam, India and Beyond* (Cambridge: Cambridge University Press, 2007); Akhil Gupta, "The Song of the Nonaligned World: Transnational Identities and the Reinscription of Space in Late Capitalism," *Cultural Anthropology* 7, no. 1 (1992): 63–79; Magnus Marsden, "Muslim Cosmopolitans? Transnational Life in Northern Pakistan," *Journal of Asian Studies* 67, no. 1 (2008): 213–47.
10 Bayly, *Asian Voices*, 6–11.
11 Bayly, *Asian Voices*, 11.
12 Maharashtra is a large state in western India. Amravati became part of British India's Berar Province in 1853 and Central Provinces and Berar in 1903. After independence and the linguistic reorganization of states, Amravati was allocated to Bombay Province in 1956 and to the new state of Maharashtra in 1960.
13 Vinay Gidwani and K. Sivaramakrishnan, "Circular Migration and Rural Cosmopolitanism in India," *Contributions to Indian Sociology* 37, nos. 1–2 (2003): 339–67.
14 Schultz, *Singing a Hindu Nation*.
15 P. S. Kane, *The Rashtrasant: The Sociopolitical Thought of Sant Tukdoji Maharaj* (Nagpur, India: Manohar Pimpalapure, 1973), 4–8; P. L. Joshi, "Saints of Vidarbha," in *Political Ideas and Leadership in Vidarbha*, ed. P. L. Joshi (Nagpur, India: Nagpur University, 1980), 288–89; R. S. Kadwe, "Life Sketch of Rashtrasant Tukadoji," in *The Gramgita (An Epic on Indian Village Life)*, Canto I to V (vol. 1), trans. R. S. Kadwe (Wardha, India: Rashtrasant Sahitya Prachar Mandal, 1979), i; Joseph Jean Lanza del Vasto, *Gandhi to Vinoba: The New Pilgrimage* (New York: Schocken Books, 1974), 173.
16 Kane, *The Rashtrasant*, 3–13; Kadwe, "Life Sketch," i.
17 Though Lanza del Vasto wrote that Tukdoji was illiterate and dictated all his writings, he is often depicted with a pen in his hand. Lanza del Vasto, *Gandhi to Vinoba*, 174. See also Kadwe, "Life Sketch," ii.
18 Kane, *The Rashtrasant*, 35–36, 40; Balvantsinha, *Under the Shelter of Bapu* (Ahmedabad, India: Navajivan Publishing House, 1962), 93–94.
19 Mohandas Gandhi, *Collected Works*, vol. 63, *June 1–November 2, 1936* (New Delhi: Publications Division, Ministry of Information and Broadcasting, Government of India, 1976), 140–43, 186, 188, 232.
20 Balvantsinha, *Under the Shelter of Bapu*, 93–94.
21 Gandhi, *Collected Works*, vol. 63, 140.
22 Gandhi, *Collected Works*, vol. 63, 158.
23 Mohandas Gandhi, *Collected Works*, vol. 88, *May 25, 1947–July 31, 1947* (New Delhi: Publications Division, Ministry of Information and Broadcasting, Government of India, 1983), 253–54; Mohandas Gandhi, *Collected Works*, vol. 90, *November 11, 1947–January 30, 1948* (New Delhi: Publications Division, Ministry of Information and Broadcasting, Government of India, Gandhi, Mohandas, 1984), 371.

24 Tukdoji Maharaj, *Gleams of New Age*, trans. S. M. Chitre (Gurukunj, India: Shri Gurudev Prakashan Mandal, 1956), 63–64. See also Joshi, "Saints of Vidarbha," 289; Balvantsinha, *Under the Shelter of Bapu*, 94.
25 Shrinivas Khandevale, "Gramgita: Gramin Sankatachya Sandarbha" [Song of the village: A plan for rural difficulties], in *Rashtrasanta Tukdoji Maharaj—Vyakti aani vangamay* [National Saint Tukdoji Maharaj—Person and literature], ed. Akshaykumar Kale (Nagpur, India: Visa Books, 2008), 83. All translations are mine unless otherwise noted.
26 Gandhi advocated for a decentralized political system of village self-rule known as Panchayat Raj, which drew inspiration from—but was distinct from—a long-standing South Asian political system whereby important local decisions were made by a group of village elders. Mohandas Gandhi, *Panchayat Raj* (Ahmedabad, India: Navajivan Publishing House, 1959); Vijandra Singh, *Panchayati Raj and Village Development*, vol. 3 (New Delhi: Sarup and Sons, 2003), 84–90.
27 Anand Patil, *Uddhav Shelke* (New Delhi: Sahitya Akademi, 2002), 42–43; Ratnakar D. Bhelkar, "The Political Reality in Tukadoji's *Gramgeeta* in the Indian Context of Self Governance and Secularism," *Asian Journal of Multidisciplinary Studies* 3, no. 6 (2015): 168–70; Tukaramdada Geetacharya, *Gramgita Online*, accessed September 18, 2015, http://www.Gramgita.org/Gramgita/i_Gramgita.htm; Tukdoji Maharaj, *Srigramgita* (Tekadi, India: Tukaramji Dada Gitacharya, Shrigurudev Aatmanusandhaan, 1982).
28 Partha Chatterjee, *Nationalist Thought and the Colonial World: A Derivative Discourse?* (Minneapolis: University of Minnesota Press, 1986), 99–100, 133–66; Anil Dutta Mishra, "Sarvodaya: A Fresh Look," in *Gandhism after Gandhi*, ed. Anil Dutta Mishra (New Delhi: Mittal Publications, 1999), 37–42; N. Jayapalan, *Indian Political Thinkers: Modern Indian Political Thought* (New Delhi: Atlantic Publishers, 2003), 219–35.
29 "'Shramdan' by 1,50,000: Fitting Tribute to Mahatma," *Times of India*, January 22, 1955, 11; Schultz, *Singing a Hindu Nation*, 83; Dadamaharaj Manmadkar, *Varkari Sampradaya: Tattvadnyan va Sadyakalin Aucitya* [Varkari tradition: Philosophy and its relevance for current times] (Pandharpur, India: Sri H.Bh.P. Guruvarya Vidyavacaspati Dr. Dadamaharaj Manmadkar Satkar Samiti, 1998), 324–29.
30 Vinoba Bhave, *Bhoodan Yajna: Land-Gifts Mission* (Ahmedabad, India: Navajivan Publishing House, 1953).
31 "Bhoodan Yagna Board Formation Announced," *Times of India*, August 21, 1953, 9; "Sant Tukdoji Maharaj . . . ," *Times of India*, March 17, 1953, 5.
32 "Bhoodan Movement," *Times of India*, June 6, 1953, 9; "205 Villages for Bhoodan: Maharashtra Area," *Times of India*, January 30, 1957, 5. Lanza reported that he collected more than fifty thousand acres of land for the bhoodan movement. Lanza del Vasto, *Gandhi to Vinoba*, 174.
33 Lanza del Vasto, *Gandhi to Vinoba*, 174.
34 Quoted in "Landlord Gives 2,100 Acres: 'Bhoodan' Movement," *Times of India*, May 4, 1953, 9.
35 "Rashtra Sant Shri Tukdoji Maharaj-Ji Speech and Bhajan Part 1," YouTube, accessed September 15, 2015, https://www.youtube.com/watch?v=OIF2Qij4JPc.

36 Balvantsinha, *Under the Shelter of Bapu*, 64; Ram Ghode, *Rashtrasantachya Sahavaasaat* (Nagpur, India: Rajiv, 1996), 34.
37 Lanza del Vasto, *Gandhi to Vinoba*, 174–75.
38 Tukdoji, *Srigramgita*, 158.
39 Tukdoji, *Srigramgita*, 358.
40 Lyrics found at "Mani Nahi Bhav Mhane," Aathvanaathli Gaani, accessed September 25, 2020, https://www.aathavanitli-gani.com/Song/Mani_Nahi_Bhav_Mhane; Translation by Anna Schultz and Hemangi Wadekar.
41 Ebenezer Burgess, *Grammar of the Marathi Language* (Bombay: American Mission Press, 1854), 170–71; Ganpatrao Navalkar, *The Student's Marathi Grammar* (Bombay: Education Society's Press, 1880), 329.
42 Even here there are irregularities, as the first stanza is composed of two lines plus refrain and the second stanza is composed of four lines plus refrain.
43 Eleanor Zelliot, "A Historical Introduction to the Warkari Movement," in *Palkhi: An Indian Pilgrimage*, by D. B. Mokashi, trans. Philip C. Engblom (Albany: State University of New York Press, 1987), 31–53; Jacqueline Jones, "Performing the Sacred: Song, Genre, and Aesthetics in Bhakti" (PhD diss., University of Chicago, 2009), 3–14; Christian Novetzke, *Religion and Public Memory: A Cultural History of Saint Namdev in India* (New York: Columbia University Press, 2008), 7–23.
44 Burgess, *Grammar of the Marathi Language*, 172–73; Navalkar, *Student's Marathi Grammar*, 330; Gail Omvedt and Bharat Patankar, trans., *The Songs of Tukoba* (Delhi: Manohar, 2012), 14, 35–38, 118–38. See also Dr. Kishor Saanap's comparison of the poetry of Tukdoji and Tukaram in "Tukdojinchya Abhangagathetil Atmapravas" [The personal journey of Tukdoji's Abhangas] (2008), in Kale, *Rashtrasanta Tukdoji Maharaj*, 191–208. Brahmins are the highest Hindu caste in ritual terms. They have traditionally been associated with scholarship and priesthood.
45 Hess, *Bodies of Song*.
46 I have not yet discovered when this bhajan was composed.
47 Sant Tukdoji Maharaj, "Mani Nahin Bhav," Apple Music, track 2 on *Santanchi Bhakti Geete*, Saregama, 2007.
48 On bhajan style, see Stefan Fiol, "Making Music Regional in a Delhi Studio," in *More than Bollywood: Studies in Indian Popular Music*, ed. Gregory Booth and Bradley Shope (New York: Oxford University Press, 2014); Anna Schultz, "Bollywood *Bhajans*: Style as 'Air' in an Indian-Guyanese Twice Migrant Community," *Ethnomusicology Forum* 23, no. 3 (2014): 383–404.
49 This stanza is from chapter 30, "Bhajan Prabhav" (The power of Bhajan), in Tukdoji, *Srigramgita*, 352–60.
50 Bulbul tarang (also sometimes called "banjo") is a two-stringed plucked, keyed instrument in which one string is used for the melody and the second string for a drone.
51 Alison Arnold, "Popular Film Song in India: A Case of Mass-Market Musical Eclecticism," *Popular Music* 7, no. 2 (1988): 177–88.
52 Musically speaking, the term *filmi* is used to describe features of popular song that derive from Bollywood film song conventions. Filmi-sounding songs (including

those not from Bollywood films) include a combination of carefully orchestrated Indian and Euro-American instruments, catchy melodies, closed rather than open/cyclical forms, and audible studio production techniques.

53 For a live recording of "Mani Nahi Bhav" by Tukdoji Maharaj, see "Rashtra Sant Shri Tukdoji Maharaj-Ji Speech and Bhajan Part 5," YouTube, accessed 15 September 2015, https://www.youtube.com/watch?v=27Ktkw-TcdE. Here he is accompanied only by a chorus, taal, his own khanjeri, and harmonium. This was his standard live performance ensemble and the typical ensemble (often with pakhawaj substituting for khanjeri) of varkari musicians.

54 Sant Tukdoji Maharaj, "Ghadi ghadi," Apple Music, track 3 on *Santanchi Bhakti Geete*, Saregama, 2007. I have not been able to find the recording date for either "Mani Nahi Bhav" or "Ghadi ghadi," but by the musical style, I would guess the 1960s.

55 Lyrics found at "Ghadi ghadi mani tujhe naam japaave," Tukdyaadaas, accessed September 25, 2020, https://tukdyadas.in/view_bhajan.php?id=1317; translation by Anna Schultz and Hemangi Wadekar.

56 "Censure Pandit Mishra: Nagpur Demand," *Times of India*, August 27, 1951.

57 "Shramdan by Sadhus," *Times of India*, March 6, 1956; Shriman Narayan, *Memoirs: Window on Gandhi and Nehru* (Bombay: Popular Prakashan, 1971), 110–11.

58 "Censure Pandit Mishra," *Times of India*, August 27, 1951.

59 B. R. Nanda, *Jawaharlal Nehru: Rebel and Statesman* (New Delhi: Oxford University Press, 1998), 185–93.

60 Ramachandra Guha, *India after Gandhi: The History of the World's Largest Democracy* (New York: HarperCollins, 2007), 214; A. R. Kamat, *Progress of Education in Rural Maharashtra (Post-Independence Period)* (New York: Asia Publishing House, 1968), 15.

61 Schultz, *Singing a Hindu Nation*, 81–83.

62 Schultz, *Singing a Hindu Nation*, 83–87; Christophe Jaffrelot, *The Hindu Nationalist Movement and Indian Politics: 1925 to the 1990s* (New Delhi: Penguin Books, 1999), 199.

63 Rajendra Prasad, *Correspondence and Select Documents: Presidency Period—The Last Phase* (Bombay: Allied, 1995), 125.

64 M. B. Lal, *Going Back to Gettysburg: Autobiography of a Corrupt Indian* (Gurgao, India: Partridge Publishing, 2014), 88.

65 "Shramdan by Sadhus," *Times of India*, March 6, 1956; "Mass Awakening Programme: Sadhu Samaj Venture," *Times of India*, June 24, 1956; "500,000 Sadhus to Help Build New Nation," *Times of India*, February 8, 1956, 9. He became president again in the mid-1960s. Jaffrelot, *Hindu Nationalist Movement*, 199.

66 Government of India, *Report of the Hindu Religious Endowments Commission (1960–1962)* (Delhi: Government of India Press, 1962), 510.

67 "500,000 Sadhus to Help Build New Nation"; Government of India, *Report of the Hindu Religious Endowments Commission*, 510–13, 515.

68 Government of India, *Report of the Hindu Religious Endowments Commission*, 516–17.

69 Amol Raut, "Rashtrasant Tukdoji Maharaj" (documentary), YouTube, June 28, 2013, at 2:25 and 8:58, https://www.youtube.com/watch?v=J15finMQ7Ws. See Schultz, *Singing a Hindu Nation*, for a discussion of rural development in the kirtans of the Marathi singer-saints Gadge Maharaj and Kaikadi Maharaj.

70 "Response to the Budget: Not Unfavourable," *Times of India*, March 17, 1956.

71 "Preventing Misuse of Religious Funds: Centre Will Take Steps, Says Prime Minister," *Times of India*, May 4, 1959, 7.

72 Jaffrelot, *Hindu Nationalist Movement*, 199–200.

73 Hansen, *Saffron Wave*, 101; Jaffrelot, *Hindu Nationalist Movement*, 197; "Inception of VHP," Vishwa Hindu Parishad, accessed August 31, 2015, http://vhp.org/organization/org-inception-of-vhp.

74 Jaffrelot, *Hindu Nationalist Movement*, 197–200.

75 Tukdoji Maharaj, *Rashtrasantace Patre*, ed. Baba Mohod (Amravati, India: Shrigurudev Publishers, 1966), 125–26.

76 "Historic World Hindu Conference," Vishwa Hindu Parishad, accessed August 31, 2015, http://vhp.org/organization/org-historic-world-hindu-conference.

77 Jaffrelot, *Hindu Nationalist Movement*, 199–200.

78 Hansen, *Saffron Wave*, 103; Manjari Katju, *Vishwa Hindu Parishad and Indian Politics* (Hyderabad: Orient Longman, 2003), 35–60.

79 Narayan Bhaskar Khare, *My Political Memoirs, or Autobiography* (Nagpur, India: Shri J. R. Joshi, 1959), 192–94; Kane, *The Rashtrasant*, 40–44.

80 Gyanendra Pandey, "Introduction: The Indian Nation in 1942," in *The Indian Nation in 1942*, ed. Gyanendra Pandey (Calcutta: Centre for Studies in Social Sciences, 1988), 11–12.

81 Arti is a prayer and song performed while waving an oil lamp in front of a deity or other object of worship, usually at the end of a longer program or ceremony.

82 Kane, *The Rashtrasant*, 40–44; Khare, *My Political Memoirs*, 192–94.

83 Khare, *My Political Memoirs*, 192. P. L. Joshi cites a similar statement but gives the year as 1938. Joshi, "Saints of Vidarbha," 289.

84 Khare, *My Political Memoirs*, 192; Kane, *The Rashtrasant*, 43.

85 Kane, *The Rashtrasant*, 154.

86 Sushama Londhe, "Unknown Hindu Revivalists," in *A Tribute to Hinduism: Thoughts and Wisdom Spanning Continents and Time about India and Her Culture* (New Delhi: Pragun Publications, 2008).

87 Shin Negami, "Invitation No. 2," in *The Report on the Third World Religion Correspondence Congress (Under Auspices of the Ananai-Kyo)* (Shimizu, Japan: International General Headquarters of Ananai-Kyo, 1955), 8.

88 *The Report on the Fifth World Religion Congress* (Shimizu, Japan: International General Headquarters of Ananai-Kyo, 1955), 15; Kane, *The Rashtrasant*, 154.

89 I have found no evidence that Tukdoji spoke English (he only completed a few years of school). He was accompanied in Japan by Acharya Tukaramji Gitacharya, who was the head of the Shri Gurudeo Sewamandal (Lord Guru Service Association). *The Report on the Fifth World Religion Congress*, 61.

90 *The Report on the Fifth World Religion Congress*, 15.

91 Deborah Kapchan, "The Promise of Sonic Translation: Performing the Festive Sacred in Morocco," *American Anthropologist* 110, no. 4 (2008): 468.
92 *The Report on the Fifth World Religion Congress*, 15.
93 Raut, "Rashtrasant Tukdoji Maharaj," at 9:41. See also *The Report of the Fifth World Religion Congress*, 16.
94 Narayan, *Memoirs*, 110–11.
95 Tukdoji, *Rashtrasantace Patre*, 41–42.
96 Tukdoji Maharaj, "The Saint Tukadoji Maharaja, India," in *The Report on the Third World Religion Correspondence Congress*, 328.
97 Kane, *The Rashtrasant*, 150–52.
98 Tukdoji, *Gleams of New Age*, 81–88.
99 Kane, *The Rashtrasant*, 150–51.
100 Jaffrelot, *Hindu Nationalist Movement*, 199.
101 A performance of this bhajan is available online. "AaoChinioMaidanMe—Rashtrasant Tukdoji Maharaj Bhajan," YouTube, accessed September 15, 2015, https://www.youtube.com/watch?v=o97xTVLV5no.
102 Raut, "Rashtrasant Tukdoji Maharaj," at 11:52.
103 Paul Kerr and Mary Beth Nikitin, *Pakistan's Nuclear Weapons: Proliferation and Security Issues* (Washington, DC: Congressional Research Service, 2010), 2.
104 Bhumitra Chakma, *Strategic Dynamics and Nuclear Weapons Proliferation in South Asia: A Historical Analysis* (Bern: Peter Lang, 2004), 134–37.
105 Schultz, *Singing a Hindu Nation*, 87.
106 "India's Nuclear Weapons Program," Nuclear Weapon Archive, accessed October 2, 2015, http://nuclearweaponarchive.org/India/index.html.
107 Tukdoji Maharaj, *Rashtrasantanci Pravacane* [The national saint's religious discourses], ed. Baba Mohod (Gurukunj: Shrigurudev Prakashan, 1965), 51–52. See also Kane, *The Rashtrasant*, 150–51.
108 A children's performance of the bhajan and the complete Marathi lyrics can be found online. Sant Tukdoji Maharaj, "Ya Bhartat Bandhubhav Nitya Vasu De," Orange Music, YouTube, accessed September 20, 2020, https://www.youtube.com/watch?v=8Qayg-UdODQ&list=RD8Qayg-UdODQ&start_radio=1.
109 Steven Feld, *Jazz Cosmopolitanism in Accra: Five Musical Years in Ghana* (Durham, NC: Duke University Press, 2012), 231.
110 Chana Bloch, "Crossing the Border," in *Crossing Borders: Stories and Essays about Translation*, ed. Lynne Sharon Schwartz (New York: Seven Stories Press, 2017), location 1383, Kindle.
111 Kweku Ampiah, *The Political and Moral Imperatives of the Bandung Conference of 1955: The Reactions of the U.S., U.K. and Japan* (Folkestone, Kent, UK: Global Oriental, 2007), 171.
112 Yonosuke Nakano, "General Remarks on the Agenda," in *The Report on the Fifth World Religion Congress*, 46.
113 Tukdoji, *Srigramgita*, 25.
114 Lanza del Vasto, *Gandhi to Vinoba*, 175.

8. YELLOW MUSIC CRITICISM DURING CHINA'S ANTI-RIGHTIST CAMPAIGN

QIAN ZHANG

The Chinese word *huangse* 黄色 (yellow) was first used in the music field around 1945 as a metaphor for "eroticism" and "obscenity."[1] The term signified a kind of criticism aimed at the "decadent" social atmosphere that allegedly remained from the period of Japanese occupation. The Japanese occupied all the Chinese-controlled parts of the city after the 1937 Battle of Shanghai. With the beginning of the Pacific War in 1941, the foreign concessions were also occupied by the Japanese military, after which the whole of Shanghai was under Japanese rule until Japan's surrender in 1945. During the occupation, the Japanese army gradually took control over the distribution and production of popular music. It first assigned the Nihon Chikuonki Shōkai 日本蓄音器商会 (Nipponophone Co., Ltd.) to take over Baidai changpian 百代唱片 (Pathé Records) and Da Zhonghua changpian 大中华唱片 (Great China Records). Then the Zhonghua dianying lianhe gufen gongsi 中华电影联合股份公司 (China Film Joint-Stock Company), which was created through a merger involving eleven small film companies, fell into the hands of the Japanese-supported collaborationist government. In these particular historical conditions, popular music constructed the city as a peaceful place for song and dance instead of revealing the truth of war—especially when compared to the anti-Japanese nationalist songs that focused on Chinese suffering. When the nationalist government returned its capital to Nanjing in 1947, it issued decrees to eliminate "yellow music" in compliance with its governance policy of "rejuvenating rituals and music."[2]

The founding of the People's Republic of China (PRC) meant the end of the metropolitan media culture of republican-era Shanghai. Such artists and producers as Liang Yueyin 梁乐音, Li Houxiang 李厚襄, Yao Min 姚敏, Bai Guang 白光,

and Gong Qiuxia 龚秋霞 moved to Hong Kong, taking the crafts and aesthetics of film and popular music with them. During the Anti-Rightist Campaign (1957–58), the popular songs of "Old Shanghai" were again criticized as yellow music. During this period, the yellow music discourse critiqued the culture and ideology of the bourgeoisie, becoming a vehicle for defining class divisions and advancing the totalitarian control of the cultural field. As a result, some musicians who produced yellow music in the republican period, such as Chen Gexin 陈歌辛 and Liu Xue'an 刘雪庵, were labeled rightists, and the sound of yellow music was quickly excluded from the public sphere and the everyday life of ordinary people. In the 1980s, as popular music from Hong Kong and Taiwan flooded into the mainland, yellow music criticism reemerged as a media buzzword in 1983, functioning as an ideological tool during the brief Anti-Spiritual Pollution Campaign when the Chinese Communist Party (CCP) became concerned that Western liberal values were posing a threat to China's socialism.[3]

In *Yellow Music: Media Culture and Colonial Modernity in the Chinese Jazz Age*, Andrew F. Jones analyzes Mandarin popular music's formation in the emerging modern business environment and colonial culture. His central argument is that Chinese popular music in the 1930s must be understood as a "musical, technological, financial, linguistic and racial transaction conducted within the boundaries of the complex colonial hierarchies peculiar to that time and place."[4] This argument indirectly deconstructs the hegemony and aesthetic prejudices of the anti–yellow music discourse put in place by CCP intellectuals. My chapter builds on Jones's pioneering work, examining the formation of yellow music discourse during the period of the Anti-Rightist Campaign, uncovering key events and figures from the historical archives. The first section illustrates how anti–yellow music criticism was generated and how it operated as part of the anti-rightist campaign. The second section focuses on textual analysis, revealing the discursive violence hidden in the criticism's key metaphors, which were structured linguistically to form a binary opposition. Taking the perspective of contextual analysis, the third section shows how other discourses such as hedonism, carnalism, and antipatriotism could finally converge in the yellow music discourse as the anti-rightist campaign expanded. The fourth section explains how anti–yellow music criticism gradually generated a set of aesthetic standards with specific ideological attributes that would continue to interfere with China's musical practices in later decades. As illustrated extensively in Jones's study, yellow music was often associated with the United States, for example in criticism of jazz. Although yellow music was often criticized as foreign or Western or American, the main focus of this chapter is on the way the binary opposition of bourgeoisie/proletariat (of Marxist-Leninism) became metaphorically imposed upon and fused with the dichotomy of yellow/red music, and the detailed way that this discourse was applied to songs, lyrics, and music. I stress the national importance of this strategy as a means of asserting ideological political control within China. Situated in relation to the themes of this book, the discourse was used to control the routes of music, allow for covers of songs, and establish a clear ideological front.

The Production and Circulation of Yellow Music Discourse during the Anti-Rightist Campaign

With the founding of the PRC, a new propaganda apparatus replaced the media environment that had previously emerged in republican Shanghai. Besides existing media such as radio and newspapers, big character posters and mimeograph printing also played an important role in promoting this shift. In this section, I describe how yellow music criticism was produced and how it operated within the new media environment of socialist China. I also show how the authoritarian power could be strengthened, not only through the efforts of the government but also by those of the people, and how it could extend to every place within China like a network of blood vessels.

The launching of the Hundred Flowers Movement in April 1956 could be considered a prelude to the Anti-Rightist Campaign. The Hundred Flowers Movement offered political support for diversity and freedom in literary and artistic creation. The *People's Daily* declared: "Since the May 4th New Cultural Movement, many excellent works of music have been an important part of our national heritage, which must be carried on."[5] In order to carry out this new principle, left-wing film songs that had not circulated since 1949 and dated from before the founding of the PRC, such as "Tianya genü" 天涯歌女 (The wandering songstress), "Siji ge" 四季歌 (Song of four seasons), "Yeban gesheng" 夜半歌声 (Song at midnight), and "Chuntian li" 春天里 (In spring), were brought back into the public sphere. During this short period, an eclectic group of popular songs were relabeled *old songs* and temporarily gained a legitimate position in broadcast media and newspapers.[6] Subsequently, however, many of the arguments that supported popular music from this period became the targets of yellow music criticism during the Anti-Rightist Campaign.[7] The Hundred Flowers Movement was therefore described as *"yin she chu dong"* 引蛇出洞 (luring snakes out of their holes) by Mao Zedong, but whether Mao's original intention was really that of identifying critics in order to punish them is still a matter of debate.[8]

On June 8, 1957, the CCP Central Committee issued "Muster Our Forces to Repulse Rightists' Wild Attacks," drafted by Mao. They outlined the specific plans and strategies for the anti-rightist struggle and demonstrated Mao's ability to mobilize the masses and manipulate public opinion. The key parts of the directive were as follows:

> Get each of these parties to organize forums with the Left, middle and Right elements all taking part, let both positive and negative opinions be voiced, and send reporters to cover these discussions.... The Party paper in each locality should have dozens of articles ready and publish them from day to day when the high tide of the attacks begins to ebb there. Make a point of organizing the middle and Left elements to write for the press. But before the tide is on the ebb, Party papers should restrict the number of articles expressing positive views (they can publish articles written by the middle elements). Give the masses a free hand in refuting the Rightists' big-character posters. Organize forums at colleges and universities to let professors speak their minds about the Party, and as far as possible try to get the Rightists to spew out all their venom, which will be published in the newspapers.... At the same time, organize some non-Party people to make speeches and state the correct views. Then, have a responsible Party cadre who enjoys prestige make a summing-up speech that is both analytical and convincing to effect a complete change in the atmosphere.[9]

This text shows the important role of "mobilizing the masses" in the CCP's political campaigns. Actually, all the people who got involved in this campaign, whether leftists or rightists, professors or students, did not know the final direction and were unaware that the results had been decided by the power center in advance. Behind an appearance of open discussion and free talk, there was an invisible authoritarian mechanism controlling the direction and process of the campaign.

The *dazi bao* 大字报 (big-character posters) referred to in the "Instructions" were an effective medium for mobilizing the masses. Usually, these posters were written in bold characters, and their language was simple, direct, and even violent. They were put up in public spaces where they were easily accessible to the common people, who would gather together and converse around them. Provoked and motivated by the big-character posters, people engaged in the affective politics of everyday life and developed a sense of their own political self-identities. In this way, a "top-down" imposition of power was transformed into a kind of "bottom-up" politics.

Various left-wing literary and art forms such as poems, caricatures, songs, and critical essays became the means for triggering emotions and promoting the Anti-Rightist Campaign. In August 1957, the magazine *Songs* published two songs especially composed for the campaign. One was "Youpai xiansheng aonao ge" 右派先生懊恼歌 (Rightist gentleman's annoyance); the other was a mass song, "Shehuizhuyi hao" 社会主义好 (Socialism is good). With its direct lyrics and simple melody, "Socialism Is Good" not only effectively fueled the Anti-Rightist Campaign but also became a widely circulated mass song that would propagate the superiority of socialism through the singing activities of the masses through the 1990s.[10]

> Socialism is good! 社会主义好
> Socialism is good! 社会主义好
> The country of socialism is defended by the people. 社会主义江山人民保
> People rule the country well. 人民江山坐得牢
> The rightists can never revolt even if they want to. 右派分子相想反也反不了
> Socialism will prevail. 社会主义一定胜利
> Communist society will surely come, surely come! 共产主义社会一定来到, 一定来到!

Starting in July 1957, the official periodical of the Zhongguo yinxie 中国音协 (Chinese Musicians' Association), *People's Music*, began to publish numerous articles exposing the rightists' "crimes against the Communist Party, the people, and socialism," thereby launching a campaign of incessant condemnation and repression in the sphere of public opinion.[11] Other music journals followed suit and fell swiftly in line.[12] These journals published a series of "criticisms" that purported to reveal the rightists' "abominable crimes"; some established special anti-rightist columns, which used large red characters for headlines and employed combative sentence structures that were compatible with the form and content of big-character posters.

In early 1958, as part of a general effort to intensify the Anti-Rightist Campaign, a wide-ranging anti–yellow music criticism campaign was initiated in the music field. Several academic institutions, government agencies, and newspapers were mobilized to produce what would be the densest concentration of anti–yellow music writings in history.[13] As Lü Ji 吕骥, the chairman of the Chinese Musicians' Association, pointed out: "The struggle against yellow music is a 'two-line struggle' in the music field. It is a tough struggle on its own, but it also forms one line of the Anti-Rightist Campaign."[14] Consequently, the Anti-Rightist Campaign, which had initially centered on reforming intellectuals, extended its criticism to include the music field, a move aimed at furthering the struggle of the proletariat against the bourgeoisie.

To help facilitate the rapid spread of the anti–yellow music criticism campaign, music-related institutions at all levels, ranging from the Chinese Musicians' Association to local Qunzhong yishuguan 群众艺术馆 (mass art centers), edited and published a large number of collections of anti–yellow music criticism in order to meet the requirements of meetings and media at various levels. Due to the low technological conditions of the time, these collections usually took the form of handwritten mimeographs.[15] These materials included not only selected critical essays by "red musicians" and "ordinary people" but also the "reactionary" opinions of rightist musicians, and sheet music to give examples of yellow music as well. The covers of most volumes were clearly marked with the words "For internal reference only and to be returned." Obviously, the various collections were to be used exclusively in activities related to the criticism campaign, and they were thus the material prerequisite for the development of anti–yellow music criticism. A report published by *People's Music* commended a collection produced by the Wuhan Mass Art Center, noting that it "has been distributed to local organizations such as labor unions, youth league committees and cultural centers, etc., thereby reaching the hands of rank-and-file members and giving them key figures with which to study."[16] Next I focus in more detail on the specific ways that the campaign used metaphors and sought to impose them on the titles, lyrics, and musical characteristics of specific songs, and the actions of the musicians composing and performing these songs.

Binary Opposition Structures in the Metaphorical Discourse

Even though the anti-rightist and the anti–yellow music criticism campaigns cannot be viewed simply as direct results of the Cold War, the external structure and condition of the Cold War deepened the ideological struggles taking place domestically. Under the pressures caused by the Cold War, the imaginary enemy planted in the popular mind unconsciously became an engine for launching a rhetorical battle without gunpowder. As Martin Medhurst argues, a Cold War is, "by definition, a rhetorical war, a war fought with words, speeches, pamphlets, public information (or disinformation) campaigns, slogans, gestures, symbolic actions, and the like."[17] Drawing on rhetorical analysis, this section examines metaphorical language in order to reveal the discourse of violence inherent in the texts that linguistically presented a structure characterized by binary opposition.

As a rhetorical tool, metaphor is the use of one thing to understand and experience another, and it has the function of representing "reality" in the symbolic order. In *Metaphors We Live By*, George Lakoff and Mark Johnson demonstrate how metaphors play an important part in structuring how people understand the world and how they have a direct impact on perception, behavior, and action.[18] As a means of ideological indoctrination and manipulation, metaphor may be used in sophisticated, subtle, or crude ways to deliberately and strategically motivate the receivers' emotions and to influence their political values, religious orientation, and social beliefs. The anti–yellow music discourse did not simply judge music as good or bad but incorporated infectious and emotional metaphors in its denunciatory texts.

Some criticisms retained the original meaning of yellow music, including "erotic," "obscene," and "pornographic" associations, and even linked the term to "brothels," "whores," or "pornography," all of which had been regarded as illegal or criminal since the founding of the PRC.[19] The most common metaphors used to describe yellow music were such drugs as opium, morphine, anesthetics; *fushou gao* 福寿膏 (opium); and *ducao* 毒草 (poisonous weeds). The various drug metaphors linking yellow musical aesthetics with hedonism, sensual pleasures, and addiction implicitly cautioned against the harmful effects of yellow music despite its momentary "delight." The metaphorical binary oppositions of *xianghua/ducao* 香花／毒草 (fragrant flowers/poisonous weeds) were also frequently used at the time, implying the aesthetic and political difference between red music and yellow music and indirectly emphasizing the illegitimacy of yellow music in daily life.

The following section uncovers the discursive violence in such metaphoric usages through an analysis of texts criticizing three important popular musicians. As the most important popular music composer in the period of the Japanese occupation, Chen Gexin 陈歌辛 composed more than two hundred works. Some of his best-known works, such as "Ye Shanghai" 夜上海 (Night in Shanghai) and "Meigui, meigui, wo ai ni" 玫瑰, 玫瑰, 我爱你 (Rose, Rose, I love you), have become symbols of the metropolitan culture of Old Shanghai, but he also composed a few anthems for the Japanese army, including "Da dongya minzu tuanjie jinxingqu" 大东亚民族团结进行曲 (The March of Greater East Asian Unification) and "Shenfeng ge" 神风歌 (Song of the Godly Wind). Due to these political "stains," he was targeted as a "rightist" and he eventually starved to death in a reeducation camp in Anhui province in 1957. In texts denouncing Chen, the metaphor of "fragrant flower/poisonous weed" was mobilized to emphasize the gravity of his "crime." As Wang Yunjie 王云阶 declared in an article: "Among the more than 200 songs composed by Chen Gexin, 'poisonous

Yellow Music Criticism · 237

weeds' account for the majority. The remaining few can at best only be identified as non-fragrant 'flowers' and non-poisonous 'weeds.' . . . As we thoroughly exposed and criticized his furious anti–Communist Party and anti-people speeches and conduct, we should also carry out a nationwide disinfection!"[20]

Liu Xue'an 刘雪庵 was the composer of the music and lyrics of "Heri jun zai lai" 何日君再来 (When will you return?), a song that remains very popular in the Sinophone world. This song was first sung by 周璇 Zhou Xuan and later made famous by Li Xianglan 李香兰 / Yamaguchi Yoshiko, a Japanese singer during the period of Japanese colonization. Even though Liu composed songs on the theme of resisting Japanese invasion and saving China from extinction, including such works as "Changcheng yao" 长城谣 (The Great Wall Ballad) and "Liuwang sanbuqu" 流亡三部曲 (Exile Trilogy), he was still categorized as a rightist. Lü Ji, the president of the Chinese Musicians' Association, exaggerated and distorted the "historical issues" found in Liu's works and used the metaphor of "fragrant flowers/poisonous herbs" to label him as a "capitalist roader" and a "counterrevolutionary":

> He [Liu Xue'an) not only seeks a legitimate position as a leader in musicians' associations, but also explicitly promotes his infamous songs, "When Will You Come Again" and "Nongjiale" 农家乐 (Happy Farmhouse) in order to allow the reactionary ruling class to present a false image of peace and prosperity. He tried to force us to accept all of those songs as *fragrant flowers*! . . . Based on his position as a reactionary bourgeois, Liu Xue'an asks us to reevaluate those malicious poisonous weeds according to his political standards.[21]

As an early pioneer of popular music in China, Li Jinhui 黎锦晖 was criticized as "the founder of yellow music." Under pressure from the critique mounted against him, he wrote an open letter of self-criticism titled "Zhanduan dugen chedi xiaomie huangse gequ" 斩断毒根彻底消灭黄色歌曲 (Cut the poisonous roots and eradicate yellow songs). It is possible that this open letter allowed Li to survive this political crisis. In its text, he borrowed common wording frequently used by others and compared his work to opium and a "drug for happiness": "I wrote many yellow songs. I was addicted to composing them in spite of the national crisis. Why? . . . I was too addicted to them and unable to resist. It was like smoking opium. The more you smoke, the more you want. And you even call these narcotics 'drugs for happiness and longevity.' You lure others to partake together with you and make them addicted too."[22]

As these texts show, the metaphors used to signify yellow music were framed as binary oppositions mirroring the class struggle of the proletariat against the bourgeoisie, an internal response to the conflict between the two camps of the Cold War. Analyzing the metaphors used in the texts of anti–yellow music criticism not only reveals the ideology and hegemony operating in the discourse but also further highlights how the discourse was mobilized in the political and aesthetic conflict between red music and yellow music.

The Expanding Boundaries of Yellow Music during the Anti-Rightist Campaign

The anti–yellow music campaign was launched immediately after the anti-rightist campaign with the goal of consolidating the latter's achievements. Musicians from the CCP such as Li Ling 李凌, Zhou Weizhi 周巍峙, Li Jiefu 李劫夫, and Lian Kang 联抗 published papers that aimed to reconstruct the category of yellow music based on the current political needs.[23] These CCP critics denounced yellow music using a wider set of connotations beyond the original meanings of obscene and pornographic. According to them, yellow music also embodied hedonism, carnality, antipatriotism, and sarcasm aimed at the working class. As a result, the boundaries of the category of yellow music were enlarged as the anti-rightist campaign expanded. By analyzing the context of yellow music, I explain how other discourses were finally able to converge into yellow music criticism during the anti-rightist campaign.

The criticism of anti–yellow music by CCP activists incorporated the discourses of patriotism and nationalism, which resonated with nationalist emotions and the popular determination to resist foreign aggression in the early twentieth century. Before the founding of the People's Republic of China in 1949, there were two ruptures in the history of Chinese popular music related to the Japanese military invasion. In the first half of the 1930s, such modern media as sheet music, radio broadcasting, records, and newspapers and magazines had achieved only a fledgling status in Shanghai. As pioneers of China's popular music, Li Jinhui and members of the Mingyue gewu yueshe 明月歌舞乐社 (Bright Moon Song and Dance Troupe) represented a first peak in the history of popular music in Shanghai. But when anti-Japanese sentiments became dominant, Li's songs were criticized by left-wing musicians, particularly Nie Er 聂耳, as products of the bourgeoisie's decadent lifestyle and as opposed to the movement.[24] In 1937, when war against Japan erupted nationwide, the production of popular music in Shanghai was forced to cease operations. From 1941 to 1945, the Japanese army controlled all media in Shanghai, including newspapers, film, and the record industry. Under the conditions of this colonized culture, a group of stars, such as Zhou Xuan, Yamaguchi Yoshiko, and Bai Guang, launched a second boom of popular music, with many songs released as records or used in films. Lacking any nationalist or patriotic discourse, these songs were rooted in the colonized and metropolitan culture and therefore ran counter to the dominant ideology of the 1950s. Compositions that directly praised Japanese colonization were severely criticized as "reactionary and traitorous," including "Yangchun xiaochang" 阳春小唱 (Spring ditty), "Manzhou guniang" 满洲姑娘 (Manchu girl), and "Zhina zhi ye" 支那之夜 (China nights).

The theory of dictatorship of the proletariat, an essential component of Marxism-Leninism, provided the theoretical basis for the critique of yellow music. Karl Marx outlines the theory in *The Communist Manifesto* and openly declares that victory could be attained only through the violent overthrow of all existing social conditions. According to *The Communist Manifesto*, "Let the ruling classes tremble at a Communistic revolution. The proletarians have nothing to lose but their chains. They have a world to win."[25] In order to eliminate bourgeois culture and finally achieve the dictatorship of the proletariat, yellow music criticism constructed musical aesthetics based on a binary opposition of proletarian/bourgeois. As a result, music that satirized the working class or the people at the bottom of society and music that complimented the bourgeoisie and their lifestyle were equally regarded as yellow music. The songs attacked included such compositions as "Cungu le" 村姑乐 (The happiness of village women), "Xiangxiaren" 乡下人 (Village people), and "Sanlunche shangde xiaojie" 三轮车上的小姐 (The lady in the pedicab). During this struggle of the proletariat against the bourgeoisie, the language of criticism inevitably invoked violence and a sense of bloodshed, as for example a poem by proletarian poet Lu Mang 卢芒 declaring that "our common task is creating 'red music and strangling yellow music by its neck.'"[26]

The anti–yellow music campaign also invoked collectivism as part of a broader effort to achieve wide-ranging public ownership. After the completion of the *San da gaizao* 三大改造 (three major transformations) of socialism (agriculture, handicrafts, and capitalist industry and commerce), public ownership was alienated into a state-dominated system that not only confiscated private property but also restrained the expression of individual feelings. In republican-era Shanghai, which saw the initial emergence of a new media culture, the so-called yellow music was introduced into private space in order to express personal feelings and aesthetic sentiments. We see this in such examples as "Xiangsi de ziwei" 相思的滋味 (Taste of lovesickness), "Bianzhou qinglü" 扁舟情侣 (Lovers on the skiff), and "Ailian zhi ge" 爱恋之歌 (Song of love). In the anti-yellow music campaign, the CCP critics denounced and tried to eliminate yellow music in an effort to confiscate the personal emotions expressed through the mediation of music. By contrast, those genres that expressed collective aspirations such as "mass songs" and "revolutionary songs" gained political legitimacy.

In May 1958, the Second Session of the Eighth National Congress of the CCP officially approved the general guidelines that would lead to the Great Leap Forward, urging members to "go all out, aim high and achieve greater, faster, better and more economical results in building socialism."[27] Confronting conditions of low economic productivity, this ultraleft policy aimed to overtake the industrial production of capitalist countries in a very short time; it called for matching value systems and ideologies, such as pulling together in hard work, diligence, and selfless laboring in the public interest. The CCP critics redefined the hedonism, carnality, consumerism, and emphasis on the body in Shanghai popular music as symptoms of bourgeois lifestyle, and the range of songs criticized as yellow music was expanded to include such works as "Man chang fei" 满场飞 (Flying around the dance floor), "Yiye xiaohun" 一夜销魂 (A night of ecstasy), "Huahua shijie" 花花世界 (This dazzling world), and "Zuiren de kouhong" 醉人的口红 (Enchanting lipstick). In short, as a tool for political movement, yellow music kept expanding its boundaries while the Anti-Rightist Campaign gathered momentum. Meanwhile, the standards for critiquing yellow music were increasingly refined and professionalized.

The Formation of Aesthetic Standards in Yellow Music Criticism

Critics not only interpreted the content and cultural meaning of yellow music lyrics from the perspective of class struggle but also took aim at the characteristics and qualities of the music, resulting in a hastily constructed aesthetic standard for judging yellow music. Yellow music, now considered a specific music genre with a defined sound structure, was broken up by CCP musicians and critics into several musical elements, including melodic rules, rhythm, ornamentation, and accompaniment. They linked these specific elements to ideological and cultural connotations, for example by expanding the discourse of "statements" with such new terms as *yellow singing style* and *yellow melody*. The rhetoric of this anti-yellow music discourse was vivid and graphic. For example, the words used to describe the melody of this style included "greasy tune," "frivolous and lingering," "desperate and decadent," and "vulgar and corrupted." Yellow music melodies were also said to be "disorganized," "chaotic," "jerking and drunk," and "hysterical." Similarly, the yellow music singing style was described with such words as "teasing," "soft," "kitsch," and "dissipated and disgusting."[28]

Due to its relationship with dance halls in republican Shanghai, jazz was constructed by CCP critics as a symbol of the bourgeoisie's lifestyle and thus also came under criticism as a kind of yellow music. Old Shanghai songs from the period of Japanese occupation such as "Night in Shanghai," "Jinxiao jinxiao" 今宵今宵 (Tonight tonight), "Yelai xiang" 夜来香 (Fragrance of the night), "Fengkuang yuedui" 疯狂乐队 (The crazy band), "Xin de ayaya" 新的啊呀呀 (New Ayaya), and "Fengyu jiaoxiangqu" 风雨交响曲 (Symphony of wind and rain) were obviously influenced by American jazz styles and were therefore cataloged as yellow music in the ongoing political campaign. Under the pressures of the Cold War, jazz was viewed as a representative genre of American imperialism, and thus criticizing jazz was considered a form of ideological struggle against the non-socialist camp. As a result, in the new categorization of yellow music, any sound structure resembling jazz (regardless of lyrical content or whether it was influenced by styles from the United States) was labeled yellow music and expunged from the public sphere.

Analyzing yellow music as a form of ideological propagation meant describing musical skills with greater specificity while drawing a stark contrast between red and yellow musical aesthetics, a binary opposition that could then serve to sharpen the distinction between the proletariat and bourgeoisie. Music criticism in socialist China gradually generated a set of aesthetic standards that came with specific ideological attributes. In particular, the following elements came under attack: overuse of ornamentation in melody; sad tunes, even those with beautiful melodies; use of jazz-derived melodies, rhythms, and arrangements; the appropriation of folk music, especially the adaptation of city ditties; the use of ballroom dance rhythms, such as tango, rumba, and waltz; and singing styles that were soft, smooth, and ornamented.[29] This definition of yellow music aesthetic had a deep impact on China's songs and directly triggered the later criticism of *Shuqing gequ* 抒情歌曲 (lyric songs) in early 1958. For example, the vivacious tune of "Jiujiu yanyang tian" 九九艳阳天 (Sunny Day in Early Spring) was used in a scene in the film *Liubao de gushi* 柳堡的故事 (*The Story of Liubao Village*, 1957) and became popular at the time. But this song was first criticized as semi–yellow music because of its use of a folk song melody and its strophic form.[30] Later, "Diu jiezhi" 丢戒指 (Losing a ring) became a target of severe criticism due to its adaption of a folk song from northeastern China and its dramatic depiction of the love between young men and women.[31]

The Power Struggle between Yellow and Red Music

The binary opposition between socialism and capitalism during the Cold War became a structural condition that contributed to the formation of the practices and aesthetics of Chinese music. Anti–yellow music criticism revolved around a "two-line struggle"—the proletarian line represented by red music and the bourgeoisie line represented by yellow music. The two-line struggle was used to show how music reflected and advanced the proletarian triumph over the bourgeoisie. As an expression of socialist culture, red music continuously expanded its dominant position in China's cultural landscape, pressuring and marginalizing yellow music in an attempt to finally eliminate it altogether. Traces of yellow music were increasingly hard to find in such media as sheet music, dance halls, and radio broadcasting, and as a result the spiritual and cultural life of the common people were increasingly unified and disciplined.

Yellow music was constructed as a class enemy, narrowing the focus of the collective imagination to the proletarian revolution and its struggles. Communist Party musicians and critics, such as Lü Ji 吕骥, Zhou Weizhi, Li Ling, Wang Yunjie, Ji Liankang 吉联抗, Li Jiefu, Ai Ke'en 艾克恩, Ma Ke 马可, and Zhao Feng 赵沨, used music criticism to denounce yellow music. At the same time, the destiny of yellow song composers such as Chen Gexing, Liu Xue'an, and Li Jinhui ranged from psychological punishment to loss of life. Yellow music criticism was not only an important discursive weapon for class struggle but also a means for expressing the political ideals that would identify oneself as proletarian, and moreover, individuals would use music criticism to pursue ambitions for political power.

During the Anti-Rightist Campaign, a large number of intellectuals, party cadres, and musicians were wrongly classified as rightists. Driven by the mindset of an imaginary enemy and a conflictual philosophy grounded in binary oppositions, the CCP critics continuously expanded the connotations and range of yellow music. As a result, the diversity of music culture was severely restricted, and literature and art ended up moving toward an ultraleftist direction, thereby contributing to the outbreak of the Great Proletarian Cultural Revolution.

NOTES

1 The term *huang* was associated with nobility and dignity in imperial China. Along with the spread of compound words into China in the modern era, such as yellow journalism or yellow press, it gradually came to connote pornographic and erotic content. After the end of the Anti-Japanese War, the new meanings of the word *yellow*

spread into the cultural fields of film, literature, and music. See Huang Xingtao 黄兴涛 and Chen Peng 陈鹏, "Jindai Zhongguo 'huangse' ciyi bianyi kaoxi" 近代中国"黄色"词义变异考析 [A study of the shift in the meaning of the word yellow in modern China], *Lishi yanjiu* 历史研究 5 (2010): 83–98. All translations are mine unless otherwise noted.

2   Liu 柳 [*sic*], "Suqing huangse yinyue bixu shuangguan qixia" 肃清黄色音乐必须双管齐下 [A two-pronged approach is a must for eliminating yellow music], *Wenhua xianfeng* 文化先锋 21 (1947): 18; Ye Baokun 叶宝琨, "Qudi huangse yinyue yiwaide genben wenti" 取缔黄色音乐以外的根本问题 [The fundamental issue beyond eliminating the yellow music], *Liyue banyuekan* 礼乐半月刊 7 (1947): 6.

3   Shu-shin Wang: "The Rise and Fall of the Campaign against Spiritual Pollution in the People's Republic of China," *Asian Affairs: An American Review*, 1986: 47–46.

4   Andrew F. Jones, *Yellow Music: Media Culture and Colonial Modernity in the Chinese Jazz Age* (Durham, NC: Duke University Press, 2001), 7.

5   *Shelun* 社论 [Editorial], "Fayang minzu chuantong fanrong yinyue yishu" 发扬民族传统 繁荣音乐艺术 [Develop national tradition, expand music art], *Renmin ribao* 人民日报, August 27, 1956.

6   Lan Daming 蓝大名, "Ting 'jiuge chongfang' yougan" 听'旧歌重放'有感 [My thoughts on "replayed old songs"], *Tianjin ribao* 天津日报, June 5, 1957; Qiao Zhengyan 乔正寅, "Dui 'jiuge chongfan' de tihui" 对'旧歌重放'的体会 [My feelings on "replayed old songs"], *Tianjin ribao* 天津日报, June 5, 1957.

7   Liu Bingyan 刘冰雁 and Chen Bohong 陈伯鸿, "Shanghai zai chensi zhong" 上海在沉思中 [Shanghai in contemplation], *Zhongguo qingnianbao* 中国青年报, May 13, 1956; Zhang Shu 张曙, "Li Jinhui wei 'shuqing gequ' mingbuping" 黎锦晖为"抒情歌曲"鸣不平 [Li Jinhui voices his grievances on "lyric songs"], *Xinwen ribao* 新闻日报, May 21, 1957; Yin 胤 [*sic*], "Wei liuxing gequ mingbuping" 为流行歌曲鸣不平 [Voice the grievances for popular music], *Jiefang ribao* 解放日报, June 8, 1957; Tu Xianruo 屠咸若, "Wo dui 'liuxing gequ' de kanfa" 我对"流行歌曲"的看法 [My opinion on "popular music"], *Jiefang ribao* 解放日报, June 23, 1957.

8   Sun Qiming 孙其明, "Mao Zedong wei shenme yao fadong zhengfeng yundong—lun 1957 nian de zhengfeng fanyou yundong" 毛泽东为什么要发动整风运动—论1957年的整风反右运动 [Why did Mao Zedong launch the Rectification Movement: On the Rectification and Anti-Rightist Campaign in 1957], *Tongji daxue xuebao* 同济大学学报 2 (2004):37.

9   毛泽东 Mao Zedong, "Zuzhi liliang zhunbei fanji youpai fen zi jingong de zhishi" 组织力量准备反击右派分子进攻的指示 [Muster our forces to repulse rightists' wild attacks, June 8, 1957], in 毛泽东选集 5 [*Selected works of Mao Zedong*, vol. 5] (Beijing: Renmin chubanshe, 1977), 431–32. English translation in *Selected Works of Mao Zedong*, vol. 5 (Beijing: Foreign Languages Press, 1977), 449.

10 The lyrics of "Socialism Is Good" are by Huo Xiyang 霍希扬 and the music is by Li Huanzhi 李焕之. The lyrics cited here are a little different from the later commonly known version. After the Anti-Rightist Campaign, the lyric "the rightists can never revolt even if they want to" was revised to "Reactionaries can never revolt even if they want to."

11 *People's Music* first adopted an anti-rightist position in July 1957. Lang Yuxiu 郎毓秀 and Huang Yijun 黄贻钧 were the first to initiate an anti-rightist campaign. In August the Editorial Department organized articles to criticize such figures as Liu Xue'an 刘雪庵, Li Yinghang 李鹰航, Lu Huabai 陆华柏, Xu Jie 徐杰, Yao Yirang 姚以让, and Hu Jingxiang 胡静翔. Liu received the most severe criticism. In September, to reinforce the achievements of the Anti-Rightist Campaign, some rightists, such as Liu Xue'an, Zhang Quan 张权, Lu Huabai, and Li Yinghang, were criticized again. In December the Shanghai Conservatory of Music announced the success of the Anti-Rightist Campaign and exposed what it called a "Wang Lisan wei shou de fandang xiao jituan" 汪立三为首的反党小集团 [small anti-Communist Party group headed by Wang Lisan].

12 The August 1957 issue of *Qunzhong yinyue* 群众音乐 [*Mass Music*] opened with the article "Yinyue gongzuozhe yao jiji touru fan youpai de douzheng" 音乐工作者要积极投入反右派的斗争 [Musicians should actively engage in the anti-rightist fight] and published two strongly anti-rightist songs on its back cover: "Fan youpai de douzheng da zhankai" 反右派的斗争大展开 [The anti-rightist fight started with great vigor] and "Bu dakua youpai bu ganxin" 不打垮右派不甘心 [Keep fighting till the rightists are razed to the ground]. In September, *Yuanlin hao* 园林好 [*The Garden is good*] magazine established an anti-rightist special issue titled "Gonggu shehuizhuyi yinyue zhendi, jianjue fanji youpai changkuang jingong" 巩固社会主义音乐阵地、坚决反击右派猖狂进攻 [Consolidate the position of socialist music, and firmly counter the rampant attack of the Rightist]. In the October issue, the title of the special issue was changed to "Jiaqiang dang dui yinyue shiye de lingdao, shenru jielu youpai de fandong yinmou" 加强党对音乐事业的领导, 深入揭露右派的反动阴谋" [Strengthen the party's leadership of music institutions and expose the reactionary conspiracy of the rightists], and *Music Life* also published numerous anti-rightist critiques. Music entities and institutions at various levels also engaged in countless attacks on rightists and published songs such as "Fensui youpaifenzi jingong" 粉碎右派分子进攻 [Shattering the assault of the rightists] and "Jinggao youpaifenzi" 警告右派分子 [Warning rightists].

13 On January 7, 1958, *People's Daily* published the editorial "Suqing huangse gequ" 肃清黄色歌曲 [Eliminating yellow songs]." On the same day, teachers and students from the Musicology Department and the Composition Department of the Central Conservatory of Music held a symposium on yellow song issues. He Qiansan 何乾三, "Dakai yin yuan zhi men, guanxin shiji—yinyue yuan shi sheng pipan huangse gequ" 打开音院之门、关心实际—音乐院师生批判黄色歌曲 [Opening the gate of the Central Conservatory of Music and caring about reality: Teachers and students from the Central Conservatory of Music criticize yellow songs], *Renmin yinyue* 人民音乐, February 1958, 9. On January 17, 1958, the Bureau of Art Administration under the Ministry of Culture and the Chinese Musicians' Association jointly held a symposium to criticize yellow music. The symposium was attended by sixty people, including such musicians as Lü Ji 吕骥, Zhou Weizhi 周巍峙, Meng Bo 孟波, Li Ling 李凌, Zheng Lücheng 郑律成, An E 安娥, Li Huanzhi, Lao Zhicheng 老志诚, and Liu Zhi 刘炽, as well as the heads of local branches of the Chinese Musicians'

Associations. "Wenhuabu guanyu suqing huangse yinyue wenti gei Zhongyang de baogao" 文化部关于肃清黄色音乐问题给中央的报告 [Report on eliminating "yellow music" issues to the CCP Central Committee by the Ministry of Culture], March 1958, drafted by the General Office, the Ministry of Culture. The report is included in *1949–1959 Wenhua gongzuo wenjian ziliao huibian* 文化工作文件资料汇编 [*Collection of documents on cultural work, 1949–1959*] edited and printed by Zhonghua Renmin Gongheguo wenhuabu bangongting 中华人民共和国文化部办公厅 (Beijing: General Office for the Ministry of Culture of the People's Republic of China, 1982), 238–41. Soon afterward, the Chinese Musicians' Association wielded its administrative authority and organized conferences attended by heads of local branches of the Chinese Musicians' Association to discuss the work plans of the association and its local branches. Editorial Department, "Jiaqiang sixiang lilun gongzuo, cujin puji yundong—gedi yinxie fuzeren zai Jing kaihui" 加强思想理论工作，促进普及运动—各地音协负责人在京开会 [Strengthen ideological and theoretical work to promote popularization—Heads of Chinese musicians' association's local branches attend the conference in Beijing], *Renmin yinyue* 人民音乐 2 (1958): 22.

14 Benbao bianji 本报编辑 [Journal editors], "Beijing yinyuejie weijiao huangse yinyue—Lü Ji haozhao yinyue gongzuozhe chuangzuo shidai yuequ ba zheyi chang liangtiao luxian de douzheng jinxing daodi" 北京音乐界围剿黄色音乐—吕骥号召音乐工作者创作时代乐曲把这一场两条路线的斗争进行到底 [Beijing's music circles siege yellow music—Lü Ji called on musicians to create songs of our times to carry out this two-line struggle to the end], *Wenhui bao* 文汇报, February 2, 1958.

15 My argument here is based on relevant historical materials published as mimeographs, including: Zhongguo yinyuejia xiehui 中国音乐家协会 [Chinese Musicians' Association], "Pipan huangse yinyue cankao ziliao—neihan 62shou huangse gequ gepu" 批判黄色音乐参考资料—内含62首黄色歌曲歌谱 [Reference Material for Criticizing Yellow Music: 62 Music Sheet of Yellow Songs], January 1958; Zhongguo yinyuejia xiehui Tianjin fenhui, Tianjinshi qunzhong yishuguan 中国音乐家协会天津分会、天津市群众艺术馆 [Tianjin Branch of Chinese Musicians' Association and Tianjin Mass Art Center], "Buxu huangse yinyue duhai qingnian: Pipan huangse yinyue cankao ziliao (wu)" 不许黄色音乐毒害青年: 批判黄色音乐参考资料（五）[Do not allow yellow music to poison youth: reference material for criticizing yellow music issues, vol. 5], February 1958; Zhongguo yinyuejia xiehui Shanghai fenhui 中国音乐家协会上海分会 [Shanghai Branch of Chinese Musicians' Association], "Guanyu huangse gequ wenti taolun de cankao ziliao (yi)" 关于黄色歌曲问题讨论的参考资料（一）[Reference material for the discussion of yellow music issues, vol. 1], January 1958; Wuhan qunzhong yishuguan 武汉群众艺术馆 [Wuhan Mass Art Center], "Wei suqing huangse yinyue er douzheng" 为肃清黄色音乐而斗争 [Fighting for the eradication of yellow music], January 1958.

16 Qiu Hong 丘红, "Wuhan chuban 'wei suqing huangse yinyue' er douzheng zhuanji" 武汉出版"为肃清黄色音乐"而斗争专辑 [Special issue of fighting for "eradicating yellow music" published in Wuhan], *Renmin yinyue* 人民音乐 1 (1958): 11.

17 Martin J. Medhurst, "Introduction," in *Cold War Rhetoric: Strategy, Metaphor, and Ideology*, ed. Martin J. Medhurst, Robert L. Ivie, Philip Wander, and Robert L. Scott (East Lansing: Michigan State University Press, 1997), xiv.

18 George Lakoff and Mark Johnson, *Metaphors We Live By* (Chicago: University of Chicago Press), 1980.

19 Feng Lou 丰楼, "Women xuyao shidai de shengyin" 我们需要时代的声音 [We need the sound of our times], *Renmin yinyue* 人民音乐 1 (1958): 9; Tang Ji 唐纪, "Chang huangse gequ you shenme haichu?" 唱黄色歌曲有什么害处? [What is the harm in singing yellow songs?], *Yinyue shenghuo* 音乐生活 3 (1958): 30–31.

20 王云阶 Wang Yunjie, "Youpaifenzi Chen Gexin de fandong yinyue daolu" 右派分子陈歌辛的反动音乐道路 [The reactionary path of Chen Gexin the rightist], *Renmin yinyue* 人民音乐 10 (1957): 22–24.

21 Lü Ji 吕骥, "Bo Liu Xue'an: Shehuizhuyi yinyue luxian bu rong youpaifenzi cuangai" 驳刘雪庵：社会主义音乐路线不容右派分子篡改 [Rebutting Liu Xue'an: The socialist music path cannot be tampered with by the rightists], *Renmin yinyue* 人民音乐 9 (1957): 2–3.

22 Li Jinhui 黎锦晖, "Zhanduan dugen chedi xiaomie huangse gequ" 斩断毒根彻底消灭黄色歌曲 [Cut the poisonous roots and eradicate yellow songs], *Renmin yinyue* 人民音乐 3 (1958): 24–25.

23 Jie Fu 劫夫, "Wei suqing huangse gequ er douzheng" 为肃清黄色歌曲而斗争 [Fighting for the elimination of yellow music], *Yinyue shenghuo* 音乐生活 11 (1957): 181–86; Li Ling 李凌, "Zenyang jianbie huangse gequ" 怎样鉴别黄色歌曲 [How to identify yellow songs], in *Rang xinde yinyue shenghuo huoyue qilai* 让新的音乐生活活跃起来 [Make new music life thrive] (Beijing: Yinyue chubanshe, 1958), 8–9. Lian Kang 联抗, "Huangse gequ shi ducao" 黄色歌曲是毒草 [Yellow songs are poisonous weeds], *Renmin yinyue* 人民音乐 9 (1957): 35–36; Zhou Weizhi 周巍峙, "Pipan huangse yinyue" 批判黄色音乐 [Criticizing yellow music, 1957], in *Lun yinyue wei gongnongbing fuwu* 论音乐为工农兵服务 [On music serving workers, farmers, and soldiers] (Beijing: Yinyue chubanshe, 1966), 281–97.

24 See Nie Er 聂耳, "Zhongguo gewu duanlun" 中国歌舞短论 [An Essay on Chinese Songs and Dances], *Dianying yishu* 电影艺术 3 (July 22, 1932). The article is signed by Nie Er's pseudonym—Hei Tianshi 黑天使, Dark Angel. See also Nie Er 聂耳, "Li Jinhui de *Bajiao ye shang shi*" 黎锦晖的"芭蕉叶上诗" [Poem written on a banana leaf by Li Jinhui], *Shenbao* 申报 (local supplement), January 6, 1935.

25 Makesi 马克思, Engesi 恩格斯 [Karl Marx and Friedrich Engels], 马克思恩格斯全集第四卷 *Makesi Engesi quanji disi juan* [The complete works of Marx and Engels, vol. 4] (Beijing: Renmin chubanshe, 1956), 504.

26 Lu Mang 卢芒, "Ezhu huangse yinyue de bozi" 扼住黄色音乐的脖子 [Strangling yellow music by its neck], *Wenhui bao*, March 29, 1958, 3.

27 Guzu ganjin, lizheng shangyou, duokuai haoshengdi jianshe shehuizhuyi 鼓足干劲，力争上游，多快好省地建设社会主义 [go all out, aim high and achieve greater, faster, better, and more economical results in building socialism] is a very important slogan in the Great Leap Forward. See Xiang Dongmin 项东民 and An Yihui 安熠辉, "Chuixiang 'dayuejin' chongfeng hao de Zhonggong bada erci huiyi" 吹响"大跃进"冲锋号的中共八大二次会议 [Blowing the bugle call of the "Great Leap Forward" in the

second session of the Eight National Congress of the Communist Party of China], 文史精华 *Wenshi jinghua* 3 (2011): 24-27.

28. Cheng Dun 成敦, "Fenxi jishou huangse gequ de biaoxian tezheng" 分析几首黄色歌曲的表现特征 [Analyzing the expressive features of several pieces of yellow music], 辽宁日报 *Liaoning ribao*, December 20, 1957. Wang Yunjie 王云阶, "Huangse gequ shi ducao, bixu chanchu!" 黄色歌曲是毒草，必须铲除！ [Yellow music is a poisonous weed and must be rooted out!], *Renmin yinyue* 人民音乐 1 (1958): 10–12. Xiao Qing 肖晴, "Zhengquede duidai Zhou Xuan de gechang yishu" 正确地对待周璇的歌唱艺术 [Have the right attitude toward Zhou Xuan's singing art], 人民音乐 *Renmin yinyue* 1 (1958): 13–14. Zhao Feng 赵沨, "Suqing fandong tuifei de huangse yinyue" 肃清反动颓废的黄色音乐 [Eliminate the reactionary and decadent yellow music], *Renmin yinyue* 人民音乐 3 (1958): 20–21.

29. The popular music of republican Shanghai frequently employed folk music melodies. For instance, "Nanmin ge" 难民歌 (A refugee song) by Yan Hua used the melody of "Jinü gaozhuang" 妓女告状 (The prostitute's complaint); the melody of "Majiang jing" 麻将经 (A Mahjong game) came from "Ju da gang" 锯大钢 (Saw the jar); "Mai xiangsi" 卖相思 (Selling lovesickness) borrowed from "Da bainian" 大拜年 (Happy new year), a folk song in Shanxi and Suiyuan, and "Tan qingjia" 探亲家 (Visiting relatives), a folk song from northern China; "Meimei wo ai ni" 妹妹我爱你 (Dear sister I love you) by Li Jinhui closely resembled "Ba ban" 八板 (*Baban*), an instrumental folk song; and the Japanese military song "Manzhou guniang" used motifs from "Fengyang huagu" 凤阳花鼓 (Fengyang flower drum). In taking up the issue of yellow music's use of folk music, CCP critiques declared that yellow music "stole," "distorted," and "destroyed" Chinese folk music.

30. Bianzhe de hua 编者的话 [Editor], "Guanyu 'Jiujiu yanyangtian' de taolun" 关于"九九艳阳天"的讨论 [Discussions on "Sunny days in early Spring"], *Renmin yinyue* 人民音乐 5 (1958): 20. Peng Chao 澎潮, "Tan dianying chaqu 'Jiujiu yanyangtian'" 谈电影插曲"九九艳阳天" [On the film song "Sunny days in early Spring"], *Renmin yinyue* 人民音乐 3 (1958): 3; Li Guifen 李桂芬, "Chang 'Jiujiu yanyangtian' yougan" 唱"九九艳阳天"有感 [My thoughts on singing "Sunny days in early Spring"], *Renmin yinyue* 人民音乐 3 (1958): 8; Li Ling 李凌, "Cong 'Jiujiu yanyangtian' tanqi" 从"九九艳阳天"谈起 [Starting from "Sunny days in early Spring"], *Beijing ribao* 北京日报, March 28, 1958.

31. Ying Yu 影予, "'Diu jiezhi' shi bu jiankangde" '丢戒指'是不健康的 ["Losing a ring" is unhealthy], *Renmin yinyue* 人民音乐 4 (1959): 21–23; Zhong Qiang 钟锵, "Yinyue yishu de chonggao mubiao—Cong 'Diu jiezhi' 'Xiao yanzi' de taolun tanqi" 音乐艺术的崇高目标—从'丢戒指''小燕子'的讨论谈起 [The noble objective of musical art: starting from the discussions on "Losing a ring" and "Small swallow"], *Renmin yinyue* 人民音乐 8 (1959): 16–19; 马可 Ma Ke, "Cong 'Diu jiezhi' tandao huixie gequ wenti" 从'丢戒指'谈到诙谐歌曲问题 [From "Losing a ring" to the problem of humorous songs], *Yinyue yanjiu* 音乐研究 2 (1959): 99–100.

AFTERWORD

Asia's Soundings of the Cold War

CHRISTINE R. YANO

This volume of "sound alignments" juxtaposes three analytic elements—popular music, Cold War, and Asia—within Kuan-Hsing Chen's political call to "de–cold war" the ways in which we examine the area and period.[1] By this intervention, Asia and its experiences of an extended and variable period recenter our thinking of global forces away from traditional East-West binaries and toward a multiplex of emergences. In this I deliberately invoke a cinema-centric spin: several movies shown at once in a large multiply divided structure, with the possibility of sound leakages between theaters. Thus sitting in the darkened viewing room of Cold War Asia within a multiplex site assumes not isolated stories to be told but overlapping, simultaneous experiences of other viewers and movies whose presence may be noted most clearly in overhearing their sounds next door. The editors' three-pronged introduction and organization of this volume—routes, covers, and fronts—serve our multiplex well. Tracing the pathways of songs overlaps with practices of covering borrowed melodies, themes, and sentiments, both pushing and pulling popular song along the forefront of political conflict. What are the backs upon which song rides? How do those backs shape song? How does song help shape publics? And how does the commercial milieu of these practices intermix with the politics of its time?

Cold War Asia provides multiplex experiences by which one may tune in to the narratives of one darkened theater or another, at will. Notably, it is sound that becomes the nagging, overlayered presence, bleeding through walls. The sounds overheard in the Cold War Asia multiplex may be most congruent when least noticed, as well as jarringly disconcerting when most disruptive (e.g., the rapid-fire explosions of a gun battle overheard just as lovers lean in for a kiss). The cinema-going experience is not confined to the narrative of one theater but assumes the cacophony of multiple narratives reminding us of their presence primarily through sound leakages.

In short, as this volume makes clear, there is no single "Cold War Asia," no music genre that singly captures the time, place, politics, or sentiment. Instead, there is the multiplex of Cold War Asias, imagined in its complexity through sound. Sound leakages demand that the framework for analysis in this volume remains flexible, open-ended, and highly contextualized. Asia's soundings of the Cold War draw out the complexities of a political environment with cultural ramifications that are not peripheral or contingent but central to Cold War concerns. The aims of this volume run broad and deep and find significant bumps along the way, as the editors point out in their organization of an international conference at the University of Chicago Beijing Center. The bumps demonstrate just how alive the topic of the Cold War is, still susceptible to ripples of political sensitivities in waves that lap across oceans.

The notion that popular music might play a part in this very political of topics holds the seductive calling card. Popular music: an industrial product dismissed by Adorno-ists, embraced by populists, debated and used by nationalists, and consumed by large swaths of the population. The ability of popular music to seep into the nooks and crannies of everyday life makes for a prime rendering of on-the-ground Cold War soundings. Even as the definition of popular music may be extended by a bandwidth of genres to include urban folk song and overtly political but youth-oriented music (see Jennifer Lindsay's chapter), it is the everyday presence (the "popular") that begs our attention. Herein lies the thrum of human conflict, tension, pleasure, and pure escape by which people may individually or as a group tap their feet, move their bodies, shed their tears, and heave a collective sigh. Popular music creates future mnemonics of being there (note the reaction to the nightclub performance described in the editors' introduction). This volume calls upon us to consider the power of songs we cannot get out of our heads.

Of course, these are not any sound alignments but ones of a specific time (Cold War) and place ("Asia"). As such, we should consider the conditions of recentering, of Chen's "de-cold war" project and its sonic ramifications. The conditions of routes, covers, and fronts include the presence of US military bases throughout Asia, particularly the Philippines, Korea, and Japan (with Okinawa carrying the disproportionate burden). Military bases may have housed American soldiers, but importantly for our consideration of music, they provided many and varied opportunities for American popular music circulation. Whether mediated (radio, such as Far Eastern Network, and recordings) or live (on-base performance venues), US military bases provided opportunities for listening, learning, and performing the latest hit-parade tunes from across the Pacific with a heady sense of coevalness. US military personnel inevitably brought some musicians among their ranks: while many of these included jazz and popular musicians from the continental US, artists such as Japanese American ukulele virtuoso Herb Ohta (b. 1934) from Hawaiʻi, who helped repopularize the Hawaiian instrument as a member of the US Marine Corps stationed in Japan, played a role as well. These forms of Cold War sonic travelings and travelers gave American popular music an immediacy and accessibility within the context of postwar Asia.

Local musicians and audiences could not fail to notice; in fact, many of them were thrilled by the opportunity to hear these riffs live. In Japan, what had been banned by the wartime regime as "enemy music" became the fodder of Cold War exhilaration. Even for those who did not live near a military base or performance hall, the airwaves of radio and eventually television brought the sounds into their homes. What piqued their listening musicianship were both the products of the US music industry (songs, instruments) as well as some of the historical processes (possibilities of particular popular song genres and practices—the singer-songwriter or urban folk song in South Korea, for example, as detailed by Hyunjoon Shin). Touring musicians on US military bases—whether from the US or other parts of Asia—created and re-created the audible pulse of Cold War empires.

When considering Cold War Asia, we should juxtapose this framework with other global historicities, particularly what is known as the Jet Age, beginning in the late 1950s with commercially scheduled flights on jet-propelled airplanes and ending by the late 1970s, when air travel by jet was taken for granted. Whereas the initial and signature travelers of the Jet Age came to be known as wealthy "jet-setters" from Europe and America, with their own culture of high-flying conspicuous consumerism, the development of economy class and affordable tours meant the eventual rise of the middle-class traveler.[2] The technological and industrial developments that coalesced into the Jet Age promoted global tourism that reinforced particular kinds of national agendas and enabled corporate strategies.[3] This shrinking of the globe included Asia, or more specifically the idea of Asia, within its context. The new Cold War jet-enabled cosmopolitanism thus juxtaposed the aesthetics of technological sleekness with exotic, often sexualized primitivism, including that of the Asian woman or man. As literary historian Christina Klein points out, the period following World War II represented both the expansion of the US human-to-human intervention in Asia as well as a concomitant popular fascination with Asia, fueled by books, musicals, and magazines.[4] Such "Cold War Orientalism" shaped middle-class America's consumption of "Asia." The Jet Age fueled not only the fantastic in Asia-framed musicals and images of wealthy jet-setters but also the everyday in middle-class tourists and sober international programs, such as the Sister Cities International movement (begun under President Dwight D. Eisenhower in 1956), student exchange programs, and other enactments of people-to-people diplomacy. Indeed, as part of the political impetus for such diplomacy, these citizen exchanges deliberately took place with former enemy nations, such as Japan. Different kinds of jet-setters thus enabled the routes of Cold War Asia and its musics.

The Jet Age and its routes extended to global airlines developed within Asia, especially with the advent of early pioneering carriers, such as Air India in 1932, Cathay Pacific (Hong Kong) in 1946, Orient Airways in 1946 (later Pakistan International Airways), Malayan Airlines in 1947 (later split into Malaysian Airline System and Singapore Airlines), Japan Airlines in 1951, All Nippon Airways in 1952, Far Eastern Air Transport in 1957 (Taiwan), China Airlines in 1959 (Taiwan), Thai Airways International in 1959, Korean Air in 1962, Bangkok Airways in 1968, and Malaysian Airline System in 1972. Although the Jet Age itself may have been based far more on American international carriers (especially Pan American World Airways), the development of Asian international carriers lent a structure of coevalness to Asia. International routes and their passengers formed some of the pathways by which music, too, could travel from abroad and between Asian sites. Thus the development of global middle-class tourism enabled by the Jet Age created Asia as a destination for primarily Western tourists and eventually placed Asia within and partly controlling the flows of global tourists. Asia as a destination—whether in person or virtually through images—became a frame within which its popular culture expressions developed. Even if those expressions did not find major audiences within Cold War visitors or Westernized versions of "Asia," these multiple sides form the complex picture this volume examines.

Jet Age routes had global musical repercussions. Cold War Asia, officially "decolonized" by postwar treaties, became, in effect, newly colonized by Western popular culture and conjoined with other exotica in commercially based "tiki culture." Asia (and the Pacific) became a culturally appropriative novelty item. Replete with bamboo-decorated bars, miniature-umbrella-decorated mixed drinks, and bird-call-infused music, tiki culture combined elements of not only Polynesian but also Asian and Latin features, devolving into Western escapism. Within this milieu, Hawai'i symbolized "paradise"—channeled historically through Tin Pan Alley, performed during the postwar era by ethnically Hawaiian and Japanese American musicians (descendants of immigrants to Hawai'i) and further reified by Asian media. As analyzed by Lindsay in this volume, Hawaiian music ("Hawaiian-style band music"), under the aegis of American popular music, pervaded Asian sonic worlds, including that of the Eurasian community in Indonesia, influencing newly created syncretic genres such as *kroncong*. Even when the music per se may not have been strictly Hawaiian, the inclusion of an iconic musical instrument, such as the ukulele—itself part of transoceanic circulations of immigrants from the Azores to Hawai'i to the continental US to Asia—retained a symbolic visual and aural connection. The ukulele's presence in places such as Okinawa, discussed by Marié Abe in this volume, speaks to historic routes. Asia, the Pacific, and specifically Hawai'i occupied various niches of sonic meanings—kitsch, novelty, escape—as part of the new symbolic Cold War order in pop-cultural terms.

Jet Age routes encompassed not only traffic between East and West, and the development of an industry that catered to "exotic" tastes, but also, importantly, circulation within Asia. Inter-Asian travel—necessarily limited by class and infrastructural access—played a role in complicating the East-West divides normally associated with the Cold War. The routes of this Jet Age mobility demand that we "follow the song/singer," as Lindsay does in tracing an Indonesian popular kroncong song in its travels to international political contexts; as Anna Schultz does in following the highly unusual path of a rural Indian singer-saint turned leader of socialist cosmopolitanism through Bombay, Amravati, and parts of Japan; and as C. J. W.-L. Wee discusses vis-à-vis an emergent (and incomplete) East Asian pop music imaginary. Mobility frames Cold War Asia as on the move, within, between, and across regions, thereby creating new political, social, cultural, and musical affiliations.

That mobility is not problem-free but comes with its own preconditions. Considering Asia's Cold War and its musical expressions forces us to consider ways by which certain countries and their immigrant families are still divided by official Communism/capitalism lines. For some within Asia, Cold War tensions remain part of their daily lives, and even developed as a top tourist attraction, such as the demilitarized zone (DMZ) between North and South Korea. The DMZ tourism represents commodified neo-nostalgia for the Cold War, even as actual families separated by the divide may reunite with heartfelt remembrances. Importantly, Chen reminds us that "the cold war is still alive within us," exactly through the everyday parade of those tears, those songs, those tastes of foods.[5] Thus DMZ tourism allows us all to become voyeurs to these emotionally wrung tensions.

With the global rise of China as a bloated capitalist power, the irony of its earlier ideologically driven Communist purge recedes into the distant past. This form of internal Asian Cold War drama gives us pause for thought when considering the musically expressive forms this history might take. Amid a backdrop of revolutionary opera, contemporary Chinese popular music brackets the past as a dated reminder for some and a living memory for others. Indeed, the scene described in the editors' introduction of the East Is Red nightclub vividly reminds us of generational differences and transmissions and the potential for kitsch in this kind of emotional mash-up.

In considering Cold War Asia, we should also place Japanese colonialism and its paternalistic co-prosperity sphere as central to intra-Asian battles, tensions, and its own version of global reconciliation. Older Japanese and even a few young ones who never lived through the war period may gather at military song (*gunka*) bars in Tokyo and sing full-throated versions of nationalistic marches. They can hear gunka in pachinko parlors, the march of game tokens and money adding another layer to the cacophony. Many older Japanese men I have spoken with disavow any personal attachment to militarism; they proclaim their own antiwar pacifism. Gunka is nothing more or less than the sound of their youth—akin to the grandmothers and grandfathers at the East Is Red nightclub. These kinds of stories demonstrate the sticking power of music, beyond words, beyond meanings. Who knew that the little ditty one heard over and over again as a teenager would be difficult to erase from one's memories, sixty or seventy years later? The Cold War needle gets stuck in the grooves of one's past.

Thinking through Cold War Asia and beyond rarely brings in the topic of religion. But in certain nations, religion plays a central role in defining affiliations and political obligations. Thus, including Hindu devotional singers within this volume, including the first International Hindu Conference in 1966, demonstrates different kinds of alliances broached in this arena. Imported, localized religion plays a significant role in a country such as Korea, where Christianity carries such spiritual, emotional, and potentially political weight. Christian churches have not only created routes for the popularity of Western urban folk song in South Korea, but as anthropologist Nicholas Harkness eloquently discusses, they have created an aesthetics of the voice itself that is linked to modernity, morality, and national prosperity.[6]

Voice, in fact, plays a central role in considering Cold War Asia musical aesthetics, for it is not only what is being sung (musical scales, lyrics, orchestration, rhythms) but how it is sung (the materiality of the voice) that reverberates with such intensity. These sonorities of identity make distinctive an Okinawan vocalization from a Japanese mainland (*naichi*) one, a Balinese-sung expression from a Javanese, much less a Korean from a South Asian. Here lie timbral idioms that a stranger—whether from a neighboring village, district, island, linguistic group, or nation—may find near impossible to duplicate. This is what may be perceived as the stubbornness of voice as natal dialect or racialized accent. Here also lie the differences of language and enunciation that cross-cultural (cross-linguistic) covers rarely achieve. But keep in mind that these kinds of covers create their own genre and political space in the popular music lexicon: not so much English-language songs with an accent but the assertion of the co-opting position of musical miscegenation. This is not failure so much as triumph, or at least a triumphalist approach to covers. The processes by which one may identify and then attempt to duplicate vocal sonorities create the bases of differences that matter. This is where Chen's project of marking out a space "in which unspoken stories and histories may be told" that "map the historically constituted cultural and political effects of the cold war" may lie.[7] Listening for the voice makes work of that project.

Cosmopolitanism—that is, traffic in ideas and sounds that go beyond the provincial—entangles Cold War Asia within a larger sphere of people, aesthetics, and institutions. This is why the concept of "vernacular cosmopolitanism" proves so useful for our consideration. The concept takes the mobility of cosmopolitanism and places it squarely upon the shoulders of people in situ, within the particularities of their histories and aesthetics. Perhaps we might consider this a kind of "rickshaw vernacular"—icon veering into stereotype—drawing upon indigenous forms of mobility on an intimate scale. Rickshaw vernacular may be predicated not so much on the large corporations or even governmental infrastructure that produce jets, trains, and cars but on downscaled human networks, person to person, kin to kin, friend to friend, by which this form of trafficking in ideas and sounds may take place. The resulting songs represent political processes and their ideological alignments on a human scale, those alignments made audible, experiential, personal, and maybe even pleasurable.

We have to keep in mind that circulations build upon existing social, political, and commercial infrastructures, even as they can seep into new routes. Censorship often guides the way: in Cold War Korea, official restrictions against Japanese popular media, including broadcast music and sales, which began immediately after the end of colonial rule in 1945, have been lifted only incrementally. Official restrictions do not necessarily stop music from traveling; instead, sometimes when music travels through what the editors of this volume call "forbidden routes," the subterfuge itself may become part of the lure. The situation keeps shifting. What only moved through illegal underground channels may now surface in retail stores (in effect, dulling the draw). New postwar generations without direct experience of colonial rule never looked back as they sought the cool of Japan's latest; ironically, they now occupy many of the sound booths and stages of Asia's global cool. As the hot spot of Asia's cool shifts, so, too, do the geopolitics of the musical encounter.

That musical encounter and the cosmopolitanism that it circumscribes point to a concept that has many governments abuzz—Joseph Nye's soft power, the ability to attract and persuade.[8] Popular music is often positioned as a source of soft power, particularly so with its sonic seductions, accruing to bodies and memories in its ability to get under one's skin. Popular music holds iconic soft power attributes. Indeed, Asian countries have taken notice. The Japanese government developed its "Cool Japan" project beginning in 2005, based upon the global fandom of its pop culture products, including J-pop. The Korean government has aggressively adopted soft power strategies in the twenty-first century, bolstering creative industries (including K-pop) with incentives and support. Such soft power cultivation has paid off, boosting the efficacy by which popular music in Cold War Asia has made global inroads. As the influence of J-pop and K-pop spreads throughout other parts of Asia as well as beyond niche markets in the West to more mainstream airwaves, we must consider how to position a Cold War Asia frame in relation to its soft power markings.

Cosmopolitanism adheres not only in sounds but in sound makers: guitars (accompaniment to jeans and draft beers) in the South Korea of which Shin writes; ukulele in the Okinawa of which Abe writes. In many cases, the very mobility of these music makers seems to befit the age. They represent portable expression, borrowed from Euro-America, poised to cover (as in the editors' introduction) but sometimes with surprise vernacularisms of their own. The accessibility of these instruments—relatively inexpensive, relatively easy to play at some level, musical democracy in action—makes them apt monikers in this newly decolonized world. Rather than the laden piano (in prestige, literal weight, and size, its burdensome history and repertoire), a guitar or ukulele may impart possibilities of particular kinds of resonant cosmopolitanism in Cold War Asia.

One form of cosmopolitanism that challenges our assumptions rests not in the urban but in the rural, as Schultz writes of Cold War India and Abe writes of Okinawa. Whereas one might assume cosmopolitanism to flourish within the urban centers of global activities, the idea of remotely based, rural cosmopolitanism suggests other possibilities. Okinawa in particular—a separate kingdom annexed by Japan in 1879, geographically distant from the four main islands of Japan, bearing the brunt of losses of World War II, occupied by US forces far longer than any other prefecture in Japan, and in the twenty-first century shouldering a disproportionate burden of US military bases amid much public controversy—in many ways has been positioned within the crossfires of its own remoteness. It is at the same time some of the most rural and distant from Japan's capital as well as central to political conflict between Japan and the United States. Ironically in trying to build its economy, Okinawa deliberately borrowed a model from the US—a template of palm trees, tropical flowers, and "island sounds"—in order to become "Japan's Hawai'i."[9] At the same time, Okinawa historically rests in the pathways of the Kuroshio (Black Current), which has brought trade, cultural practices (including music, as evidenced by its shared musical scales with islands in Southeast Asia), and shipwrecks from different parts of Asia to its shores. If one searches for a rurally based cosmopolitanism, Okinawa represents the historically remote superconnecter, evidenced in its language, culture, food, music, clothing, and social organization. Furthermore, its very positioning at the margins enables its centrality to ongoing Cold War concerns. Okinawa may serve as a unique confluence of factors that combine remoteness with connectivity, the rural and the cosmopolitan. In many ways, rural cosmopolitanism disentangles the assumptions of global connections, filtered through the metropole and connecting laterally, point to point. And why not? Why not search beyond the bounds of the metropole to find a vantage point whose very remoteness enables a fresh approach? And perhaps in not restricting our viewfinder to urban sites of cosmopolitanism, we may find new sites by which we may frame ideas and sounds embedded within the provincial that prod the metropole.

In considering Cold War Asia, let us locate the time frame of our examination within other global simultaneities. One of these is the emergence of the "teenager" in the US and elsewhere, variably as a consumer force, a site of rebellion, a portent of incipient adulthood. Of course individuals between the ages of thirteen and nineteen have always existed, but the creation of an age grade around this developmental period speaks to particular symbolic elements that have gone global: youth-based rebellion, generational divides, consumer affiliations in music, fashion, and movies. Much of this reads as white and middle class in the US, but these social demographics demonstrate not only the source of the characterization but their global influence, as discussed in Lindsay's chapter, which includes details of the World Festivals of Youth and Students held primarily in Eastern Europe in the 1940s and 1950s. The fact that these festivals drew youth ("teenagers") from all over the world, including Asia, suggests the potent combination of music, youth, and politics. The corralling power of rock music proved pivotal in building a youth generation committed to distinguishing themselves from their parents. Teenagers bought the records, filled the concert venues, turned the dials of their radios and televisions, and twisted their way to rebellion. And it was their music that traveled the globe, including to Asia. Some of the musical groups traveled to Asia; for example, in Japan in the 1960s alone, the Ventures performed in 1964, the Beatles in 1966, and the Beach Boys in 1966.[10] (Notably, the Ventures perform there still, touring Japan with regularity to aging audiences.)

The presence of live performances by these famous foreigners on Asian soil extended the frenzy of global fandom. Asian fans may have had different ways of expressing their allegiances to these superstars, but the excitement lay in their very co-presence. Thus the touring groups from America and Britain confirmed the global status of youth cultures in Asia—the boys picking up guitars, the girls reading fan magazines and swooning to the music. Indeed, the time period we examine occurred as the Western popular music industry flourished with the electrified sounds of masculinist rebellion as well as the acoustic sounds of new urban folk compositions. Both of these represent forms of countercultures predicated upon youth, individuality, and notions of freedom as sonic challenges to the status quo. These were anthems of and to the teenager with images of cars (and motorcycles), young romance, and implicit rebellion. Even when these forms of expression themselves became a new status quo, it was still possible to discern some of their origins in discontent ("angst") that was iconic to the notion of a teenager.

That youth-based discontent in the US turned on the political targets of the period: the Communist domino-theory justification of the Vietnam War (and militarism generally), women's liberation, ethnoracial pride. Musicians, especially from the urban folk movement, led the political activism, performing as part of antiwar demonstrations. The groundswell of youthful rebellion and music spread to parts of Asia as well, as detailed by Shin in this volume. By the late 1960s, political activism captivated at least certain Asian youth, in particular in Japan, which saw student uprisings at its most prestigious institutions of learning. The scene cast Cold War Asia as an internal battleground, especially with the best and brightest refusing to inhabit the established mantle of privilege.

Part of what drew people in the US together during the Cold War was fear of the unknown. This included fear of an atomic bomb, fear of Communist takeover of Asian countries ("domino theory"), and fear of World War III. In Asia, fear understandably permeated national consciousness, especially as the site of the only two atomic bombings in human history. However, with the cataclysmic changes after the end of World War II, including reordered colonial affiliations and national boundary lines, fear of the unknown paled by comparison with the jumblings of a new political order. The popular music of Cold War Asia thus expressed different kinds of anxieties within the confusions of occupying presences and scrambled allegiances.

Popular music resonates in the lives of Cold War Asia as soundtrack to the untold stories that refuse to be ignored or glamorized. In this volume's project to de–Cold War, decolonize, de-Americanize Asia, popular music holds a central position as its own story to be told. Part of that story undeniably rests in the hands of its makers, for the most part a capitalist-driven music industry, but leaving space for noncapitalist music-making endeavors as well. Part of that story rests in the voices of its singers—quivering, belting, crooning, whispering, growling, sobbing. It is the sob that astonishes and serves as the prompt for many of the chapters in this volume. Some of those redolent voices reach back to cultural, even religious, traditions that well predate the industrial manipulations of recording studios. Other voices reach across oceans to borrowed lyrics and sounds that become theirs. Those voices travel pathways gilded by power and prestige as the infrastructure of public expression. They also traverse contentious arenas, often on the front lines of conflict. These voices cover America (or "Amerika"), they cover global pop, they cover globalized Asias. And in doing so, they enact the negotiations of lives pulled by regimes far from their homes yet shaped by profound attachments to their own domesticity. Call these soundings domestic or vernacular if you will, but this so-called minoritizing positionality only amplifies their power. This is what the de-X project is about—singing the lowercase *cold war* as both a unifying framework and diversifying rubric for the heated complications of Asia. Indeed, the sound alignments gathered here may not be quite so sound (that is, tightly unified) or aligned. There is no canonical Asian Popular Music of the Cold War. Rather, this volume revels in bringing together juxtapositions within a conceptual framework—the multiplex of Cold War Asia. Sounds bleed from one theater to the other, the shared cool darkness informed by the walls between them. The framework of routes, covers, and fronts set forth by this volume challenges us to rethink the Cold War in Asia in newly configured ways—following the song, comparing its iterations, politicizing its sometime-glamor. The book's framework forces us to query previous binaries and periodizations in favor of an ongoing, ever present, "long-fade-out" Cold War Asia that is necessarily multiplex. The volume disrupts the notion of the Cold War as peaceful: turn the focus away from Europe and America and one encounters plenty of conflict and turmoil, much of it aimed at refiguring a world order. As Schultz aptly puts it in her chapter of this volume, these are the "ambivalences of a 'cold' war marked by 'hot' antagonisms."

In this long fade-out of Asia's Cold/Hot War, consider again the grandmothers and grandfathers in the East Is Red restaurant, singing and dancing with their families to Cultural Revolution schmaltz, memories of authoritarian regimes taken down to the dance floor. In many ways, these "folk" represent the place of popular music in thinking through the Cold War in Asia that the editors and contributors seek. What happens when we examine the soundtracks that in-fill lives? How might soundtracks humanize, politicize, aestheticize, sentimentalize, and narrativize an already complex political picture? How does popular song create nuanced publics, including of music overheard? How might song communicate, less logogenically, more melogenically, or as pure sound, timbre, vibration, pulse? This may be especially significant within an Asian country with many incomprehensible dialects as well as between Asian countries without a common lingua franca. I am certainly not advocating music as a universal language; ethnomusicologists have long disputed that naive notion. But I do entertain the possibility of felt intimacies, translations, communications for which music might be particularly apt. Cold War Asia lives in the voices and bodies moving to the reverberations of the East Is Red restaurant. Guilty yet adamantly not-so-guilty pleasures lie in the sways of grandmothers and grandfathers, their feet moving to the rhythms of their youth, as they teach yet younger feet their dance. These elderly lives span the fade-out that this volume embraces. Dreams of forbidden fruit pervade the moment: "yellow music" turns red, shades very human and deeply yellow.

NOTES

1 Kuan-Hsing Chen, *Asia as Method: Toward Deimperialization* (Durham, NC: Duke University Press, 2010), 120.
2 Christine R. Yano, *Airborne Dreams: "Nisei" Stewardesses and Pan American World Airways* (Durham, NC: Duke University Press, 2011), 28–29.
3 Christopher Endy, *Cold War Holidays: American Tourism in France* (Chapel Hill: University of North Carolina Press, 2004); Jenifer Van Vleck, *Empire of the Air: Aviation and the American Ascendancy* (Cambridge, MA: Harvard University Press, 2013); Christine R. Yano, "'Flying Geisha': Japanese Stewardesses with Pan American World Airways," in *Modern Girls on the Go: Gender, Mobility, and Labor in Japan*, ed. Alisa Freedman, Laura Miller, and Christine R. Yano (Stanford: Stanford University Press, 2013), 85–106.
4 Christine Klein, *Cold War Orientalism: Asia in the Middlebrow Imagination, 1945–1961* (Berkeley: University of California Press, 2003).
5 Chen, *Asia as Method*, 118.

6   Nicholas Harkness, *Songs of Seoul: An Ethnography of Voice and Voicing in Christian South Korea* (Berkeley: University of California Press, 2014).
7   Chen, *Asia as Method*, 120.
8   Joseph Nye, *Soft Power: The Means to Success in World Politics* (New York: Public Affairs, 2004).
9   Osamu Tada, "Constructing Okinawa as Japan's Hawai'i: From Honeymoon Boom to Resort Paradise," *Japanese Studies* 15, no. 3 (2015): 287–302.
10 Carolyn Stevens, *The Beatles in Japan* (London: Routledge, 2018).

Bibliography

Abbas, Ackbar. "Cosmopolitan De-scriptions: Shanghai and Hong Kong." In *Cosmopolitanism*, edited by Carol A. Breckenridge, Sheldon Pollock, Homi K. Bhabha, and Dipesh Chakrabarty, 209–28. Durham, NC: Duke University Press, 2002.
Abelman, Nancy. "Minjung Theory and Practice." In *Cultural Nationalism in East Asia: Representation and Identity*, edited by Harumi Befu, 139–68. Berkeley: University of California Press, 1993.
Agamben, Giorgio. *State of Exception*. Chicago: University of Chicago Press, 2005.
Adorno, Theodor. "On Popular Music" [with the assistance of George Simpson]. *Studies in Philosophy and Social Science* 9 (1941): 17–48.
Aidit, D. N. *Seni dan Sastra*. Jakarta: Radja Minjak, 2002.
Amemiya, Kozy K. "The Bolivian Connection: U.S. Bases and Okinawan Emigration." In *Okinawa: Cold War Island*, edited by Chalmers Johnson, 53–69. Cardiff, CA: Japan Policy Research Institute, 1999.
Ampiah, Kweku. *The Political and Moral Imperatives of the Bandung Conference of 1955: The Reactions of the U.S., U.K. and Japan*. Folkestone, UK: Global Oriental, 2007.
Aoki, Shin. "Singing Exoticism: A Historical Anthropology of the G.I. Songs 'China Night' and 'Japanese Rumba.'" *Journal of American History* 13, no. 4 (2017): 943–55.
Aoyagi, Hiroshi. *Island of Eight Million Smiles: Idol Performers and Symbolic Production in Contemporary Japan*. Cambridge, MA: Harvard University Asia Center, 2005.
Apeland, Nils M. *World Youth and the Communists: The Facts about Communist Penetration of WFDY and IUS*. London: Phoenix House, 1958.
Appiah, Kwame Anthony. *Cosmopolitanism: Ethics in a World of Strangers*. New York: W. W. Norton, 2010.
Arnold, Alison. "Popular Film Song in India: A Case of Mass-Market Musical Eclecticism." *Popular Music* 7, no. 2 (1988): 177–88.
Asato, Eiko. "Okinawan Identity and Resistance to Militarization and Maldevelopment." In *Islands of Discontent: Okinawan Responses to Japanese and American Power*, edited by Laura Hein and Mark Selden, 228–42. Oxford: Rowman and Littlefield, 2003.

Balakrishnan, E. *History of the Communist Movement in Kerala*. Ernakulam, India: Kurukshethra Prakasan, 1998.

Balakrishnan, Hemma. "Towards an Understanding of the Use of English and Malay in Malaysian-Tamil Hip-Hop Songs." *South Asian Diaspora* (2018): 1–15.

Balvantsinha. *Under the Shelter of Bapu*. Ahmedabad, India: Navjivan Publishing House, 1962.

Baranovic, Nimrod. *China's New Voices: Popular Music, Ethnicity, Gender, and Politics, 1978–1997*. Berkeley: University of California Press, 2003.

Barnhisel, Greg. *Cold War Modernists: Art, Literature, and American Cultural Diplomacy*. New York: Columbia University Press, 2015.

Baskaran, S. Theodore. "Music for the Masses: Film Songs of Tamil Nadu." *Economic and Political Weekly* 26, nos. 11/12 (1991): 775–58.

Bate, Bernard. "'To Persuade Them into Speech and Action': Oratory and the Tamil Political, Madras, 1905–1919." *Comparative Studies in Society and History* 55, no. 1 (2013): 142–66.

Bayly, Susan. *Asian Voices in a Postcolonial Age: Vietnam, India and Beyond*. Cambridge: Cambridge University Press, 2007.

Beaster-Jones, Jayson. "Evergreens to Remixes: Hindi Film Songs and India's Popular Music Heritage." *Ethnomusicology* 53, no. 3 (2009): 425–48.

Beaster-Jones, Jayson. *Bollywood Sounds: The Cosmopolitan Mediations of Hindi Film Song*. Oxford: Oxford University Press, 2015.

Belgrade, Daniel. *The Culture of Spontaneity: Improvisation and the Arts in Postwar America*. Chicago: University of Chicago Press, 1999.

Benbao bianji [Editorial]. "Beijing yinyuejie weijiao huangse yinyue—Lü Ji haozhao yinyue gongzuozhe chuangzuo shidai yuequ ba zheyichang liangtiao luxian de douzheng jinxing daodi [Beijing's music circles siege yellow music—Lü Ji called on musicians to create songs of our times to carry out this two-line struggle to the end]." *Wenhui bao*, February 2, 1958.

Beng, Huat Chua. "Southeast Asia in Postcolonial Studies: An Introduction." *Postcolonial Studies* 11, no. 3 (2008): 231–40.

Bermani, Cesare. *Guerra guerra ai palazzi e alle chiese: Saggi sul canto sociale* [War war to palaces and churches: Essays on the social song]. Rome: Odradek, 2003.

Berry, Michael. *Speaking in Images: Interviews with Contemporary Chinese Filmmakers*. New York: Columbia University Press, 2005.

Berry, Michael. *Xiao Wu, Platform, Unknown Pleasures: Jia Zhangke's "Hometown Trilogy."* London: Palgrave Macmillan/BFI, 2009.

Beus, Yifen. "On Becoming Nora: Transforming the Voice and Place of the Sing-Song Girl through Zhou Xuan." In *Vamping the Stage: Female Voices of Asian Modernities*, edited by Andrew N. Weintraub and Bart Barendregt, 65–82. Honolulu: University of Hawai'i Press, 2017.

Bhabha, Homi. "Unsatisfied: Notes on Vernacular Cosmopolitanism." In *Text and Nation: Cross-Disciplinary Essays on Cultural and National Identities*, edited by Laura Garcia-Morena and Peter C. Pfeifer, 191–207. London: Camden House, 1996.

Bhave, Vinoba. *Bhoodan Yajna: Land-gifts Mission*. Ahmedabad, India: Navjivan Publishing House, 1953.

Bhelkar, Ratnakar. "The Political Reality in Tukadoji's Gramgita in the Indian Context of Self Governance and Secularism." *Asian Journal of Multidisciplinary Studies* 3, no. 6 (2015): 168–71.

Bianzhe de hua [Editorial]. "Guanyu 'Jiujiu yanyang tian' de taolun" [Discussions on "Sunny days in early Spring"]. *Renmin yinyue* 5 (1958): 20.

Bohnenkamp, Max. "Turning Ghosts into People: *The White-Haired Girl*, Revolutionary Folklorism, and the Politics of Aesthetics in Modern China." PhD diss., University of Chicago, 2014.

Booth, Gregory D. "Preliminary Thoughts on Hindi Popular Music and Film Production: India's 'Culture Industry(ies),' 1970–2000." *South Asian Popular Culture* 9, no. 2 (2011): 215–21.

Bourdaghs, Michael K. *Sayonara Amerika, Sayonara Nippon: A Geopolitical Prehistory of J-Pop*. New York: Columbia University Press, 2012.

Boyd-Barrett, Oliver. "Reconfiguring Media and Empire." In *The Korean Wave: Korean Media Go Global*, edited by Youna Kim. Abingdon, UK: Routledge, 2013.

Breckenridge, Carol A., Sheldon Pollock, Homi K. Bhabha, and Dipesh Chakrabarty, eds. *Cosmopolitanism*. Durham, NC: Duke University Press, 2002.

Burgess, Ebenezer. *Grammar of the Marathi Language*. Bombay: American Mission Press, 1854.

Burhan, Firdaus. *Ismail Marzuki: Hasil karya dan pengabdiannya*. Jakarta: Proyek Inventarisasi dan Dokumentasi Sejarah Nasional, Direktorat Sejarah dan Nilai Tradisional, Departemen Pendidikan dan Kebudayaan, 1983/1984.

Bustam, Mia. *Sudjojono dan Aku*. Jakarta: Pustaka Utan Kayu, 2006.

Campbell, Emma. *South Korea's New Nationalism: The End of "One Korea"?* Boulder, CO: First Forum Press, 2016.

Carlsson, Chris. *Critical Mass: Bicycling's Defiant Celebration*. Oakland, CA: AK Press, 2002.

Chakma, Bhumitra. *Strategic Dynamics and Nuclear Weapons Proliferation in South Asia: A Historical Analysis*. Bern: Peter Lang, 2004.

Chatterjee, Partha. *Nationalist Thought and the Colonial World: A Derivative Discourse?* Minneapolis: University of Minnesota Press, 1986.

Chen, Kuan-Hsing. *Asia as Method: Toward Deimperialization*. Durham, NC: Duke University Press, 2010.

Cheng, ChenChing, and George Athanasopoulos. "Music as Protest in Cold-War Asia: Teresa Teng (Deng Lijun), the Enlightenment for Democracy in the 1980s and a Case of Collective Nostalgia for an Era That Never Existed." *Lied and populäre Kultur / Song and Popular Culture* 60–61 (2015–16): 41–59.

Cheng Dun. "Fenxi jishou huangse gequ de biaoxian tezheng" [Analyzing the expressive features of several pieces of yellow music]. *Liaoning ribao*, December 20, 1957.

Cheng Qingsong and Huang Ou, eds. *Wode sheyingji bu sahuang: Xianfeng dianyingren dang'an—shengyu 1961–1970* [My camera doesn't lie: Files on avant-garde directors born in 1961–1970]. Beijing: Zhongguo youyi chubanshe, 2002.

Chew, Matthew M. "The Subversive Sociocultural Meanings of Cantopop Electronic Dance Music." *Chinese Sociology and Anthropology* 42, no. 2 (2010): 76–93.

Chinese Musicians' Association Editorial Department. "Jiaqiang sixiang lilun gongzuo, cujin puji yundong—gedi yinxie fuzeren zai Jing kaihui" [Strengthen ideological and theoretical work to promote popularization—heads of Chinese musicians' association's local branches attend the conference in Beijing]. *Renmin yinyue* 2 (1958): 22.

Chiu, Stephan, Lui Tai-Lok, and Yung Sai-Shing, eds. *Xionghuai zuguo: Xianggang aiguo zuopai yundong* [Passion for the country: Hong Kong "patriotic leftist" movement]. Hong Kong: Oxford University Press, 2014.

Cho, Hae-Joang. "Reading the 'Korean Wave' as a Sign of Global Shift." *Korea Journal* 45, no. 4 (2005): 147–82.

Chua, Jocelyn Lim. *Pursuit of the Good Life: Aspiration and Suicide in Globalizing South India*. Berkeley: University of California Press, 2014.

Chun, Allen, and Ned Rossiter. "Introduction: Cultural Imaginaries, Musical Communities, Reflexive Practices." In *Refashioning Pop Music in Asia: Cosmopolitan Flows, Political Tempos and Aesthetic Industries*, edited by Allen Chun, Ned Rossiter, and Brian Shoesmith, 1–14. London: Routledge, 2000.

Chung Po-Yin, *Xianggang yingshiye bainian* [A hundred years of the Hong Kong film industry]. Hong Kong: Joint Publishing, 2004.

Clews, John C. *Communist Propaganda Techniques*. Westport, CT: Praeger, 1964.

Clifford, James. *Routes: Travel and Translation in the Late Twentieth Century*. Cambridge, MA: Harvard University Press, 1997.

Conceison, Claire. "Eating Red: Performing Maoist Nostalgia in Beijing's Revolution-themed Restaurants." In *Food and Theatre on the World Stage*, edited by Dorothy Chansky and Ann Folino White, 100–115. New York: Routledge, 2016.

Cordier, Adeline. *Post-War French Popular Music: Cultural Identity and the Brel-Brassens-Ferré Myth*. Farnham, UK: Ashgate, 2014.

Cumings, Bruce. *Parallax Visions: Making Sense of American–East Asian Relations at the End of the Century*. Durham, NC: Duke University Press, 1999.

Damodaran, Sumangala. "Music and Resistance: The Tradition of the Indian People's Theatre Association in the 1940s and 1950s." NMML Occasional Paper: History and Society, New Series 56. New Delhi: Nehru Memorial Museum and Library, 2014.

Damodaran, Sumangala. *The Radical Impulse: Music in the Tradition of the Indian People's Theatre Association*. New Delhi: Tulika Books, 2017.

De Kloet, Jeroen, and Jaap Kooijman. "Karaoke Americanism Gangnam Styl [sic]: K-pop, Wonder Girls, and the Asian Unpopular." In *Unpopular Culture*, edited by Martin Lüthe and Sascha Pöhlmann, 113–28. Amsterdam: Amsterdam University Press, 2016.

Dennehy, Kristine. "Overcoming Colonialism at Bandung, 1955." In *Pan-Asianism in Modern Japanese History: Colonialism, Regionalism and Borders*, edited by Sven Saaler and J. Victor Koschmann, 213–25. London: Routledge, 2007.

Denning, Michael. *Noise Uprising: The Audiopolitics of a World Musical Revolution*. London: Verso, 2015.

Denning, Michael. *Culture in the Age of Three Worlds*. London: Verso, 2004.

Dower, John W. *Empire and Aftermath: Yoshida Shigeru and the Japanese Experience, 1878–1954*. Cambridge, MA: Council on East Asian Studies, Harvard University, 1979.

Dungga, J. A. "Perkembangan Musik Indonesia." In *Almanak Seni*, edited by Zaini, 107–15. Jakarta: BMKN, 1957.

Dungga, J. A., and L. Manik. *Musik di indonesia dan Beberapa Persoalannja*. Jakarta: Balai Pustaka, 1952.

Efimova, Larisa. "Indonesia's Cultural Traffic Abroad 1950–1965." Unpublished paper presented at KITLV, Leiden, Netherlands, April 2009.

Endy, Christopher. *Cold War Holidays: American Tourism in France*. Chapel Hill: University of North Carolina Press, 2004.

Esha, Teguh, et al. *Ismail Marzuki: Musik, tanah air dan cinta*. Jakarta: Pustaka LP3ES, 2005.

Esha, Teguh. "'Pembersih Kolam Musik' vs 'Gembong Kebudayaan' Kritik terhadap Ismail Marzuki." In *Ismail Marzuki, Musik, Tanah Air dan Cinta*, edited by Teguh Esha et al., 81–103. Jakarta: LP3ES, 2005.

Eyerman, Ron, and Andrew Jamison. *Music and Social Movements: Mobilizing Traditions in the Twentieth Century*. Cambridge: Cambridge University Press, 1998.

Feld, Steven. *Jazz Cosmopolitanism in Accra: Five Musical Years in Ghana*. Durham, NC: Duke University Press, 2012.

Feng Lou. "Women xuyao shidai de shengyin" [We need the sound of our times]. *Renmin yinyue* 1 (1958): 9.

Finchum-Sung, Hilary. "New Folksongs: Shin Minyo of the 1930s." In *Korean Pop Music: Riding the Wave*, edited by Keith Howard, 10–20. Folkestone, UK: Global Oriental, 2006.

Fiol, Stefan. "Making Music Regional in a Delhi Studio." In *More than Bollywood: Studies in Indian Popular Music*, edited by Gregory Booth and Bradley Shope. New York: Oxford University Press, 2014.

Fuhr, Michael. *Globalization and Popular Music in South Korea: Sounding Out K-Pop*. New York: Routledge, 2016.

Furmanovsky, Michael. "A Complex Fit: The Remaking of Japanese Femininity and Fashion, 1945–65." *Kokusai bunka kenkyū* 16 (2012): 43–65.

Galbraith, Patrick W., and Jason G. Karlin. "Introduction: The Mirror of Idols and Celebrity." In *Idols and Celebrity in Japanese Media Culture*, edited by Patrick W. Galbraith and Jason G. Karlin, 1–32. Houndmills, UK: Palgrave Macmillan, 2012.

Gandhi, Mohandas. *Collected Works*, vol. 63, *June 1–November 2, 1936*. New Delhi: Publications Division, Ministry of Information and Broadcasting, Government of India, 1976.

Gandhi, Mohandas. *Collected Works*, vol. 88, *May 25, 1947–July 31, 1947*. New Delhi: Publications Division, Ministry of Information and Broadcasting, Government of India, 1983.

Gandhi, Mohandas. *Collected Works*, vol. 90, *November 11, 1947–January 30, 1948*. New Delhi: Publications Division, Ministry of Information and Broadcasting, Government of India, 1984.

Gandhi, Mohandas. *Panchayat Raj*. Ahmedabad, India: Navjivan Publishing House, 1959.

George, Siby K. "The Cosmopolitan Self and the Fetishism of Identity." In *Questioning Cosmopolitanism*, edited by Stan van Hooft and Wim Vandekerckhove, 63–82. New York: Springer, 2010.

Getter, Joseph, and B. Balasubrahmaniyan. "Tamil Film Music: Sound and Significance." In *Global Soundtracks: Worlds of Film Music*, edited by Mark Slobin, 114–51. Middletown, CT: Wesleyan University Press, 2008.

Ghode, Ram. *Rashtrasantachya Sahavaasaat*. Nagpur, India: Rajiv Publishers, 1996.

Gokulsing, K. Moti, and Wimal Dissanayake, eds. *Routledge Handbook of Indian Cinemas*. London: Routledge, 2013.

Government of India: Ministry of Law. *Report of the Hindu Religious Endowments Commission (1960–1962)*. Delhi: Government of India Press, 1962.

Gregory, Derek. "Imaginative Geographies." *Progress in Human Geography* 19, no. 4 (1995): 447–85.

Gregory, Derek. *The Colonial Present: Afghanistan, Palestine, Iraq*. Malden, MA: Blackwell, 2004.

Grossberg, Lawrence. *Cultural Studies in the Future Tense*. Durham, NC: Duke University Press, 2010.

Guha, Ramachandra. *India after Gandhi: The History of the World's Largest Democracy*. New York: HarperCollins, 2007.

Guilbault, Jocelyne. "Audible Entanglements: Nation and Diasporas in Trinidad's Calypso Music Scene." *Small Axe* 9, no. 1 (2005): 40–63.

Gupta, Akhil. "The Song of the Nonaligned World: Transnational Identities and the Reinscription of Space in Late Capitalism." *Cultural Anthropology* 7, no. 1 (1992): 63–79.

Hansen, Kathryn. "Who Wants to Be a Cosmopolitan? Readings from the Composite Culture." *Indian Economic and Social History Review* 47, no. 3 (2010): 291–308.

Hansen, Thomas Blom. *The Saffron Wave: Democracy and Hindu Nationalism in Modern India*. Princeton, NJ: Princeton University Press, 1999.

Harkness, Nicholas. *Songs of Seoul: An Ethnography of Voice and Voicing in Christian South Korea*. Berkeley: University of California Press, 2014.

Hawley, John Stratton. *A Storm of Songs: India and the Idea of the Bhakti Movement*. Cambridge, MA: Harvard University Press, 2015.

Hawley, John Stratton. *Saints and Virtues*. Berkeley: University of California Press, 1987.

He Qiansan. "Dakai yinyuan zhi men, guanxin shiji—yinyueyuan shisheng pipan huangse gequ" [Opening the gate of the Central Conservatory of Music and caring about reality: Teachers and students from the Central Conservatory of Music criticize yellow songs]. *Renmin yinyue* 2 (1958): 9.

Hein, Laura, and Mark Selden, eds. *Islands of Discontent: Okinawan Responses to Japanese and American Power*. Oxford: Rowman and Littlefield, 2003.

Herrera, Eduardo. *Elite Art Worlds: Philanthropy, Latin Americanism, and Avant-garde Music*. Oxford: Oxford University Press, 2020.

Hess, Linda. *Bodies of Song: Kabir Oral Traditions and Performative Worlds in North India*. New York: Oxford University Press, 2015.

Ho, Tung-hung. "The Social Formation of Mandarin Popular Music Industry in Taiwan." PhD diss., Lancaster University, 2003.

Honda, Shiro. "The Spreading of Japan's Popular Culture in East Asia." *Japan Echo* 21, no. 4 (1994): 75–79.

Hosokawa, Shūhei. "Soy Sauce Music: Haruomi Hosono and Japanese Self-Orientalism." In *Widening the Horizon: Exoticism in Post-war Popular Music*, edited by Philip Hayward, 114–44. Sydney, Australia: John Libbey, 1999.

Howard, Keith. "Coming of Age: Korean Pop in the 90s." In *Korean Pop Music: Riding the Wave*, edited by Keith Howard, 82–98. Folkestone, UK: Global Orient, 2006.

Howard, Keith. "Exploding Ballads: The Transformation of Korean Pop Music." In *Global Goes Local: Popular Culture in Asia*, edited by Timothy J. Craig and Richard King, 80–95. Vancouver: University of British Columbia Press, 2002.

Hu, Brian. "Worldly Desires: Cosmopolitanism and Cinema in Hong Kong and Taiwan." PhD diss., University of California, Los Angeles, 2011.

Huang Xingtao and Chen Peng. "Jindai Zhongguo 'huangse' ciyi bianyi kaoxi" [A study of the shift in the meaning of the word "yellow" in modern China]. *Lishi yanjiu*, no. 5 (2010): 83–98.

Huat, Chua Beng. *Structure, Audience and Soft Power in East Asian Pop Culture*. Hong Kong: Hong Kong University Press, 2012.

Huat, Chua Beng, and Koichi Iwabuchi, eds. *East Asian Pop Culture: Analysing the Korean Wave*. Hong Kong: Hong Kong University Press, 2008.

Hubbert, Jennifer. "Revolution Is a Dinner Party: Cultural Revolution Restaurants in Contemporary China." *China Review* 5, no. 2 (2005): 123–48.

Hwang, Okon. "Kim Min-ki and the Making of a Legend." In *Made in Korea: Studies in Popular Music*, edited by Hyunjoon Shin and Seung-ah Lee, 133–41. New York: Routledge, 2017.

Igarashi, Yoshikuni. "Mothra's Gigantic Egg: Consuming the South Pacific in 1960s Japan." In *In Godzilla's Footsteps: Japanese Pop Culture Icons on the Global Stage*, edited by William M. Tsutsui and Michiko Ito, 83–102. New York: Palgrave Macmillan, 2006.

Iwabuchi, Koichi, ed. *Feeling Asian Modernities: Transnational Consumption of Japanese TV Dramas*. Hong Kong: Hong Kong University Press, 2004.

Iwabuchi, Koichi. "Pop Culture's Lingua Franca: Language and Regional Popular Cultural Flows in East Asia." In *Babel or Behemoth: Language Trends in Asia*, edited by Jennifer Lindsay and Tan Ying Ying, 161–74. Singapore: Asia Research Institute, National University of Singapore, 2003.

Iwabuchi, Koichi. *Recentering Globalization: Popular Culture and Japanese Transnationalism*. Durham, NC: Duke University Press, 2002.

Jaffrelot, Christophe. *The Hindu Nationalist Movement and Indian Politics: 1925 to the 1990's*. 3rd English ed. New Delhi: Penguin, 1999.

Jameson, Fredric. "Notes on Globalization as a Philosophical Issue." In *The Cultures of Globalization*, edited by Fredric Jameson and Masao Miyoshi, 54–80. Durham, NC: Duke University Press, 1998.

Jameson, Fredric. *Signatures of the Visible*. New York: Routledge, 1990.

Jang, Gunjoo, and Won K. Paik. "Korean Wave as Tool for Korea's New Cultural Diplomacy." *Advances in Applied Sociology* 2, no. 3 (2012): 196–202.

Jayapalan, N. *Indian Political Thinkers: Modern Indian Political Thought*. New Delhi: Atlantic Publishers, 2003.

Jeffrey, Robin. *Politics, Women and Well-Being: How Kerala Became a "Model."* Houndmills, UK: Macmillan, 1992.
Jie Fu. "Wei suqing huangse gequ er douzheng" [Fighting for the elimination of yellow music]. *Yinyue shenghuo* 11 (1957): 181–86.
Jin, Dal Yong, and Woongjae Ryoo. "Critical Interpretation of Hybrid K-Pop: The Global-Local Paradigm of English Mixing in Lyrics." *Popular Music and Society* 37, no. 2 (2014): 113–31.
Johnson, Chalmers, ed. *Okinawa: Cold War Island.* Cardiff, CA: Japan Policy Research Institute, 1999.
Jones, Andrew F. *Like a Knife: Ideology and Genre in Contemporary Chinese Popular Music.* Ithaca, NY: Cornell University Press, 1992.
Jones, Andrew F. *Yellow Music: Media Culture and Colonial Modernity in the Chinese Jazz Age.* Durham, NC: Duke University Press, 2001.
Jones, Andrew F. *Circuit Listening: Chinese Popular Music in the Global 1960s.* Minneapolis, MN: University of Minnesota Press, 2020.
Jones, Jacqueline. "Performing the Sacred: Song, Genre, and Aesthetics in Bhakti." PhD diss., University of Chicago, 2009.
Joshi, P. L., ed. *Political Ideas and Leadership in Vidarbha.* A Project Sponsored by the Silver Jubilee Committee of the Department of Political Science and Public Administration. Nagpur, India: Nagpur University, 1980.
Jung, Eun-Young. "The Place of Sentimental Song in Contemporary Korean Musical Life." *Korean Studies* 35 (2011): 71–92.
Jung, Eun-Young. "Transnational Cultural Traffic in Northeast Asia: The 'Presence' of Japan in Korea's Popular Music Culture." PhD diss., University of Pittsburgh, 2007.
Jung, Sun. *Korean Masculinities and Transcultural Consumption: Yonsama, Rain, Oldboy, K-Pop Idols.* Hong Kong: Hong Kong University Press, 2011.
Kadwe, R. S. "Life Sketch of Rashtrasant Tukadoji." In *The Gramgita* [An epic on Indian village life]. Cantos 1–5 of vol. 1. Translated from Marathi by R. S. Kadwe. Wardha, India: Rashtrasant Sahitya Prachar Mandal, 1979.
Kamat, A. R. *Progress of Education in Rural Maharashtra (Post-Independence Period).* New York: Asia Publishing House, 1968.
Kane, P. S. *The Rashtrasant: The Sociopolitical Thought of Sant Tukdoji Maharaj.* Nagpur, India: Manohar Pimpalapure, 1973.
Käng, Dredge Byung'chu. "Idols of Development: Transnational Transgender Performance in Thai K-Pop Cover Dance." *TSQ: Transgender Studies Quarterly* 1, no. 4 (2014): 559–71.
Kapchan, Deborah. "The Promise of Sonic Translation: Performing the Festive Sacred in Morocco." *American Anthropologist* 110, no. 4 (2008): 467–83.
Katju, Manjari. *Vishwa Hindu Parishad and Indian Politics.* Hyderabad: Orient Longman, 2003.
Katsumata, Hiro. "Japanese Popular Culture in East Asia: A New Insight into Regional Community Building." *International Relations of the Asia-Pacific* 12, no. 1 (2011): 133–60.
Kawabata, Shigeru. "The Japanese Record Industry." *Popular Music* 10, no. 3 (1991): 327–45.

Kendall, Gavin, Ian Woodward, and Zlatko Skrbis, eds. *The Sociology of Cosmopolitanism*. London: Palgrave Macmillan, 2009.

Kerr, Paul, and Mary Beth Nikitin. *Pakistan's Nuclear Weapons: Proliferation and Security Issues*. Washington, DC: Diane Publishing, 2010.

Kesavadev, P. *From the Gutter*. Translated by E. M. J. Venniyoor. New Delhi: Orient Longman, 1978.

Khandevale, Shrinivas. "Gramgita: Gramin Sankatachya Sandarbha" [Song of the village: A plan for rural difficulties]. In *Rashtrasanta Tukdoji Maharaj—Vyakti aani vangamay* [National Saint Tukdoji Maharaj—person and literature], edited by Akashyakumar Kale, 83–92. Nagpur, India: Visa Books, 2008.

Khare, Narayan Bhaskar. *My Political Memoirs, or Autobiography*. Nagpur, India: Shri J. R. Joshi, 1959.

Kim, Ch'ang-nam, ed. *Kim Min-ki*. Seoul: Hanul, 1986.

Kim, Jeongmee, and Basil Glynn. "'Oppa'-tunity Knocks: PSY, 'Gangnam Style' and the Press Reception of K-Pop in Britain." *Situations: Cultural Studies in the Asian Context* 7, no. 1 (2013–14): 1–20.

Kim, Pil Ho, and Hyunjoon Shin. "The Birth of 'Rok': Cultural Imperialism, Nationalism, and the Glocalization of Rock Music in South Korea, 1964–1975." *positions: east asia cultures critique* 18, no. 1 (2010): 199–230.

Kim, Youna. "Introduction: Korean Media in a Digital Cosmopolitan World." In *The Korean Wave: Korean Media Go Global*, edited by Youna Kim, 1–28. Abingdon, UK: Routledge, 2013.

Klein, Christine. *Cold War Orientalism: Asia in the Middlebrow Imagination, 1945–1961*. Berkeley: University of California Press, 2003.

Kommattam, Nisha. "Malayalam Poetry." In *The Princeton Encyclopedia of Poetry and Poetics*, edited by Roland Greene. Princeton, NJ: Princeton University Press, 2013.

Korean Culture and Information Service. "The Korean Wave: A New Pop Culture Phenomenon." Seoul: Korean Culture and Information Service, Ministry of Culture, Sports, and Tourism, 2011.

Kumar, Priya. *Limiting Secularism: The Ethics of Coexistence in Indian Literature and Film*. Minneapolis: University of Minnesota Press, 2008.

Kun, Josh. *Audiotopia: Music, Race, and America*. Berkeley: University of California Press, 2005.

Kwok Ching-Ling and Au-Yeung Fung-Ki. *Xianggang yingren koushu lishi congshu zhiwu: Modeng secai xianggang—maijin 1960 niandai* [Oral history series (5): An emerging modernity: Hong Kong cinema of the 1960s]. Hong Kong: Hong Kong Film Archive, 2008.

Kwon, Heonik. *The Other Cold War*. New York: Columbia University Press, 2010.

Kwon, Seung-Ho, and Joseph Kim. "The Cultural Industry Policies of the Korean Government and the Korean Wave." *International Journal of Cultural Policy* 20, no. 4 (2014): 422–39.

Lakoff, George, and Mark Johnson. *Metaphors We Live By*. Chicago: University of Chicago Press, 1980.

Lal, M. B. *Going Back to Gettysburg: Autobiography of a Corrupt Indian*. Gurgao, India: Partridge Publishing, 2014.

Lan Daming. "Ting 'jiuge chongfang' yougan" [My thoughts on "replayed old songs"]. *Tianjin Ribao*, June 5, 1957.

Lanza del Vasto, Joseph Jean. *Gandhi to Vinoba: The New Pilgrimage*. Translated by Philip Leon. New York: Schocken Books, 1974.

Lee, Jung-Yup. "Managing the Transnational, Governing the National: Cultural Policy and the Politics of 'the Cultural Archetype Project in South Korea.'" In *Popular Culture and the State in East and Southeast Asia*, edited by Nissim Otmazgin and Eyal Ben-Ari, 123–43. London: Routledge, 2011.

Lee, Namhee. *The Making of Minjung: Democracy and the Politics of Representation in South Korea*. Ithaca, NY: Cornell University Press, 2007.

Leheny, David. "A Narrow Place to Cross Swords: 'Soft Power' and the Politics of Japanese Popular Culture in East Asia." In *Beyond Japan: The Dynamics of East Asian Regionalism*, edited by Peter J. Katzenstein and Takashi Shiraishi, 211–34. Ithaca, NY: Cornell University Press, 2006.

Levi, Pavle. *Disintegration in Frames: Aesthetics and Ideology in the Yugoslav and Post-Yugoslav Cinema*. Stanford, CA: Stanford University Press, 2007.

Leydi, Roberto, and Bruno Pianta. "La possibile storia di una canzone" [The possible story of a song]. In *Storia d'Italia*, vol. 5, edited by Corrado Vivanti e Ruggiero Romano. Turin: Einaudi, 1973.

Li Guifen. "Chang 'Jiujiu yanyangtian' yougan" [My thoughts on singing "Sunny days in early Spring"]. *Renmin yinyue* 3 (1958): 8.

Li Jinhui. "Zhanduan dugen chedi xiaomie huangse gequ" [Cut the poisonous roots and eradicate yellow songs]. *Renmin yinyue* 3 (1958): 24–25.

Li Ling. "Cong 'Jiujiu yanyangtian' tanqi" [Starting from "Sunny days in early Spring"]. *Beijing ribao*, March 28, 1958.

Li Ling. "Zenyang jianbie huangse gequ" [How to identify yellow songs]. In *Rang xinde yinyue shenghuo huoyue qilai* [Make new music life thrive], 8–9. Beijing: Yinyue chubanshe, 1958.

Li, Stephen. *Gangshi xiyangfeng—liushi niandai xianggang yuedui chaoliu* [Hong Kong style western music: Hong Kong 1960s band trends]. Hong Kong: Zhonghua Book Company, 2016.

Lian Kang. "Huangse gequ shi ducao" [Yellow songs are poisonous weeds]. *Renmin yinyue* 9 (1957): 35–36.

Lindsay, Jennifer. "Making Waves: Private Radio and Local Identities in Indonesia." *Indonesia* 64, no. 1 (1997): 105–24.

Lindsay, Jennifer, and Maya Liem, eds. *Heirs to World Culture: Being Indonesian 1950–1965*. Leiden: KITLV, 2012.

Lipsitz, George. *Footsteps in the Dark: The Hidden Histories of Popular Music*. Minneapolis: University of Minnesota Press, 2007.

Liscutin, Nicola. "Surfing the Neo-Nationalist Wave: A Case Study of Manga Kenkanryū." In *Cultural Studies and Cultural Industries in Northeast Asia: What a Difference a Region Makes*, edited by Chris Berry, Nicola Liscutin, and Jonathan D. Mackintosh, 171–94. Hong Kong: Hong Kong University Press, 2009.

Liu [sic]. "Suqing huangse yinyue bixu shuangguan qixia" [A two-pronged approach is a must for eliminating yellow music]. *Wenhua xianfeng* 21 (1947): 18.

Liu, Jin. *Signifying the Local: Media Productions Rendered in Local Languages in Mainland China in the New Millennium*. Leiden: Brill, 2013.

Liu, Lydia. "A Folksong Immortal and Official Popular Culture in Twentieth-Century China." In *Writing and Materiality in China: Essays in Honor of Patrick Hanan*, edited by Judith Zeitlin and Lydia Liu, 553–609. Cambridge, MA: Harvard University Asia Center, 2003.

Liu Bingyan and Chen Bohong. "Shanghai zai chensi zhong" [Shanghai in contemplation]. *Zhongguo qingnianbao*, May 13, 1956.

Lockard, Craig. *Dance of Life: Popular Music and Politics in Southeast Asia*. New York: Oxford University Press, 1999.

Londhe, Sushama. *A Tribute to Hinduism: Thoughts and Wisdom Spanning Continents and Time about India and Her Culture*. New Delhi: Pragun, 2008.

Lu Mang. "Ezhu huangse yinyue de bozi" [Strangling yellow music by its neck]. *Wenhui bao*, March 29, 1958, 3.

Lu, Sheldon Hsiao-peng. *Transnational Chinese Cinemas: Identity, Nationhood, Gender*. Honolulu: University of Hawai'i Press, 1997.

Lü Ji. "Bo Liu Xue'an: shehuizhuyi yinyue luxian bu rong youpaifenzi cuangai" [Rebutting Liu Xue'an: the socialist music path cannot be tampered with by the rightists]. *Renmin yinyue* 9 (1957): 2–3.

Ma, Jean. *Sounding the Modern Woman: The Songstress in Chinese Cinema*. Durham, NC: Duke University Press, 2015.

Ma Ke. "Cong 'Diu jiezhi' tandao huixie gequ wenti" [From 'Losing a ring' to the problem of humorous songs]. *Yinyue yanjiu* 2 (1959): 99–100.

Manabe, Noriko. *The Revolution Will Not Be Televised: Protest Music after Fukushima*. Oxford: Oxford University Press, 2015.

Manmadkar, Dadamaharaj. *Varkari Sampradaya: Tattvadnyan va Sadyakalin Aucitya* [Varkari tradition: Philosophy and its relevance for current times]. Pandharpur, India: Sri H.Bh.P. Guruvarya Vidyavacaspati Dr. Dadamaharaj Manmadkar Satkar Samiti, 1998.

Manuel, Peter. "Popular Music and Media Culture in South Asia. Prefatory Consideration." *Asian Music* 24, no. 1 (1992): 91–100.

Manuel, Peter. *Popular Musics of the Non-Western World: An Introductory Survey*. New York: Oxford University Press, 1988.

Mao Zedong. *Mao Zedong xuanji* [Selected works of Mao Zedong], vol. 5. Beijing: Renmin chubanshe, 1977. English translation in *Selected Works of Mao Zedong*, vol. 5. Beijing: Foreign Languages Press, 1977.

Marsden, Magnus. "Muslim Cosmopolitans? Transnational Life in Northern Pakistan." *Journal of Asian Studies* 67, no. 1 (2008): 213–47.

Makesi, Engesi [Marx, Karl, and Friedrich Engels]. *Makesi Engesi quanji disi juan* [The complete works of Marx and Engels, vol. 4]. Beijing: Renmin chubanshe, 1956.

Marx, David W. "The Jimusho System: Understanding the Production Logic of the Japanese Entertainment Industry." In *Idols and Celebrity in Japanese Media Culture*, edited by Patrick W. Galbraith and Jason G. Karlin, 35–55. Houndmills, UK: Palgrave Macmillan, 2012.

Mason, Kaley. "On Nightingales and Moonlight: Songcrafting Femininity in Malluwood." In *More than Bollywood: Studies in Indian Popular Music*, edited by Gregory D. Booth and Bradley Shope, 75–93. New York: Oxford University Press, 2014.

Massey, Doreen. *Space, Place and Gender*. Minneapolis: University of Minnesota Press, 1994.

Mazierska, Ewa, ed. *Popular Music in Eastern Europe: Breaking the Cold War Paradigm*. London: Palgrave Macmillan, 2016.

Mazumder, Premendra. "Music in Mainstream Indian Cinema." In *Routledge Handbook of Indian Cinemas*, edited by K. Moti Gokulsing and Wimal Dissanayake, 257–68. New York: Routledge, 2013.

McCarthy, Kathleen D. "From Cold War to Cultural Development: The International Cultural Activities of the Ford Foundation, 1950–1980." *Daedalus* 116, no. 1 (1987): 93–117.

McClure, Steve. *Nippon Pop*. Tokyo: Charles E. Tuttle, 1998.

McGrath, Jason. "The Independent Cinema of Jia Zhangke: From Postsocialist Realism to a Transnational Aesthetic." In *The Urban Generation: Chinese Cinema and Society at the Turn of the Twenty-first Century*, edited by Zhang Zhen, 81–114. Durham, NC: Duke University Press, 2007.

McGrath, Jason. *Postsocialist Modernity: Chinese Cinema, Literature, and Criticism in the Market Age*. Stanford, CA: Stanford University Press, 2008.

McIntyre, Bryce T., Christine W. S. Cheng, and Weiyu Zhang. "Cantopop: The Voice of Hong Kong." *Journal of Asian Pacific Communication* 12, no. 2 (2002): 217–43.

Medhurst, Martin J. "Introduction." In *Cold War Rhetoric: Strategy, Metaphor, and Ideology*, edited by Martin J. Medhurst, Robert L. Ivie, Philip Wander, and Robert L. Scott, xiii–xvi. East Lansing: Michigan State University Press, 1997.

Meyers, John Paul. "Still Like That Old Time Rock and Roll: Tribute Bands and Historical Consciousness in Popular Music." *Ethnomusicology* 59, no. 1 (2015): 61–81.

Middleton, Richard. *Studying Popular Music*. Philadelphia: Open University Press, 1990.

Miller, Christopher J. "Cosmopolitan, Nativist, Eclectic: Cultural Dynamics in Indonesian Musik Kontemporer." PhD diss., Wesleyan University, 2014.

Mishra, Anil Dutta. "Sarvodaya: A Fresh Look." In *Gandhism after Gandhi*, edited by Anil Dutta Mishra, 37–50. New Delhi: Mittal Publications, 1999.

Mittler, Barbara. *A Continuous Revolution: Making Sense of Cultural Revolution Culture*. Cambridge, MA: Harvard University Press, 2012.

Mittler, Barbara. "Cultural Revolution Model Works and the Politics of Modernization in China: An Analysis of *Taking Tiger Mountain by Strategy*." *The World of Music* 45, no. 2 (2003): 53–81.

Molasky, Michael S. *The American Occupation of Japan and Okinawa: Literature and Memory*. 2nd ed. New York: Routledge, 2005.

Mōri, Yoshitaka. "J-Pop: From the Ideology of Creativity to DiY Music Culture." *Inter-Asia Cultural Studies* 10, no. 4 (2009): 474–88.

Mōri, Yoshitaka. "Winter Sonata and Cultural Practices of Active Fans in Japan: Considering Middle-Aged Women as Cultural Agents." In *East Asian Pop Culture: Analysing the Korean Wave*, edited by Chua Beng Huat and Koichi Iwabuchi, 127–42. Hong Kong: Hong Kong University Press, 2008.

Moskowitz, Marc L. *Cries of Joy, Songs of Sorrow: Chinese Pop Music and Its Cultural Connotations*. Honolulu: University of Hawai'i Press, 2010.

Mularski, Jedrek. *Music, Politics, and Nationalism in Latin America: Chile during the Cold War Era*. Amherst, NY: Cambria Press, 2015.

Muller, Carol A. "'American Musical Surrogacy': A View from Post-World War II South Africa." *Safundi: The Journal of South African and American Studies* 7, no. 3 (2006): 1–18.

Myers-Moro, Pamela A. "Songs for Life: Leftist Thai Popular Music in the 1970s." *Journal of Popular Culture* 20 (1986): 93–113.

Nakano, Yonosuke. "General Remarks on the Agenda." In *The Report on the Fifth World Religion Conference*, International General Headquarters of Ananai-Kyo, Shimizu, Japan, 1955.

Nakano, Yoshiko. "Who Initiates a Global Flow? Japanese Popular Culture in Asia." *Visual Communication* 1, no. 2 (2002): 229–53.

Nakassis, Constantine, and Melanie Dean. "Desire, Youth and Realism in Tamil Cinema." *Journal of Linguistic Anthropology* 17, no. 1 (2007): 77–104.

Nanda, B. R. *Jawaharlal Nehru: Rebel and Statesman*. 2nd ed. New Delhi: Oxford University Press, 1998.

Narayan, Shriman. *Memoirs: Window on Gandhi and Nehru*. Bombay: Popular Prakashan, 1971.

Navalkar, Ganpatrao. *The Student's Marathi Grammar*. Bombay: Education Society's Press, 1880.

Negami, Shin. "Invitation No. 2." In *The Report on the Third World Religion Correspondence Congress (Under Auspices of the Ananai-Kyo)*, 7–9. Shimizu, Japan: International General Headquarters of Ananai-Kyo, 1955.

Negus, Keith. *Popular Music in Theory: An Introduction*. Cambridge: Polity Press, 1996.

Negus, Keith. *The South Korean Music Industry: A Literature Review*. CREATe (Centre for Copyright and New Business Models in the Creative Economy) Working Paper Series. Glasgow: CREATe, 2015.

Nettl, Bruno. "We're on the Map: Reflections on SEM in 1955 and 2005." *Ethnomusicology* 50, no. 2 (2006): 179–89.

Ng, Benjamin Wai-ming. "Japanese Popular Music in Singapore and the Hybridization of Asian Music." *Asian Music* 34, no. 1 (2002): 1–18.

Ng Yuet-Wah. "Geying paihe: Yueyu qingchun gewupian gequ yu dianying de guanxi (1966–1969)" [Songs in tune with movies: The relationship of movie songs and Cantonese youth musicals in 1966–1969]. MPhil diss., Hong Kong Baptist University, 2006.

Nie Er [Hei Tianshi]. "Zhongguo gewu duanlun" [An essay on Chinese songs and dances]. *Dianying yishu* 3, July 22, 1932.

Nie Er. "Li Jinhui de *Bajiao ye shang shi*" [*Poem written on a banana leaf* by Li Jinhui]. *Shenbao* (local supplement), January 6, 1935.

Nossiter, Thomas. *Communism in Kerala: A Study in Political Adaptation*. Berkeley: University of California Press, 1982.

Novak, David. *Japanoise: Music at the Edge of Circulation*. Durham, NC: Duke University Press, 2013.

Novetzke, Christian. "Divining an Author: The Idea of Authorship in an Indian Religious Tradition." *History of Religions* 42, no. 3 (2003): 213–42.

Novetzke, Christian. *Religion and Public Memory: A Cultural History of Saint Namdev in India*. New York: Columbia University Press, 2008.

Nowicka, Magdalena, and Maria Rovisco. "Introduction: Making Sense of Cosmopolitanism." In *Cosmopolitanism in Practice*, edited by Magdalena Nowicka and Maria Rovisco, 1–18. London: Routledge, 2016.

Nye, Joseph. *Soft Power: The Means to Success in World Politics*. New York: Public Affairs, 2004.

Ogawa, Masashi. "Japanese Popular Music in Hong Kong: What does TK present?" In *Refashioning Pop Music in Asia: Cosmopolitan Flows, Political Tempos, and Aesthetic Industries*, edited by Allen Chun, Ned Rossiter, and Brian Shoesmith, 144–56. London: RoutledgeCurzon, 2004.

Okakura, Kakuzō. *Ideals of the East: The Spirit of Japanese Art*. Mineola, NY: Dover, 2005.

Osborne, Peter. *Anywhere or Not at All: Philosophy of Contemporary Art*. London: Verso, 2013.

Osumare, Halifu. *The Africanist Aesthetic in Global Hip-Hop: Power Moves*. New York: Palgrave Macmillan, 2006.

Ota, Masahide. "Re-examining the History of the Battle of Okinawa." In *Okinawa: Cold War Island*, edited by Chalmers Johnson, 13–37. Cardiff, CA: Japan Policy Research Institute, 1999.

Pandey, Gyanendra. "Introduction: The Indian Nation in 1942." In *The Indian Nation in 1942*, edited by Gyanendra Pandey, 1–18. Calcutta: Centre for Studies in Social Sciences, 1988.

Park, Ae-kyung. "Modern Folksong and People's Song (Minjung Kayo)." In *Made in Korea: Studies in Popular Music*, edited by Hyunjoon Shin and Seung-ah Lee, 83–93. New York: Routledge, 2017.

Park, Chung-Shin. *Protestantism and Politics in Korea*. Seattle: University of Washington Press, 2003.

Park, Yong-Shin. "Protestant Christianity and Its Place in a Changing Korea." *Social Compass* 47, no. 4 (2000): 507–24.

Patankar, Bharat. *The Songs of Tukoba*. Translated by Gail Omvedt. Delhi: Manohar Publishers, 2012.

Patil, Anand. *Uddhav Shelke*. New Delhi: Sahitya Akademi, 2002.

Peng Chao. "Tan dianying chaqu 'Jiujiu yanyangtian'" [On the film song "Sunny days in early Spring"]. *Renmin yinyue* 3 (1958): 3.

Pestelli, Carlo. *Bella Ciao: La Canzone della Libertà* [Bella ciao: The song of freedom]. Turin: ADD editore, 2016.

Pollock, Sheldon, Homi K. Bhabha, Carol Breckenridge, and Dipesh Chakrabarty. "Cosmopolitanisms." *Public Culture* 12, no. 3 (2000): 577–89.

Pollock, Sheldon. "The Cosmopolitan Vernacular." *Journal of Asian Studies* 57, no. 1 (1998): 6–37.

Prasad, Rajendra. *Correspondence and Select Documents: Presidency Period—The Last Phase*. Bombay: Allied Publishers, 1995.

Prashad, Vijay. *The Poorer Nations: A Possible History of the Global South*. London: Verso, 2012.

Puri, Bindu. *The Tagore-Gandhi Debate on Matters of Truth and Untruth*. New Delhi: Springer, 2015.

Qiao Zhengyan. "Dui 'jiuge chongfan' de tihui" [My feelings on "replayed old songs"]. *Tianjin ribao*, June 5, 1957.

Qiu Hong. "Wuhan chuban 'wei suqing huangse yinyue' er douzheng zhuanji" (Special issue of fighting for "eradicating yellow music" published in Wuhan]. *Renmin yinyue* 1 (1958): 11.

Rabson, Steve. "Assimilation Policy in Okinawa: Promotion, Resistance, and 'Reconstruction.'" In *Okinawa: Cold War Island*, edited by Chalmers Johnson, 133–48. Cardiff, CA: Japan Policy Research Institute, 1999.

Radano, Ronald, and Tejumola Olaniyan, eds. *Audible Empire: Music, Global Politics, Critique*. Durham, NC: Duke University Press, 2016.

Rao, Anupama. *The Caste Question: Dalits and the Politics of Modern India*. Berkeley: University of California Press, 2009.

Regev, Motti. *Pop-Rock Music: Aesthetic Cosmopolitanism in Late Modernity*. Cambridge: Polity, 2013.

Rhee, Rosaleen. "The Shifting Censorship and Emergent Politics of South Korean P'ok'ŭ Music in the 1970s." Paper presented at the Association for Asian Studies (AAS) Annual Conference, Denver, Colorado, March 21–24, 2019.

Roberson, James. "Uchina Pop: Place and Identity in Contemporary Okinawan Popular Music." In *Islands of Discontent: Okinawan Responses to Japanese and American Power*, edited by Laura Hein and Mark Selden, 192–227. Oxford: Rowman and Littlefield, 2003.

Roberts, Martin. "'A New Stereophonic Sound Spectacular': Shibuya-kei as Transnational Soundscape." *Popular Music* 32, no. 1 (2013): 111–23.

Rovisco, Maria, and Magdalena Nowicka, eds. *The Ashgate Research Companion to Cosmopolitanism*. Farnham, UK: Ashgate, 2013.

Russell, James. *POP Goes Korea: Behind the Revolution in Movies, Music, and the Internet Culture*. Berkeley, CA: Stone Bridge Press, 2008.

Saanap, Kishor. "Tukdojinchya Abhangagathetil Atmapravas" [The personal journey of Tukdoji's Abhangas]. In *Rashtrasanta Tukdoji Maharaj—Vyakti aani vangamay* [National Saint Tukdoji Maharaj—person and literature], edited by Akashyakumar Kale, 191–208. Nagpur, India: Visa Books, 2008.

Said, Edward W. *Culture and Imperialism*. New York: Vintage Books, 1993.

Said, Edward W. *Reflections on Exile and Other Essays*. Cambridge, MA: Harvard University Press, 2000.

Sakai, Naoki. "'You Asians': On the Historical Role of the West and Asia Binary." *South Atlantic Quarterly* 99, no. 4 (2000): 789–818.

Sakamoto, Rumi, and Matthew Allen. "Hating 'The Korean Wave' Comic Books: A Sign of a New Nationalism." *Asia Pacific Journal/Japan Focus* 5, no. 10 (2007). apjjf.org/-Rumi-SAKAMOTO/2535/article.html. Accessed July 1, 2016.

Samuels, David, Louis Meintjes, Ana Maria Ochoa, and Thomas Porcello. "Soundscapes: Toward a Sounded Anthropology." *Annual Review of Anthropology* 39 (2010): 329–45.

Sarbhadikary, Sukanya. *The Place of Devotion: Sitting and Experiencing Divinity in Bengal-Vaishnavism*. Oakland: University of California Press, 2015.

Sasidharan, K. P. *Kesava Dev*. New Delhi: Sahitya Akademi, 1990.

Satō, Yasuko. "Retorosupekutivu na kakumei: 70-nendai fōku·songu [Retrospective revolution: Folk songs in the 1970s]." In *Sengo seron no media shakaigaku* [The sociology of media on postwar popular opinion], edited by Satō Takumi, 167–92. Tokyo: Kashiwa shobō, 2003.

Schmelz, Peter J. "Introduction: Music in the Cold War." *Journal of Musicology* 26, no. 1 (2009): 3–16.

Schomer, Karin, and W. H. McLeod. *The Sants: Studies in a Devotional Tradition of India*. Berkeley, CA: Berkeley Religious Studies Series, 1987.

Schultz, Anna. "Bollywood *Bhajans*: Style as 'Air' in an Indian-Guyanese Twice Migrant Community." *Ethnomusicology Forum* 23, no. 3 (2014): 383–404.

Schultz, Anna. *Singing a Hindu Nation: Marathi Devotional Performance and Nationalism*. New York: Oxford University Press, 2013.

Sen, Amartya Kumar. *Amartya Sen on Kerala*. New Delhi: Institute of Social Sciences, 2000.

Shamoon, Deborah. "Re-creating Traditional Music in Postwar Japan: A Prehistory of Enka." *Japan Forum* 26, no. 1 (2014): 113–38.

Shank, Barry. *The Political Force of Musical Beauty*. Durham, NC: Duke University Press, 2014.

Shelun [Editorial]. "Fayang minzu chuantong fanrong yinyue yishu" [Develop national tradition, expand music art]. *Renmin ribao*, August 27, 1956.

Shelun [Editorial]. "Suqing huangse gequ" [Eliminating yellow songs]. *Renmin ribao*, January 7, 1958.

Shin, Gi-Wook, and Joon Nak Choi. "Paradox or Paradigm? Making Sense of Korean Globalization." In *Korea Confronts Globalization*, edited by Chang Yun-Shik, Hyun-Ho Seok, and Donald L. Baker, 250–72. London: Routledge, 2009.

Shin, Hyunjoon. "Have You Ever Seen the Rain? And Who'll Stop the Rain? The Globalizing Project of Korean Pop (K-Pop)." *Inter-Asian Cultural Studies* 10, no. 4 (2009): 507–23.

Shin, Hyunjoon. "Reconsidering Transnational Cultural Flows of Popular Music in East Asia: Transbordering Musicians in Japan and Korea Searching for 'Asia.'" *Korean Studies* 33 (2009): 101–23.

Shin, Hyunjoon, and Pil Ho Kim. "Birth, Death, and Resurrection of Group Sound Rock." In *The Korean Popular Culture Reader*, edited by Kyung Hyun Kim and Youngmin Choe, 275–95. Durham, NC: Duke University Press, 2014.

Shin, Hyunjoon, and Tung-hung Ho. "Translation of 'America' during the Early Cold War Period: A Comparative Study on the History of Popular Music in South Korea and Taiwan." *Inter-Asia Cultural Studies* 10, no. 1 (2009): 83–102.

Shiraishi, Takashi. "The Third Wave: Southeast Asia and Middle-Class Formation in the Making of a Region." In *Beyond Japan: The Dynamics of East Asian Regionalism*, edited by Peter J. Katzenstein and Takashi Shiraishi, 237–72. Ithaca, NY: Cornell University Press, 2006.

Sin, Hyŏn-chun, Yi Yong-u, and Ch'oe Chi-sŏn. *Hanguk pap ŭi kogohak 1970* [The archaeology of Korean pop 1970s]. Seoul: Hangil Art, 2005.

Singh, Vijandra. *Panchayati Raj and Village Development*. Vol. 3. New Delhi: Sarup and Sons, 2003.

Siriyusavak, Ubonrat. "Popular Culture and Youth Consumption: Modernity, Identity and Social Transformation." In *Feeling Asian Modernities: Transnational Consumption of Japanese TV Dramas*, edited by Koichi Iwabuchi, 177–202. Hong Kong: Hong Kong University Press, 2004.

Siriyuvasak, Ubonrat, and Hyunjoon Shin. "Asianizing K-Pop: Production, Consumption and Identification Patterns among Thai Youth." *Inter-Asian Cultural Studies* 8, no. 1 (2007): 109–36.

Solis, Gabriel. "I Did It My Way: Rock and the Logic of Covers." *Popular Music and Society* 33, no. 3 (2010): 297–318.

Soja, Edward. *Postmodern Geographies: The Reassertion of Space in Critical Social Theory*. London: Verso, 1989.

Song, Ŭn-yŏng. "Taejung munhwa hyŏnsang ŭrosŏ ŭi Ch'oe In-ho sosŏl: 1970nyŏndae ch'ŏngnyŏn munhwa/munhak ŭi sŭt'ail kwa sobi p'ungsok" [Choi Inho's novel as a phenomenon of mass culture: The style and consumption of youth culture/literature in 1970s Korea]. *Sanghŏhakpo* 15 (2005): 419–45.

Stankovic, Peter. "1970s Partisan Epics as Western Films: The Question of Genre and Myth in Yugoslav Partisan Film." In *Partisans in Yugoslavia: Literature, Film and Visual Culture*, edited by Miranda Jakisa and Nikica Gilic, 245–64. Bielefeld, Germany: Transcript-Verlag, 2015.

Sterne, Jonathan. "Sonic Imaginations." In *The Sound Studies Reader*, edited by Jonathan Sterne, 1–18. New York: Routledge, 2012.

Stevens, Carolyn S. *Japanese Popular Music: Culture, Authority, and Power*. Abingdon, UK: Routledge, 2008.

Stevens, Carolyn S. *The Beatles in Japan*. London: Routledge, 2018.

Stoler, Ann Laura, and Frederick Cooper. "Between Metropole and Colony." In *Tension of Empire: Colonial Cultures in a Late Bourgeois World*, edited by Frederick Cooper and Ann Laura Stoler, 1–36. Berkeley: University of California Press, 1997.

Storey, Ian, and Malcolm Cook. "The Trump Administration and Southeast Asia: America's Asia Policy Crystalizes." *ISEAS Perspectives* 77 (2018). www.iseas.edu.sg/images/pdf/ISEAS_Perspective_2018_77@50.pdf. Accessed October 16, 2020.

Su, Hŏ. "1970 nyŏndae ch'ŏngnyŏnmunhwaron" [The discourse on 1970s youth culture]. In *Nonjaeng ŭro pon han'guk sahoe 100 nyŏn* [100 years of Korean society seen from debates], edited by Yŏksabip'yŏng p'yŏnjip wiwŏnhoe, 318–24. Seoul: Yŏksabip'yŏngsa, 2011.

Sugatha, Bose, and Kris Manjapra. *Cosmopolitan Thought Zones: South Asia and the Circulation of Global Ideas*. New York: Palgrave Macmillan, 2010.

Sun Qiming. "Mao Zedong wei shenme yao fadong zhengfeng yundong—lun 1957 nian de zhengfeng fanyou yundong" [Why did Mao Zedong launch the Rectification Movement: On the Rectification and Anti-Rightist Campaign in 1957]. *Tongji daxue xuebao* 2 (2004): 37.

Suzuki, Taku. *Embodying Belonging: Racializing Okinawan Diaspora in Bolivia and Japan*. Honolulu: University of Hawaiʻi Press, 2010.

Tada, Osamu. "Constructing Okinawa as Japan's Hawaiʻi: From Honeymoon Boom to Resort Paradise." *Japanese Studies* 15, no. 3 (2015): 287–302.

Taira, Koji. "Okinawa's Choice: Independence or Subordination." In *Okinawa: Cold War Island*, edited by Chalmers Johnson, 171–85. Cardiff, CA: Japan Policy Research Institute, 1999.

Tang Ji. "Chang huangse gequ you shenme haichu?" [What is the harm in singing yellow songs?]. *Yinyue shenghuo* 3 (1958): 30–31.

Taussig, Michael. *Mimesis and Alterity: A Particular History of the Senses*. New York: Routledge, 1992.

Toer, Koesalah Soebagyo. *Kampus Kabelnaya: Menjadi mahasiswa si Uni Soviet*. Jakarta: Kepustakaan Populer Gramedia, 2003.

Toynbee, Jason, and Byron Dueck, eds. *Migrating Music*. London: Routledge, 2011.

Tu Xianruo. "Wo dui 'liuxing gequ' de kanfa" [My opinion on "popular music"]. *Jiefang ribao*, June 23, 1957.

Tukdoji Maharaj. *Gleams of New Age*. Translated by S. M. Chitre. Gurukunj, India: Shri Gurudev Prakashan Mandal, 1956.

Tukdoji Maharaj. *Rashtrasantace Patre* [The National Saint's letters]. Edited by Baba Mohod. Amravati, India: Shrigurudev Publishers, 1966.

Tukdoji Maharaj. *Rashtrasantanci Pravacane* [The National Saint's religious discourses]. Edited by Baba Mohod. Gurukunj, India: Shrigurudev Prakashan, 1965.

Tukdoji Maharaj. "The Saint Tukadoji Maharaja, India." In *The Report on the Third World Religion Correspondence Congress (Under Auspices of the Ananai-Kyo)*, 327–29. Shimizu, Japan: The International General Headquarters of Ananai-Kyo, 1955.

Tukdoji Maharaj. *Srigramgita*. Tekadi, India: Tukaramji Dada Gitacharya, Shrigurudev Aatmanusandhaan, [1954] 1982.

Turino, Thomas. "Signs of Imagination, Identity and Experience: A Peircean Semiotic Theory for Music." *Ethnomusicology* 43, no. 2 (1999): 221–55.

Udornpim, Kant, and Arvind Singhal. "Oshin, a Pro-Social Role Model, in Thailand." *Keio Communication Review* 21 (1999): 3–21.

Ugaya, Hiromichi. *J-Poppu to wa nani ka* [What is J-pop?]. Tokyo: Iwanami Shoten, 2005.

Um, Haekyung. *K-Pop on the Global Platform: European Audience Reception and Contexts*. Seoul: KOFICE [Korean Foundation for International Cultural Exchange], 2014.

Van Vleck, Jenifer. *Empire of the Air: Aviation and the American Ascendancy*. Cambridge, MA: Harvard University Press, 2013.

Vogel, Ezra F. *Japan as Number One: Lessons for America*. Cambridge, MA: Harvard University Press, 1979.

Von Eschen, Penny. "Di Eagle and Di Bear: Who Gets to Tell the Story of the Cold War?" In *Audible Empire: Music, Global Politics, Critique*, edited by Ronald Radano and Tejumola Olaniyan, 187–208. Durham, NC: Duke Univeristy Press, 2016.

Vu, Tuong. "Cold War Studies and the Cultural Cold War in Asia." In *Dynamics of the Cold War in Asia: Ideology, Identity, and Culture*, edited by Tuong Vu and Wasana Wongsurawat, 1–16. New York: Palgrave Macmillan, 2009.

Wade, Bonnie C. *Music in Japan: Experiencing Music, Expressing Culture*. Oxford: Oxford University Press, 2005.
Wade, Peter. "Hybridity Theory and Kinship Thinking." *Cultural Studies* 19, no. 5 (2006): 602–21.
Wang, Hui. *The Politics of Imagining Asia*. Cambridge, MA: Harvard University Press, 2011.
Wang Yunjie. "Huangse gequ shi ducao, bixu chanchu" [Yellow music is a poisonous weed and must be rooted out]. *Renmin yinyue* 1 (1958): 10–12.
Wang Yunjie. "Youpaifenzi Chen Gexin de fandong yinyue daolu" [The reactionary musical path of Chen Gexin the rightist]. *Renmin yinyue* 10 (1957): 22–24.
Wardaya, S. J., and T. Baskara. "Global Solidarity against Unilateralism." *Inter-Asia Cultural Studies* 6, no. 4 (2005): 476–86.
Wee, C. J. W.-L. "Staging the Asian Modern: Cultural Fragments, the Singaporean Eunuch, and the Asian Lear." *Critical Inquiry* 30, no. 4 (2004): 771–99.
Wee, C. J. W.-L. "Is Consumption-Oriented Popular Culture in Singapore Being 'Japanized'?" *Gaiko Forum* 74 (1994): 66–68.
Weidman, Amanda. "Iconic Voices in Post-Millennium Tamil Cinema." In *Music in Contemporary Indian Film: Memory, Voice, Identity*, edited by Jayson Beaster-Jones and Natalie Sarrazin, 120–32. New York: Routledge, 2017.
Weintraub, Andrew N., and Bart Barendregt. "Re-Vamping Asia: Women, Music, and Modernity in Comparative Perspective." In *Vamping the Stage: Female Voices of Asian Modernities*, edited by Andrew N. Weintraub and Bart Barendregt, 1–39. Honolulu: University of Hawai'i Press, 2017.
Weintraub, Andrew. *Dangdut Stories: A Social and Musical History of Indonesia's Most Popular Music*. Oxford: Oxford University Press, 2010.
Wenhuabu bangongting. "Wenhuabu guanyu suqing huangse yinyue wenti gei Zhongyang de baogao" [Report on eliminating "yellow music" issues to the CCP Central Committee by the Ministry of Culture]. In *Wenhua gongzuo wenjian ziliao huibian* [Collection of documents on cultural work, 1949–1959]. Zhonghua renmin gongheguo wenhuabu bangongting, 1982, 238–41.
Werbner, Pnina. "Vernacular Cosmopolitanism." *Theory, Culture and Society* 23, nos. 2–3 (2006): 496–98.
Westad, Odd Arne. *The Global Cold War*. New York: Cambridge University Press, 2005.
Withers, Jonathan Sanjeev. "Kurdish Music-Making in Istanbul: Music, Sentiment, and Ideology in a Changing Urban Context." PhD diss., Harvard University, 2016.
Wong, Ain-ling, and Pui-tak Lee, eds. *Lengzhan yu Xianggang dianying* [The Cold War and Hong Kong Cinema]. Hong Kong: Hong Kong Film Archive, 2009.
Wong, Chi-wah. *Qu ci shuangjue: Hu Wensen zuopin yanjiu* [Music and lyrics: Study on the works of Hu Wensen]. Hong Kong: Joint Publishing, 2008.
Woo, Jung-en. *Race to the Swift: State and Finance in Korean Industrialization*. New York: Columbia University Press, 1991.
Woodward, Jude. *The US vs China: Asia's New Cold War?* Manchester, UK: University of Manchester Press, 2017.
World Bank. *The East Asian Miracle: Economic Growth and Public Policy*. New York: Oxford University Press, 1993.

Xiang Dongmin and An Yihui. "Chuixiang 'dayuejin' chongfeng hao de Zhonggong bada erci huiyi" [Blowing the bugle call of the "Great Leap Forward" in the second session of the Eight National Congress of the Communist Party of China]. *Wenshi jinghua* 3 (2011): 24–27.

Xiao Qing. "Zhengquede duidai Zhou Xuan de gechang yishu" [Have the right attitude toward Zhou Xuan's singing art]. *Renmin yinyue* 1 (1958): 13–14.

Xiao, Ying. *China in the Mix: Cinema, Sound, and Popular Culture in the Age of Globalization*. Jackson: University Press of Mississippi, 2017.

Xu Shujian. "Shengming—meili de hua: 'Ah, Pengyou' xinshang" [Life—a beautiful flower: Appreciating "Ah, friend"]. In *Liuxing gequ jianshang* [Appreciating popular music], edited by Jiang Chaowen and Zheng Chengwei. Guangzhou: Guangdong gaodeng jiaoyu chubanshe, 1987.

Yampolsky, Philip. "Kroncong Revisited: New Evidence from Old Sources." *Archipel* 79, no. 1 (2011): 7–56.

Yampolsky, Philip. "Music and Media in the Dutch East Indies: Gramophone Records and Radio in the Late Colonial Era 1903–1942." PhD diss., University of Washington, 2013.

Yang, Hon-Lun. "Socialist Realism and Chinese Music." In *Colloquium Musicologicum Brunense 36/2001: Socialist Realism and Music*, edited by Geoffrey Chew, Petr Macek, and Mikuláš Bek, 135–44. Prague: Bärenreiter-Verlag, 2004.

Yang, Hon-Lun. "Gendering '1968': Womanhood in Model Works of the People's Republic of China and Movie Musicals of Hong Kong." In *Music and Protest in 1968*, edited by Beate Kutschke and Barley Norton, 222–36. Cambridge: Cambridge University Press, 2013.

Yang, Hon-Lun. "People's Music in the People's Republic of China: A Semiotic Reading of Socialist Musical Culture from the Mid to Late 1950s." In *Music, Meaning and Media*, edited by Erkki Pekkila, David Neumeyer, and Richard Littlefield, 195–208. Helsinki, Finland: International Semiotics Institute, 2006.

Yano, Christine R. "'Flying Geisha': Japanese Stewardesses with Pan American World Airways." In *Modern Girls on the Go: Gender, Mobility, and Labor in Japan*, edited by Alisa Freedman, Laura Miller, and Christine R. Yano, 85–106. Stanford, CA: Stanford University Press, 2013.

Yano, Christine R. *Airborne Dreams: "Nisei" Stewardesses and Pan American World Airways*. Durham, NC: Duke University Press, 2011.

Yano, Christine R. "Covering Disclosures: Practices of Intimacy, Hierarchy, and Authenticity in a Japanese Popular Music Genre." *Popular Music and Society* 28, no. 2 (2005): 193–205.

Ye Baokun. "Qudi huangse yinyue yiwaide genben wenti" [The fundamental issue beyond eliminating the yellow music]. *Liyue Banyuekan*, no. 7 (1947): 6.

Yin [sic]. "Wei liuxing gequ mingbuping" [Voice the grievances for popular music]. *Jiefang ribao*, June 8, 1957.

Ying Yu. "'Diu jiezhi' shi bu jiankangde" ["Losing a ring" is unhealthy]. *Renmin yinyue* 4 (1959): 21–23.

Yoda, Tomiko. "A Roadmap to Millennial Japan." *South Atlantic Quarterly* 99, no. 4 (2000): 659–62.

Yoneyama, Lisa. *Cold War Ruins: Transpacific Critique of American Justice and Japanese War Crimes*. Durham, NC: Duke University Press, 2016.

Yoshimi, Shunya. "'America' as Desire and Violence: Americanization in the Postwar Japan and Asia in the Cold War." *Inter-Asia Culture Studies* 4, no. 3 (2003): 433–50.

Yoshimi, Shunya. "Consuming 'America': From Symbol to System." In *Consumption in Asia: Lifestyles and Identities*, edited by Chua Beng Huat, 202–24. London: Routledge, 2000.

Yuan, Qingfeng. "Nansilafu yingpian yu Zhongguo dalu dianying wenhua yujing de duijie—Yi Beijing dianying zhipianchang 1973 nian yizhi de *Qiao* (1969) wei lie" [The cultural contexts of Yugoslavian movies and mainland Chinese cinema—The case of *Bridge* (1969), dubbed by Beijing film studio in 1973]. *Shantou daxue xuebao* 30, no. 2 (2014): 12–17.

Yuliantri, Rhoma Dwi Aria. "Lekra and Ensembles: Tracing the Indonesian Musical Stage." In *Heirs to World Culture: Being Indonesian 1950–1965*, edited by Jennifer Lindsay and Maya Liem, 421–52. Leiden: KITLV, 2012.

Yung, Bell. *Cantonese Opera: Performance as Creative Process*. Cambridge: Cambridge University Press, 1989.

Zachariah, Kunniparampil Curien, and Sebastian Irudaya Rajan. *Migration and Development: The Kerala Experience*. New Delhi: Daanish Books, 2009.

Zelliot, Eleanor. "A Historical Introduction to the Warkari Movement." In D. B. Mokashi, *Palkhi: An Indian Pilgrimage*, translated by Philip C. Engblom, 31–53. Albany: State University of New York Press, 1987.

Zhang Shu. "Li Jinhui wei 'shuqing gequ' mingbuping" [Li Jinhui voices his grievances on "lyric songs"]. *Xinwen Ribao*, May 21, 1957.

Zhao Feng. "Suqing fandong tuifei de huangse yinyue" [Eliminate the reactionary and decadent yellow music]. *Renmin yinyue* 3 (1958): 20–21.

Zhong Qiang. "Yinyue yishu de chonggao mubiao—Cong 'Diu jiezhi' 'Xiao yanzi' de taolun tanqi" [The noble objective of musical art: starting from the discussions on "Losing a ring" and "Small swallow"]. *Renmin yinyue* 8 (1959): 16–19.

Zhou Weizhi. "Pipan huangse yinyue" [Criticizing yellow music, 1957]. In *Lun yinyue wei gongnongbing fuwu* [On music serving workers, farmers, and soldiers], 281–97. Beijing: Yinyue chubanshe, 1966.

Contributors

MARIÉ ABE is Associate Professor of Music in the Department of Musicology and Ethnomusicology at Boston University. Her scholarship explores the intersection of sound, space, and sociality, bridging sound studies and cultural human geography. She is particularly invested in the politics of sound in social movements. She is the author of *Resonances of Chindon-ya: Sounding Space and Sociality in Contemporary Japan* (2018), which is the first English-language ethnographic monograph on *chindon-ya*, a live advertisement street music in Japan. Her most recent projects involve the politics of sound and the anti–US military base movement in Okinawa, and the uncanny musical affinity between 1950s Japanese sentimental pop music and 1970s Ethiopian popular music. She is also a coproducer of the NPR radio documentary *Squeezebox Stories*, which tells stories of Californian immigration history using the accordion as a common trope.

MICHAEL K. BOURDAGHS is Robert S. Ingersoll Professor in East Asian Languages and Civilizations and the College at the University of Chicago. He previously taught at UCLA and received his PhD in Asian Literature from Cornell University. A specialist in modern Japanese literature and culture, he is the author of *The Dawn That Never Comes: Shimazaki Tōson and Japanese Nationalism* (2003) and *Sayonara Amerika, Sayonara Nippon: A Geopolitical Prehistory of J-Pop* (2012; Japanese translation, 2012). He is also a prolific translator, most recently of Kojin Karatani, *The Structure of World History: From Modes of Production to Modes of Exchange* (2014). He is the recipient of a 2019 Guggenheim Fellowship and numerous other fellowships and awards.

PAOLA IOVENE received her PhD from Cornell University and is Associate Professor of Modern Chinese Literature at the University of Chicago. She is the coeditor (with Judith Zeitlin) a special issue of *Opera Quarterly* on Chinese opera film (2010) and the author of *Tales of Futures Past: Anticipations and the Ends of Literature in Contemporary China* (2014).

NISHA KOMMATTAM is an Associate Instructional Professor in the Department of Comparative Literature at the University of Chicago. She works at the intersection of South Asian literatures and Gender & Sexuality studies, with a focus on Southern India (Malayalam Literature, Kerala Studies). She is also interested in literatures of migration, inter-Asia comparisons, and in the transnational entanglements of pioneering queer German writers in fin-de-siècle Europe. Recent publications include *Are they Women? A Novel concerning the Third Sex* by Aimée Duc (2020, translated and edited with Margaret Breen) and *Sind es Frauen? Roman über das dritte Geschlecht* by Aimée Duc (2020, edited with Margaret Breen).

JENNIFER LINDSAY, an honorary Associate Professor in the School of Culture, History and Language at Australian National University, studied in New Zealand, the United States, and Australia. She has lived in Indonesia on and off for some thirty years. She led an international research project into Indonesian cultural history in the 1950s and early 1960s, and directed a documentary film about Indonesia's cultural missions abroad of that period. She has translated many literary works from Indonesian into English and now spends most of her time writing and translating. She divides her life between Indonesia and Australia.

KALEY MASON is Assistant Professor of Music at Lewis and Clark College. Before moving to Portland, Oregon, he taught at the University of Chicago and received his PhD in Ethnomusicology from the University of Alberta. In addition to contributing to *The Cambridge History of World Music* (2013) and other edited volumes, he recently coedited a special issue of the journal *MUSICultures* (2017). He is the author of the forthcoming book *The Labor of Music: South Indian Performers and Cultural Mobility*.

ANNA SCHULTZ is Associate Professor of Music at the University of Chicago, where she is also an associate member of the Department of South Asian Languages and Civilizations and a member of the Greenberg Center for Jewish Studies. The core issue animating her research in India and beyond is music's power to activate profound religious experiences that in turn shape other identities. She is the author of *Singing a Hindu Nation: Marathi Devotional Performance and Nationalism* (2013) and *Songs of Translation: Bene Israel Gender and Textual Orality* (forthcoming).

HYUNJOON SHIN is Professor in the Faculty of Social Science and the Institute for East Asian Studies (IEAS) at Sunkonghoe University. Having received his PhD with a thesis on the transformation of the Korean music industry, he has carried out broader research projects on popular culture, international migration, and urban space in Korea and East Asia. He was a Visiting Scholar at National University of Singapore, Leiden University in the Netherlands, Leuven University in Belgium, and Duke University in the United States. He is currently a member of the International Advisory Editors of *Popular Music* and the Editorial Collective of *Inter-Asia Cultural Studies*. His publications have appeared in *positions*, *Popular Music*, *Inter-Asia Cultural Studies*, and *City, Culture and Society*.

C. J. W.-L. WEE is Professor of English at the Nanyang Technological University, Singapore. He has held visiting fellowships at—among other institutions—the Centre for the Study of Developing Societies, Delhi, India; the Society for the Humanities, Cornell University; and the National Humanities Center (the last in 2020). Wee is the author of *Culture, Empire, and the Question of Being Modern* (2003) and *The Asian Modern: Culture, Capitalist Development, Singapore* (2007), and is a coeditor of *Contesting Performance: Global Genealogies of Research* (2010). Among his recent research interests are the formation of contemporary art practices in theater and the visual arts and curatorial practices in showcasing modern and contemporary Asian art in East and Southeast Asia.

HON-LUN (HELAN) YANG is Professor of Music at Hong Kong Baptist University. She is the coeditor of *China and the West: Music, Representation, and Reception* (2017) and the lead author of *Networking the Russian Diaspora: Russian Musicians and Musical Activities in Interwar Shanghai* (2020). Her book chapters have appeared in *The Bloomsbury Handbook of Popular Music and Social Class* (2019), *The Oxford Handbook of Music Censorship* (2018), *Composing for the State* (2016), and *Music and Protest in 1968* (2013). She has published articles in *Music and Politics* (2013), *Journal of Musicological Research* (2019), *Journal of the American Liszt Society* (2018), *Twentieth-Century Music* (2018), *Twentieth-Century China* (2012), *International Review of Aesthetics and Sociology of Music* (2011), and *Asian Music* (2010).

CHRISTINE R. YANO, Professor of Anthropology at the University of Hawai'i, has conducted research on Japan and Japanese Americans with a focus on popular culture. She has served as Vice President (President-Elect, 2019) and President (2020) of the Association for Asian Studies. Her publications include *Tears of Longing: Nostalgia and the Nation in Japanese Popular Song* (2002), *Crowning the Nice Girl: Gender, Ethnicity, and Culture in Hawai'i's Cherry Blossom Festival* (2006), *Airborne Dreams: "Nisei" Stewardesses and Pan American World Airways* (2011), and *Pink Globalization: Hello Kitty and Its Trek across the Pacific* (2013). She has also coedited a number of volumes: *Modern Girls on the Go: Gender, Mobility, and Labor in Contemporary Japan*, with Alisa Freedman and Laura Miller (2013); *Making Waves: Traveling Musics in Hawai'i, Asia, and the Pacific*, with Fred Lau (2018); and *Straight A's: Asian American College Students in Their Own Words*, with Neal Akatsuka (2018).

QIAN ZHANG is Associate Professor at the Communication University of China. Trained in ethnomusicology and media studies, she has conducted ethnographic research in China and the United States and was a visiting scholar at the Massachusetts Institute of Technology and the Chinese University of Hong Kong. She specializes in Asian popular music focusing on industry, digitalization, and transnationalism. Her current research interests include K-pop fandom in China and historicizing globalization in Asia.

Index

Page numbers followed by f refer to illustrations.

"Aamuca Desh Sukhaci Khan" [Our nation is a wellspring of happiness] (Sant Tukdoji Maharaj), 222
acoustic guitar, 136
"A E I O U" (film song), 83
Afro-Asian Writers Union, the, 23
aidoru, 103
AKB 48 (band), 117
Akimoto Yasushi, 117
Americanization, 117, 134
Amuro Namie, 102
Anpo protest, the, 23
anti-communism, 3, 146
Anti-Rightist Campaign, 234, 235–36, 243
"A pengyou zaijian" [Good-bye, friend]. *See* "Bella ciao"
Arashi (band), Taipei concert in 2006, 115–16
Around Indonesia (documentary), 53
"Aru koi no monogatari" (the Peanuts), 22
Asia: American middle class' consumption of, 251–52; a multicultural New Asia, 97, 109; "Economic Asia" and "Security Asia," 95, 97. *See also* the Cold War and Asia
Asian financial crisis, 96, 110, 113
Asian national music societies, 5
Asian studies, 4
"Auto, Auto," 81
Avex Group, 113

Aye Auto! (Venu Nagavally), 80–85

Baby V.O.X. (band), 126n99
"Balikudeerangale" (Monuments of martyrdom), 25–26, 28–30
"Banana Boat Song" (Harry Belafonte), covers of, 158–59
bans on Japanese content, 103, 112
Bandung Conference, 32n11, 223
Bandung movement, 3, 22
Baskaran, Theodore, 74, 89n14
Bayly, Susan, 204
Beatles, the (band), influence in Hong Kong, 155–56
"Bella ciao," 12–15
Berry, Michael, 12
Bhabha, Homi, 87, 160
bhajan, 205
bhakti, 202; poetry, 211
Bharat Sadhu Samaj (BBS, Indian Society of Ascetics), 215
Bhave, Vinoba, 207
binary oppositions: in Cold War aesthetics, 3; East vs. West, 249; escape from, 23; North vs. South (Korea), 17–18; proletariat vs. bourgeoisie, 240
Big Hit Entertainment, 117
Birmingham School of Cultural Studies, the, 6
Bloch, Ernst, 87

BoA (Kwon Boa), 113
bhoodan movement, the, 207–8
Bourdaghs, Michael K., 132, 160
Bridge, The (Most) (Krvavac), 13–14
BTS (Bangtan Sonyeondan [Bulletproof Boy Scouts]) (band), 117
bubble economy, 103–4, 106
Bucharest, 52
Budapest, 49

campus song (*taehakkayo*), 144
Campus Song Festival, 144
Cantonese, 165n4
Campbell, Emma, 147
"camp show," 134
campus song (*taehakminyo*), 144
"Candy" (H.O.T.), 111
Cantopop, 156, 164
canzone, 109, 136
Caramel Mama [Tin Pan Alley] (studio musician group), 151n17
cassette, 72, 145
Castro, Fidel, 52
censorship, 255–56; in South Korea, 143
C'est Si Bon (listening hall), 134
Chan, Connie, 162
chanson, 109, 136
Chen, Gexin, 237
Chen, Kuan-Hsing, 17
China, People's Republic of, 93
China Central Television (CCTV), 99–100, 113
Chinese economic reforms, 11–12
Chinese Musicians' Association, 235
Chinese popular music, 9; contemporary, 254; Japanese military invasion and, 239–40. *See also* "yellow music"
Cho Hae-Joang, 121n31
Cho Yong-pil, 109
Christian Broadcasting Station (CBS), 139
Christian church-based organizations, in Korea, 134, 139–40
Christianity, Korean, 140
Chua Beng Huat, 99, 120n21
CIA: Comrade in America (Amal Neerad), 28
Chun, Allen, 197n6
Chun Doo Hwan, 144
Clifford, James, 11
Cold War, the: Asia and, 2–3, 7, 16, 154, 250–51; fear and, 258–59; ideological struggles and, 236; knowledge formation of, 4; politics, internalization of, 143; rethinking, 259. *See also* popular music and the Cold War
Colorful Youth (Wong Yiu), 161–62
"comfort women" issues, 114
commodity, as objectified containers of meaning, 157
communism, in Kerala, 75, 90n28;
Communist Party of India (CPI): popular culture and, 25, 74; the split-off from the Marxist branch, 79. *See also* Kerala
cosmopolitanism, 5, 8, 69, 78, 88n1, 154–55, 251, 256–57; in Communist Kerala, 83–85, 91n51; in Korean folk song, 136, 151n18; "rural cosmopolitanism," 204, 256–57; "vernacular," 153–54, 160, 200n37
covers, 16, 18, 31, 255; alignment and, 19, 20, 23–24
covers of Western songs: Cantonese, 157; Korean, 136, 150n5
cultural studies, 6, 7
Cumings, Bruce, 3, 94, 96

Daiku Tetsuhiro, 179–81. *See also individual works*
Damodaran, Sumangala, 74, 75, 78, 90n35
dazi bao (big-character posters), 234
de–cold war, 249
decolonization and deimperialism, derailed, 17
Demilitarized Zone (DMZ), 131
dictatorship of the proletariat, 240
disputes over territories: in East Asia, 96–97
Dong-A Ilbo (newspaper), 114
"Double 10 Riot," 169n38
Dylan, Bob, 140

East Asia: in an *incomplete contemporary*, 97; regionalization in, 99. *See also* Asia: "Economic Asia" and "Security Asia"; Asian financial crisis; bubble economy
Eighth US Army, the. *See* military bases in South Korea
English: in East Asia, 99; in Kerala, 83–85, 91n51
enka, 109
Exodus (Utada Hikaru), 107

"Fa giu bat chih yuhk yahn meih" [The flower is not as pretty as the girl], 163
Fei chaak gam si maau (*The Golden Cat*) (film), 159, 161, 163

"Fei go dit lok hang keui" [Teddy boy in the gutter], 157–58
festivals. *See* youth festivals
film songs, 8; in Kerala cinema, 71–72, 89n14, 89n21; Hindi, 212
Fīrin Guddo: Pīnattsu no atarashii sekai [Feeling good: The Peanuts' new world] (the Peanuts), 20
First Love (Utada Hikaru), 107
Folk Crusaders, the (band), 17
folk music: in Indonesia, 50; Japanese, 132; national song and, 59–60. *See also* kayōkyoku; *sanchi minyō*; South Korean folk music
four "mini-dragons," the, 96, 99, 155. *See also* Hong Kong; Singapore; South Korea; Taiwan
Frankfurt School, the, critique of popular music from, 6
freedom, 3
fronts, 5, 24–25; beyond national, 31

Gandhi, Mahatma, 205–6, 213
"Gangnam Style" (PSY), 117
Gembira (vocal ensemble), 50–51
"Ghadi ghadi" [Every single moment] (Sant Tukdoji Maharaj), 212–13
"Git buhn yauh cheun" [Spring outing], 159
Glaser, Bonnie, 119n14
Glay (band), 102
Global South, the, 2, 5
Golden Cat, the. *See Fei chaak gam si maau*
"Gou go hei mouh" [Sing and dance], 158
Gramgita (Sant Tukdoji Maharaj), 206–7, 209, 223
Gregory, Derek, 177
Gwangju Uprising, the, 145–46

Hallyu. *See* the Korean Wave
Hamasaki Ayumi, 102
Han Tae-su, 131–32, 137, 141f, 142, 146
"Hātorando" [Heartland] (Daiko Tetsuhiro), 173
Hattori Ryōichi, 98
Harkness, Nicholas, 254
"Haruch'im" [One Morning] (Han Tae-su), 131
"Harupam" [One night] (Han Tae-su), 131
Hawai'i, Okinawa and, 191, 192, 257
Hein, Laura, 195

"Hitotsubo Taritomo Watasumai" [We shall give up not even one tsubo] (Daiku Tetsuhiro), 186
"Hiyamikachi Bushi" [Cheer up!] (Daiku Testuhiro), 192
hōgaku, 102
Hong Kong, 101, 116; film industry of, 153; "vernacular cosmopolitanism" and, 161–62; western pop music in, 156–57
Hōrai, 174
Hōraikō: Exo Patirohma (Daiku Tetsuhiro), 181–83, 190, 193
"Hore Hore Bushi" [Hore hore song] (Daiku Tetsuhiro), 191
Hosono Haruomi, 200n34
H.O.T. (High-Five of Teenagers), 110–11
Hui, Sam, 163–64
Hundred Flowers Movement, the, 233
Hwang Sŏk-yŏng, 145
"Hyōjungo Reikō no Uta" (Standard Japanese encouragement song), 183–84

I Am (documentary), 149
ideologies. *See* Americanization; anticommunism; communism; modernization theory
idol: Japanese (aidoru), 103; Korean, 109
"Idŭngbyŏngŭi p'yŏnji" [The letter from a private] (Kim Kwang-sŏk), 131
"Imugin-gawa" [Imjun River] (the Folk Crusaders), 17
India: anticolonial struggle of, 214; the liberation of market in, 84; nonalignment in, 201, 222; tension with Pakistan, 221
Indonesia, 99, 196; K-pop and, 108; participation in WFYS, 47, 48–50
International Association for the Study of Popular Music (IASPM), 6
Iron Curtain, the, 2, 3
Iwabuchi Koichi, 120n23, 121n24, 123n50

Jameson, Fredric, 99–100
Japan: "Cool Japan," 256; participation in the Bandung movement, 22–23; relationship with China, 93; relationship with the US, 103, 176. *See also* the Anpo protest; the economic agenda of the United States in Asia
Japanese cultural products, 101
"Japanese Rumba" (Daiku Tetsuhiro), 191

jazz, criticism of, 240
Jet Age, the, 251–52; Cold War Asia in, 252–53
Jia Zhangke, 8–10, 11
jimusho, 111
Joe Junior, 155
Johnny and Associates, 111–12, 115
Johnson, Chalmers, 199n27, n28
Jones, Andrew F., 232
J-pop, 100, 102; K-pop and, 112, 114–15; as "*local-and-metropolitan*," 107; nationalism and, 104, 108; the recede of, 107; the spread of, 101–3, 124n77
JSA (*Joint Security Area*) (Pak Ch'an-uk), 131, 147
JYP Entertainment, 111

"Kaette kita yopparai" [The drunkard's return] (the Folk Crusaders), 17
"Kaette kita yopparai" (*Three Resurrected Drunkards*) (Ōshima Nagisa), 17
Käng, Dredge, 153
Kapchan, Deborah, 219
kayo. See South Korean folk song
kayōkyoku, 123n56
Kerala, 72–74, 91n46; migration, 99n55
Kerala cinema, 70, 88n6. *See also* film songs in Malayalam cinema
Kerala People's Arts Club, the (KPAC), 25
Kerala rikshawala, 69, 79–80, 85–86, 87, 88n3. *See also* Aye Auto!; "Oh Rikshawala!"
Kesavadev, P., 75, 90n39. *See also* Odayil Ninnu (novel)
Kim Chi-ha, 140
Kim Dae-jong administration, 112
Kim Kwang-sŏk, 131–32, 146
Kim Min-ki, 137, 138–39f, 140, 144, 151n14
Kim Pyŏng-ik, 151n18
Kim Young-sam government, 110
Klein, Christina, 251
Kōhaku Uta Gassen, 113
"Koi no vakansu" (Vacance de l'amour) (the Peanuts), 21
Kongjangŭi pulbit [The light of the factory] (song drama), 145
Koo, Joseph, 163–64
Korean talent agencies, 111
Korean War, the, 133
Korean Wave, the, 98, 100, 108, 120n23
K-pop: economics of, 113; history of, 110–11; industry, 109; and J-pop, 112, 114–15; nationalism and, 109, 111, 147; routes of, 114; stars learning other languages, 113; as a term, 98, 111–12, 125n81; as a translocal formation of the contemporary, 108
kroncong, 45–46, 58
Kun, Josh, 31
Kwon Heonik, 1

Lee Sooman (Yi Suman), 147–49
Legend of the Super Voices 101: Hong Kong's Muzikland of the 60/70s (album), 155
Leung so yau dei yuk (*Two Fools in Hell*) (Tang Kee-Chan), 157
Li Guyi, 35n35
Li Jinhui, 9, 98, 238, 239
Li Xianglan [Yamaguchi Yoshiko], 238, 239
literature, and Kerala institution, 90n39. *See also* socialist realism
Liu, Lydia, 9
liuxing, 10, 34n29
Liu Xue'an, 238
Lü Ji, 235, 238

Maharashtra, 214–15, 224n12. *See also* Marathi
Malayalam cinema. *See* Kerala cinema
Malayalam literature, 74–75, 90n33. *See also* Odayil Ninnu (novel)
Manga Kenkanryū (Hating the Korean wave) (Yamano Sharin), 114
Manik, Liberty, 55–56
"Mani Nahi Bhav" [If you pray without faith] (Sant Tukdoji Maharaj), 209–12
Manuel, Peter, 72
Mao Zedong, 38n81, 233–34
Marathi, 210–11
Marxism, in Kerala, 86–87. *See also* cosmopolitanism in Communist Kerala
Marzuki, Ismail, 43–44
Massey, Doreen, 183
mass culture, 100
Matsushita, 99, 103
Matsuyama Takeshi, 17
Meari (student song group), 144–45
metaphor, as a means of ideological indoctrination and manipulation, 237
middle class: American, consumption of East Asian by, 251–52; in East Asia, 97, 99
Middleton, Richard, 203

military bases: in Japan, 133; in South Korea, 133–34
Minch'ŏnghangnyŏn (National League of Democratic College Students), 142
minjung, 140, 151n16
minjung kayo, 145–46
minyo, 132
Misora Hibari, 17
Miyagawa Hiroshi, 21, 22
mobility, 253
modernization theory, 19–20
Moment (SPEED) (album), 102
Mōri Yoshitaka, 104
Muller, Carol, 23
Munhwa Broadcasting Corporation (MBC), 143
My Boss (Jeethu Joseph), 81–82

Na Hyŏn-ku, 151n17
"Nan arayo" (I know) (Seo Taiji and Boys), 110
Nanda, Guzarilal, 215
Narayan, Shriman, 218
nationalism, 90n35, 118; Hinduism and, 216; J-pop and, 100, 104, 108; Korean folk song and, 133, 140; K-pop and, 109, 111, 147; nationalist response to Japanese cultural products, 117; nationalist response to the Korean wave, 114. *See also* bans on Japanese content
national music, debate in Indonesia over, 55
Negami Shin, 218
Nehru, Jawaharlal, 201, 213, 214, 215
Nettl, Bruno, 5
Nie Er, 239
"Nimŭl wihan haengjin'gok" [The march for the beloved] (Meari), 145
"Nobody" (Wonder Girls), 117
Non-Aligned Movement (NAM). *See* the Bandung Movement

Odayil Ninnu (novel) (P. Kesavadev), 75–76, 77–78
Odayil Ninnu (film) (K. S. Sethumadhavan), 76–78
official popular culture, 9
"Oh Rikshawala!" (Mehboob), 78–80
Okinawa, 174–78, 196n3, 197n5; as a confluence of factors, 257; cultural outreach of, 200n39; emigration from, 190–91; Japanese colonial rule of, 183–84, 198n16; "Okinawan difference," 185, 198n15; struggle against land dispossession, 185–86; Taiwan and, 192–93; US occupation of, 178
Okinawa Jinta (Daiku Tetsuhiro), 179
"Okinawa o Kaese" [Return Okinawa] (Daiku Tetsuhiro), 187–89
Organization for Economic Cooperation and Development [OECD], 108
original soundtracks (OST), 101
Osborne, Peter, 97, 109
Oshin (drama), 98
Ōta Masahide, 199n22

Pacchigi! (Break Through! / We Shall Overcome Someday) (Izutsu Kazuyuki), 16
Park Chung Hee, regime, 17, 133
Peanuts, the (band), 19–22
People's Daily (newspaper), 245n13
People's Music (magazine), 235
piracy, of J-pop content, 101
Pizzicato Five (P5) (band), 105
Platform (*Zhantai*) (Jia Zhangke), 8–12
p'ok'ŭ song. *See* South Korean folk song
Pollock, Sheldon, 160
pop-rock genres, 5
popular (as a concept), the: capitalism and, 60–61; as everyday presence, 3, 250
popular anthems, 26–27
popular culture, 6, 60; in China, 8–10; inter-Asian commercial, 94–95
popular music, 203; the academic study of, 6; the Cold War and, 3–4, 60, 94, 133, 250; in East Asia, 98; inter-Asian flow, 109; Malayalam, 89n12; soft power and, 256; in South Asia, 72. *See also* liuxing; *yuhaengga*
professional music associations, 5; International Council for Traditional Music (ICTM), 4; Society for Ethnomusicology (SEM), 4
public ownership, 240
"Puch'iji anhŭn p'yŏnji" [The unmailed letter] (Kim Kwang-sŏk), 131

qunzhong yinyue (*Mass Music*) (magazine), 245n12

Rain (Korean star), 112, 126n99
rashtrasant, 202
"Rayuan Pulau Kelapa" (Lure of the Coconut Isles), 44–46, 51–52, 57–58; criticism of, 55–56; in the USSR as "Indonesia Lubov Moya," 53–55

Index · 293

Regev, Motti, 5
religion, 254
resistance, in India, 217, 221. *See also* South Korean folk song and resistance
Richard, Cliff, 155
rikshawala. *See* Kerala rikshawala
"Rimjingang" [Imjun River], 17–18
rock music, 134
Rolling Stones, the (band), 155
Rossiter, Ned, 197n5
route, 4, 8; of South Korean folk song, 134; "forbidden," 10; of K-pop, 114; military bases as, 4, 15, 250–51
Ryūkyū. *See* Okinawa

Sakamoto Kyū, 117
sanchi minyō, 193
Sant Tukdoji Maharaj [Manik Ingle], 201–2, 204, 205–7, 208, 211, 213; cosmopolitanism of, 211–12; nationalist side of, 216–17, 219–20. *See also individual works*
Sarangi mwŏgillae [What is love?], 100
sarvodaya, 207
Sasidharan, K. P., 76, 90n35, 91n41
Segyehwa Ch'ujin Wiwŏnhoe (Globalization Promotion Committee), 110
Seldon, Mark, 195
Seo Taiji [Jung Hyun-chul]. *See* Seo Taiji and Boys
Seo Taiji and Boys [Sŏ Taejiwa aidŭl] (band), 110
seriosa, 58
Se7en (pronounced "Seven"), 126n99
Shanghai, 231, 239, 240; Old, 242
Shank, Barry, 26–27
"Shehuizhuyi hao" [Socialism is good], 235
Shibuya-kei, 102, 104, 107
shidai qu, 9
Shiraishi Takashi, 119n13, 120n23
Siao, Josephine, 162
Simon and Garfunkel (band), 109, 136
Singapore, 116; the impact of J-pop on, 101–2
"'67 Riot," 169n38
SMAP (Sports, Music Assemble People) (band), 93, 111, 118n1
SM Entertainment, 110. See also *I Am* (documentary); Korean talent agencies
socialist realism, in Malayalam literature, 74–75, 91n48

soft power, 99, 113, 256
Solis, Gabriel, 22
Song Ch'ang-sik, 140, 142. *See also* Twin Folio
Songs (magazine), 235
sound studies, 6–7
South Asia, 203
South China Sea, 96, 119n14
South Korea (Republic of Korea): Christian church-based organizations in, 134, 139–40; Cold War and, 133, 146–47; relations with Japan, 96; reunification and, 132, 147
South Korean folk song, 109, 131–32, 134–36, 149n4; alignment of, 146; campus song (*taehakkayo*), 144; *minjung kayo*, 145–46; resistance and, 137, 142, 145; sing-alongs, 134, 136; university song clubs, 144–45; youth culture and, 136, 142
Southeast Asia, 113; as the center of power competition, 96–97; ethnic Chinese communities in, 98
Sony Cooperation, 99, 103
state-sponsored model. *See* official popular culture
"Sukiyaki" (Sakamoto Kyū), 117
Summer Holiday (musical), 161
Sundar, Gopi, 28–30

Taira Shinsuke, 192
Taiwan, 8–9, 96, 101, 115–16; folk music, 193; Okinawa and, 192–93
"Taiwan Yuki Kazoe Uta" (Going to Taiwan song) (Daiku Tetsuhiro), 192
Tamil cinema, 74, 88n6
Taussig, Michael, 18, 20
technology, evolution of, 86
"Teddy Boy in the Gutter." *See* "Fei go dit lok hang keui"
teenagers, 257–58
television, 100
television dramas: Japanese, 101; Korean, 108. *See also* Oshin (drama)
Teng, Teresa [Deng Lijun], 8–9, 33n23
Thailand, 99, 101, 115–16, 146
This Year's Girl (Pizzicato Five), 105
Tin Pan Alley, 203, 252
Tobing, Gordon, 52
"Toganisuza" (Daiku Tetsuhiro), 190
Toi et Moi (band), 136

Tosisanŏpsŏn'gyohoe (Urban Industrial Mission), 145
"Travessia" (Bridge) (Milton Nascimento), 196
Trump, Donald, administration, 97
Tukdoji. *See* Sant Tukdoji Maharaj
Turino, Thomas, 26
TVXQ (band), 113, 126n91
"Twiggy, Twiggy" (Pizzicato Five), 105–6
Twin Folio (band), 136, 140

United States, the: the Cold War and the institutions of, 4; as a conflicting presence, 134; cultural products of, in Asia, 103; economic agenda of, in Asia, 95–96
Utada Hikaru, 107

varkari movement, the, 202
"vernacular cosmopolitanism," 153–54, 160, 200n37
vernacular languages. *See* Cantonese; Malayalam; Marathi
video compact disc, the (VCD), 101
Vishwa Hindu Parishad (VHP, World Hindu Council), 216
visual-kei (visual-style), 102
voice, 254–55, 259

Wang Hui, 95
Watanabe Productions, 19
We Hate All Kinds of Violence (H.O.T.), 110–11
Wen Jiabao, 93
Werbner, Pnina, 160
Westad, Odd Arne, 1, 2
Wong Yiu, 161
World Federation of Democratic Youth, the, 34n30

World Festivals of Youth and Students, the (WFYS), 13, 46–48
world music, 117–18
World Religion Congress, the, 218, 223

X-JAPAN (band), 102

Yamaguchi Yoshiko. *See* Li Xianglan
Yamanouchi Seihin, 192
Yanagita Kunio, 198n18
Yang Hŭi-ŭn, 137, 139, 147, 151n14, 151n18
Yang Pyŏg-chip, 142
"Yat san ngaih" [Ants all over the body], 158–59
"yellow music," 166n14, 231–32; and the Cold War, 243; critical metaphors of, 237; criticism of, 232, 236, 239–42
YG Entertainment, 111
Yi Chang-hŭi, 140, 141f, 151n18
Yi Chŏng-sŏn, 142
Yingyu gequxuan (Selected songs in English), 14–15
YMCA, 135f. *See also* Christian church-based organizations
"Yonaguni Kouta" (Daiku Tetsuhiro), 190
Yoneyama, Lisa, 4
Yoshimi Shunya, 103, 134
youth culture: in Hong Kong, 153; in Japan, 104, 107; in Korea, 136, 142–43
youth festivals, 10
"youth movie musical," 165n3
Yuan, Qingfeng, 14
yuhaengga (song in fashion), 112
"Yusakuya" (Daiku Tetsuhiro), 190
YWCA, 134, 139. *See also* Christian church-based organizations

Zainichi, 17
Zhou Xuan, 9, 238, 239

www.ingramcontent.com/pod-product-compliance
Lightning Source LLC
Chambersburg PA
CBHW072019290525
27270CB00018BA/276